INSIGHT GUIDES

TRINIDAD & TOBAGO

TOGETHER WE ASPIRE · TOGETHER WE ACHIEVE

APA PUBLICATIONS

Part of the Langenscheidt Publishing Group

L

INSIGHT GUIDE
TRINIDAD & TOBAGO

Editorial

Editor
Lesley Gordon
Editorial Director
Brian Bell

Distribution

UK & Ireland
GeoCenter International Ltd
The Viables Centre, Harrow Way
Basingstoke, Hants RG22 4BJ
Fax: (44) 1256 817988

United States
Langenscheidt Publishers, Inc.
36–36 33rd Street 4th Floor
Long Island City, NY 11106
Fax: 1 (718) 784 0640

Canada
Thomas Allen & Son Ltd
390 Steelcase Road East
Markham, Ontario L3R 1G2
Fax: (1) 905 475 6747

Australia
Universal Publishers
1 Waterloo Road
Macquarie Park, NSW 2113
Fax: (61) 2 9888 9074

New Zealand
Hema Maps New Zealand Ltd (HNZ)
Unit D, 24 Ra ORA Drive
East Tamaki, Auckland
Fax: (64) 9 273 6479

Worldwide
**Apa Publications GmbH & Co.
Verlag KG (Singapore branch)**
38 Joo Koon Road, Singapore 628990
Tel: (65) 6865 1600. Fax: (65) 6861 6438

Printing

Insight Print Services (Pte) Ltd
38 Joo Koon Road, Singapore 628990
Tel: (65) 6865 1600. Fax: (65) 6861 6438

©2005 Apa Publications GmbH & Co.
Verlag KG (Singapore branch)
All Rights Reserved
First Edition 1987
Third Edition 2000
Updated 2005

CONTACTING THE EDITORS
We would appreciate it if readers
would alert us to errors or out-
dated information by writing to:
**Insight Guides, P.O. Box 7910,
London SE1 1WE, England.
Fax: (44) 20 7403 0290.
insight@apaguide.co.uk**

www.insightguides.com

ABOUT THIS BOOK

This guidebook combines the interests and enthusiasms of two of the world's best known infor-mation providers: Insight Guides, whose titles have set the standard for visual travel guides since 1970, and Discovery Channel, the world's premier source of nonfiction televi-sion programming.

The editors of Insight Guides pro-vide both practical advice and general understanding about a destination's history, culture, institutions and people. Discovery Channel and its Web site, www.discovery.com, help millions of viewers explore their world from the comfort of their own home and also encourage them to explore it first hand.

This fully updated edition of *Insight Guide: Trinidad and Tobago* is care-fully structured to convey an under-standing of the islands and their culture as well as to guide readers through their sights and activities:

◆ The **Features** section, indicated by a yellow bar at the top of each page, covers the history and culture of the islands in a series of informative essays.

◆ The main **Places** sec-tion, indicated by a blue bar, is a complete guide to all the sights and areas worth visiting. Places of special int-erest are coordinated by number with the maps.

newspaper, effectively rewrote *Modern Times* and *New Horizons*. He also compiled *Decisive Dates*. A colleague at the *Express*, **David Brewster**, a sport journalist, wrote the witty and informative feature on sport called *Liming and Leisure*.

Caribbean and Latin America specialist **James Ferguson** updated the authoritative *Trinbagonians*, written by novelist **Merle Hodge**.

The bulk of the updating and new material was produced by **Simon Lee**, a Caribbean specialist who lived in Trinidad for many years, and **Raymond Ramcharitar**, a Trinidad-based arts journalist and novelist. Lee updated **Knolly Moses** and **Therese Mills**' *Roti on the Run* and **Ernest Brown**'s *A Musical Nation*. He also updated *Festivals* and *Caribbean Carnival* both written by **Molly Ahye**.

Lee also updated the *Northern Range* and the two touring Tobago chapters and wrote *Insight On... Flora and Fauna*, *Birds and Butterflies* and *Carnival Costume*. Ramcharitar updated *A Colourful Capital*, *Chaguaramas and the Dragon's Islands*, *Coast to Coast* and *Down in the South* and wrote the religion chapter, *A Matter of Faith*. The dynamic duo also co-wrote the arts feature, *Artistic Influence*. **Aneka Roberts-Griffith** compiled the Travel Tips.

The current edition builds on the foundation created most notably by **Elizabeth Saft**, project editor of the original guide, and **Clara Rosa de Lima** who contributed to the Places chapters. **David Weintraub**, **Sean Drakes** and **Lesley Player** provided new images, adding to those of photographers **Junia Browne** and **Bill Wassman**. **Laura Hicks** proofread, and **Isobel McLean** indexed this edition.

◆ The **Travel Tips** listings section, with an orange bar, provides a handy point of reference for information on travel, hotels, shops, restaurants and more.

The contributors

This edition of *Insight Guide: Trinidad and Tobago* was supervised by managing editor **Lesley Gordon** at Insight Guides' London office. The book has been completely updated with the invaluable help of several people, including editor **Caroline Radula-Scott** and TIDCO in Trinidad. The original history chapters, written by **Kim Nicholas Johnson**, were appraised for this edition by historian **Bridget Brereton**, Deputy Principal at the University of West Indies in Trinidad. Johnson, a journalist on the *Trinidad Express*

Map Legend

—··—	International Boundary
————	Parish Boundary
—·—·—	National Park/Reserve
————	Ferry Route
✈ ✈	Airport: International/Regional
🚌	Bus Station
❶	Tourist Information
✉	Post Office
✝ ✝ ✝	Church/Ruins
✝	Monastery
☾	Mosque
✡	Synagogue
⛫	Castle/Ruins
∴	Archaeological Site
∩	Cave
⚐	Statue/Monument
★	Place of Interest

The main places of interest in the Places section are coordinated by number with a full-colour map (e.g. ❶), and a symbol at the top of every right-hand page tells you where to find the map.

INSIGHT GUIDE
TRINIDAD & TOBAGO

CONTENTS

Maps

Beach at
Plaisance,
Trinidad.

THE PARADISE ISLANDS

Trinidad and Tobago is rich in nature and wildlife, with a unique culture and, most precious of all, people who love life

Sir Walter Raleigh envisioned it as the gateway to the gold of El Dorado; Robinson Crusoe sustained himself on the fruits of its earth and sea; 18th-century Europeans travelled thousands of arduous miles hoping to become as "rich as a Tobago planter". For hundreds of years the beauty and fecundity of these paradisiacal islands have entranced and inspired dreamers, visitors and inhabitants.

Southernmost of the islands in the Caribbean archipelago, the Republic of Trinidad and Tobago lies only 11 km (7 miles) from the South American mainland, just off the coastal plains of Venezuela. Trinidad and Tobago are not the remnants of ancient volcanoes but rather the serendipitous result of a gradual and gentle breach between South America and a small mountainous region on its northeastern coast. This geological fact creates a sea of difference between these two islands and those further north, with geography, flora and fauna as multiform as those of the neighbouring great continent.

For aeons the islands lay in relative obscurity in an elysian corner of the uncharted world, but in the few hundred years since they appeared on the European map the peoples and lands of Trinidad and Tobago have exerted a subtle influence on the culture and history of countries all over the world.

When Trinidad and Tobago were "discovered" by Europeans, the promise they held of riches and beauty brought four of the most powerful nations in the Western world to struggle with one another for control. Their greed involved even more distant peoples in their future. The cruel commerce of slavery transplanted the people of African nations to these islands, and when that practice was ceased, labourers from India, China and the Middle East were compelled by both despair and hope to make new homes in Trinidad.

Indirectly, Trinidad and Tobago were involved in the American Civil War, and since then the Trini people and their music have filtered northwards to entwine themselves in the growth of the USA and its music. Calypso and steel drums have brought their rhythms to folk songs, jazz, R&B and rock 'n' roll, while hundreds of thousands of Trinidadians have become an integral part of American life.

The immigrants who made Trinidad and Tobago their home forged an independent and original nation. The number of visitors to the islands is increasing, but the natural beauty and indigenous culture remain unspoiled. Those who come to enjoy the scintillating beaches and lilting music also discover a land and peoples as diverse as those of countries many times the size, and a population eager to welcome the traveller to a unique and vibrant culture. ❏

PRECEDING PAGES: "jumping up" with the Poison band; on the beach at Las Cuevas; a black grouper, part of a rich marine life; a Tobagonian roadblock. **LEFT:** a Trini-style wedding scene.

Decisive Dates

Around 5000 BC Mesolithic Indians from the Orinoco delta in Venezuela arrive in Trinidad in dug-out canoes; this makes it the first island of the Caribbean archipelago to be settled.

300 BC–AD 1500 More skilful ceramic-using agricultural Saladoid Indians arrive. By 1500 several Indian nations are living in Trinidad, with Caribs in Tobago.

THE SPANISH COLONISTS 1498–1757

After Columbus's landfall, Trinidad becomes the much fought-over launching pad for El Dorado expeditions.

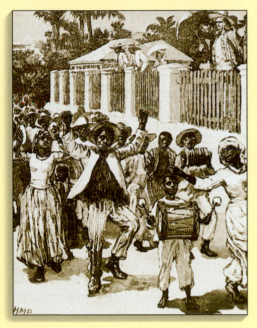

1498 Columbus, on his third voyage, names the island after the Holy Trinity because he can see three hills.

1530 Antonio Sedeno receives a commission to settle Trinidad. He fails.

1592 Domingo de Vera founds St Joseph, the first European settlement in the Lesser Antilles, for Antonio de Berrio, who dies in 1596 after the failure of his El Dorado expedition.

1595 Sir Walter Raleigh sacks St Joseph before entering the Orinoco. He is later executed for attacking a Spanish fort.

1625–42 Several British and Dutch settlements in Tobago are wiped out by Amerindians and Spaniards.

1654 The Dutch wipe out a Courlandian (Latvian) settlement in Tobago, which in 1674 is ceded to the Dutch.

1699 Amerindians at Arenales mission in Trinidad revolt, and jump off the cliffs at Toco to their deaths.

PLANTATION SLAVERY 1699–1834

A latecomer to plantation slavery, Trinidad develops a large population of French planters eager to farm the island's fertile soil. Insurrection festers in Tobago.

1764 The British encourage settlement in Tobago; slavery expands on sugar and cotton plantations.

1777 Trinidad is placed under the jurisdiction of the captain-general of Venezuela. The first French planters arrive to develop Trinidad's slave plantations.

1778 Americans, like the warring Spanish, Dutch, British, French and Courlanders, make an unsuccessful attempt to settle Tobago, a pirate stronghold.

1783 Madrid issues a Cedula of Population to attract Roman Catholic (mainly French) immigrants to Trinidad with grants of land.

1784 The *cabildo* (council) moves to Port of Spain.

1796 Spain declares war on Britain.

1797 Britain captures Trinidad, and the dictatorial Thomas Picton is appointed governor.

1801 A planned slave revolt in Tobago is quashed.

1803 Britain takes Tobago from France once and for all.

1807 The slave trade is abolished by Britain, and five years later slave registration begins.

1810 Trinidad becomes a Crown Colony under the direct supervision of Britain.

1829 Legal equality for all free men is established.

1834 Slavery is replaced by a temporary "apprenticeship" system.

EMANCIPATION AND IMMIGRATION 1834–1903

After the end of slavery, cheap labour is drawn from Asia, and a multi-racial middle class develops in Trinidad. Tobago sinks deeper into recession.

1838 Apprenticeship ends, and former slaves are granted full freedom.

1845 Immigrants indentured to the sugar and cocoa plantations arrive from India. Later, more immigrants pour in from Madeira, China, Venezuela, Africa and other West Indian islands.

1857 The first successful oil well is sunk in Trinidad.

1876 A riot at Roxborough Estate in Tobago spreads into a major rebellion; scared planters abolish self-government in favour of becoming a Crown Colony.

1881 An attempt to curb the Carnival Canboulay torch-lit procession sparks rioting. In 1884 the East Indian Hosay festival is brutally suppressed in San Fernando.

1883 Ordinance bans drum dances and African musical instruments.

1897 Chemist Walter Mills forms the Trinidad Working-men's Association (TWA).

1898 Tobago is made a ward of the colony of Trinidad and Tobago; the first popular calypso in English attacks the governor.
1903 Riots against the government's water policy leave the Red House burnt and 16 dead.

POLITICAL AND CULTURAL PIONEERS 1903–39

The 1930s' world recession sparks labour unrest, precipitating the formation of trade unions and the first steps to democracy, spurred on by the calypsonians.
1919 Disaffected soldiers from World War I join the dockworkers' strike.
1920 Cocoa and sugar estates are abandoned as a result of the recession.
1922 "Chieftain" Walter Douglas forms the first commercial calypso revue or "tent".
1923 Radicalised by World War I, white planter Captain Arthur Andrew Cipriani takes the leadership of the TWA, and in 1925 wins a seat in the first Legislative Council elections.
1931 Albert Gomes founds the cultural and political journal *The Beacon*.
1934 Sugar workers riot; the Negro Welfare, Cultural and Social Association (NWA) is formed.
1937 Tubal Uriah "Buzz" Butler starts an oil workers' strike which leads to rioting; trade unions are formed.
1939 The formation of the first steel band, Alexander's Ragtime Band.

ROAD TO DEMOCRACY 1939–62

The rise of cultural and political nationalism is embodied in Carnival and the People's National Movement (PNM).
1941 The US Army occupies Chaguaramas and Wallerfield, creating well-paid employment.
1945 World War II ends and the steel band movement goes public, accompanied by violent rivalry.
1946 The first Carnival for six years is held, as are the first general elections with universal suffrage.
1950 The Trinidad & Tobago Steelbandmen's Association is formed to end the bands' feuding; in 1951 the Trinidad & Tobago All Steel Percussion Orchestra, the first symphonic steel band, visits the Festival of Britain.
1956 Eric Williams's PNM wins 13 seats to become the first responsible government; calypsonian Mighty Sparrow debuts with "Jean and Dinah".
1958 Federation of the British West Indies is formed; the PNM loses federal elections, and racial political antagonism increases.
1961 A.N.R. Robinson wins one of two Tobago seats in Parliament.

LEFT: slaves celebrate their freedom.
RIGHT: the flag of the Republic of Trinidad and Tobago.

1962 Following Jamaica, Trinidad and Tobago withdraws from the Federation to become independent.

AN INDEPENDENT NATION 1962–TODAY

Eric Williams dominates political life until his death in 1981. Tobago's autonomy continues to grow.
1963 Lord Kitchener returns after 17 years in England to challenge Sparrow's calypso dominance; the Panorama steel band competition is launched.
1970 Black Power rises against racial discrimination, and the army mutinies.
1971 Elections boycotted by all opposition parties.
1975 Bloody Tuesday repression of "peace, bread and justice" demonstration.

1980 First elections held for the newly formed Tobago House of Assembly.
1981 Eric Williams dies.
1986 Led by A.N.R. Robinson, the four-party National Alliance for Reconstruction wins the election.
1990 Muslim insurgents capture the Cabinet for five days; 24 people die in the violence.
1991 The PNM is returned to power.
1995 The United National Congress (UNC) and the PNM win 17 seats each. Basdeo Panday is the first East Indian prime minister.
2000 Calypsonian Lord Kitchener dies.
2003 Distinguished musician Andre Tanker dies.
2005 The Caribbean Court of Justice is inaugurated in Port of Spain. ❏

IN THE BEGINNING

When Christopher Columbus arrived in Trinidad in 1498, looking for fresh water,
35,000 Amerindians were already living there and on Tobago

When the Mesolithic Indians established communities in Trinidad from around 5000 BC, they made it the first settled island in the Caribbean, hunting, fishing and gathering in the swampy coastal areas. Their tools of stone, bone and shell were left behind like fingerprints.

Around 300 BC Amerindians of the Saladoid archaeological era arrived from the South American mainland, and their skills were even greater. They could spin and weave, make and paint pottery, cultivate sweet potato and cassava, and process the latter into a long-lasting bread. At around the time of Christ, these people were living only in Tobago, but they slowly moved up the island chain of the Lesser Antilles to the Virgin Islands and Puerto Rico, colonising the islands as they went. In around AD 250 the Barrancoid people settled in Trinidad and Tobago, and Saladoid pottery was replaced by Barrancoid. (The names come from archaeological sites in Venezuela.)

Land of the Hummingbird

A sharp break occurred around AD 1000 when central and southern Trinidad developed close cultural links with the Paria coast of Venezuela. Tobago and north Trinidad kept their ties with the Windward Islands to the north. Formerly all the tribes of Trinidad and Tobago had spoken Arawakan dialects, but after this time, and for the next 500 years, Amerindians speaking Cariban dialects are believed to have arrived from the South American lowlands to settle on Trinidad – then called Ieri, "Land of the Hummingbird". They also moved on up the Caribbean archipelago.

So when Columbus came to fill up with fresh water in 1498, who was there? Shebaio and Arawak-speaking tribes (now referred to as Taínos) were on the south coast, Nepoio on the southeast and east coasts, and Yao on the

southwest coast. In the northwest were the Carinepagoto who, like the Yao and Nepoio, spoke Cariban dialects, as did the Kalina, or Island Caribs, of Tobago. All in all, they totalled about 35,000.

The Trinidad and Tobago Amerindians were described by the Spanish as well-proportioned

and of fairer complexion than the Island Caribs. They went naked but for girdles and head bands, painted their bodies red and wore feathers for decoration. Chiefs wore crowns and ornaments of gold, while normal folk contented themselves with beaded decorations of stone, bone and teeth.

Amerindian lifestyle

Living in villages of no more than a few hundred inhabitants, the Amerindians moved their bell-shaped thatched houses regularly. Theirs were loose societies, and chiefs, who held little secular power, were easily replaced. This allowed them to resist the Spaniards much more

LEFT: one of the last remaining Carib Indians poses for a 19th-century guidebook to British Guiana.
RIGHT: Amerindian artefact at the Tobago Museum.

successfully than did the hierarchic Incas and Aztecs of Central and South America, for the death of a chief did not immobilise the tribe.

The main social divisions were between men and women: men cleared the forest, hunted and fished; women planted, weeded, harvested and prepared meals. The economy was based on the shifting cultivation of cassava, maize, tobacco, beans, squash and peppers for food, cotton for clothes and hammocks, and annatto for body paint. The Amerindians fished, hunted and gathered shells,

> **TAÍNO TRADE FAIRS**
>
> Several villages would join up for a feast and trade in a fair-like atmosphere, bartering many items: cassava graters for salt, pearls for axes, trumpets for hammocks.

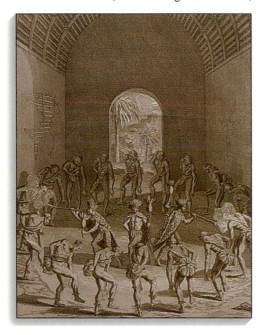

crabs and turtle eggs, and they traded and made war. Villages fought with one another, formed and dissolved alliances, and captured slaves. Their weapons were darts, stones, bows and poisoned arrows. Yet most war expeditions resulted in no more than a minor skirmish.

Cannibal myths

What of the notorious man-eating habits of the Caribs, whose very name has given us the world cannibal? It is believed that most Amerindian tribes in the region may have practised some form of ritual cannibalism, for example eating the heart of a courageous enemy or a beloved chieftain. Certainly nothing

like the voracious flesh-eaters portrayed in many history books existed. This scurrilous myth was the creation of Spanish slave traders who sought to justify their unChristian activities of capturing Indians for slavery.

In 1510 the Spanish declared that the only peaceful Indians in the region were living in Trinidad, and King Ferdinand of Spain forbade slave raiding from the island. Despite that, in 1511 Trinidad was categorised as Carib, and thus cannibal; but, following protests from the Spanish priest Bartolomé de Las Casas, who came to be known as the "Protector of the Indians", it was eventually excluded from the list of Carib islands in 1520. Nonetheless, this did not stop the island's first governor, Antonio Sedeno, asking in 1532, for permission to catch slaves in Trinidad for, he claimed that, the inhabitants were "Caribs and people who eat human flesh and have other rites and evil customs and are very warlike".

But the Spanish soon realised that it was not in their interest to capture the Taínos as the latter participated in a trade network that stretched for thousands of miles, which proved to be very useful to the invaders. The trade base included what is now Guyana, northeastern Venezuela and the Orinoco basin. Each tribe had its specialities which it traded for those of others. A Taíno tribe called the Lokono, whose villages were found in Trinidad and along the Orinoco, specialised in trade itself, travelling hundreds of miles up the river with the wares of other tribes, for water in those days did not separate people but brought them closer.

One particular Lokono village called Arucay, on the left bank of the lower Orinoco, was larger than the others because of its admirable position for trade upriver, downstream and along the coasts. Its inhabitants supplied many a Spanish expedition with food, earning the Taínos the title "friends of the Christians". Spanish dependence on them enhanced the tribe's economic strength, for they had access to the coveted iron tools. It also exempted them from Spanish slave raiding, and so other tribes found it expedient to describe themselves as Taínos. However, a reverse logic worked for many Spanish slave raiders, for whom it was convenient to find as few "friends of the

Christians" as possible, and as many cannibals as there were Amerindians.

Spanish Trinidad

It was a well-populated island that Christopher Columbus sighted on 31 July 1498. This was the admiral's third trip to the New World. Becalmed at the Equator on his way to South America (the other half of his six-ship fleet had sailed straight to Hispaniola), he changed his plans out of desperation and sailed due west and north. It was on this course, just as the drinking water on his ships was about to run out, that the crew sighted three peaks joined at

on their deck. The Indians let loose a flight of arrows, and the Spaniards responded. The Indians approached one of the caravells and invited the pilot to come ashore, but then lost their nerve and fled. The admiral departed for Hispaniola, never to land again on Trinidad. En route he espied two islands which he named "Concepcion" and "Assumpcion". They were Grenada and Tobago.

God or man?

During the 16th century, further Spanish incursions into Trinidad began as a search for slaves to work the nearby pearl islands of Cubagua and Margarita. The story is told that when the

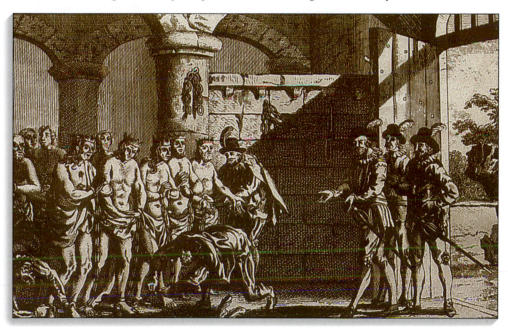

the base. Overjoyed at their deliverance he named the land La Trinidad after the Holy Trinity.

Columbus cruised along the south coast, and landed at Punta de la Playa (now Erin) where his men saw only footprints in the sand. He continued along to the southwestern tip, naming places in a godlike fashion as he went. Next day his ship was approached by a dug-out canoe manned by 20 Amerindians. The men from the two worlds stared at one another for some time until the Spaniards began singing and dancing

LEFT: priests breathe courage into their subjects.
ABOVE: Sir Walter Raleigh, on his way to El Dorado, sets free five Amerindian kings.

Indians finally decided to rid themselves of the Spaniards' burdensome presence, they were unsure whether these white people could be killed. A sceptical chief named Brayoan devised a plan: they found a Spaniard passing through their lands and offered to escort him. At a river the Indians courteously offered to take the Spaniard across on their shoulders, but in the deepest part they threw him off and held him under the water until he was still. They dragged him to the bank and wept copious tears, apologising for keeping him under for so long. The chief then inspected the corpse; once it was proved to be dead, they knew it was possible to wage war against the Spaniards.

Sir Walter Raleigh drops in

For the Spaniards, Trinidad was a starting point for expeditions into Guyana in search of El Dorado – the mythical city of gold – and it was not until 1592 that the first Spanish settlement of St Joseph was established by Domingo de Vera. He marked out the sites of the church, the governor's residence, the *cabildo* (council) and the prison, founding a colony which, for the next two centuries, would be characterised by poverty and anarchy, and would be repeatedly attacked by foreign adventurers, including Sir Walter Raleigh – also on a quest for El Dorado. While passing through he ransacked St Joseph, killing

IN SEARCH OF EL DORADO

Throughout the 16th century, European explorers and fortune hunters were intent on finding El Dorado, a mythical land of gold which they were convinced existed somewhere between the Orinoco and Amazon rivers in the Guyana highlands of South America.

Spanish governors of Caribbean colonies competed for funds to finance expeditions, and Sir Walter Raleigh was among those who had heard tales of a tribe that once a year rolled its king in gold dust. He was one of a few who returned alive from expeditions up the Orinoco. Many were foiled by Amerindians who would direct them deep into the jungle; they would never be seen again.

the inhabitants because "to leave a garrison in my back interested in the same enterprize, who also dayly expected supplies out of Spaine, I should have savoured very much of the asse".

Raleigh then freed any imprisoned Indians, telling them of his "Queene, who was the great *cacique* (chief) of the North, and a virgine". When the Dutch invaded, they merely took all the Spaniards' belongings, including their clothes, turning Trinidad into a nudist colony.

Missions and malaise

Having staked their claim in Trinidad, the Spaniards allotted communities of Amerindians to privileged colonists in four *encomiendas* (plantations). The failure of these to see to the Indians' conversion to Christianity led to the setting up of Catholic missions. In 1699 the Indians at Arenales (the site is marked at San Rafael) rebelled and killed the missionaries, the governor and several soldiers. They were pursued by a vengeful army to Toco where, rather than surrender, they leapt off a cliff to their deaths. By then, however, the missions had fallen foul of the planters who wanted labour, not religious devotion. The missions were eventually abolished in 1708, although four – Savana Grande (Princes Town), Guayria (Naparima), Savanetta and Montserrate – survived the 18th century as Amerindian villages.

The early Spanish settlers grew tobacco, an Amerindian drug for which Europeans had acquired a taste. It was produced for illegal trade with the Dutch and English. The Spanish policy of destroying all foreign ships in the Gulf of Paria in the early 17th century, and competition from North American colonies, ended that industry.

Cocoa became the next main crop, cultivated by Indian labourers on the *encomiendas*. But in 1725 a disease wiped out the cocoa farmers, and in 1739 a smallpox epidemic ended all pretence of civilised life; the settlers abandoned St Joseph for the bush, only emerging to intrigue against the governor. The cabildo even staged a coup in 1745, imprisoning the governor until a force from Venezuela was sent to the rescue. Eventually, in 1757, the representative of Spain moved to Puerto de España, a small fishing village on the west coast. ❑

LEFT: a humanised image of the slave.
RIGHT: the enslaved Taíno Amerindians mined for gold.

ENTER FRANCE AND BRITAIN, EXIT SPAIN

As the islands changed hands – Tobago many times – the sugar industry prospered, and the number of slaves increased

The winds of change had begun to blow, even through the moribund Spanish state, even through sleepy Port of Spain, described in 1777 as "several cannons on a battery, a church, and about 80 houses covered with straw". Trade within the Spanish Empire was liberalised (though foreigners were still excluded) and, under the influence of his French allies, Charles III sought to strengthen his empire's defences by developing the more neglected provinces. In 1776 Manuel Falquez was appointed governor of Trinidad, with instructions to attract Roman Catholic immigrants, especially French planters, by offering land grants and tax incentives. But it was the Africans, whose labour had enriched islands such as Barbados and Martinique, who were really in demand.

Enticing Roman Catholic settlers

The first trickle of immigrants came from Grenada, where the French suffered discrimination under a new British government. One such man was Roume de St Laurent; this energetic planter supported the scheme by lobbying in Caracas and Madrid for its expansion. In 1783 his opinions were embodied in a Cedula of Population issued from Madrid, offering very generous terms to planters willing to emigrate with their slaves to this wilderness. Every white immigrant was entitled to approximately 53 hectares (130 acres) of land for each member of his family, and half as much again for each slave he brought with him, and there were tax exemptions as well. Free coloured and free black settlers were granted half the amount. The settlers only had to be Roman Catholic and from a nation friendly to Spain.

It is a strange coincidence that Tobago, kicked around between different metropolitan countries for the previous two centuries, was

at this time in the hands of the French, who pursued a similar immigration policy: a French colony offering monetary bribes to attract French settlers from a Spanish colony.

In 1784 there were almost 4,500 non-native

people and only 1,495 Amerindians in Trinidad. By 1797 there were 16,000 non-natives, including Europeans, slaves and people of mixed blood, and only 1,000 or so Amerindians. Trinidad was not yet a plantation society based on African slavery in the way that some of the other islands were, but it was getting there, with a slave population that nearly twice outnumbered the freemen.

The man in charge from 1784 was Governor Don José María Chacon, an educated multilingual Spaniard with a black mistress and mulatto children. Chacon set about encouraging new colonists, to the detriment of the old Spanish settlers. A decree was passed by which lands

LEFT: slaves landing from the ships.
RIGHT: a rebel slave with musket.

left uncultivated were forfeited to the Crown, for Chacon thought the old Spanish settlers lazy and crooked. His advisers were Spaniards from Spain or Venezuela and French settlers, and by 1788 six out of nine members of the *cabildo* (council) were foreign.

As Trinidad grew less like the mainland colonies in social structure, Chacon's powers grew more autonomous and extensive, and Trinidad's links with the captaincy-general of Venezuela, under whose jurisdiction the island lay, grew weaker. It was as if the longstanding connection with the mainland, that had continued in an Amerindian cultural unity and a Spanish administrative unity, had at last been broken. And so the old Spanish and Amerindian society was superseded, and new actors replaced the old ones in the drama.

A plantation bureaucracy

Very soon Trinidad was a Spanish colony whose mind and heart were French. French planters filled the important public offices such as the Commissioner of Population, the Commandant of Quarters and the members of the *cabildo*; the predominant language was French or French Creole *(patois)*, and social customs were French as well. This was when Carnival,

LES GENS DE COULEUR

The free coloureds, or *gens de couleur* as they were referred to by the French, were the result of interracial unions that were commonplace in the older slave-owning colonies of the Caribbean. It was unusual for a white planter not to have a slave for his mistress, who would bear him many children.

These mulatto offspring grew up to become a highly significant group in West Indian society, occupying a marginal position between the whites and the slaves. If the father's marriage had been childless, it was not unheard of for a mulatto to inherit his father's sugar estate. But mulattos were still discriminated against, whatever their

position, and many came to Trinidad hoping for better lives.

Although they were given no official public posts in Trinidad, coloureds faced no public apartheid as they did in the British and French colonies. Some became wealthy slave-owning planters, some were republicans. Most were smallholders and artisans with no more ideology than a desire for equality.

Already these *gens de couleur* possessed the contemporary characteristics of large numbers, beautiful women and deep conservatism. But they were thought of as just like those on the French islands, and every coloured man claiming equality was seen as a wild revolutionary.

which lasted then from Christmas to Ash Wednesday, was introduced. And while French and French Creole would die out in the 20th century, Carnival would grow from an exclusively white festival to today's one that includes all races and classes, providing both an idiom for the Trinidadian social mind in general and a wellspring of the nation's arts.

The leaders of society at this time were all wealthy white planters, but in the 1790s, as the fortunes of the French Revolution waxed and waned in the Caribbean, immigrants in Trinidad began to reflect the entire ideological spectrum, much to the dismay of the island's governor and the planters. More numerous than the whites were the free coloureds, who fled the older French slave colonies such as Grenada, where they had suffered systematic discrimination. The largest group of immigrants, however, was the African slaves. Roman Catholic, *patois*-speaking, at first they came with their owners. Some were brought or kidnapped from neighbouring colonies. But the development of the colony required more slaves, and soon the slave trade was flourishing in Trinidad and was declared open to all nationalities in 1790.

British at the controls

It is sometimes argued that slavery was less harsh under the Spanish than in the French and British islands; the Spanish Slave Code of 1789 was quite liberal by comparison. But Spanish laws were implemented in Trinidad by French planters, and the mortality of slaves in Trinidad was higher than the birth rate, especially in the early phase of clearing the land. Yet the scarcity of slaves, the accessibility of the bush and the influence of Southern European culture made for a more intimate master-slave relationship than that in other territories. The issue is clouded, but certainly the Spaniards tolerated, even encouraged, much of the Africans' culture in a way not found in other nations' colonies.

For Governor Chacon the 1790s were definitely the worst of times. The slaves were

getting revolutionary ideas, and Britain and France were fighting the Revolutionary wars, which often spilled into Spanish colonial territories, especially the poorly defended island of Trinidad. French privateers and British warships battled in the Gulf of Paria, and in May 1796 open fighting broke out in Port of Spain between British sailors from the *Alarm*, the warship which had just sunk some privateers in the Gulf of Paria, and the town's French inhabitants.

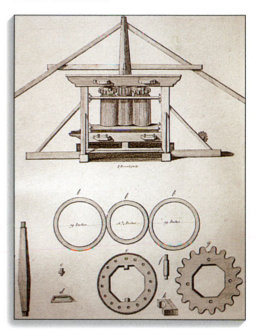

Chacon did what he could: he organised a militia, armed a few Amerindians with bows and arrows, and pleaded with Madrid for reinforcements. But when the French Jacobin emissary Victor Hugues offered his assistance, Chacon demurred: "Should the King send me aid, I will do my duty to preserve his Crown to this colony; if not, it must fall into the hands of the English who I believe to be generous enemies, and are more to be trusted than treacherous friends".

In September 1796 a Spanish squadron of five ships commanded by Admiral Apodaca arrived in Trinidad from Puerto Rico with 740 soldiers, many of whom immediately fell ill

LEFT: a cartload of sugarcane used as cattle fodder.
RIGHT: one type of sugar mill in use throughout the West Indies.

with yellow fever. In October Spain declared war on Britain; the *Alarm* incident was mentioned. A corvette bringing money and ammunition from Puerto Rico was captured by the British, who had long had their eyes on Trinidad. On 16 February 1797 their invasion force sailed into the Gulf: 18 ships to Apodaca's five, 7,000 soldiers to Chacon's 2,000 (most of them deserted, if healthy enough).

That night the Spaniards burnt their own ships. The next day they surrendered to the British with hardly a shot. For this, Chacon would be later vilified by the Trinidad planters and humiliated by the King of Spain.

colony, or a French, or Dutch one. Abercromby next appointed one of his officers, Thomas Picton, as governor of Trinidad with near absolute powers. "Do justice according to your conscience", ordered Abercromby, and then left the island. The results were horrendous.

A brutal governor

Thomas Picton was a harsh soldier who had been early advised to rule with an iron rod because the island was full of revolutionaries and assassins. Arbitrary imprisonment and execution, judicial torture and mutilation were the hallmarks of Picton's six-year reign, and slaves

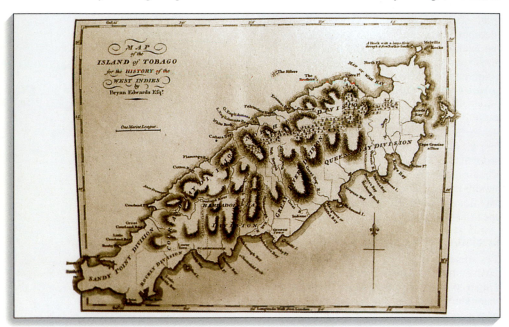

Generous terms

The terms of the capitulation offered by Sir Ralph Abercromby were generous: Chacon's soldiers were to surrender and would be allowed to return to Spain – but not to take up arms against Britain; officers in the judiciary and administration were allowed to remain at their posts, and Spanish law was to be maintained; everyone, except the prisoners of war, was to swear allegiance to Britain and, having done so, was allowed to retain his property; men of property were allowed to keep their weapons; and those who considered themselves to be citizens of the French Republic were to be given safe conduct to some other Spanish

and free coloureds bore the brunt of it. The blunt soldier with the frightening laugh had overnight become an absolute dictator and a planter; his cruelty was merely the logic of his powerful position.

Picton's transformation was a gradual departure from British policy. When Britain first captured the island, its aim, apart from the tactical one, was to foster an illegal trade with Venezuela by two methods: first, to encourage the contraband trade through Port of Spain, up the Orinoco and into Venezuela; secondly, to encourage the embryonic nationalist revolution on the mainland, knowing that a liberated Venezuela would trade openly with Britain. For a while, Picton diligently assisted the Venezuelan revolutionaries, turning Port of Spain into a den of spies and conspirators, much to the dismay of the Governor of Cumana who offered $20,000 for Picton's head. Picton offered $20 for the Governor's.

Praised in 1801 for his "zeal", by 1802 Picton was an embarrassment to the British Government, for he had promoted a slave colony. London had wanted a colony of free white settlers. Therein lay Picton's great mistake, and a commission was set up to govern the colony. Picton, William Fullarton and Samuel Hood were its three members, but the first two became involved in a sordid feud over Picton's methods of government. The commission was dissolved, Fullarton secured an indictment against Picton for torturing a coloured girl, and the problem of how to rule the country was, in 1803, once again painfully raised.

Meanwhile, over in Tobago

In the same year, 1803, a British force took Tobago away from the French without any opposition. Tobago, the region's most knocked-about island, had changed hands for the last time, and Britain's ownership was confirmed in 1815 at the Congress of Vienna, never to be challenged until independence. But let us start from the beginning.

At the time of Columbus, the island was thought to be occupied by Kalina Indians, or Island Caribs, and in the 17th century more Kalinas arrived from St Vincent. Although the admiral, seeing the island from a distance in 1498, had named it "Assumpcion", it later came to be called Tavaco – after an Indian smoking instrument, it is sometimes said.

Whatever the name, it was a nominally Spanish island on which the first English settlers arrived in 1625. The Amerindians wiped them out, but the English claimed the island anyway. The Dutch landed settlers in 1628, but a Spanish and Amerindian force from Trinidad invaded in canoes and put them to the sword; as Eric Williams explains, "Trinidad and Tobago went to war". The English landed again in

CHRISTENING GIFT

Charles I of England (1625–49) is believed to have given Tobago to his infant godson, the Duke of Courland, as a christening present in 1642.

1639, and again the Amerindians chased them off. It is believed that Charles I then gave the island to the Duke of Courland (Latvia), as a christening present, so Courlanders attempted to settle in 1642. Indians chased them off, along with a party from Barbados. Courlanders returned in 1650, and again in 1654, but the Dutch came again, and suppressed them. Louis XIV of France then gave the island to the victorious Dutch, who were expelled by the English, who were in turn driven off by the French, who

razed the settlement and abandoned the island.

By 1674, when Tobago was ceded to the Dutch, the island had changed flags over a dozen times, and so it continued – Dutch, French, Latvian, English, Dutch, French, English – even the Americans took a turn, in 1778, at capturing the half-deserted, undeveloped island which was, for most of the time, just a nest of pirates.

Rum and rebellion

Dutch policy for Tobago was that the island should be "so laid waste as will hinder all settlement", partly to appease other colonies which feared competition. It was formally ceded to

LEFT: a map of Tobago showing British divisions.
RIGHT: a shackled slave.

Britain in 1763; the British began to encourage settlers once again in 1764, and five years later 9,300 hectares (23,000 acres) were already under cultivation. The colony developed rapidly, and huge numbers of slaves were imported from Africa. Seven years after the first shipment of sugar was exported, Tobago was producing 1,200 tonnes of sugar, 6 million litres (1.6 million gallons) of rum, 680,000 kg (1.5 million lb) of cotton, and 2,300 kg (5,000 lb) of indigo. The corollary of this expansion was that by the early 1770s slaves

SLAVES IN TOBAGO

To keep the anti-slavery movement in Europe at bay, Tobago planters pretended that they were kinder to their slaves, giving them more rights – but little was implemented.

outnumbered whites by twenty to one. It was a ratio higher than anywhere else in the British West Indies, and as a result Tobago experienced almost annual slave revolts on a small scale until 1784. One rebellion, in 1774, brought savage punishments on the rebels.

In French hands again

The French captured Tobago once more in 1781, but the island's land and slave owners remained predominantly British, and sugar production continued to grow. In 1793 Britain took Tobago back until 1802, when the French intervened once again, but only for a year. In 1803 the British took the island back again, once and for all.

Between 1771 and 1791 Tobago's population rose from 5,084 to 15,020; 14,170 of these were black slaves, and only five Amerindians could be found. But the black-white ratio had fallen to a less dangerous level, or so the planters thought.

The British and the French made Tobago productive and populous, an exporter of sugar and cotton, at the cost of creating a typical West Indian slave society. In 1798, to deflect anti-slavery attacks from abroad, a legislative committee produced a report on the state of the slaves, unique for its liberality. In summary, land was to be distributed to slaves and time to cultivate it allowed, more food was to be given to them, slave imports were discouraged, and the Creole population was to be increased naturally. Matrimony was encouraged, children and pregnant mothers were protected, and midwives paid by planters. And Guardians of the Rights of Negroes were to be appointed in every parish.

Foiled slave revolt

The planters were pleased with themselves, despite the fact that little of what the report said was implemented, and mistakenly confident of their slaves. Early in 1801 Sir William Young, stated that "here the planters talk of their Negroes as their resort to be depended on against either a licentious garrison, an arbitrary Governor, or the mad democracy of French hucksters". Imagine their surprise when a Christian slave exposed a massive plan for insurrection, scheduled for Christmas Day.

Martial law was declared, 200 suspects were rounded up, and the whole conspiracy was exposed. Slaves from 16 estates were involved. Roger, a driver at the Belvedere estate, was the "governor", and Thomas, a cooper, the "colonel". There were five "captains" on various estates and five "chiefs" in Scarborough. These men had formed companies of slaves, and the plan had been to set alight five estates, killing any whites who came to control the fire. In the town, the governor and the commander in chief of the garrison were to be assassinated. It was expected that the whole slave population would then rise up in revolt. By 4 January 1802, sentences had been handed down and the whole affair ended. Because the slaves were needed, only six rebel leaders were executed. Four other rebels were banished, and the rest sent back to work after a severe flogging. Tobago was quiet for the next 60 years.

Trinidad under the Crown

In 1812 it was written: "Trinidad is a subject for an anatomy school or rather a poor patient in a country hospital on which all sorts of surgical experiments are tried, to be given up if they fail and to be practised on others if they succeed". The first experiment sought to find out what kind of government the colony should have. The issue had been forced by Thomas

Britain, however, was less willing to grant laws to new colonies than before. The government had grown too familiar with the difficulties and obstructions of which West Indian colonial assemblies were capable, but could not ignore the demand which came from Trinidad. However, then the free coloureds petitioned for consideration on the matter, fearing that a local assembly would merely entrench the power of a small and bigoted élite. Hislop was furious, but in contrast Smith was elated, reasoning that if the free coloureds were excluded from an assembly there would be difficulties, so there could be no assembly. Including the free

Hislop, the governor who replaced Picton. He became embroiled in a struggle with Chief Justice George Smith, an irascible man whose rigorous application of Spanish laws angered the planters. Smith despised them in return.

"Generally colonies are peopled by the refuse of the Mother Country", he said, "but Trinidad is peopled by the refuse of the other colonies". In 1810 Hislop, his Council of Advice and the *cabildo* petitioned the king for a British Constitution and British laws.

LEFT: view over Scarborough, Tobago.
ABOVE: proclaiming emancipation to slaves on a sugar plantation.

coloureds, even the wealthiest, was never considered, and the matter was closed: Trinidad would be a Crown Colony under direct supervision of Britain. This signalled the beginning of the end of colonial self-government in the British West Indies.

Demand for slaves

The next problem to contend with was that of development. Trinidad was mostly forest, and large slave-owning plantations were rare. The planters wanted more slaves, although their number had doubled in Picton's time. But the British Parliament was under pressure from abolitionists to make no extensions of the slave trade. Other sugar colonies agreed with the abolitionists because they feared competition. So Britain suggested a scheme of free labourers, but implemented it halfheartedly. In 1806 the slave trade was prohibited to new colonies, and in the following year it was abolished. Trinidad never became a mature slave society like the other West Indian territories, although sugar came to dominate land use and exports.

However, the illegal importation of slaves was now a major problem which had to be addressed, and a registry of slaves was set up by an Order in Council. Every slave was to be registered within a month of March 1812, and

no unregistered person could be held as a slave. The registrar was a slave owner, and both he and the governor, Sir Ralph Woodford, hardly implemented the Order at all. The deadline was ignored or extended, and the whole exercise rendered useless. Slave smuggling continued, many brought in as "domestics" from other territories and sold in Trinidad where the prices were high. A new governor, Sir Lewis Grant, prosecuted many who had illegally imported slaves, but too late – only a year before the Act of Emancipation in 1833.

Another experiment tested whether the harshness of slavery could be ameliorated by legislative measures. In 1824 an Order in Council

was passed restricting an owner's right to punish his slaves and giving slaves limited legal, religious and social rights: no more whipping of women; for men no more than 25 strokes; no more Sunday labour; manumission must be facilitated, even without the owner's consent; slave evidence was admissible in court; and a Protector of Slaves was to act on their behalf.

Howls of protest went up from the planters, and, they subverted the Order and made it nugatory. By 1830 this was apparent to Britain, and a tougher Order was drawn up. The planters' reaction grew hysterical as they resisted with the assistance of officials, especially those in the *cabildo*. In so doing they paved the way for the abolition of Spanish laws and the *cabildo* in the 1840s. But, more importantly, the planters themselves convinced Britain that it was time to end slavery completely.

The "Great Experiment"

And so the Act of Emancipation – the "Great Experiment" – was passed in August 1833 to take effect on 1 August 1834. Slave owners were compensated for their loss of property; field slaves were immediately apprenticed to their former owners for six years, other slaves for four; special magistrates were appointed to administer the system. On the big day, hundreds of slaves assembled in Port of Spain to protest at the apprenticeship period. The militia was called out, arrests were made, and the most dismal era of Caribbean history ended.

Or did it? On 17 June 1837 a Yoruba African called Makandal Daaga led a mutiny of liberated slaves from the First West Indian Regiment. The mutineers attacked and fired on the barracks at St Joseph and then set off to walk back to Africa. After days of skirmishing with the regular forces the rebels were put down, and the affair was over, having cost 40 lives, most of them of rebels. On 16 August 1837 Daaga and two others were executed.

Much later, in 1971, Daaga was to be the inspiration for another man with flashing eyes and a deep voice. The leader of a "Black Power" movement which had caused an unsuccessful mutiny in the army changed his name from Geddes Granger to Makandal Daaga. ❑

LEFT: slaves celebrate Emancipation, 1 August 1834.
RIGHT: a letter from the Governor of Trinidad is a mixture of fear and paternal reassurance.

THE HISTORICAL SOCIETY OF TRINIDAD AND TOBAGO.

Publication No. 882.

General Hislop to the Under Secretary of State.

Source:- Public Record Office. State Papers Colonial. C. O. 295/14.

Published by the courtesy of the Master of the Rolls and the Deputy Keeper of the Public Records.

Private.   Trinidad.
                                 8th January 1806.
Dear Sir

X   X   X

You will learn from my public dispatches which are forwarded by this packet, of the alarming situation into which the Colony has recently been thrown, and in which it still exists to a certain degree.

Our neighbouring Island of Tobago, is also under Martial Law in consequence of a discovery of an intention to poison the cistern of the garrison. It is also reported that a plan of an insurrection among the negroes in Guadeloupe has fortunately been discovered; and that General Evreux caused six of the Chiefs to be burnt alive. They were said to belong to San Domingo.

I can assure you that our situation is far from being pleasant but I trust that with proper examples in the first instance and a strict observance of discipline in the next, we shall succeed in preserving the Colony from a recurrence of so shocking a state as that from which it has so miraculously escaped.

THE PROBLEMS OF FREEDOM

After Emancipation, a shortage of labour in Trinidad opened the doors to desperate immigrants from India. Meanwhile, Tobago was bankrupt

A pprenticeship of the former slaves ended two years before schedule, in 1838, owing to the insistence of abolitionists in Britain and the intransigence of the ex-slaves, who decided not to work after 1 August 1838. On that day the old society died, and the future offered only the challenge of building freedom.

For the former slaves, liberty meant choosing how they wished to live: culturally, socially and, most important, economically. It involved no retreat to the bush – largely the preserve of Spanish-Amerindian *peons* – and any movements were to the urban areas. Most of all, in an island where labour was scarce, freedom for the former slaves meant using their bargaining power to improve their economic conditions, and this they did successfully. The average wage per task throughout the Caribbean was 30 cents; in Trinidad it was 50. In 1841 the planters collectively tried to reduce wages to 30 cents, but the workers withdrew their labour and the planters backed down: a success for Trinidad's first strike.

New labour force

Planters sought to retain a dependable labour force by allowing freed slaves to occupy estate huts and provision grounds, but most former slaves left the estate anyway. Many settled in or around the towns, and a large internal trade network grew up. For others, land was abundant, and if they were unable to meet the price they squatted illegally. The Crown showed no inclination to distribute land to the landless, but could not stop the squatting. This pull and tug was interrupted in 1846 when the Sugar Duties Act was passed in Britain, allowing cheaper foreign sugar into the mother country. Many estates were abandoned, and wages fell. The industry recovered with the British Government agreeing to the immigration of indentured labourers from India and to modernise the sugar industry.

LEFT: a young woman wearing traditional Martiniquan costume.
RIGHT: breaking cocoa during harvest.

The 1860s and 1870s saw two important and closely related developments. Under Governor A. H. Gordon, Crown lands were opened up to smallholders. His predecessor, Lord Harris, had sought to prevent the former slaves from becoming landowners by authorising the sale of large lots of land only, and at high prices. In

1869 Gordon reduced the smallest lot to 2 hectares (5 acres), the price to £1, and conveyance costs to a minimum. Many of the most intransigent squatters, it was discovered, were willing purchasers, and Gordon also offered land to the Indians who had served their indentures, in lieu of return passages to India.

The cocoa boom

The second change was the expansion of cocoa cultivation. Completely owned by locals, and often in peasant hands, cocoa had always been cultivated in Trinidad in small quantities. When chocolate touched the British sweet tooth in the 1860s, and cocoa blossomed in Trinidad to become the largest export. It was an achievement mainly of the *peons*, although blacks and Indians later contributed. These peasants bought small plots of Crown land which they cleared and planted with cocoa. When the trees began to bear, they sold the plots to a plantation and were paid for both land and trees. They then repeated the process. Alternatively, the plantation, already owning the land, contracted with *peons* for its clearance and cultivation. They did this but simultaneously used it for cash crops. At the end the *peons* were paid for each tree and moved on. Thus the French Creole élite shifted their wealth from depressed

incentive, half those in Trinidad, and the Treasury could not afford to pay for immigration. A hurricane in 1847 devastated the island and made prospects more grim. Even the British capitalists, usually willing to buy out bankrupt estates at knockdown prices, considered Tobago a bad deal. A different approach was required, and the planters looked to St Lucia and Antigua for inspiration. What they came up with was known as the *Metairie*, or *Métayage*, System (sharecropping).

This was an arrangement whereby the workers took no pay for their labour but instead shared the crop with the owner. An oral agree-

sugar to buoyant cocoa, growing richer until the 1920s, when the cocoa market crashed.

Tobago's travail

Tobago, a more classic plantation society than Trinidad, found itself bankrupt on Emancipation Day. "This Colony," stated an 1823 petition, "has now arrived at a pitch of distress of a deeper nature than we can possibly detail." As everywhere else in the British West Indies, in Tobago the labour force lost its tractability once freed, so planters sought to encourage the immigration of British convicts, Barbadians, Africans from Sierra Leone and free blacks from America. But wages were too low to be an

ment, it worked well enough until, in the late 1870s, the sugar industry declined further. Then planters began to renege on their agreements, and the almost feudal relationship showed its cracks. Riots broke out in May 1876 at Roxborough Estate; there had been fires on the estate – arson by Barbadian workers, it was said. Corporal Belmanna and five privates were sent to arrest the alleged arsonists but, as the warrants were being executed, the people grew restive. The corporal was knocked down, and shot a woman. She died, and the flame of justice was ignited. The manager's house was gutted, and the people besieged the court house. The police released their prisoners, but Belmanna, especially hated, was beaten to death. A warship was sent from Grenada to help.

Under the Crown

As the Morant Bay Rebellion did for the Jamaican planters in 1865, the Belmanna Riots scared the Tobago planters into surrendering their self-government in favour of Crown Colony government. So at the beginning of 1877 the 215 eligible voters in Tobago lost their democratic right to elect representatives, and Tobago became a Crown Colony. A Royal Commission was appointed

BRAVE SHARECROPPER

When a sharecropper was evicted by a planter in 1886, he took him to court for damages and won on appeal. But an ensuing enquiry then found in favour of the planter.

and Tobago (following the union of 1889). Sir John castigated the planter for his shamelessness and upheld the old man's claim for damages. And the planters raised their voices in the same centuries-old protest: "…the labouring classes of the Island are in an unsettled state and… this condition of affairs is attributable to an impression which has been created amongst them, with which your Honour's name is unfortunately associated." A commission of enquiry was set up and the chief justice was repri-

LEFT: farmworkers at the end of the 19th century.
ABOVE: a family of young farmhands pauses for a picture in a cornfield.

in 1882 to look into the impoverishment of Tobago (and other colonies). The Commission found an empty Treasury, but it was the labourers who felt the pinch hardest.

In 1886 a sharecropper, Joseph Franks, was evicted by a planter from his plantation. The 73-year-old Franks, a former slave, took the planter to court, and lost the case. He appealed and, in February 1890, received the judgement of Sir John Gorrie, the chief justice of Trinidad

manded. More immigration was suggested instead of the *Metairie* System; Tobago should try to inveigle some Indians over from Trinidad.

Joining up with Trinidad

The Commission of 1882 had recommended a federation of St Vincent, St Lucia, Grenada and Tobago to reduce administrative costs and to combat the (fiscal) "evils of isolation", and in 1885 this was effected, although Tobago retained its bureaucracy. In 1886 Britain decided to tack Tobago on to Trinidad, either as a dependency or as a wholly incorporated ward (an administrative district in Trinidad). The planters opted for the former, demanding fiscal autonomy.

As Tobago resisted, so Britain insisted, and in 1889 a union was forced upon the two grumbling partners, although Tobago retained some autonomous institutions. Britain solved the issue by fiat, and in 1899 Tobago was made a ward of Trinidad and Tobago. A shotgun marriage, yes, but only for the wealthy; for ordinary people it was a union long-consummated by their migrations and the communities of Tobagonians living on Trinidad's north coast.

New system of slavery

Labour in Trinidad had always been scarce, but after Emancipation things grew worse, for ex-

slaves could no longer be compelled to work 18-hour days. Recruitment agents were sent to the other islands to tell of job opportunities, high wages and cheap land. Many people came, but few remained on the plantations. And if they brought their crafts and skills, they were still inadequate because planters wanted only sugar-cane fodder. Next the United States was considered as a source, but the few free blacks who responded were even more urbanised. Sierra Leone, a colony of liberated slaves yielded over 3,000 Africans. But, although they remained discrete tribal groups – Radas in Belmont, Yoruba and Congo in Laventille – they, too, abandoned sugar. Some Europeans

came, but they either took overseas jobs or left for America. Portuguese came from Madeira and quickly set up as shopkeepers, as did the Chinese. But eventually the planters found what they were searching for, when in May 1845 a windjammer, the *Fatel Rozack*, docked at Port of Spain, bringing 225 immigrants from Calcutta.

India had a large destitute population forced by poverty, oppression and economic dislocation to consider emigration. Largely under British control, it had a tropical climate, and its people were mainly agriculturalists. Transportation costs, though high, were not prohibitive. One problem remained: the first immigrants from India had already deserted the estates. The solution was an indentureship contract, later described as "a new system of slavery".

A financial crisis temporarily halted the scheme between 1848 and 1851, after which a steady flow of Indians arrived in Trinidad until the Indian Government stopped it in 1917. By then about 144,000 Indians had come. Most were from the Gangetic plain, especially the provinces of Uttar Pradesh, Bihar and Oudh. Smaller numbers came from Bengal and the Punjab, and a tiny minority from Madras in the south. They were escaping extreme poverty, famine caused by a decaying economy and exploitative ruling classes, dislocation caused by British imperialism and the savage repression which took place after the Indian Mutiny (1857).

On arrival, immigrants were assigned to a plantation and bound to work for three years. After that they had to complete a two-year "industrial residence", during which they could re-indenture to any plantation, or pursue another occupation – provided that they paid a special tax. Only after five years was completed did immigrants receive their "free paper". However, they were not entitled to free return passage for another five years. And after 1895 indentureds were forced to pay a proportion of the cost of returning to India.

Cruel conditions

The indentureship "contract" signed in India laid down minimum wages, working hours and working conditions. These were often ignored by planters, especially in the 1880s when the sugar industry almost collapsed. On the other hand, breaches of the contract by the indentured labourers were treated as criminal offences punishable by imprisonment.

Conditions were wretched. Indentured labourers lived in single-room barrack ranges reminiscent of early slave quarters, cramped and insanitary, and suffered from malaria, hookworm, anaemia and ground itch. Some plantation hospitals were so deplorable that the cure was often worse than the illness. Perhaps the cruellest cut was the unbalanced sex ratio which made women scarce and generated the notorious 19th-century Indian crimes of passion, when Indian men murdered wives who had succumbed to the enticements of other men. Between 1872 and 1900, 87 Indian women were murdered, 65 by their husbands.

CRIMES OF PASSION

Owing to a lack of Indian women in Trinidad in the 19th century, Indian men would seduce other men's wives. These women were then often killed by their husbands.

Isolated community

On the plantations the Indians were an isolated community, desperately poor yet despised by the wider society who thought them amoral, deceitful, revengeful, barbarous and dirty. Their customs were considered "degrading practices", "vile" and "painted devilry". Even the former black slaves held them in contempt for their languages, customs, appearance, poverty and bondage. And yet most remained.

Once released, many Indians remained as labourers on the plantations. Some picked up the crafts they had practised in India, while others became petty traders. Moneylending made a few rich, but many more subsisted as labourers, gardeners, porters, scavengers, domestics and other menial "coolie" jobs. Most importantly, they became peasant proprietors, growing "wet" rice, sugar cane and vegetables on land received either in lieu of return tickets or purchased from the Crown. By 1905 a labour committee would find that they "are industrious and useful citizens".

The creation of a peasantry allowed Indians to recreate their customs as best they could and the countryside became dotted with Hindu temples. An Indian sense of community with middle-class leadership developed. In 1897 the East Indian National Association was created to protest at the discrimination suffered by Indians, and in 1898 the *Kohinoor Gazette* was published – the first Indian newspaper.

LEFT: a 19th-century East Indian West Indian.
RIGHT: the wealthy middle classes enjoy a city view.

Trinidad's pecking order

At the top of Trinidadian society were the whites, the ruling class which controlled the wealth and power. Yet whites did not form a single homogeneous group, but were divided between the British and the "French Creoles".

Today "French Creole" refers to any white person whose family has resided in Trinidad for generations, but in the 19th century it was a very different matter. The French Creoles then were Roman Catholic, French-speaking and

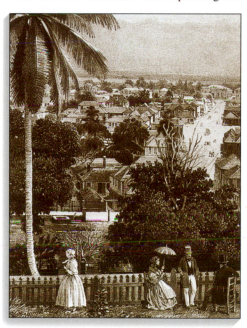

descended mainly from Royalist French settlers. They were racially exclusive and saw themselves as an aristocracy.

The British on the islands were Protestant, often born abroad, mostly colonial officials, managers of sugar estates or merchants. Conflict between the two groups took the form of local versus foreign whites, or merchants and planters versus government officials, but most consistently it was French lined up against British, the latter wanting to Anglicise the colony in language and manners, the former wanting some say in government policies. Otherwise, the two groups were very similar in their outlook, and by the end of the century the gap had narrowed.

Free education

Yet this sparring had important consequences. First was the creation in the 1850s, under the Anglicising Governor Lord Harris, of a series of free Ward Schools (primary) and a Normal School (teacher training). Second was the fact that when, in the 1880s, the government sought to abolish the black Carnival because of its rowdiness, the French Creoles protested. Finally, a tradition of French Creole opposition to government was established, a tradition which produced

ISLAND SCHOLARS

The Island Scholarship was a much coveted award that allowed its winners to leave Trinidad and study abroad. They usually returned as lawyers or doctors.

schools, which qualified them to become junior clerks, journalists and store assistants. Every few years one of the sons of the middle and respectable working classes won the Island Scholarship to study abroad, from whence they returned doctors and lawyers, almost to a man. Two notable 20th-century exceptions read literature and history: they were V.S. Naipaul *(see page 107)* and Eric Williams *(see page 59)*. But it was the teachers who formed the backbone of this class, producing even at an early stage men such as

men like Philip Rostant *(see page 44)* and Captain Cipriani *(see page 50)*.

When Lord Harris's Normal School began taking in graduates from the Ward Schools, most black children remained outside the doors, but for a few of the brightest the state-funded Ward Schools provided the means of social mobility. They could, on graduation, study to become teachers in the Normal School and make the first faltering steps out of manual labour. This ensured the growth of the black and coloured middle class, whose origins lay in the free coloured property-holders and professionals of the slavery era. A smaller group of fortunates won free places in the secondary

John Jacob Thomas, a philologist of international repute.

Among the Indian community, largely ignored by the state, the Canadian Mission began to set up schools in 1868, creating a parallel Indian middle class. The largest sector of the population was the black working classes. Predominantly rural, they worked as agricultural labourers, small farmers and tradesmen. In the sugar industry they were replaced in the fields by Indians but kept many of the skilled factory jobs. In the Northern Range, shaded by immortelle trees, they worked on cocoa estates as labourers, contractors or smallholders alongside the *mestizo* – black *peons* – known today as *cocoa payols*. Even within the black community there were distinct groups: those who spoke French patois and the immigrants who spoke English, the "Americans" (demobilised US soldiers in the Company Villages), the demobilised soldiers of the West Indian regiment, and the freed Africans, who numbered about 8,000. They had in common poverty, lack of education and exclusion from political power.

Squalid and overcrowded

Yet Trinidad was a rapidly urbanising colony, and by the end of the 19th century Port of Spain contained a quarter of the population. The

crime. It also practised African and syncretic religions, indistinguishable in respectable eyes from the illegal *obeah* (witchcraft) of slavery. It was a tightly packed community with an exuberant demi-monde and intense loyalties.

The French Creole élite and the British governing class grew closer, two obstacles remained. The first was a land distribution policy of Governor Gordon (1866–70), who allowed the peasants to buy Crown land – the planters were not happy. Second was the impartiality of Chief Justice Gorrie, who reformed judicial procedure to make the courts more accessible to the lower classes – even the governor disliked that.

urban black plebeians were found in various menial jobs, as domestics, messengers, washerwomen, longshoremen and petty traders. Many were periodically or permanently unemployed; living in overcrowded, squalid barrack houses in the city or the labyrinthine hills of Laventille and Belmont, racked with dysentery, malaria, sometimes cholera and smallpox: camping, as Earl Lovelace puts it, "on the eyebrow of the enemy". This group exhibited the symptoms of urban unemployment: juvenile delinquency, vagrancy, prostitution and petty

The blacks, and in particular the urban working class, felt the brunt of upper-class fear and loathing from the long end of a police baton, wielded more often than not according to J.J. Thomas, by "Barbadian rowdies, whose bitter hatred of the older residents had been often brutally exemplified." The law prohibited lower-class music and religion, frowned upon their language and sexual mores, and punished even trivial offences with beatings.

The most outrageous were the *jamets*, described in the *San Fernando Gazette* as "hordes of men and women, youthful in years but matured in every vice that perverts and degrades humanity, [who] dwell together in all

LEFT: urban blacks enjoy Queens Park around 1903.
ABOVE: early Carnival *circa* 1888.

the rude licentiousness of barbarian life". The *jamets* had taken over the Carnival celebrations in recent years with sexual horseplay, gang warfare, ribald songs and drumming. At the Canboulay procession on the Sunday before Carnival Monday, gangs tramped around with lit torches (Canboulay from *cannes brulées*, meaning burning canes), singing, and dancing and challenging rivals to duels in Kalenda, a traditional martial art performed with sticks.

Carnival mayhem

In 1877 the inspector commandant of police, Captain Baker, decided to destroy the Kalenda

gangs and reform Carnival. In the following two years he clamped down, and in 1880 called on all marchers to surrender their torches, sticks and drums. Taken by surprise, they complied. The next year he armed the force with clubs and tried the same tactic, but the *jamets* were ready with bottles and stones and sticks, and a riot started. The governor conciliated the revellers and confined the police to barracks.

Three years later the Canboulay was made illegal, and warfare erupted in San Fernando. Two gangs laid siege to the police station; police shot into the crowd, leaving two dead and five wounded. Thus ended the *jamet* Carnival, and the respectable classes joined the fête

once more. Noticeably, throughout it all, the French Creoles, despite their high moral tone, criticised Baker's high-handedness and condemned government intention to ban Carnival.

A similar fate befell Hosay, a Shi'ite Muslim festival in which bands of masqueraders, carrying a large ornate tomb, reenact a famous battle of Islamic history. Despite its origins, this celebration was mainly supported by Hindus, and by the 1870s it had become "a sort of national Indian demonstration". Gatka – an Indian martial art with staves – was performed, and Hosay bands from different estates competed with one another. In the 1880s the festival grew riotous, more a demonstration of class and ethnic solidarity, owing to worsening conditions in the sugar industry. In 1884 regulations were passed to exclude Hosay bands from San Fernando and Port of Spain, and to stop the *jamets* joining in. The bands ignored the order, and police opened fire, killing 12 and injuring 104. After that the festival became a more domesticated affair.

Hankering after change

The emergent middle class sought changes, in the reform movement begun in the 1880s by Philip Rostant, a white French Creole journalist. Rostant organised a petition in favour of elected members for the Legislative Council, but the Colonial Office rejected the idea in 1889. Thereafter the banner was carried by black and coloured professionals such as C. P. David, Henry Alcazar, J. S. de Bourg and Emmanuel Lazare. The reform movement appeared a useless passion, the suffrage sought was exclusive and the tactics were courteous, but the Secretary of State for the Colonies, Joseph Chamberlain, ended the matter in 1895 by refusing point blank. In 1898 he also abolished the Port of Spain Borough Council and the unofficial majority in the Legislative Council.

Eventually reform members engaged in black nationalist and working-class politics, foreshadowing key developments of the 20th century. In 1897 Walter Mills, a chemist, formed the Trinidad Workingmen's Association, and in London a lawyer, Henry Sylvester Williams, formed the Pan-African Association, opening enthusiastic branches at home in 1901. ❑

LEFT: the harbour at Port of Spain *circa* 1860.
RIGHT: the French aristocracy watch while the slaves enjoy their own festival.

POLITICAL AND ECONOMIC TURMOIL

Riots and strikes throughout the first half of the 20th century

paved the way for a better deal for the working classes

Amazing scenes were witnessed in Port of Spain on Monday 23 March 1903, when the Red House, the seat of government in Trinidad and Tobago, was burnt to the ground in the course of a riot over water charges. In

postpone its water legislation in 1902, then again in February 1903, and yet again on 16 March. Leading the struggle was the Rate Payers Association (RPA), a middle- and upper-class group led by reform agitators of the 1890s. This

the previous months the government had announced its intention to control the wastage of water by installing a metering system in houses (for the wealthy were known to bath indulgently), and by visiting homes to cut off the water supply to leaking taps. The culprits were unrepentant: "We know that rheumatics is the only evil resulting from the use of these baths", complained one writer. Besides, government inefficiency was thought to be the cause of much of the wastage anyway. But the underlying issue was really the middle-class demand for a more representative and less high-handed government.

The objectors had forced the government to

time, however, the RPA was supported by the lower classes.

Tension mounted. The RPA leaders were denied entry to the Council Chamber in the Red House, and the crowd roared outside. A woman threw a rock, and a rain of stones fell on the building; Governor Maloney hid with one official, and the rest fled. The Red House was set alight, and the RPA leaders of the crowd decamped; the hidden official escaped, disguised as a policeman, but the governor had to be escorted by the police, under a shower of stones, away from the conflagration. Firemen came to the rescue, but were repelled by the crowd. The Riot Act was read, and the police fired into the crowd and charged with bayonets, leaving 18 dead and 42 wounded. And the Red House was left a smoking pile of ashes.

An investigative commission absolved the police, and found the riots unrelated to the issue of representative government. Joseph Chamberlain, the Secretary of State for the Colonies, was more perceptive. He told the governor to begin talks to restore the abolished Port of Spain Borough Council, and in 1913 it was agreed that an elected council would be created.

Ten years on, the franchise that had eventually arrived was limited, but local politicians now had a platform on the council. Significantly, in

in the world was drilled by the Merrimac Oil Company at La Brea in southern Trinidad. The company folded soon afterwards, and two other 19th-century firms were no more successful. Then in the 1890s the internal combustion engine became a commercial proposition. Things were never the same again.

The oil industry was pioneered by an Englishman called Randolph Rust, who had migrated to Trinidad in 1881. Rust sought to explore for oil in the Guayaguayare forests with local backing. None was forthcoming, so he obtained Canadian capital, and the first well was drilled in 1902, followed by eight others

the waiting the RPA disappeared, but the older Trinidad Workingmen's Association (TWA) grew in the struggle, only to lapse once the 1914 franchise excluded its members.

The discovery of "black gold"

It was in the same year that World War I began in Europe that the first major oil refinery in Trinidad was opened at Pointe-à-Pierre.

The history of the oil industry in Trinidad dates from 1857, when perhaps the first oil well

in the next five years. He lobbied tirelessly for government support in Port of Spain and London, and in 1905 an engineer was sent from England to prospect for a British company. His successful drilling prompted a conference in 1909 at 10 Downing Street with the governor of Trinidad and representatives of the Colonial Office and the Admiralty. The Royal Navy, which was converting to oil-powered ships, had become interested. In 1910 Trinidad Oilfields Ltd was formed, to be joined in 1913 by both United British Oilfields of Trinidad and Trinidad Leaseholds Ltd.

Drilling for oil in those days was hard work. The fields which were found in Guayaguayare,

LEFT: the beginning of the water riot that left the Red House in ashes and 18 people dead.
ABOVE: the original Red House.

Palo Seco, Rousillac, Siparia, Erin and Tabaquite had to be wrested from dense jungle through which heavy equipment had to be dragged. It was, in Rust's words, "one terrible fight against nature". Blowouts, gushers, fires, explosions: all of these were common occurrences, and as late as 1929 a fire killed several people near Fyzabad. It was one of the last, however, and technology and safety standards improved rapidly thereafter.

The Great War

World War I revolutionised Russia; in Trinidad and Tobago changes were less spectacular but

opposition delayed its passage until 1920) in an attempt to keep the Indians tied to the estates. The Colonial Secretary thought that the law went "considerably beyond anything in the UK, in that it makes the mere fact of refusing to work and being without visible means of subsistence a punishable offence". It was eventually passed anyway. It tells much of the society that in 1911, the year of Trinidad's future prime minister Eric Williams's birth, £62,000 was spent on education, and £66,000 on the police, £18,000 on prisons, and £4,000 on the military.

The British West Indian soldiers had fared no better in Europe. As good British subjects,

nevertheless important. The war years and after were hard; inflation was high, especially for basic foods, and wages remained low. The diet of the labouring classes became, in the words of the Surgeon General, "somewhat deficient in protein". A strike by oil and asphalt workers in 1917 resulted in imprisonment for the leaders, and for a Seventh-Day Adventist who had displayed a placard saying "Awake ye Stevedores and be men". The East Indian Destitute League was formed, only to have its founder deported in 1918; Indian immigration was curtailed because of agitation against it in India.

The Government drafted the infamous Habitual Idlers Ordinance (although widespread

they had volunteered to fight for the Empire, but the British Government refused to let blacks serve, and only when King George V interceded did the War Office agree to a West Indian contingent. They formed a separate regiment, not part of the British Army, with lower pay and lower allowances; and only those of "unmixed European blood" were eligible for commissions. Furthermore, perhaps to preserve them from acquiring a taste for white people's blood, the West Indians were excluded from actual combat with Europeans.

Some of these soldiers were sent to Egypt where a few, briefly, saw action against Turkish troops; most performed labour services, like the others who had gone to Europe, digging trenches and carrying ammunition.

When the war ended on 11 November 1918, the British West Indian Regiment was sent to Taranto, Italy, for demobilisation under a South African camp commander. There the soldiers were given menial tasks; when they refused to do them, several were court martialled and sentenced to up to three years. As a postscript, some West Indian soldiers created the clandestine Caribbean League, which

---

COURT-MARTIALLED

After World War I, members of the British West Indian Regiment were made to wash linen and clean latrines because "the men were only niggers". If they refused they were sometimes court-martialled.

---

celebrations held on 19 July, and a few British marines from HMS *Dartmouth* were attacked. White businessmen requested arms from the governor. They also sought the suppression of newspapers which informed the public of conditions in Britain, like the *Argos*, a paper for the coloured middle class which, with Marcus Garvey's *Negro World*, advocated racial pride.

In 1918 the TWA had come under new and more radical leadership: James Braithwaite and David Headley, two dockers

advocated economic, social and political reforms for the West Indies. The league was reported to the authorities and disbanded, but ideas leavened with experience cannot be set aside so easily, and the soldiers, especially Captain Arthur Andrew Cipriani, returned home to make their mark.

In July 1919 there were anti-black demonstrations in Britain, and news of this inflamed the returned soldiers. British Honduras saw rioting. In Trinidad, soldiers boycotted the victory

influenced by international socialism, J. S. de Bourg from the reform movement and Howard Bishop, a journalist. From early 1919 the revamped TWA participated in agitation for high wages, supporting a wave of strikes throughout the island. Workers on the railways, city council employees, electricity and telephone workers, and labourers at the Pitch Lake all called strikes in 1919. But it was the Port of Spain dockers who changed the tempo.

"Scum of the wharves"

Called the "scum of the wharves" by the *Trinidad Guardian*, the dockers were the most well-informed and cosmopolitan workers in the

LEFT: sailing boats at anchor in Port of Spain harbour. **ABOVE:** a passenger ship steaming into port while dockhands and greeters watch.

colony. Many had travelled abroad as sailors, and all had access to smuggled literature and new ideas. In November 1919 they went on strike. Led by the TWA, the dockers demanded wage increases. When the shippers refused to negotiate, they walked off the job. The shippers brought in scab labour, and on 1 December the dockers retaliated, smashing warehouses and driving off the scabs. Then they marched through the city, closing businesses and encouraging others to join them, and the

GARVEYISM

Jamaican black political activist Marcus Garvey (1887–1940), who advocated black unity and racial pride throughout the British West Indies, was blamed for many a riot during the 1920s and 1930s.

workers throughout the colony downed their tools in support. Even the black police, thought the governor, "could not be relied upon". He formed a conciliation board which, on 3 December, offered the dockers a 25 per cent wage increase.

The same day, around noon, HMS *Calcutta* steamed into the harbour, and the tide of conciliation turned to one of repression. The government, backed up by British troops and a white volunteer force of colonial vigilantes, cracked down heavily on the strikers. Ninety-nine people were arrested, 82 people imprisoned and four of the leading TWA members promptly deported.

In Tobago, on 6 December, a crowd attacked the government wireless station with bottles and stones. But it was already too late for that kind of violent behaviour – the armed forces had imposed order next door only the day before. Emboldened, the police fired on the crowd, killing one and wounding six. The marines were left to mop up.

The rise of Captain Cipriani

The immediate outcome of the dockers' strike, which had almost become a general strike, was repression. The government passed both the Strikes and Lockouts Ordinance and the Industrial Court Ordinance, which made strikes illegal. The *Trinidad Guardian* expressed "profound gratitude". The government also wrote to the TWA threatening deportation for any strike instigators. Next, the Sedition Ordinance, which banned Garveyite and socialist literature, was passed and saw to the closure of the *Argos*. A Wages Committee, set up when conciliation was necessary, recommended a minimum wage of 68 cents for men and 45 cents for women; the government threw out the report.

Although a Colonial Office man had described the dockers as "the most gentlemanly rioters I have ever heard of", they revived in the planters a fear which had possessed them since the 18th-century Haitian revolution: that of a black takeover. People spoke of a secret organisation led by six foreigners, dedicated to the destruction of organised government and "elimination of the white population".

Out of this turmoil rose the Captain. Arthur Andrew Cipriani was born in 1875 to Albert Cipriani, a white planter of Corsican stock with blood ties to the Bonaparte family. Arthur had lost both parents by the time he was seven, and was brought up by an aunt. He left school at 16, distinguished only by atrocious handwriting. His next 25 years were equally unremarkable, divided between managing cocoa estates and horse-racing.

A few months before his 40th birthday, World War I broke out. Cipriani lobbied for a West Indian contingent and eventually found himself a captain in the British West Indian Regiment, stationed in Egypt. There he earned the respect of his compatriots by defending them against army racism. He wrote letters, sent off protests, and argued at court martials, and continued to do so until demobilised. By the time he returned to Trinidad in 1918, he was loved as a man of the people, both owing to and in spite of his white planter background.

Captain Cipriani, who retained his army title, joined the TWA in 1919 and became its president in 1923. The organisation had shifted its focus from trade union struggle to political agitation, and Cipriani, the white planter who sided with the "unwashed and unsoaped bare-footed men", was seen to be the perfect man for the job. In 1925 he won a seat in the first

black and strongly influenced by Garveyism, the TWA also attracted support from the Indians. Sarran Teelucksingh and Timothy Roodal, two Indian leaders elected to the Legislative Council, joined the organisation. Krishna Deonarine, later known as Adrian Cola Rienzi, was president of its San Fernando branch in 1925; some years later he became "Buzz" Butler's emissary *(see page 55)*.

However, Cipriani sacrificed trade unionism on the altar of reformist politics. Worsening economic conditions in the 1930s made many followers disillusioned with his limited ambition "to propose and oppose legislation". Two

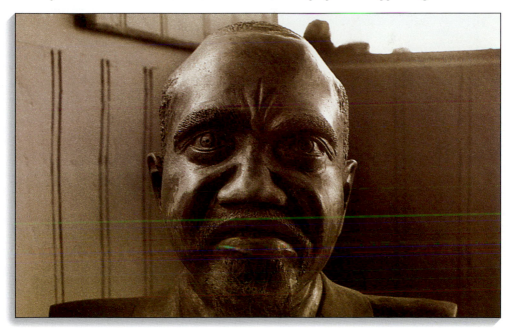

Legislative Council elections – despite a limited franchise – on a platform favouring workmen's compensation, an eight-hour day, abolition of child labour, compulsory education, competitive examinations for entry into the Civil Service and repeal of the Sedition Ordinance. He kept the seat until his death in 1945.

Cipriani was autocratic but an effective speaker, and under his joint leadership with Howard Bishop the TWA grew to 33,000 members in 1928. Although predominantly urban,

incidents foreshadowed this. In 1931 the government proposed a Divorce Bill which was opposed by the Roman Catholic French Creoles. The TWA was neutral, but Cipriani broke ranks in favour of the French Creoles. Howard Bishop criticised him in the *Labour Leader*, the TWA organ. The publication was closed in 1932.

That same year the Trade Union Ordinance gave limited rights to trade unions. After two years of consultation with the British TUC, Cipriani decided not to register the TWA as a union, and it was renamed the Trinidad Labour Party. Again his colleagues grumbled; having made colonial people politically aware, Cipriani found his star begin to fall.

LEFT: Captain Arthur Andrew Cipriani, champion of the rights of black people, mulattos, children and workers. **ABOVE:** a woodcarving of Uriah "Buzz" Butler.

Poets and writers

The 1930s began with dark clouds on the horizon. The world economy was depressed, and fascism was growing. In Trinidad unemployment rose, and planters tightened the screws, lowering wages and extending tasks. In Tobago the peasants "wrestled with the earth with their bare hands for sustenance". So wrote their poet, Eric Roach, of a people who were "like figures in bas-relief, half-emerged from the heavy clay of our tragic past".

In this context a cultural movement was started by men such as C. L. R. James, Alfred Mendes, Albert Gomes and Ralph de Boissière,

essays. In their "barrack yard" literature, the members of the *Beacon* group celebrated urban lower-class life for its spontaneity, and criticised the respectable classes for their hypocrisy. Nor were they merely middle-class romantics; the *Beacon* group also condemned the exploitation of the working classes.

As Gomes described it, *The Beacon* was "the debunker of bourgeois morality, obscurantist religion and primitive capitalism". And inevitably the magazine came under attack from the establishment: the police harassed its leading writers, and businessmen organised advertising boycotts. It folded before the end

who had been influenced by World War I and the Russian Revolution.

"Those were the two events in our lives at that time which drove us into writing about our islands", recalls Mendes. This marked the beginning of West Indian creative writing. The movement started around *Trinidad*, a magazine began in 1929 by James and Mendes. It folded after two issues, for the colony was just a small philistine backwater. Then, in 1931, the 20-year-old Albert Gomes brought out *The Beacon*, editing and financing it through 28 issues for three years.

The Beacon published fiction and poetry, cultural criticism, political analysis and historical

of 1934. (That was a bad year for culture, for the government legislated to censor calypsos). But in its short life *The Beacon* did its job well; it created the beginning of a Trinidadian literature, and politicised men who would play leading roles in times to come.

Before the storm

From the late 1920s onwards, prices climbed with unemployment, but workers were earning less in 1935 than in 1929. Like a bad joke, the Wages Advisory Board found that workers' needs were lower in 1935 than in 1920; malnutrition was endemic. A commission of enquiry found working-class houses in Port of

Spain "indescribable in their lack of elementary needs of decency". Conditions were worse in the rural areas, where in places 80 percent of the population was infested with hookworm. Life was even harder in Tobago, and Roach remembers "clinging to life by the skin of our teeth … [although we] did not realise our hardship because we knew nothing else".

By 1934 the National Unemployment Movement (NUM), formed by Jim Headley, Dudley Mahon and Elma François, was organising hunger marches in Port of Spain. But it was the Indian sugar workers who started the ball rolling. That July, sugar workers from San Fernando to Tunapuna demonstrated against their desperate situation. A hunger march fought its way from Caroni to Port of Spain, attacking bosses and policemen, burning buildings and looting shops. A police barricade just outside the city halted the angry marchers, and a delegation of "leaders", all unknowns, went to parley with the governor; Cipriani's new Trinidad Labour Party (TLP) was by-passed. The situation was defused, but only for the moment.

ABYSSINIA

The NWA established communist links all over the world, and when fascist Italy invaded Abyssinia, in 1935, the organisation held large demonstrations in Port of Spain supporting the Africans.

Oil workers down tools

The torch passed to workers at the Apex oilfields. In March 1935 they downed tools and tramped to Port of Spain, protesting over low wages and harsh conditions. Cipriani had sanctioned no such action, but the workers went ahead under the leadership of John Rojas and "Buzz" Butler, a fire-and-brimstone preacher with a pronounced limp and a loud voice. The two broke with Cipriani, and from then on Butler began mobilising oil workers in the south.

Bertie Percival, a friend of Butler, was an Apex worker with a talent for public speaking. He gave a speech in Port of Spain about conditions at Apex and was invited to join a new organisation, formed by Elma François, Jim Barrat and others, called the Negro Welfare, Cultural and Social Association (NWA). It was the successor to the NUM. Denouncing Cipriani as "Britain's best policeman in the colonies", the NWA saw to mobilising the workers in the north.

LEFT: Labour leader Albert Gomes.
RIGHT: pouring asphalt, a by-product of oil.

Oil was important. Trinidad supplied most of the Royal Navy's fuel, and the oil companies made large profits in the colony. White expatriate staff, some South African, lived luxuriously. Black workers, however, were treated shabbily; their wages lagged behind inflation, the bosses were insufferably racist, workers were liable to instant dismissal, and a blackballing system made it difficult for a man dismissed by one company to find employment with another. There was no compensation for industrial accidents. Yet the oil workers were a concentrated modern industrial proletariat, better off than sugar workers, and easier to mobilise.

Buzz Butler to the rescue

Tubal Uriah "Buzz" Butler was a Grenadian who came to Trinidad in 1921 to work in oil. In 1929 an industrial accident left him lame, and, unfit for oil work, he turned to the Moravian Church. After the Apex strike of 1935, Butler left Cipriani's TLP to form his own party, the Workers' and Citizens' Home Rule Party (WCHRP). By the early months of 1937, he was moving up and down the southlands, holding meetings, singing hymns, rallying workers for the "heroic struggle for British justice for British Blacks in a British colony". Buzz Butler had indeed become the "Chief Servant".

On 18 June 1937, having exhausted the "prayers, petitions and bootlicking tactics of a suffering class", oil workers at Forest Reserve began a sit-down strike for better wages and working conditions. Police swarmed into the area. On 19 June the strikers were dispersed, and at 5.30am on 20 June two oil wells at the Apex oilfields were set on fire. The authorities thought it was the call to strike; more police were sent to the area and closed in on Butler,

The strike escalates

At Point Fortin, on 21 June, the police fired on strikers, killing three and wounding four. The strike moved on, closing down San Fernando and Ste Madeleine, shutting off the power station. At the telephone station the strikers met police, who killed two and wounded eight. Another siege left one policeman dead and four civilians wounded. Yet the strike grew, closing Waterloo Estate, Wyaby Estate and Woodford Lodge (one dead, two wounded) and receiving succour from the NWA in Port of Spain, where shops closed. At Rio Claro and Dinsley, work stopped on the estates; police killed one man.

who was addressing a large crowd, with a warrant for his arrest. He asked that the warrant be read, but the crowd grew restive and chased off the police. Corporal King, a plain-clothes officer, then tried to arrest him.

King was one of the most unpopular policemen around, and the threatening crowd closed in on him. He ran into a shop and tried to escape from a high window. He broke his leg in the fall, and as he lay utterly helpless he was set alight by the uncontrollable crowd. That was the real signal, for there was no turning back. Later, when 40 policemen attempted to recover the corpse, the crowd repelled them with bottles and bullets, killing another policeman.

That was 22 June, the same day that HMS *Ajax* steamed into Port of Spain. HMS *Exeter* arrived the next day, and by July labourers were returning to work. On 6 July the *Trinidad Guardian* reported that the strike was finally over.

While the marines were mopping up, the governor and the Colonial Secretary tried to appease the masses. A mediation committee was set up, and public workers were granted an eight-hour day and a new minimum wage. Both officials castigated the employers for their rapacity: "Tact and sympathy [would be] a shield far more sure than any forest of bayonets to be planted here", stated the governor. "Industry has no right to pay dividends at all until it pays a fair wage to labour", added the Colonial Secretary. For this the governor was recalled to London and forced to resign in December 1937, and the Colonial Secretary was transferred in 1938. The Forster Commission of Enquiry submitted a tough law-and-order report in February 1938. However, the Moyne Commission, which investigated conditions in the whole region, produced a report so damning that its publication was delayed until after World War II.

Hold the fort, we are coming!

Butler got the ball rolling, but after the riots he went into hiding, only to emerge straight into the arms of the police and two years in prison. The man who held, or rather built, the fort in Butler's absence was Adrian Cola Rienzi.

Born Krishna Deonarine, the grandchild of indentured labourers, Rienzi left school at 14. In 1925 he was a solicitor's clerk and president of the San Fernando branch of Cipriani's TWA. Already this young man took enough interest in world politics to be considered by the governor to have "markedly seditious views". Deonarine was unimpressed. He organised protests, formed a Young Socialist League, and became president of the Indian National Party.

Frustrated in Trinidad, he changed his name to Adrian Cola Rienzi (fair skinned, he hoped to pass as Spanish) and migrated to Ireland, where he joined the Sinn Féin Movement and studied jurisprudence. Then on to London, where he qualified as a barrister, came under the watchful eyes of the police, and tried unsuccessfully to go to India. Rienzi returned to Trinidad where he was refused admittance to the Bar until he promised to "not indulge in agitation".

A union man

Maintaining links with Butler, Rienzi gave advice, and when the strike started he operated as Butler's emissary. In September and November 1937 the Oilfield Workers' Trade Union (OWTU) and the All Trinidad Sugar Estates and Factory Workers' Trade Union (ATSEFWTU) were both legally registered, and Rienzi was the president-general of both

unions. Oil and sugar, African and Indian, had joined hands.

In the north, the Transport and General Workers' Union was established. The dock workers formed a union, as did the workers in the building and those in Public Works trade. By the end of 1939 there were 12 unions, and labour was finding a voice. All this was in keeping with numerous official recommendations of the time, which considered unions to be the best protection against social anarchy. But in practice neither government nor employers were convinced of that, and the police relentlessly harassed the unionists.

A hero's welcome

When Butler was released from prison in May 1939 he was given a hero's welcome and made General Organiser in the OWTU. But his messianic combativeness and Rienzi's organisational discipline did not mix, and when Butler began urging workers to go on strike in defiance of executive decisions he was expelled. Four months later he was again arrested for sedition and imprisoned until the end of the war.

Rienzi withdrew from the trade unions in 1944, fulfilling his own prophecy: "Individuals are subordinate to the movement, they play their role, then take their exit, to be succeeded by others; but the movement itself goes on". ❏

LEFT: "Buzz" Butler gives a passionate speech at a meeting in London.
RIGHT: Adrian Cola Rienzi, who continued Butler's work in a more moderate vein.

MODERN TIMES

With the end of World War II, radical changes lay ahead in the political

arena, and these set the colony on the road to independence

The years of World War II, coming on the heels of the Butler riots, marked the transition from one era to another. The government jailed Butler, banned Carnival, and whipped up British patriotism.

"This war with England and Germany/Going to mean more starvation and misery", sang a

one at Chaguaramas, which contained everything necessary for the good life – baseball grounds, golf course, marina. Here the US formed its Atlantic oil convoys and tested its carriers and aeroplanes before they went to the Pacific. Thousands of American soldiers were processed here, and the culture of the small

sceptical calypsonian *(see page 137)*, Growling Tiger. "But I going plant provision and fix me affairs/And the white people could fight for a thousand years". He could not have been more wrong. Many Trinidadians signed up to go to the war in Europe, but, more importantly, the war came to Trinidad. British Prime Minister Sir Winston Churchill offered huge tracts of land in Trinidad to the US in return for 50 old destroyers. The governor, Sir Hubert Young, suggested the Caroni Swamp; the Americans chose the northwest peninsula (Chaguaramas) and the Valencia district (Wallerfield), and Sir Hubert was eased out of office.

Two huge military bases were built, the main

colony of Trinidad and Tobago shifted orbit.

The Americans provided well-paid jobs for tens of thousands, and poor people lost their servility. The soldiers laboured stripped to the waist, swore, got drunk and brawled, and white dignity crumbled. Nightclubs and brothels sprang up everywhere to cater for their needs. Calypsonians prospered, and their music grew more up-tempo and risqué. Nor was it all hunky-dory. The racist arrogance of the American soldiers irritated the population, and the defection of local women into the arms of the Yanks rubbed salt into the wound. "Both mother and daughter", sang the calypsonian Invader, "working for the Yankee dollar".

Victory and new music

On Victory in Europe (VE) Day, 6 May 1945, music filled the streets of every town and village in the colony. It was the first Carnival for four years, only the sound was different, new. Before Carnival had been banned, people tramped around to string-and-brass orchestras, or to the thumping of bamboo tubes – tamboo bamboo these percussion groups were called, and they had reigned since the drums were outlawed in the 19th century. On VE Day, however, there was a ringing, clanging, booming rhythm being pounded out on metal pans – the steel band had arrived.

in elaborating their invention, pushing these drums to greater melodic capacity. But as their music grew in complexity, partisanship increased, and these successors to the 19th-century stickfighting Kalenda bands fought one another with unprecedented fury.

Streetfighting bands

When bands met, especially in the city, there was a good chance that a fight would break out with bottles and stones, machetes and knives. Furthermore, feuds developed which lasted for years and pitted entire neighbourhoods against one another. The upper classes recoiled in fear

During the war, and unknown to most of respectable society, young black men throughout the country, but especially in Port of Spain, had collectively fashioned a range of metallic percussion instruments, especially from empty oil drums. Over the next few years steel bands, as their ensembles came to be called, multiplied throughout the country, taking from the movies aggressive names such as Desperadoes, Destination Tokyo and Red Army. They competed

LEFT: a mounted policeman watches over a public gathering.
ABOVE: prefabricated houses being assembled on an American base.

and loathing. "Steel band fanaticism is a savage and bestial cult and it must be completely wiped out" was a typical complaint in the *Trinidad Guardian*. And the forces of law and order turned the heat on, the police with their batons and the judges with stiff sentences, on the slightest pretext.

Steel band warfare continued well into the 1960s, but a winding down began as early as 1950 when the Trinidad & Tobago Steelbandmen's Association was formed. By then even the movement's critics had to admit its music was marvellous, for if five years earlier the bands could only generate loud rhythms they were now attempting Chopin. The middle-class avant garde, such as dancer Beryl McBurnie, whose folklore studies revolutionised West Indian choreography, embraced the steel band. After the Trinidad & Tobago All Steel Percussion Orchestra went to the Festival of Britain in 1951, the steel band, came of age. Alongside the growing professionalism of calypsonians such as Lord Kitchener, the Mighty Spoiler and others, here was the culture that would provide the foundation of nationalism.

FESTIVAL OF BRITAIN

The steel band won respectability when an 11-man ensemble, the Trinidad & Tobago All Steel Percussion Orchestra, was formed to represent the colony at the 1951 Festival of Britain.

"If you let this movement die", cautioned a

recently returned historian and political scientist who supported McBurnie's Little Carib Folk Dance Theatre, "then you drive a nail in the coffin of our aspirations". The speaker was Dr Eric Williams.

Election free-for-all

In 1946 and 1950 the first two rowdy elections were held under universal suffrage, and all of Trinidad and Tobago's anarchic individualism came to the fore. Thus 141 candidates, 90 without any party, vied in 1950 for 18 seats. It was the heyday of the independent politician, subject to no party discipline or programme, who offered the moon to a gullible electorate: from higher pensions to more scholarships, cleaner water to a better Carnival. One candidate vowed to abolish dog licences, another promised to "demobilise unemployment". They exploited every possible social division to capture votes, this one angling for the black trade-union votes, that one for the small farmers in the east, the other for the Indians. Bhadase Sagan Maraj manipulated his Hindu organisation, the Sanatan Dharma Maha Sabha; Norman Tang remained absolutely inscrutable so as to offend no one; Ajodha Singh relied on his fame as a masseur. Few candidates were above using *obeah* (magic) in their causes.

Much of the to-do in these first two general elections was reported by Seepersad Naipaul, a journalist who had married into a well-known political family, the Capildeos. Years after, Seepersad's son, Vidiadhar Surujprasad, would relive his adolescent memories to produce two brilliant political satires: *The Mystic Masseur* and *The Suffrage of Elvira*.

On the left were the United Front (1946) and the Caribbean Socialist Party (1950), but both fared badly, and all progressive eyes focused on two men: Butler and Albert Gomes. Butler, released from prison in 1945, challenged Gomes in the middle-class St Ann's seat in 1946 and lost. But demobilisation of the US bases was creating unemployment, and Butler's popularity was growing. He won in San Fernando in 1950, when his coalition party held the most seats in the Legislative Council. Yet no Butlerite was nominated by the governor to sit in the Executive Council. "Political blasphemy", railed Butler, to no avail. The man given the limelight was Albert Gomes.

Gomes makes waves

A corpulent man of Portuguese extraction, Gomes had been the founder/editor of the radical *The Beacon* magazine in the early 1930s. After the 1937 riots, he established the Federated Workers' Union and entered City Council politics, bitterly attacking the colonial government and Captain Cipriani. He championed the rights of the common people, supporting the calypsonians in their fight against censorship, the steel bands in their quest for acceptance, and the Shouter Baptists in their struggle to be legalised. One of his notorious tactics was to be so offensive in a council meeting that he was ejected. When the police came to remove him, Gomes would prostrate himself on the floor and have to be carried out. "But the Captain had reckoned without a technicality… The Standing Orders did not provide against my immediate return", he gleefully recalled in his autobiography. "I, therefore, promptly returned".

All that changed when he was nominated to the Executive Council. "In different positions we were bound to assert different claims", Gomes said, excusing the break with his erstwhile comrades. Elected again in 1950, he was

Rise of Williams the Conqueror

The pace of life quickened in 1956. Down south a radical young trade unionist, George Weekes, captured the key Pointe-à-Pierre branch of the Oilfield Workers' Trade Union (OWTU). The British oil company Trinidad Leaseholds was bought by the American Texaco. "Money start to pass, people start to bawl", the Mighty Sparrow would later sing. "Pointe-à-Pierre sell the workmen and all".

That year Sparrow sang the song which won him both the Calypso King and Road March competitions: "The Yankees gone and Sparrow take over now". He instantly became the hero

nominated to head the Ministry of Labour, Commerce and Industry, and so was pulled over to the governor's side. There he spent his time implementing an industrialisation policy that required restraining the unions and encouraging foreign investment.

"O what an awful thing", lamented the Roaring Lion, "to see Gomes in a lion skin". And although he went on to contest both 1956 and 1961 elections, he was overtaken by the nationalist movement and, perhaps unfairly, cast aside.

LEFT: soldiers enjoying the perks of the Yankee dollar.
ABOVE: Eric Williams addresses a class at the University of Woodford Square in 1956.

of the black working class, second only to another man – Dr Eric Williams – who also made his debut in 1956, but on the political stage.

Williams had been born in 1911 into a declining lower-middle-class family. "Family fortunes were reflected in the descent from the water closet to the cesspit", he would later write. Yet his parents were ambitious, and young Eric was rigorously drilled to win whichever scholarships were on offer. At Tranquillity Intermediate School he won the Government Exhibition, which funded him through five years at the Queen's Royal College. There he won the House Scholarship, in 1931 and went on to gain the Island Scholarship too.

The following year Williams left for Oxford to read history, determined to follow in the footsteps of those teachers whom he had admired. One of them, C. L. R. James, hoping to make his way as a writer, had gone to England only a few months earlier, bearing in manuscript the first Trinidadian novel, *Minty Alley*. James, a brilliant polymath, was soon cricket correspondent for the *Manchester Guardian* – today his *Beyond A Boundary* is considered one of the most important books on cricket and perhaps on any sport. James also became well known as a Trotskyist and a Pan-African speaker, producing several important books,

politics and Williams to teach political science at Howard University where he expanded his thesis into the great work *Capitalism and Slavery* and wrote *The Negro in the Caribbean*.

University of Woodford Square

Williams also began part-time work with the Washington-based Anglo-American Commission, a British-American organisation set up in the early 1940s to encourage Caribbean co-operation. He went full time in 1944, and four years later he was put in charge of the Commission's research. This post enabled him to return to Port of Spain, where he fell in love

including *A History of Negro Revolt*, *The Life of Captain Cipriani*, *World Revolution* and the enduring *The Black Jacobins*.

Meanwhile, Williams pursued his academic career single-mindedly, studying through the "excessively long vacations" and graduating with first-class honours. The chairman of his board of examiners asked about his interest in colonial history, and Williams replied that scholarship had to be connected with the environment. When he was rejected for a Fellowship, James suggested a PhD on the economic factors underlying British slave emancipation.

Just before war broke out in Europe both men went to the US, James to continue his leftist

with and married a beautiful Chinese woman.

Williams had always been interested in education; while in the US he had submitted a memorandum on the proposed West Indian University to the colonial Committee on Higher Education. But after he returned home his biggest impact was made in the sphere of adult education. He launched the *Caribbean Historical Review*, wrote a weekly series on Caribbean history in the *Trinidad Guardian*, and regularly gave public lectures.

By the early 1950s he was a local celebrity in great demand. His lectures under the auspices of the Teachers' Educational and Cultural Association were wildly popular. He spoke on a wide range of topics: West Indian history, the sugar industry, small-scale farming, Caribbean education, Locke and Rousseau, Toussaint L'Ouverture, Carlyle and Aristotle. But the lectures were always variations on the theme of nationalism and anti-colonialism. And Williams, now dubbed the "Third Brightest Man in the World", drew ever larger crowds which spilled out of the public library and into Woodford Square, the adjoining park. There they heard the words of "The Doctor" over a loudspeaker, and were

FLORAL TRIBUTE

The motto of the People's National Movement (PNM) is "Great is the PNM, it shall prevail", and its symbol is the balisier palm flower, a bright red and yellow heliconia.

if it had not been for the Caribbean Commission (as the Anglo-American Commission was now called) declining to renew his contract on 21 June 1955. That same evening he told the public at length about the injustice of his dismissal. "I am going to let down my bucket where I am", he vowed, "right here with you in the British West Indies".

A new lecture series was launched, and it founded a new politics based on public education and nationalism. A speech on constitutional reform ended with a call to

mesmerised by his scholarship, uplifted by his vision and fired by his passion.

Williams was a solitary man. He was shy, but also a football injury during childhood had left him almost deaf. Yet by 1955 a People's Education Movement had been formed from the teachers' association to sponsor his lectures. And the Political Education Group, a nucleus of committed supporters, secretly crystallised around Williams to promote his entry into politics. Perhaps he might not have made the leap

sign a petition. Within weeks the embryonic party had collected 28,000 signatures. The cocky eloquence of a brilliant academic had captured the black middle class and proletariat. "Now that I have resigned my position at Howard University in the USA", the Doctor promised, "the only university in which I shall lecture in future is the University of Woodford Square and its several branches throughout the length and breadth of Trinidad and Tobago".

"Master! Giant!" enthused the masses, and on 15 January 1956 Williams's party, the People's National Movement (PNM), was born. And that September the general elections postponed from the previous year were finally held.

LEFT: the first Trinidad and Tobago Cabinet of 1962.
ABOVE: young girls at the festivities welcoming Queen Elizabeth II in 1983.

The path to glory

There were only 39 independent candidates this time and seven parties – similar in programmes but diverse in style and tone, each one seen as representing a different social group. The PNM, comprised mainly of black professionals, emphasised morality and discipline, intelligence, nationalism and modernity.

Progressives of all races rallied behind the PNM, which especially had the support of the artistic community. However, it was still considered to be merely the black people's party versus the rest, categorised by Williams as reactionaries, but who were in effect the French

Williams used a divide-and-conquer strategy against the PDP. He wooed the Muslim Indians by labelling the PDP a racist party akin to the Hindu Maha Sabha in India, seeking to alienate from it Muslim and Christian Indians as well as reformist Hindus. He attacked it as a Brahmin (upper caste) party linked to big business.

Surprise results

The elections results surprised everyone. The PNM, an organised political party, won the majority of elective seats – 13 out of 24. Even some French Creoles had voted PNM. The PDP won five seats, the Butler Party two, Captain Cipriani's

Creoles, Hindus, trade unionists, independent politicians, the media and the Catholic Church.

The PNM's greatest enemy was the People's Democratic Party (PDP), led by Bhadase Sagan Maraj. Considered by many to be little short of a gangster, Maraj was nevertheless enormously popular by virtue of the Sanatan Dharma Maha Sabha, over which he presided, and its role in opening scores of primary schools for Hindus.

Additionally, Maraj was president of the sugar workers' union, and was viewed by rural Indians as their equivalent of Williams: a man whose achievements had elevated the entire ethnic group. In return, Maraj categorised the PNM as "Pure Negro Men".

TLP two, and the independents two. Trinidad had redeemed itself, it seemed, and the governor decided to give the winning party a working majority. The Legislative Council also contained four nominated members and two officials, so Williams was allowed to nominate two, and the rest were chosen from people not hostile to the party. The constitution against which Williams had protested so bitterly was invoked to give the PNM a chance to govern effectively with him as prime minister at the helm.

The new government took over the administration of Carnival from private hands, ended the Carnival Queen beauty pageant and offered larger prizes to calypsonians.

The nationalist struggle

The years leading to independence in 1962 were acrimonious ones for the country. After victory the PNM offered peace to the upper class by nominating two white members to the Legislative Council. This was more than an olive branch, though, and was integral to the government's continuation of Gomes's industrialisation strategy. The trade unions were conspicuously ignored.

Williams also sought to court the Hindus, but with little success. The whites and the Hindus combined to form the Democratic Labour Party (DLP), which immediately launched an unrelenting war against the government. And when the West Indies Federation, set up in 1957, held its first elections in 1958, the DLP won six seats to the PNM's four. Williams was furious. He invited C. L. R. James to return home and edit a more aggressive PNM organ, *The Nation*.

The nationalist struggle intensified. A strike in the oil industry had businessmen clamouring for state intervention. Williams folded his arms and turned away, saying: "Industrial democracy is based on the right of workers to withhold their labour by way of strike, even if the community is thrown into turmoil".

He criticised Britain for giving the bases to the US, and demanded that Chaguaramas be returned to the nation. He described the lease as "a callous anachronism" and called a demonstration to demand its return for 22 April 1960. Rain fell "bucket-a-drop" but did not deter the thousands who marched behind the Doctor.

Capildeo – the "Big God"

Meanwhile, the DLP leadership had slipped from Maraj to Dr Rudranath Capildeo – V.S. Naipaul's uncle, satirised as the "Big God" in his book *A House for Mr Biswas*. Capildeo was frail and sensitive as a youth, volatile and tormented by his family life. Unlike Vidia and Seepersad, his nephew and brother-in-law, Capildeo had difficulty with English. But he was nonetheless bright, and in 1938 he won the Island Scholarship and left to study in England the following year. His career in there was also marked by loneliness and uncertainty, but he

---

LEFT: a military regiment salutes.

RIGHT: workers on a sugarcane plantation.

> **ODE TO THE PNM**
>
> Well, the way how things shaping up
> All this nigger business go stop
> I tell you, soon in the West Indies
> It's please Mister Nigger, please.
> MIGHTY SPARROW, 1956

still graduated with first-class honours in mathematics and physics. In 1944 Capildeo was elected president of the Men's Union, and in 1945 he returned home to Trinidad as a teacher. Alas, he soon fell foul of the Director of Education, who held the power to make his life miserable, so Capildeo packed his bags and returned to England. By 1950 he had a doctorate and was lecturing at the University of London. Over the next few years he studied law, visited Trinidad and took up the post of principal of the Trinidad

Polytechnic under the PNM government. In March 1960 Capildeo was invited to lead the DLP into next year's elections. So it was that "Trinidad's Most Educated Man" had come to match knowledge with the "Third Brightest Man in the World".

The DLP launched its campaign with a blistering PNM onslaught. Trade unions demonstrated for the PNM. "Hooligans", complained the *Trinidad Guardian*. So Williams told the demonstrators: "March where the hell you like!" The party was loved by the steel bands, whose fighters interpreted him as meaning "Mash up what the hell you like" and went on a rampage.

Capildeo threatened "bloodshed and riot,

revolution or civil disobedience". On 15 October he incited a large crowd: "Arm yourselves with weapons in order to take over this country". Violence erupted in the east: one man was killed and a state of emergency declared. The country went to the December elections riven by Afro-Indian hatred. The PNM won in 20 of the 30 constituencies, even taking for the first time the two Tobago seats.

Collapse of the Federation

The next bone of contention was the West Indies Federation. Jamaica was unenthusiastic about an economic and political alliance with

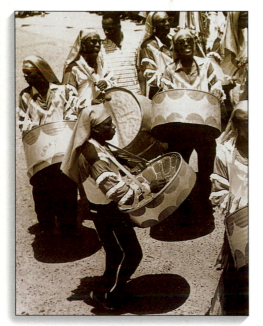

nine other British islands, unwilling to assist the smaller territories financially. The Jamaicans were further repelled by Trinidad and Tobago's proposals for the highly centralised federal government, based in Trinidad, whose prime minister, Grantley Adams, was Barbadian. In September 1961 Jamaica pulled out to move towards independence alone.

Hearing the news, Williams refused to saddle Trinidad and Tobago with the poorer islands. "One from ten", he quipped, "leaves nought". It was a bitter defeat for Pan-Caribbean idealists. "Federation boil down to simply this", rhymed the Mighty Sparrow, "Is dog eat dog and survival of the fittest".

A rocky road

With the PNM and the DLP at each other's throats, Trinidad and Tobago began moving towards independence as well. The government organised a public conference to discuss a draft constitution; the DLP, the Sanatan Dharma Maha Sabha and the Hindu Youth Organisation, boycotted it. The DLP claimed elections were rigged and demanded safeguards against political interference with the Elections Commission, the police and the judiciary. Indians and whites feared Williams as an incipient dictator; independence meant no Britain to protect them.

The deadlock dragged on into June 1962. For days the conference with the Colonial Office at Marlborough House in London was unable to agree on anything, and the British delegation was losing patience. On the sixth day, as the conference teetered on collapse, the British tactfully broke for tea. Capildeo was sipping tea with a colleague when Williams strode up and said: "Rudy – come, I want to talk with you".

Agreements over tea

The two went off for a brief tête-à-tête, and returned shortly. Although no one knows what was said, after the tea break Williams declared that he would always consult the leader of the opposition on matters of national interest, and everything was ironed out that same day.

Who compromised what? Capildeo no longer demanded that voting machines be abandoned, elections be held before independence, and the police be removed from the Home Affairs minister. Williams claimed he made no concessions, but the truth is the opposition won independence from political interference for the judiciary, the auditor general and the elections and boundaries commission. These provisions were entrenched in the Constitution, and could only be changed by special majorities in Parliament. Capildeo also achieved a Bill of Rights which could be enforced against the government by every individual, including – as has recently been discovered – those on death row.

And at midnight on 31 August 1962 the Union Jack was lowered for the last time after 165 years, and the country became a sovereign state, a full member of the community of nations. ❏

LEFT: an oil-drum orchestra.
RIGHT: the Duchess of Kent attends a service to mark the independence of Trinidad and Tobago.

NEW HORIZONS

During the years following Independence, Dr Eric Williams's party stood firmly at the helm. Then Black Power started rocking the boat

Culturally, the 1960s were blessed years. Samuel Selvon was past his peak, but V. S. Naipaul was reviving the moribund art of travel writing. C. L. R. James wrote what is perhaps his greatest book, *Beyond A Boundary*, fired by the achievements of West Indian cricketers such as Frank Worrell and Garfield

Velasques, Chang and many others, including those who created the brilliant, surreal Fancy Sailor costumes with their huge elaborate headpieces. It was they who paved the way for the world-renowned designer Peter Minshall, who went on to design the Olympics' opening ceremonies in Barcelona and Atlanta.

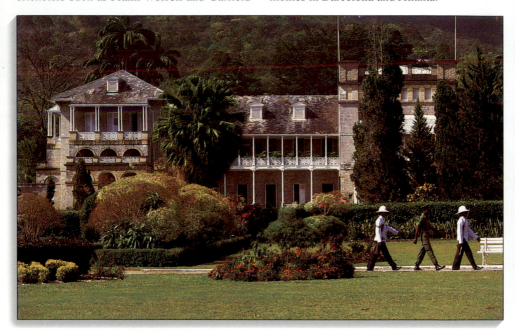

Sobers – considered by some to be the sportsman of the century. St Lucian Derek Walcott, who had come to stay in the 1950s and founded his Trinidad Theatre Workshop, was now in his full bloom as a poet. Artists such as Alfred Codaillo and Carlysle Chang, inspired by the nationalist movement, produced their most important work, Codaillo in his folklore studies and Chang in his public murals and, even more significantly, his Carnival designs.

Indeed, the many dimensions of Carnival attained levels of artistry never before known or even suspected. In the masquerade there was the work of now legendary designers such as George Bailey, Harold Saldenah, Cito

Carnival fever

Musically, a rivalry between the Mighty Sparrow and Lord Kitchener pushed calypso to greater and greater heights. Steel bands had evolved into huge wheeled caravans which dominated Carnival, producing vast rivers of sensuous, irresistible music – new world symphonies if ever there were any.

Ironically, none of this exuberance was reflected in the political parties. After Independence the DLP accepted its fate of permanent opposition, and Dr Rudranath Capildeo, while still the leader of the party, returned to his post at London University. The PNM ejected radicals, such as C. L. R. James, and Dr Eric Williams abandoned his University of Woodford Square. Even parliamentary politics declined, and the public lost interest in its debates.

But the militant nationalism which Williams had invoked in the run up to Independence persisted. Unionised workers translated independence into a rash of strikes against foreign-owned companies. The government's development policy involved granting concessions to foreign investors, so in 1963 the Commission of Enquiry into Subversive Activities was

whereas all candidates from the newly-formed Workers' and Farmers' Party lost their deposits, including C. L. R. James, trade unionist George Weekes and a barrister back from England, Basdeo Panday.

Poor get poorer

Development still seemed to elude Trinidad and Tobago. Independence, it seemed, was a matter of making the rich richer and the poor poorer. The poorest 20 percent of the population received 3.4 percent of total wealth in 1957, and 2.2 percent

set up. In 1964 the finance minister criticised "a developing strike consciousness" which threatened investor confidence. In 1965 sugar workers struck, contrary to the orders of their leader Bhadase Sagan Maraj, a company man if ever there was one. The government seized the opportunity to declare a state of emergency in the sugar areas, and within 24 hours rushed through parliament an Industrial Stabilisation Act making strikes virtually illegal.

The PNM won elections the following year,

in 1970, while the wealthiest 10 percent increased its share from 33.3 to 37.8 percent.

The favoured manufacturing sector did not perform as expected; oil prices stagnated; foreign capital trickled into the country, whereas repatriated profits poured out; unemployment rose. By 1968 youths who had benefited from the PNM's expansion of secondary education were entering an over-saturated job market. And what was more galling, the few white collar jobs for which they had been trained were not available to blacks.

A transport strike in 1969 broke the law, and a confederation of radical groups, the National Joint Action Committee (NJAC), was formed to

LEFT: the president's residence in Port of Spain.
ABOVE: the Oilfield Workers' Trade Union building in Fyzabad with a statue of "Buzz" Butler in front.

join the fight. The police moved in and arrested strikers, and the union was defeated. But the trade union movement had flexed its muscles and realised its strength. Three man days lost in 1967 grew to 17,568 in 1968, 19,972 in 1969 and 99,600 in 1970.

Black Power

On Carnival Monday 1970 bands of masqueraders appeared in demonstration mode, portraying topics such as The Truth About Blacks, King Sugar and 1001 White Devils. The more sensitive noses smelled a storm. To prevent this, the PNM decided to formulate a programme "to

protesters were supported by a crowd of thousands chanting "Power!".

The leaders were released from prison on 4 March 1970, and a dishevelled generation took to the streets, marching into the shanty town, a ghetto of cardboard and tin shacks. The movement swelled to over 10,000, and several Black Power groups addressed the crowd. Over the following weeks the Black Power movement held enthusiastic meetings at Woodford Square, renaming it "The People's Parliament". The activists trudged around the country by day, but at night the movement bared its teeth, firebombing businesses and banks. The government

achieve dignity and self-respect for the numerically dominant groups".

On the anniversary of a protest against racial discrimination in Canada (the Sir George Williams University incident) the NJAC took 200 protesters into Port of Spain where they tramped around for an hour or two, scuffled with the police at the Canadian High Commission and the Royal Bank of Canada, and made speeches from the pulpit of the Roman Catholic Cathedral on Independence Square, draping the statues in black. That day the Cabinet met in an emergency session, and the following morning the leaders of the demonstration were arrested. Taken to court and refused bail, the

offered concessions with unemployment relief, small business assistance and a commission of enquiry into racial discrimination. "We do not want crumbs," replied the movement, "we want the whole bread."

Musical backing

The steel band movement joined the ranks. Tobago organised a rally in support, and the deputy prime minister, A. N. R. Robinson, a Tobagonian, resigned from Cabinet. "The law will have to take its course," announced Williams, and the police clamped down on the demonstrations. When Basil Williams, a young Black Power activist, was shot by the law enforcers, the movement brought 60,000 people to his funeral. "By God we will fight fire with fire," declared a Black Power leader, Geddes Granger *(see page 34)*. "This is war."

The disquiet was contagious; wildcat strikes were breaking out. Oil workers, postal workers, water workers, civil servants, all were being swept along by the movement. On 19 April the sugar workers walked off the job, and marched into Port of Spain two days later. As in 1965 they called for assistance

CULTURAL SWING

With Black Power, the nation's culture changed: African names and *dashikis* (bright shirts); Afro hairstyles and an emphatic brogue; redemption songs from a new breed of political calypsonians, and musical extravaganzas.

The coastguard patrols stopped them by shelling the road and starting landslides. Some soldiers took to the hills; most remained at the army camp, and all eventually surrendered.

When the burning and looting in Port of Spain subsided, and a dusk-to-dawn curfew had been imposed, there were 87 soldiers and 54 Black Power militants behind bars.

A guerrilla group, the National Union of Freedom Fighters, was formed, only to be swiftly and brutally suppressed. Hence-

from George Weekes and the oil workers' union. Transport workers in another militant union also gave their support.

A state of emergency was declared, and in the small hours of 21 April the NJAC leaders and the trade unionists were arrested. The police and the army were called out. A section of the soldiers had different plans, however. Led by Lieutenants Raffique Shah and Rex Lassalle, they mutinied, took over the army camp in Chaguaramas and set off for the city.

LEFT: a stream of Black Power demonstrators marching into Port of Spain.
ABOVE: protesters chant slogans in the city centre.

forth Black Power, a movement containing much of the theatrical, lapsed into cultural concerns. Even Eric Williams occasionally shed his jacket and tie in favour of hot-coloured shirts and bright scarves. But the movement had politicised a generation and removed the grossest forms of racial discrimination from many social institutions.

Unconventional politics

Elections were due in 1971. The PNM renegade A. N. R. Robinson, who had lately taken to wearing gold chains and Nehru shirts, formed the Action Committee of Dedicated Citizens (ACDC), which merged with the DLP. The DLP was led by Vernon Jamadar, much to the chagrin of Bhadase Sagan Maraj who felt he should have been the one to replace Capildeo. Retaliating, he formed a new party with the same acronym: the Democratic Liberation Party.

Then there were the smaller groups advocating unconventional politics, such as the NJAC, whose brand of revolutionary politics had become identified in the public mind with anarchy, violence and tiring marches in the hot sun. Further left was the Union of Revolutionary Organisations (URO). This was largely comprised of ex-NJAC groups, and consequently its tone varied from pink to scarlet, from vaguely

left to orthodox Communist. URO's vital contribution to the times was to spearhead a campaign to boycott the elections. Finally there was the Tapia House Movement, a collection of non-socialist intellectuals led by a social theorist, Lloyd Best. An insightful, witty man, Best nevertheless aroused no public enthusiasm. "Cobo [turkey vultures]," he explained, "can't eat sponge cake".

The no vote campaign won in A. N. R. Robinson a last-minute convert, so only the PNM, Bhadase Sagan Maraj's DLP (which offered no programme) and an obscure African National Congress entered the elections. Consequently, the PNM, supported by 28 percent of

the electorate, won all 36 seats. A new state of emergency was called, subversives were put away, and a commission of enquiry was set up to look into constitutional reform.

Changes in the air

Bhadase Sagan Maraj died in October 1971. An unlettered, violent man who rose to prominence through intimidation and bribery, he was nevertheless a genuine leader of the East Indian community, through the orthodox Hindu organisation, the Sanatan Dharma Maha Sabha, he had formed, and the many primary schools it sponsored, and through the sugar workers' union he led. As Leader of the Opposition, he made deals with the PNM and vilified his own party. As a union leader, he fêted with the bosses and beat up workers who tried to strike. He was notorious for flashing guns in public and showing off huge wads of dollars. And when this picaresque, dangerous man died, people knew there would be changes. Into the vacuum stepped two men: Basdeo Panday and Raffique Shah.

Panday, a barrister, had studied politics and drama in England. He returned home on a doctoral scholarship which he abandoned to contest the 1966 elections. While others challenged Maraj's leadership of the sugar workers (and were often beaten by thugs for their efforts) Panday gave the union legal advice and watched from the sidelines, and after Maraj's death he was approached by the union's talent scouts.

Peace, bread and justice

Shah had been a leader of the mutiny of the army in 1970. Sentenced to 20 years' imprisonment, he appealed, and was set free in 1971 on grounds that he had not received a fair trial. The following year the new Islandwide Cane Farmers' Trade Union (ICFTU) needed a leader, someone well known who could unite the scattered sugar cane farmers against the old PNM farmers' association. The union settled on Shah and Winston Lennard. By 1974 it had the support of most cane farmers and was fighting to win recognition from the unwilling sugar producers. Simultaneously Panday was fighting for wage increases for sugar workers, and the Oilfield Workers' Trade Union (OWTU) was fighting Texaco for the same thing.

Despite hostility between Shah and Panday, a meeting of the unions came up with a proposed rally, named the United Labour Front

(ULF), under the guidance of George Weekes, President General of the OWTU.

Over 30,000 turned up to hear the militant speeches of the union leaders, who all vowed to continue their struggles. A march for "peace, bread and justice" was scheduled for Tuesday 18 March 1975. Thousands of marchers were led by priests and pundits as well as the trade unionists, but the police told the marchers to disperse, and immediately clouded the air with tear gas before wading into the panic-stricken crowd, swinging truncheons. All the leaders were arrested and several beaten for participating in an illegal march; and the day went down in history as Bloody Tuesday.

But the ULF could not be repressed so easily. On 4 January 1976 a conference of shop stewards passed a resolution: "Be it resolved that the ULF, while not sacrificing the unity it represents, takes all necessary steps to bring into being with all speed a party of the working class…", and so as motley a collection of leftists, radicals, trade unionists and black nationalists as can be imagined banded together under the leadership of Basdeo Panday.

Party political self-criticism

In the 1976 elections, 12 parties and six independents were standing, but the PNM's main challengers were the ULF, Lloyd Best's Tapia House Movement and A. N. R. Robinson's party, now called the Democratic Action Congress (DAC). The surprise came from Williams himself. He campaigned against his own party, and described five PNM candidates as "millstones" with a total lack of awareness.

In fact, Williams was the PNM's most severe critic, and he stole much of the other parties' thunder. "Heads will roll," he promised the electorate. Best thought the bottom had dropped out of Williams's bucket; Robinson thought the party was over. Williams laughed: while a Carnival atmosphere pervaded the crowds moving from meeting to meeting, he was already planning for the 1981 elections.

The campaign was peaceful, the polling low, and the electorate mostly fell into the racial

LEFT: the young Eric Williams.
RIGHT: the writing on the wall in Tobago.

> ### COMIC RELIEF
>
> Many of the parties standing in the 1976 elections provided comic relief: Dr Ivan Perot argued that he was a "younger and better-looking" doctor than Eric Williams. The two DLPs spent their energies attacking each other.

voting patterns of the 1960s. The PNM won 24 seats, having lost two Tobago seats to the DAC and picked up the same number from the ULF, which won the 10 Indian seats. "The other side too stupid," explained one PNM member. "We are winning by default." And the ULF, after the elections, attempted to prove him correct. Panday was voted out of leadership by the Central Committee and Shah put in his place. Then they swapped places again and again, until the *Trinidad Guardian* inquired:

"Are we to resign ourselves to having a new leader of the opposition every morning?" But Panday had always been the party's main attraction, and when the dust finally settled he emerged as leader of the ULF and Leader of the Opposition in Parliament.

Tobago breaks away

Since 1961 Tobago had been considered a PNM stronghold and was left to languish in its beautiful, idyllic, neglected state, lacking in social amenities. Even administrative facilities were absent, and the Tobagonians had to travel to Port of Spain for land titles, birth and death certificates and planning approval. So by 1976 they resented their poor-relation status and, unencumbered by anti-Indian fears, they voted out the PNM.

"If you want to go, go," fumed Williams, angry at the DAC victory in Tobago, which he blamed on a desire for secession. "Whatever used to be said in the past, we don't live in any world of true eternal love. The greatest thing today is the divorce celebration."

Two decades before, Williams had felt a need to "insist on the development of Tobago virtu-

ally as a self-contained unit". Now Robinson quoted him in order to lay a motion in Parliament "that all proper and necessary steps be taken to accord to the people of Tobago internal self-government in 1977". And the PNM complied, creating a Tobago House of Assembly (THA) to replace the County Council.

The PNM had won a large majority in local government elections and expected to control the THA, which was accordingly granted fairly wide self-governing powers in all spheres, including infrastructure and tourism, except national security and international treaty-making. When the first enthusiastic THA elections were held in November 1980, however, Robinson's

DAC won eight seats and the PNM four. And the THA and central government settled down to wrangle over finances.

Money? No problem

Back in September 1973, at the 15th Annual Convention of the PNM, Williams had shocked everyone by announcing his decision to retire. Choose a new leader by 31 December, he had instructed the party, claiming that he was weary, that he desired a return to academic research, that his daughter Erica had been begging him to abandon politics. Immediately two contenders emerged: Karl Hudson-Phillips, the autocratically inclined attorney general and Kamaluddin Mohammed, a founding PNM member. The choice was to be made on 2 December. Instead, at the meeting Williams was begged to stay, and he acceded.

Why? Many felt it all had been a ploy to flush ambitious rats such as Hudson-Phillips out of hiding. But more importantly, towards the end of 1973 the cartel of Oil Producing and Exporting Countries (OPEC) raised the price of oil to astronomical heights.

Over the next five years, Trinidad and Tobago's economy ballooned. A deficit trade balance became a huge surplus, and for the first time ever the government had the wherewithal to do as it pleased. "Money," as Williams famously announced, "is no problem."

Sharing the booty

And indeed there were positive developments, such as Williams's regionalism in which he lent more money to insolvent Caribbean countries than any other country, including the US with its highly publicised Caribbean Basin Initiative. Then there was the equalising impact of wealth: blacks, browns, whites and Indians were no longer inevitably separated by occupation, geographic residence, schooling or income. Consequently, race relations became more intimate, miscegenation more open. And finally, there was the rising status of women who had benefited from increased higher and tertiary education and a job market which accepted everyone. Significantly, the number of women who contested elections increased from nine in 1966 to 26 a decade later.

The government invested in ambitious pro-

MANNA FROM HEAVEN

With the influx of petrodollars in the 1970s, most Trinidadians could afford telephones and cars. They were jokingly described as having strong index fingers from dialling phones, and strong left legs from mashing clutches in traffic.

jects, such as the production of iron and steel. Wages increased; inflation increased and so did the import bill. Millionaires were made overnight as petrodollars lubricated a freewheeling economy. Fast food outlets sprang up like weeds. Every home had a telephone, a stereo and a television. The number of cars multiplied.

A speedy downfall

At the same time, productivity fell, agriculture disappeared, and inefficiency and corruption clogged the arteries of the state. Trinidad and Tobago plunged into an obscene and philistine materialism. "Check out they house and look,"

political advocate – and he considered resigning. The oil boom which had come along in the nick of time had only made things worse. For if in 1962 he criticised "the pronounced materialism and disastrous individualism (which) have spread to all parts of the fabric of the society", by 1981 the economy was even more skewed, society even more vulgar.

In March 1981, a month in which sugar workers, hospital workers and teachers demonstrated around Parliament, Williams ceased taking his diabetic medicines and paid off his domestic helpers. He slipped into a coma and, on 29 March, quietly abandoned this world.

lamented poet Derek Walcott of the educated classes, "You bust your brain before you find a book." By 1980 social commentators were complaining that the oil boom was the worst thing ever to have happened to the country.

None of this was lost on Williams. A solitary, arrogant man, he used to turn off his hearing aid at the sound of an opposing voice. But he saw the mess. Intolerant of criticism over the years, he had surrounded himself with mediocrities whom he despised. Black Power shook him to the core – after all, he was its first

We must do better

In the political landscape Eric Williams had towered like a giant among pygmies. After his death, politics were more evenly balanced, more unpredictable, every five years seeing a new party and a new prime minister. First to rise was George Chambers, the finance minister, who succeeded Williams. Chambers was an unintellectual, down-to-earth man whom some compared unfavourably with Williams. Others, however, saw in his informal style the key to a regeneration of the moribund PNM, just the man to lead the party into the 1981 elections.

Chambers's campaign of heckling and insinuation set the tone for the fight against the new

LEFT: oil wells in southern Trinidad.
ABOVE: Port of Spain with the twin towers behind.

Organisation for National Reconstruction (ONR). This party was the creation of former PNM Attorney General Karl Hudson-Phillips, and was a catch-all for disillusioned PNMs (including the calypsonian Mighty Sparrow), dissatisfied businessmen and urbanised middle-class Indians. With what appeared to be inexhaustible funds, the ONR launched a US-style public relations campaign attacking PNM corruption and inefficiency. "We must do better," was their slogan, to which Chambers

POLITICAL *PICONG*

At election time the politicians are at the mercy of the calypsonians, when a form of musical heckling called *picong* (from the French word meaning stinging, *piquant*), comes into its own.

NJAC's and a promise, like the ONR's, to be more efficient. According to the Tapia leader: "You can't do better than Best."

The campaign resembled Carnival, with *picong* (*see left*) hitting where it hurt. The ONR got the worst of it, and was successfully labelled a big business party of authoritarian bent. The masses hadn't forgotten Hudson-Phillips' role as attorney general in 1970, and although when the votes were counted his party won the second highest number, there was indeed "not a damn seat for them". The ULF lost two more seats to the PNM, and captured only eight. The DAC won the two Tobago seats, Tapia and NJAC none. And the PNM took power for the sixth time with 26 seats: its largest majority ever. George Chambers became prime minister just as the price of oil dipped, and the balance of trade showed its first deficit since 1974.

responded: "Not a damn seat for them!"

Meanwhile, the NJAC had changed its mind about "conventional politics"; members roamed the country holding strident, angry meetings, and painted ominous graffiti in red, green and black everywhere. They attracted small audiences of curiosity-seekers who were served a mild "black" nationalism (stretched to include Indians) and a vague "philosophy of man".

Then there was the National Alliance coalition, comprising the ULF, Tapia and the DAC. Lloyd Best wistfully called it the "party of parties", representing the three main "tribes": Trinidad blacks, Indians and Tobagonians. Its programme was a mild nationalism like the

Captain, the ship is sinking

Immediately after victory Chambers launched an austerity drive. "Fête over, back to work," he declared. His timing was unfortunate, however, coming shortly before Carnival, and many people replied: "The fête now start." The new stress on productivity brought the employer class back into the PNM fold and out of the ONR camp, but soon it was clear that the government was unable to discipline workers, and that corruption and inefficiency remained the same.

Opposition parties further consolidated themselves, and by 1982 the three-party National Alliance had joined with the ONR to form a tentative accommodation which won 66 out of 120 local government seats. In Tobago the DAC won 11 of the House of Assembly's 12 seats.

Social conditions were deteriorating rapidly. As oil revenues plummeted, unemployment rose; as trade unions retreated, wages shrank; as the TT dollar devalued, inflation rose. The education system was producing illiterates, and the health system bordered on collapse. Most importantly, the electorate was tired of the PNM, and perhaps the party itself was exhausted. As Chambers's stupidity became the subject of hundreds of humiliating jokes, the "accommodation" parties papered over their differences to form a National Alliance for Reconstruction (NAR). And this party of "one love" was led by

A. N. R. Robinson, on whose birthday, 16 December, it won 33 out of 36 seats in 1986. Chambers lost his seat and became a recluse, never to be seen again.

Kidnapped...

The country celebrated its new-found unity with a spontaneous street party which continued for days in some parts. Alas, it was not to last beyond the honeymoon. During 1987 acrimonious rifts appeared, and the following year the Panday faction was thrown out, much to the bitter disappointment of most Indians. Nor did Robinson endear himself to black hearts when

He formed the radical and self-righteous Jamaat-al-Muslimeen sect which absorbed many young drop-outs, the human debris created by the recession. The group occupied a large parcel of land which the government had once promised to the Muslim community, and there were several confrontations with the state, both in and out of the courts. Finally, on Friday 27 July 1990, when the court decided they had no right to the land, over a hundred of them fetched their hidden cache of arms and attacked.

One group of insurgents, led by Abu Bakr, took over the television station and announced that the government had fallen. Another group

he unilaterally reduced government salaries by 10 percent. A stiff, unspontaneous Tobagonian, Robinson never understood the more anarchic psyche of Trinidadians, who named a virulent flu after him. When he and his Cabinet were kidnapped by a radical Muslim group in July 1990, many people approved of the violence.

Islam Yaseen Abu Bakr used to be a mounted policeman by the name of Lennox Phillip. In the 1970s he converted to Islam – some say after he was kicked in the head by his mount.

LEFT: processing fertiliser.
ABOVE: an Amoco oil platform at Galeota Point, which is dominated by the oil industry.

bombed the police headquarters, stormed Parliament and holed up there with a captive Cabinet. Two dozen people were killed, and the city was trashed by looters. The army surrounded the insurgents, who remained entrenched for five days until they were able to bargain for the amnesty which eventually set them free.

Back in the driving seat

The coup had unleashed considerable animosity that had built up against Robinson among Indians and lower- and middle-class blacks. Meanwhile Patrick Manning, young and chubby-faced and amiable, had eased out the old PNM guard, and was seen as representing a renewal of the party. In December 1991 the NAR was voted out of every seat except the two in Tobago, and Manning's PNM took 21 seats, leaving 13 for Panday's UNC *(see page 90)*.

The crime rate soars

The PNM met an economy on the mend from Robinson's medicine and, despite the prophecies of all economists, things improved, aided by rising oil prices. Unemployment fell. But the main problem confronting society now was crime. Children of the boom years had grown into cynical, materialistic teenagers who listened to Jamaican music. They set the tone for

insolvent and had to be fired after a few days. The Speaker of Parliament, Occah Seapaul, an Indian woman appointed by the government, became involved in a dirty court battle with an estranged lover. Asked to resign, she refused, and a state of emergency was declared to remove her.

East Indian celebrations

The 150th anniversary of the first arrival of East Indians was massively celebrated in 1995. Members of the community had acquired a new confidence and sense of belonging, of their right to be there as equal citizens of the country.

a nihilistic young generation whose criminals were more casually brutal than ever. There were also the cocaine cartels, their murderous turf wars and their corruption of the justice system.

While respectable society cowered in terror, politics became an argument over how to outsmart constitutional lawyers and hang the murderers – something not achieved since the 1970s. Then on 16 July 1994, through a series of low dodges and judicial slip-ups, convicted murderer Glen Ashby was hanged while his constitutional appeal was being processed.

Ashby's death was like a jinx. Manning came to be perceived as insensitive, dim-witted and indecisive. One new minister turned out to be

What is more, Indians were now the single largest group, no longer concentrated in a few constituencies. So when Manning called early elections, Panday won four more seats than before. It was a tie: PNM 17, UNC 17. While Manning dithered, Panday dealt with Robinson. He bartered the two Tobago seats for Robinson's later appointment as president, and, as a result, Panday, controlling a slim majority, was made prime minister.

Fondly known as the Silver Fox, the grey-haired Panday far surpassed Manning in wit and political savvy. Yet he dissipated public goodwill with surprising rapidity. Unaccustomed to power, its limits and decorum, Panday resented criticism from both the media and calypsonians. He threw tantrums and sulked, refusing to talk to reporters. He accused critics of racism, of "lies, half-truths and innuendoes", and repeatedly encouraged his supporters to declare war on the enemy.

Tainted by corruption

Although lower-class Afro-Trinidadians' fears of victimisation by the UNC did not materialise, Panday's government was associated with high-level corrupt deals and a general lack of sophistication. Drug baron Dole Chadee and eight of his henchmen were hanged by a gleeful government in 1999, only for it to be discovered that one man might indeed have been innocent. A few months before the 2000 general elections, the inexplicable murder of a local government chairman, who had complained to Panday about threats from the minister of local government, tainted the party, as did the continuing mud-slinging between the power-hungry attorney general and the autocratic chief justice.

Like everywhere else, violent crime and drug abuse, teenage pregnancy and educational non-performance have continued their relentless growth – even in idyllic Tobago, whose booming tourism industry has taken its toll on the island's fragile marine environment.

By 2002 the PNM had returned to power and future elections are likely to be close contests. This is partly a result of the racial voting, which is indifferent to intellectual and moral considerations. But other factors contribute to the balance between the parties, such as PNM leader Patrick Manning's lacklustre performance when compared with the aggressive, well-oiled UNC party machine.

Flourishing economy

Most important, however, is the flourishing economy. Neither trade liberalisation nor the 1993 floating of the TT dollar had the disastrous effects predicted; instead the dollar has remained stable, and unemployment is lower than ever (11 percent, claims the government). As for Tobago, which handles more international flights than Trinidad, tourism and hotel

construction have provided both licit and illicit jobs for whoever wants them. Over the past five years the price of oil has risen; energy-based industries, such as methanol and urea production, have taken off, and even local manufactured goods have swamped the regional market. Investment in one liquefied natural gas plant has exceeded US$1 billion, with advance sales beyond the next 12 years. New cars crowd the roads; huge office complexes and luxury apartment blocks are sprouting like mushrooms, and steep mountain sides are being scraped clean so that mansions can cling to them.

But the flux of party politics hardly affects

the deeper tidal shifts in the society. More significant than the general election results were the deaths of two of calypso's greatest exponents – the Roaring Lion and Lord Kitchener – in July 1999 and February 2000 respectively. Their passing symbolised the end of the 20th century, its changing culture and decline of parochial civilities.

But the worst legacies of colonialism are equally on the way out, including the racial animosities and self-contempt bred of slavery and indentureship. And if the new century challenges the young to create a humane and exciting society, at least it need not be attempted under conditions of poverty or racial hostility. ❑

LEFT: Islam Yaseen Abu Bakr, the leader of the Jamaat-al-Muslimeen, surrenders after the siege in 1990.
RIGHT: Carib lager is brewed in Trinidad.

TRINBAGONIANS

The complex culture of the sister islands reveals not only a people proud of their individuality, but also a combined joy of what makes a "Trini" unique

Trinidadians may be the most heterogeneous people on Earth, for they are a people in a sense that other societies which contain multi-racial populations are not. The favourite national myth is that Trinidad and Tobago is a paradise of interracial harmony, and T&Ters view with self-righteous horror the ugly racial strife that seems endemic to other countries. Race is mentioned casually and openly in daily conversation, and Trinidadians appear unconcerned when racial stereotypes and differences are discussed.

The truth, however, is infinitely more complex than either of these two extremes. Trinidadians do not, today, fight pitched battles, race against race, but neither can the question of race be too glibly glossed over.

There is a nation of Trinidad and Tobago with a central core of culture in which all the races participate, and there is a significant percentage of the population which is of mixed race. But history has not succeeded in melting the peoples down entirely – either culturally or genetically – into one homogeneous block; and so, in Trinidad and Tobago, race is very much an issue, albeit an issue so subtle that it is not likely to assail the attention of the visitor.

Trinbagonians

Who are the Trinidadians and Tobagonians? (The term "Trinidadian" will be used hereafter to refer to the combined peoples of the two islands, at the risk of causing offence to the Tobagonian sector of the population.)

The first people to inhabit the country were, of course, Amerindians, who migrated from the South American continent, discovering the Caribbean centuries before Christopher Columbus. As happened elsewhere in the region, they were all but exterminated in the onslaught of European colonisation. There is a

tiny handful of people in Trinidad calling themselves "Caribs", and there are many among T&Ters whose physical features suggest an Amerindian admixture in their ancestry. The Amerindian strain has fed into the pool, but it is no longer a distinct racial presence.

Most territories of the Caribbean bear the

mark of one European culture, at most two. The European element of Trinidad and Tobago hails from no less than three main sources. Spanish, French and British have all, at one time or another, ruled these islands, and in addition to these three major groups of European settlers there were minority groups of Portuguese, Italians and others.

But the bulk of the people of Trinidad and Tobago today are the descendants of Africans and Indians brought to work in the sugar-cane and other plantations: the Africans transported by force and enslaved, the Indians arriving under a system of indentureship not too far removed from slavery. Together the Indians and

---

PRECEDING PAGES: two faces of Trinidad; floral hats and parasol on Republic Day.
LEFT: Carnival smile.
RIGHT: watching the world go by.

Africans constitute upwards of 80 percent of the population. During the long turbulent years of the 20th century Trinidad received, and in the 21st century continues to receive, immigrants from China and the Middle East who come as traders.

The ethnic groups which make up the population of Trinidad and Tobago all arrived, then, under different circumstances. They came from different roots, thousands of miles and continents apart; they came for different reasons; and they came to fulfil different roles. Inevitably they continue to be different from each other in many ways.

managers of major business concerns – manufacturing, hotel industry, banking, the import and distribution trades.

Some whites work in education, in schools run by religious orders which function as the old "prestige" ones originally founded for white and mulatto children, and in the new private schools set up for the still predominantly light-skinned children of today's upper classes. All in all, the white Trinidadian is a white-collar worker. A white street cleaner, chambermaid or bus driver would be a decided oddity. The recreational activities of white society in Trinidad and Tobago are the traditionally upper-

Plantation legacy

Whites in Trinidad and Tobago remain a privileged minority, fairly aloof from the rest of the population. They live in affluent suburban settlements or on large inherited landholdings scattered around the country, and a few still earn incomes from large estates passed on by their forebears – relics of the plantation system.

Whites are the traditional "aristocracy" of the society, who for centuries controlled the resources and reaped the benefits of all economic activity. Although today members of other groups have emerged to share the "commanding heights" of the economy with the old masters, whites remain the owners and

class pursuits of water sports (yachting, boat-racing, windsurfing, swimming), lawn tennis, golf, cocktail and dinner parties, or simply meeting at their exclusive clubs.

And it is whites who have kept European artistic traditions such as ballet and opera alive in Trinidadian society. The major national festival of Trinidad and Tobago – Carnival – has its origin in a European celebration (French, to be exact), and although it has been developed to its present state by the African population, white Trinidadians continue to participate in Carnival activities. Indeed, the most widely-acclaimed Carnival mas artist to emerge in recent times is a white man, Peter Minshall.

African echoes

Next in order of arrival were the Africans. Alienated from the land by the experience of slavery, the African population has tended to gravitate towards urban centres, though the population of Tobago is almost entirely African. (Tobago was a separate entity and developed apart from Trinidad until a century ago, when the two islands were unified. The smaller island does not have the same history of multi-ethnic immigration).

Blacks engage in a wide variety of occupa-

> **TRINI *JOIE DE VIVRE***
>
> The *joie de vivre* of the Afro-Trinidadian is proverbial, and the duty of enjoying all that is put on the Earth for God's children to enjoy is taken very seriously.

It was the Africans who forged the calypso-steel band-carnival arts, and they remain the chief proponents of this aspect of the vibrant Trinidad and Tobago culture.

It was they, too, who perfected the "lime", and this item has no translation because the concept belongs exclusively to this part of the world. To those who disapprove of the activity, liming means loitering, as in groups of aimless men standing around at street corners or sitting on a culvert watching the world go by. To the limers it means pointedly not doing

tions, but shy away from agriculture. Black businessmen are also thin on the ground. The Afro-Trinidadian is a salaried worker – menial, semi-skilled and skilled. For years the Civil Service was monopolised by this ethnic group, which still occupies nearly the whole of its upper levels. There is also a large class of black professionals: doctors, lawyers and other university-trained people. The means of social mobility for the African population has always been education, rather than the route of entrepreneurship, the pattern for other ethnic groups.

LEFT: a legacy of European settlement.
ABOVE: a man of African heritage.

anything too purposeful, or serious, or strenuous, whiling the time away in the company of cronies, talking or not talking, drinking or not drinking, playing all fours, going in a gang to the beach, to a party, to a cricket match...

The *joie de vivre* of the Afro-Trinidadian is proverbial, and the duty of enjoying all that is put on the Earth for God's children to enjoy is taken very seriously indeed.

The staple food of the black population is rice, a taste acquired from the Indians. While African people in the rest of the Caribbean make extensive use of root vegetables and green bananas, in Trinidad and Tobago these take second place to rice. Blacks retain a taste for the salted meat and fish which were an essential part of the food rations given out to their enslaved ancestors on the plantations. Today salted beef and pork and dried codfish are mainly used as flavouring for other dishes – rice and peas, stewed peas, *callaloo*.

The family patterns of Africans in Trinidad and Tobago, as in the rest of the Caribbean, do not adhere too strictly to the official norms of marriage and the patriarchal family. Common-law unions are prevalent, and women have a great deal of authority in the context of the family. A large percentage of households are headed by women. Extended-family habits are

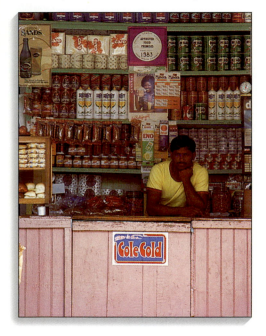

still alive, mainly among the lower classes. Promotion into the growing middle class generally means adoption of the life-style beamed out from American television, which includes the restricted nuclear family pattern. The more affluent people become, the less use they have for the larger family.

New religions which combine elements of Christianity with African religious practices and beliefs were developed by the African population on Caribbean soil. But Trinidad and Tobago is officially a Christian country, with the Catholic Church being particularly powerful, so the syncretic sects are severely frowned upon. Practically every known form of Chris-

tianity claims a portion of the black population: Roman Catholic, Church of England, Church of Scotland, Methodist, Moravian, Seventh-Day Adventist, Jehovah's Witness, Pentecostal and more. A more recent development in Trinidad and Tobago is the "Black Muslim" movement: that is Africans, turning to Islam, but in their own Muslim organisations, not as part of the established Indian Muslim community. It was one such organization, Imam Yasin Abu Bakr's Jamaat-al-Muslimeen sect, that was responsible for the violent attempted coup and kidnapping of the Cabinet in 1990.

An indigenous population

The mulatto did not, of course, come as an immigrant arriving from distant shores, but is a racial type produced on Caribbean soil, being the offspring of African and European.

There are very many people of mixed blood in Trinidad and Tobago, but they do not, by and large, constitute a separate group. They are, culturally, black Trinidadians. Within a "black" family, complexions may range from black to palest brown, reflecting miscegenation somewhere along their ancestry. But there is a group of brown Trinidadians which has to be viewed as distinct from the mass. It contains the heirs of the original "middle class" of the Caribbean – a privileged, carefully inbred social class.

This group has a very strong sense of being an élite. It jealously guards its racial "purity" – members choose only mates of the same colour or lighter. There is not much to distinguish them, in terms of life-style, from the whites. Indeed, in the popular mind, whites and upper-class mulattos are lumped together under the loose label of "French Creoles", although many families in this class bear Spanish, Portuguese, Scottish or English names. The designation "French Creole" has to do with the fact that, in the 18th century, whites and mulattos were attracted to Trinidad from the French Caribbean by enticements such as grants of land, and soon became a powerful economic and political force in the century.

Eastern elements

The East Indian presence in Trinidad and Tobago is not much more than one and a half centuries old, but it is already the largest single group in the republic, claiming over 40 percent of the population. The majority of Indians still live in rural communities, and farming remains their chief occupation. With increased access to secondary and tertiary education, however, Indians have entered the clerical and professional fields once occupied almost exclusively by Africans. Indian political leaders, long confined to opposition, finally tasted electoral success in the 1990s. Small and medium-sized businesses are owned mainly by Indians, and a great number of such concerns have grown into major business enterprises.

A TASTE OF BOLLYWOOD

The Indian film industry based in Mumbai (Bombay) is known as "Bollywood". A multi-million dollar business, it has captured audiences all over the world, including Indians in Trinidad.

Indians brought to Trinidad and Tobago a relatively intact and functional culture, which adapted itself to the new environment and shaped the fabric of life in Indian communities for generations. Inevitably the life-style of Indian Trinidadians has been and continues to be affected by the influences which prevail in society, namely the culture of their African counterparts and the essentially Western-orientated education system and mass media. But there remains a core of cultural traits which constitutes a distinctive Indian way of life.

A minority of Indians have been Christianised, notably by the Presbyterian Church. But the religions which the Indian immigrants brought with them, Hinduism and Islam, remain firmly in place. The majority religion is Hinduism, and both religions have very strong organisations which, like the Christian churches, set up their own schools. Eastern religions may be said to have gained rather than lost ground, for today they enjoy an official recognition not accorded them during the colonial period. Marriage ceremonies, for example, were not recognised. Major Hindu and Muslim festivals like Diwali and Eid-ul-Fitr are now public holidays.

Indian family organisation in Trinidad and Tobago has been eroded somewhat by Westernisation. The traditional status of the Indian is challenged by both near-universal education to secondary level and the influence of the media. But extended-family networks are generally stronger than in the African population. Many Indians live in large multi-generation households, of the type made famous by V. S. Naipaul,

although the patterns of authority which previously obtained in such households may not be operational today. But even where Indians split off into nuclear family households, there remains a strong bond of responsibility towards the larger family, which may include economic cooperation.

Indian food, of course, is quite distinctive. Among their standards are aubergine (baigan), a string bean known as bodi, tomatoes, green mangoes, potatoes (aloo), a variety of spinach known as bhaji, split peas,

chick peas (channa) and pumpkin. A favourite seasoning is curry, in addition to other spices such as cumin seed, saffron and massala. Rice is basic to the Indian diet, and so is roti – a flat, supple pastry combined with split peas, that is eaten with vegetable or meat preparations.

Indian Trinidadians are as fond of the game of cricket as their African compatriots. A favourite form of recreation, too, is going to the cinema to watch movies from India. Indian music and dance are also greatly appreciated, and there are highly accomplished Trinidadian Indian musicians, dancers and singers, some of whom trained in the ancestral country. In recent years some modern fusion forms of Indian-

LEFT: an Indian shopkeeper.
RIGHT: an East Indian West Indian woman.

inspired music, such as "chutney", have moved more firmly into the mainstream, and are now part of the sound of Carnival.

Trading places

The Chinese and Lebanese came as traders, and remain largely engaged in commercial activity – small trading and big business. The Lebanese are a tightly-knit urban community, whereas the Chinese are scattered all over the country: the "Chinese shop" is an institution in rural communities. Both groups are relative newcomers and tend to keep active links with their countries of origin, so items of their material

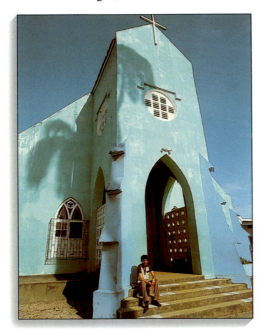

culture are ever present. In the home of a Chinese family one is likely to be surrounded by Oriental decorations and kitchen utensils. Because the Chinese and Lebanese are recent immigrants, their cultures remain fairly closed – practised "privately" while the people participate in the common culture of the country. But there is a greater level of integration on the part of the Chinese than by the Lebanese, and there has been some intermixture of Chinese blood with that of Africans and Indians; many people in Trinidad and Tobago bear no fewer than four different racial strains in their blood.

The mixing of races is part of the reality of Trinidad and Tobago, but what is the real nature of relationships among the various peoples?

Status and stereotypes

Race relations in Trinidad and Tobago are defined by the old hierarchy of "white down to black", and by the newer and more volatile current of mistrust which runs between the two largest groups in the country: the Africans and the Indians.

Europeans constitute a very small minority in Trinidad and Tobago – less than 1 percent – but they retain their economic supremacy and attendant prestige. Today the traditional attitudes towards white people have been reinforced by the impact of the foreign (mainly American) media. Moreover, deep in the ethos of the Indian population of Trinidad and Tobago is the great esteem in which their ancestral culture held the Aryan racial type of northern India.

Thus it is that the physical features of the Europeans are the yardstick against which Trinidadians evaluate beauty and worthiness in general. At the lower end of the scale of desirability lie dark skin and kinky hair; at the top, pale skin and straight hair. It stands to reason, then, that great approval also accrues to the physical features of the Chinese, the Lebanese, the light-skinned Indian, the mulatto (or "Spanish") and the "mixed" (provided that one part of the mixture is light-skinned).

There are many manifestations of this race-and-colour scale of assessment. For years a Trinidad and Tobago beauty queen was, by definition, a white or pale-skinned woman. The Black Power movement of the 1970s made some inroads into changing that tradition and attitudes, and today it is more politic to choose

CLASS CONSCIOUSNESS

Race relations in Trinidad and Tobago are far from ideal. Trinidadians mix at school and at work, but on the whole not too much at play.

Perhaps the most interaction among races is to be found at the top of the pile, where money and paleness of skin unite into one mélange of whites, mulattos, Lebanese and the successful Chinese. The middle class, mostly African and Indian, can range from professionals to civil servants to well-paid skilled workers (especially in the wake of the oil boom). There are practically no lines of communication between the middle and lower classes and the light-skinned upper class.

a queen of the indeterminate khaki mix (not too pale, but not quite black, either) that is becoming the ideal physical type in Trinidad and Tobago.

When, for bureaucratic purposes, black Trinidadians are called upon to identify their race (e.g. in passport applications, ID documentation, census exercises), many choose to write the ambiguous "mixed".

Black men on the rise up the social ladder acquire light-skinned, straighthaired wives as part of the trappings of promotion, and certain high-visibility "women's" jobs – bank teller, air hostess – until fairly recently were filled only by light-skinned types.

THE POLITICS OF RACE

Since the beginning of party politics, in the era leading up to Independence, major political parties formed along racial lines (Indian and African), and elections were perceived as a struggle for African or Indian supremacy.

side but also actively cooperate, and the miscegenation which has produced a whole new race called, the "Dougla".

But there exists a fundamental mistrust between Indians and Africans in the mass, a rivalry that dates from the Indians' arrival to replace the Africans as plantation workers in the wake of Emancipation. Each has traditionally accused the other of wanting to "take over" the country, and the two groups monitor each other's numbers with continual apprehen-

sion. Nowhere is this numbers game more evident than in politics.

The arrival in 1995 of an Indian, or Indian-dominated, government for the first time since Independence marked a major shift in racial political power. The People's National Movement (PNM), closely identified with Afro-Trinidadian interests, had monopolised government since 1962, helped by votes from the minority and mixed-raced electorate as well as a deliberately skewed system of constituency boundaries that favoured urban over rural voters. Indians were, for the most part, excluded from government, their leaders tending to engage in damaging in-fighting and short-term

Education, politics and economy

Africans and Indians constitute the bulk of the population, and relations between them are uneasy. This fact does not preclude healthy relations at the personal level: firm friendships between individuals and families, communities in which the two races not only live side by

LEFT: a black-German-Portuguese man outside a Portuguese church in Arouca.
ABOVE: an elder in the Creole village of Blanchisseuse.

alliances with any anti-PNM grouping. Yet Indian spokesmen like Bhadase Sagan Maraj refused to show support for the anti-PNM Black Power protesters in 1970, probably out of fear that the Black Power movement would eventually turn its anger on the Indian population. They were also fearful that any such wider and non-racial coalition would loosen their own stranglehold over their trade-union constituents.

Indians also traditionally had less access to education under the colonial regime, and for this reason, as well as PNM dominance, the Civil Service was until recently an Afro-Trinidadian preserve. Indian families rarely aspired to a

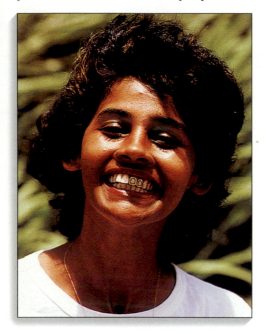

career in the public sector in the way that Afro-Trinidadians did. Their ambition, on the whole, was to succeed in business.

Meanwhile the Indian population grew steadily in the 1970s, 1980s and 1990s as a percentage of the national total (from 36.4 percent in 1960 to more than 40 percent in 2000). But still Indian voters lacked a party which would truly represent their mounting influence. The breakthrough occurred in 1988 after the leading Indian politician, Basdeo Panday, left the coalition National Alliance for Reconstruction (NAR), accusing its black majority leadership of anti-Indian racism. The following year the former lawyer and sugar union boss founded a new party, the United National Congress (UNC). In the 1991 elections the UNC could manage only 29 percent of the vote, confined – as usual for an Indian-based party – to mainly rural constituencies in the south and centre, but in 1995 it received almost 46 percent, allowing Panday to form a government in alliance with A.N.R. Robinson (the same man he had accused of anti-Indian racism in 1988).

Although the previous PNM administration had included a couple of Indians in the Cabinet, this was the first Indian-dominated government in the country's history. Its popularity was short-lived, however, for it both failed to win new friends and alienated many supporters. Continuing many of the same policies as its predecessors, the UNC administration did not, as many Afro-Trinidadians had feared, purge the Civil Service and install its own Indian candidates. But Panday was all too often hostile towards what he saw as black Trinidadian interests, labelling critics as "racist". Neither those Indians hoping for a radical shift in the control of state resources, nor blacks (few of whom were disposed to sympathise with Panday under any circumstances) were happy with a government that used racial rhetoric freely but changed little. In the December 2000 general election the UNC won 19 out of the 36 seats in the House of Representatives. But after losing its parliamentary majority following the dismissal of three cabinet ministers in September 2001, a hung parliament was elected in December 2001. This impasse was only resolved at the October 2002 elections which gave the PNM 20 seats and a clear majority.

Africans continue to perceive Indians not only as political opponents but also as taking over the economy of the country, because they are so visibly engaged in business activity, ranging from the selling of vegetables by the roadside to ownership of the sophisticated hardware store, while the Africans have chosen a different route to success, the way of education.

What perhaps exacerbated relationships in the last two decades of the 20th century was that the Indians caught up in education. With the increase in oil revenue in the 1970s, the incumbent government was able to increase educational facilities dramatically, notably at secondary level. This gave the Indians a new ubiquity which disturbs their African counterparts: the Indian who was once safely tucked away out of sight in the canefield, the rice patch or the family vegetable garden is now turning up everywhere, in every kind of job.

The juxtaposition of two different cultures has been an inevitable source of friction. The original encounter between Africans and Indians was the classic case of "host population" versus immigrants who had a foreign, therefore disturbing, culture which (as is the case in such situations) they showed no inclination of relinquishing in favour of the culture of the hosts.

But, in addition, in Trinidad and Tobago the host population had no strong sense of its own cultural identity. The circumstances under which Africans had been brought from their

The confidence of Indians in their own culture, the strength and the cohesiveness which this culture gave to Indian communities, the Indians' refusal to be assimilated, tended to be interpreted by the Africans as arrogance. Africans take a dim view of the Indian population's continuing emotional relationship with their ancestral land – Trinidad and Tobago has been brought to the brink of civil war by the spectacle of Indian Trinidadians cheering on a cricket team from India playing in Trinidad against a Trinidadian team! And Indian music on the radio and Indian movies on national television were until recently a great affront to the rest of the population; but

ancestral land made cultural continuity very difficult. Africans from different cultures had been mixed together, languages forgotten, religions garbled – even their birth and tribal names were erased. Africans now practised a new culture that was decidedly African-based, but the official, approved culture was European, and the way of life of the black population was not even seen as "culture". The attitude of the Afro-Trinidadian to his own culture was one of rejection, at best ambivalence. Salvation lay in being assimilated into the white man's culture.

LEFT: a smile as good as gold.
ABOVE: schoolgirl smiles.

this is changing, and it is in the area of culture that the republic is experiencing a shift from confrontation to intermingling. Carnival, long the preserve of the Afro-Trinidadians, is perhaps symptomatic of the growing ethnic synthesis, as Indian music and Indian singers (even women) are entering that once black-only cultural arena.

Racial mosaic

The fact that the different ethnic groups of Trinidad and Tobago have some fairly distinct cultural traits does not pose any real threat to the concept of nationhood. "Cultural pluralism" is a term which has entered the vocabulary, and although race relations are not exemplary,

Trinidadians set great store by their multi-ethnic image. At the heart of the mosaic, however, is a growing area of shared culture which makes it possible for T&Ters to coexist without major explosions of antagonism.

Creole conversation

There is, on the one hand, the shared language. In all the Caribbean territories, Creole (or hybrid) languages have developed out of the meeting of European and African. They are the achievement, in the first instance, of Africans, who in each society developed a lingua franca which allowed communication between themselves and

the Europeans as well as among the Africans themselves. It is believed that Africans transported to Trinidad and Tobago took the vocabulary of their European overlords and poured it into the mould of a standard West African syntax, retaining some words from their own languages. As Africans lost their own languages over the years, what would have started out as a pidgin for basic communication grew into a language capable of the whole range of expression.

The vocabulary of Trinidad and Tobago Creole is mainly English-derived, but it also contains words which can be traced back to languages spoken in West Africa, among them Twi and Yoruba. But Trinidad also spoke French

(and its Creole counterpart) for about a hundred years of its history, so there is in the everyday language a large stock of French vocabulary and French constructions using English words.

Trinidadians will say "It making hot", as the French say "*Il fait chaud*"; and the expression "It have", meaning "There is or are" is from the French "*Il y a*". T&Ters retain many French names for the native vegetation of the country – *balisier* (wild banana), *pomme cythère* (golden apple), *pomme rac* (otaheite apple), *cerise* (a cherry-like fruit). Damaging gossip is *mauvais-langue*; a female crony is a *macom-mère*; a term of endearment is *doo-doo*, from the French *doux* meaning "sweet"; and the spirits who people Trinidadian mythology have French-derived names: *lajablesse, soucouyant, Papa Bois, lagahou*.

Traces of Spanish in the everyday language are relatively sparse, considering Trinidad's proximity to Latin America. Words for some of the dishes introduced by the Spaniards are derived from their language – *pelau, sancoche, pastelle* – and there is the terminology surrounding the activity known as *parang* (Christmas music) which is moving into the general vocabulary. Some fruits are called by their Spanish names – *sapodilla* and *granadilla*.

And today people in Trinidad and Tobago of every racial type use some Hindi words as part of their everyday speech. Non-Indians living in integrated rural communities have used Hindi expressions for a long time, and know a great many more of them than the average Trinidadian, but some Hindi vocabulary has become the common property of all.

Hindi has mainly provided words to do with food, cooking, clothes, religion and family. In the markets the Hindi *beigun* is steadily replacing "melongene" as the word all Trinidadians use for aubergine. Indeed, the vegetables in Trinidad and Tobago are largely grown and marketed by Indians, so their Hindi names are passing into the vocabulary: *bhaji, bodi, aloo*. Some names of commonly-known Indian seasonings are *geera, massala* and *amchar*, and Trinidadians know that *roti* is baked on a *tawa*, and more and more people are becoming familiar with the cooking process known as *chungkay*. The *orhni*, the *sari* and the *dhoti* are articles of clothing familiar to all. Terms from the two major religions practised by Indian Trinidadians are household words – from Hinduism: Phagwa, Diwali, *Ramleela, puja*, *deya*, Lakshmi; from Islam: Ramadan, Eid-ul-Fitr, Hussein (Hosay). And Trinis know that the members of the Indian extended family (including grandparents and in-laws) are called by names such as *agee*, *bhowji* and *dulahin*.

The Amerindians have also made some mark on Trinidad and Tobago language, again in the form of words for food – *cassava*, *balata*, *roocoo*, *tatoo* – but also in the wealth of place names they have left behind. Trinidadians use the language of their Amerindian predecessors daily in every part of the country when they speak of Tunapuna, Mucurapo, Guayaguayare, Naprima, Curepe, Tacarigua, Carapichaima, Maitagual and many others.

Indeed, all the placenames bestowed by the various groups must be considered as part of the common language of the people of Trinidad and Tobago. English place names are not predominant – they are to be found in greatest concentration on the smaller island of Tobago: Scarborough, Roxborough, Plymouth. Spanish and French place names abound in Trinidad, which is itself a Spanish name. Some of the Spanish place names are San Rafael, Las Cuevas, Sangre Grande, Sangre Chiquito, San Fernando, El Soccorro, Los Iros.

Part of the legacy of French language is place names like Blanchisseuse, Sans Souci, Matelot, Champs Fleurs, Lopinot, Petit Bourg and L'Anse Mitan. These are some of the ingredients that go into the common language – basically a Caribbean Creole, but given its distinctive character by the special blending of peoples that took place only in Trinidad and Tobago.

A common accent

Creole differs from Standard English in its syntax – the linguists have found a common syntax across Caribbean Creoles, and have traced it back to the West African family of languages. The intonation of each Caribbean Creole is distinctive, and so is the pronunciation of individual sounds (specifically vowels) from Creole to Creole. So there is an unmistakable Trinidad and Tobago "accent" common to all people, of every ethnic classification, which appears even when they are speaking Standard English. What is significant is that older Indian-Trinidadians sound markedly different from the younger

generation: the full acquisition of the common language was not an instant process, but one which has taken several generations.

A most interesting indicator of the extent to which Trinidad and Tobago Creole (or, strictly speaking, Trinidadian Creole) has been shaped by its polyglot population is the fact that the Standard Creole of the smaller island, Tobago, is not quite the same as that of Trinidad, and has been found to have striking similarities with Jamaican Creole. Tobago is at the southern end of the Caribbean chain of islands and Jamaica is pretty near the top – the two are separated by more than 1,600 km (1,000 miles)

LEFT: echoes of Asia at Icacos.
RIGHT: a smile from Charlotteville, Tobago.

of sea – but they are both different from Trinidad in that on both islands Africans constitute the majority of the population.

There is a certain amount of controversy over Creole: its validity, its propriety, whether it is a language or not, or just "bad English". But meanwhile everybody uses it, including many who think that they are talking English all the while. Since the vocabulary is mainly English, people can be vague about where Creole ends and Standard English begins.

Creole is used actively or passively by all the peoples of Trinidad and Tobago. It is safe to say that the great majority of people do not

dard diet: every self-respecting cook can make chow mein, and delicacies such as wontons have become part of snacking habits.

The American fast-food industry is a feature of the landscape today, and has made all T&Ters (or the children, at any rate) eaters of chicken and chips, hot-dogs and hamburgers.

But what makes the diet of Trinidad and Tobago distinctive among Caribbean diets is the addition of the Indian influence. The preference for rice over what is called "ground provisions" or root crops has already been mentioned. The Indian *roti* is a real rival to American-style fast foods, and standard snack-

fully possess Standard English, and for many of those who do it tends to remain a language written rather than spoken. But Creole is inevitably one of the media through which people send and receive communications. It is the language of calypso, for example, and the calypsonian is one of the most influential and important communicators in the society.

Food is another area where T&Ters share and share alike. There is a long-standing Creole cuisine which incorporates African and Amerindian elements with contributions from each of the European cultures (whose cooking is fairly different one from the other).

Chinese influence has also gone into the stan-

foods are Indian: *channa, kurmah, polorie, bara* (served as "doubles"). Curry is taken very much for granted as one of the everyday options for food preparation, and there is a very high level of tolerance for hot pepper. *(For details on local cuisine, see page 120.)*

The merrymakers

There are three tangible areas in which a shared culture has developed – language, food and music. T&Ters, of course, share a great many other institutions which are not necessarily of their own making but which also constitute common ground – cricket, American soap operas and the latest in Western fashion.

The subjective characteristics which the people share are, of course, harder to pinpoint. Are there any attitudes, values or behaviours which distinguish Trinidadians from other peoples? Is there a "Trini" personality that cuts across race? Here we have to rely, in part, on the image thrown back by other people's perceptions – how Trinidadians are seen, in particular by their sisters and brothers in the rest of the Caribbean.

There is, first of all, the perception of Trinidadians as a people whose lives are a permanent "fête" (this being the word for T&Ters' brand of partying) and, the corollary of this assessment, who are not terribly serious.

One cannot deny the element of hedonism in their make-up – T&Ters are not in the habit of apologising for it. It has its source in the cultures of certain of the peoples who settled here, the Africans and the Latin peoples – Spanish, French and Portuguese – and it has been transmitted in the course of time to the whole population.

Trinidad and Tobago is the Caribbean country in which Carnival is the most highly developed. Indeed, there is nothing in the rest of the Caribbean to which the Trinidad and Tobago version can be compared. One has to go further afield – to Brazil, for example, another African-Latin culture – to find anything like its peer. Carnival in Trinidad and Tobago is a "season", which lasts for two to three months. It follows hard on the heels of the Christmas "season" which consists of a month-long run-up to Christmas Day peppered with *parang*, office Christmas parties, school Christmas parties and Christmas parties held by every self-respecting organisation in Trinidad and Tobago, and then a one-week binge stretching from Christmas Day to New Year's Day.

In addition, Trinidad and Tobago has a full calendar of public holidays which, along with weekends, give scope for serious fêting and liming throughout the year. There are no fewer than 15 public holidays in Trinidad and Tobago, mainly long-standing Christian holy days, to which have been added Hindu and Muslim days of observance, and dates which commemorate

What's in a Name?

There have been calls to change the name of the islands and its people. Proposals include Trinago or Trinbago, which would allow Trinagonian or Trinbagonian. But for now Trinidadian remains the most used umbrella term.

events in the political evolution of the country.

It is perhaps more accurate to say that there are 13 public holidays, because the two days of Carnival on the road have never been declared official holidays. This is a curious carry-over from the colonial era, when the authorities and the upper classes viewed the street festival of the black mob with decided repugnance and would not dream of dignifying it with official recognition. In an 1833 newspaper, Carnival was described as "the shameful violation

of the Sabbath by the lower order of the population, who are accustomed at this time of year to wear masks and create disturbances on a Sunday" (*Port-of-Spain Gazette*, 22 January 1833).

Today Carnival has active government approval and sponsorship, but Carnival Monday and Tuesday are still officially working days for government employees. Suffice it to say that on these two days the state of the nation is such that it is only the essential services which actually keep on working. Hence there are 15 holidays.

Trinidad and Tobago stops work to celebrate New Year's Day, Carnival Monday, Carnival Tuesday, Spiritual Baptist Shouter Liberation Day, Good Friday, Easter Monday, Corpus

---

Left: life's a fête in Port of Spain.
Right: jammin' during Parade of the Bands.

Christi, Eid-ul-Fitr, Labor Day, Emancipation Day, Independence Day, Diwali, Christmas Day and Boxing Day.

Trinis earn the accusation of being unserious partly because they respond to hardship, repression and disaster with a determination to continue enjoying life. When during the 1970 Black Power upheaval the authorities imposed a dusk-to-dawn curfew for a period of time, Trinidadians gathered indoors before the mandatory hour and held all-night "Curfew fêtes". When the oil bubble burst and the economy crashed, bringing widespread retrenchment, unemployment, inflation, shortages,

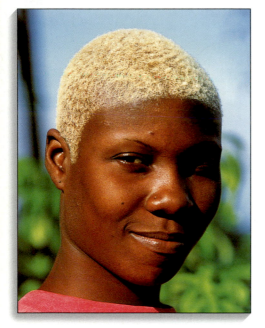

poverty – all the problems associated with a dire economic slump – a new kind of fête began to be advertised on the characteristic large posters seen around the country proclaiming where the upcoming action is: people began to throw "Recession fêtes". Come hell or high water, Trinidad and Tobago will go down fêting. It is one way of coping with existence: who is to say that it is not a valid one?

Another feature of Trini personality which might contribute to a general impression of unseriousness is the decided irreverence of the Trinidadian, his refusal to be too impressed by anything or anybody, including himself. An important part of the tradition of calypso is what

is known as *picong*, or sniping satire against individuals and institutions great or small. In the calypso tent, no personage, no office, no august creation of human beings is sacrosanct. There is no telling where the calypsonian will strike, and he strikes with exquisite humour, on behalf of all – Trinis cheer and egg him on.

This function of the calypsonian has spilled over into the phenomenon of the weekly newspaper. Weeklies proliferate in Trinidad and Tobago today, and are read just as avidly as the traditional dailies. A major part of the attraction of the weeklies is their practice of punching holes in public figures.

Constantly exposed to the wider world through the multiple arms of the media, Trinidad and Tobago has the highest density of newspaper production in the English-speaking Caribbean. For a population of just over 1 million there are three dailies, a fluctuating number of weeklies, and innumerable perodicals put out by political and other organisations. Trinidad has three television channels, plus cable TV, and 21 FM and two AM radio stations. In addition, Trinidadians have always done a fair amount of travelling to other countries. Thus there is in them an almost metropolitan sophistication, with some of the negative attributes of metropolitan behaviour.

The "Trickidadians"

The experience of growing up in a multicultural setting, and the continuous exposure to international currents, make the Trinidadian an eminently flexible person, able to adapt to a variety of situations and continually to absorb new experiences and learn new roles. Trinis sometimes are referred to by other Caribbean people as "Trickidadians", for what may be perceived as chameleon behaviour. Their capacity for adaptation also reveals itself in a great capacity for imitation, and very successful imitation at that. An important aspect of what Carnival is about is the temporary borrowing of another persona – one may be, for two days, a king or queen, a devil, a commando.

It may be said that Trinidadians are entirely too eager to mimic, and that they are a nation of copycats. Amazingly, though, their flair for imitation does not appear rob them of their originality or creativity. ❑

LEFT: a modern Trini.
RIGHT: a young Paramin boy.

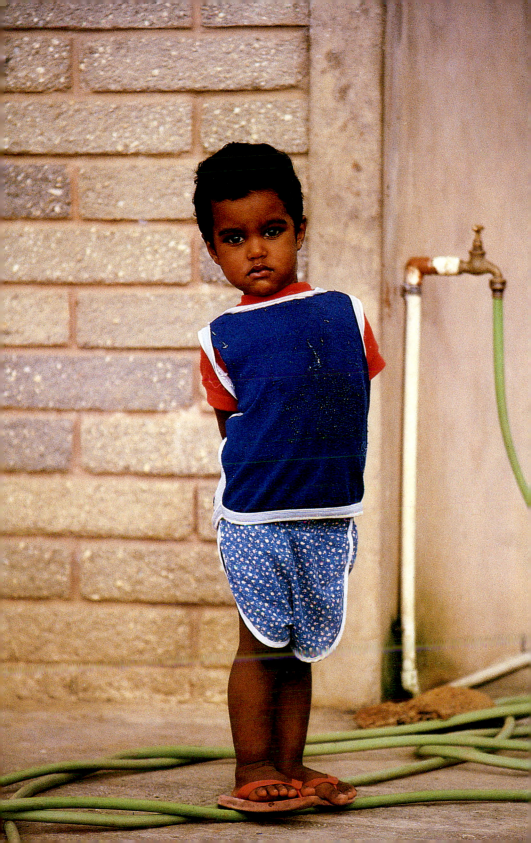

A MATTER OF FAITH

Religion is thriving on the islands: whether it's Christianity, Hinduism, Islam or an underground sect, diversity and freedom to worship are fundamental rights

If there is a defining characteristic of West Indian, and particularly Trinidadian, life, it is the ability to embrace several mutually exclusive realities simultaneously and comfortably. Nowhere is this facility for reconciling apparent contradictions more completely exercised than in the Trinidadians' religious life.

A good place to start is the official version. According to the 1990 census, 68 percent of the population are Christian, 30 percent non-Christian, and the remaining 2 percent unaffiliated. And in truth, as you drive through the country, whether city, village or rural backwater, or look at its newspapers and institutions, religion appears to be thriving.

Faith begins at school

Religious denominations dominate significant sections of the islands' education system. The Roman Catholics, Anglicans and Presbyterians control networks of primary and secondary schools, some run by various orders of priests and monks, such as the Catholic Holy Ghost Fathers and the Dominicans. Various other religious representatives work closely with the management boards of the schools. The Hindus and Muslims control mainly primary schools.

All religious groups use the schools unashamedly as vehicles for religious indoctrination as well as reading, writing and arithmetic – though there is no coercion of students of other faiths to participate in religious instruction.

Outside the schools there is no shortage of places to worship. Port of Spain has a Roman Catholic and an Anglican cathedral, a large Presbyterian church, a Pentecostal Deliverance Centre and a mosque, all within a kilometre (half a mile) of each other. Drive through the outlying districts and you will see temporary bamboo or timber structures, covered with canvas, offering deliverance and baptism; the green-and-white turrets and domes of mosques;

the trident-tipped cupolas of Hindu *mandirs*, with the colourful prayer-flags called *jhandis* arrayed outside.

The roots of religion

The roots of religion run deep in society; it has been a contentious issue from the early days of

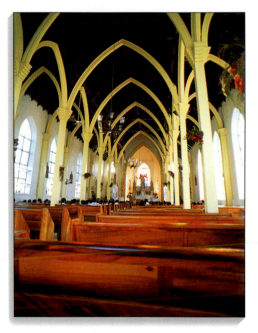

settlement because the African slaves, forcibly brought to the islands, were forbidden to practise their religious rites. The first Europeans, the Spaniards, were Roman Catholic, but it was the French settlers and planters in the late 18th century who established that church. The first church in Trinidad was built in 1781 on what is now Brian Lara Promenade in Port of Spain. The building was subsequently modified into a Gothic structure with stained-glass windows and a pipe organ, and is now known as the Cathedral of the Immaculate Conception *(see page 212)*.

The slaves the French brought with them were instructed in Catholicism, but retained

LEFT: a Diwali Nagar site.
RIGHT: the lofty interior of St Joseph's Roman Catholic Church.

memories of their own religions, which resulted in the development of syncretic Christian-animist forms of worship such as that seen in the Spiritual Baptist sect. The Orisa faith brought by the Yoruba tribesmen was forced underground during slavery and after Emancipation, but resurfaced some time around the last decade of the 20th century and is now being embraced by Trinidadians who are rediscovering their African heritage.

With the advent of British rule in 1797 the Church of England established itself, though at first it was preoccupied with the white planters and Creoles (whites born in the islands). Even

not to have to face religious prohibitions, and so continued their religious observances openly.

In spite of relative freedom of religion East Indians were forced to live in poverty and squalor; this caught the attention of the Reverend John Morton, a Canadian Presbyterian who arrived in 1865, and when he returned home he petitioned his church to send a mission to help them.

A Protestant mission

John Morton offered himself as the first missionary, and in January 1868 arrived to convert the East Indians. He set up schools, hospitals

today its flock numbers only about ten percent of the population, a third of the total of the Roman Catholics. The Cathedral of the Holy Trinity rivals the Catholic Cathedral in both size and grandeur.

Islam existed within the first slave populations, though exactly how many followers there were is not certain since in secret they followed native religions. Of the 143,000 indentured East Indians brought to the West Indies between 1845 and 1914, about 23,000, or 15 percent, were Muslims. However, Islam did not become a significant force in the islands until the 1960s.

The remaining indentured labourers were probably Hindus, who were fortunate enough

and churches, and today about three percent of the population are Presbyterian. The influence of the schools (72 primary and five secondary) and the other institutions has affected society disproportionately.

The first Presbyterian church in the island, the Susamachar Church in San Fernando, was built in 1872. Prior to Morton's arrival there had been a Scottish mission from the Greyfriars Church, but its ministry was small and was concentrated in the north of Trinidad.

Other denominations and sects filtered in from the late 19th century, including Jehovah's Witnesses, the Church of the Nazarene, the Church of God, the Ethiopian Orthodox Church,

Christian Scientists, Calvinists, Methodists, Lutherans and various other strains of mostly Protestant Christianity.

Missionaries continue to come, and on a busy day in modern Port of Spain or San Fernando you may see a few neatly-dressed young men in white shirts and ties walking through the city wearing backpacks and beatific expressions – the typical uniform of Mormon missionaries.

Hinduism

Outside Christianity the *mandirs* offer services according to the elaborate Hindu religious calendar. It is not uncommon to be driving along the coast on any day of the year and come upon hundreds of cars and thousands of people gathered for a religious festival, which must be celebrated on the banks of a river or near the sea.

The Hindus' seeming panoply of deities in fact contains many facets of the indefinable God-head. Each facet – like the aspect concerned with health, or wealth, or knowledge – has its own particular needs, which the *pandits* (priests) prescribe with the aid of astrological texts imported from India.

A fairly common sight in the rural districts is a *ramayan yagya*, the rough equivalent of a thanksgiving service or prayer meeting. At the celebrant's house, guests gather to listen to readings from the *Ramayana* along with commentaries on the text and singing of *bhajans* (hymns). What is remarkable about Hinduism here is that it survived for almost a century without a central organisation, through the efforts of *pandits* who served their particular communities. It is only relatively recently that some measure of centralisation has come to the Hindus, through organisations such as the Sanatan Dharma Maha Sabha (SDMS) and the Hindu Prachar Khendra.

Homegrown religion

Outside conventional religions there are a few homegrown strains. The Bobo Shantis, a group of Rastafarians, practise a fusion of Ethiopian Christianity, Judaism and Garveyism (based on the philosophies of Marcus Garvey, the Jamaican leader of the Back to Africa Movement), while Spiritual (Shouter) Baptists practise a syncretic blend of African spiritism and Catholicism. The Shantis live off the land in communes, to which they welcome visitors. Their theology promises a return to Africa on Black Star Line ships (taken from Garveyism). The Baptists have churches, but can be seen on the street in gowns, heads tied up, and feet bare, witnessing to the public.

Powerful propaganda

The pervasive power of religion is tangible. The *Trinidad Guardian* newspaper runs popular columns written by Ravi Ji, a Hindu activist who devotes significant space to religious matters, and from Pastor Clive Dottin, a Seventh Day Adventist preacher, who provides a straight-talking Christian perspective on affairs both spiritual and temporal.

These examples in the media point to the inordinate influence that religion and its representatives have on everyday island life and society. Not surprisingly, a conservatism bordering on puritanism pervades most conventional religious attitudes.

LEFT: boys ready for Sunday morning church at Mount Pleasant.
RIGHT: a Hindu shrine.

Indeed the Hindu perspective, promoted most often by Satnarayan Maharaj, secretary general of the Hindu organisation, SDMS, and his associates, is overwhelmingly concerned with politics, and is decidedly right-wing, supporting child marriage and ethnic segregation and frowning on intermarriage. The puritanism, though without the political aspirations, is also part of the Islamic conservative line.

The churches' official positions on sexuality and public morality are uniformly rigid and misogynistic and, for the most part, meet with public approval. In 1989 the Catholic archbishop, Anthony Pantin, had the film *The Last*

Secret sects

Only a few of the better-known religions are not fully established in Trinidad and Tobago; they include Judaism. Even so, beneath the level occupied by the formal religious bodies are small cells of quasi-religious movements. Transcendental Meditation, Freemasonry, Rosicrucianism, various schools of Yoga, Eckankar, Mahikari, Kabbalah and Western Magic are all here. Most will not be listed in the telephone book, but they exist and can be accessed through their adherents.

Tell-tale signs indicating that Trinidad is perhaps not a nation of God-fearing religious

Temptation of Christ banned from public screening by simply telephoning the prime minister. A visit by the American televangelist Benny Hinn in 1998 drew crowds of about 100,000 people to Queen's Park Savannah, including the leader of the opposition, members of the judiciary and other prominent citizens.

None of this overlapping between the religious and the secular evokes any serious criticism, or even concern about the independence of public institutions: the style guide of the *Trinidad Guardian* newspaper lists as the first cornerstone of its editorial policy "A belief in the Almighty", and parliamentary sessions begin with prayers.

ITS OWN BRAND OF ISLAM

The Muslims are, as everywhere else in the world, a closed community. Mosques are open for the Friday Juma prayer, to which all are welcome, but the main organisations on the island, including the Trinidad Muslim League (TML), the Tackveeyatul Islamic Association (TIA) and the Anjuman Sunnat-ul-Jamaat Association (ASJA), rarely make public statements.

Muslims usually celebrate Eid-ul-Fitr in the first few months of the year, though it has no fixed date because timing is governed by the position of the moon. The festival indicates the start of the Islamic New Year and the end of Ramadan and its month-long fast.

conservatives, and that alternatives definitely exist, dot the landscape. On the east coast in Salybia, on parts of the Man-zanilla-Mayaro beach and along the banks of the deserted Caura and Maracas Valley rivers there are brightly-coloured flags on bamboo poles, stumps of candle wax on the rocks, and small rings of blackened earth, ash and stumps of burnt wood on the river banks. In other places, too, there may be a few drops of (animal) blood, and on rare occasions you

AFRICAN FOLK BELIEF

Obeah is a form of witchcraft and magic brought to the Caribbean from West Africa by slaves who practised a religion called Obi. It exists in a diluted form in Trinidad and Tobago.

is Yesenia Gonzalez, whose predictions are carried about three or four times a year in the daily newspapers. Most local psychics work by referral; few of them would allow their names to be published. Several claim to have influential clients from the highest political, social and corporate echelons of the land. But this is hardly ever publicly acknowledged, or brought up in polite conversation – at least not with strangers.

The schisms in the modes of life were recog-

might even come across the remains of a dis-membered chicken or a goat's head.

These are evidence of religious customs whose adherents and practitioners do not have columns in the national newspapers. Some, which involve animal sacrifice, are the work of *Obeah* men (magic) or the worshippers of *Kali* (the Hindu goddess of destruction); others are carried out by the Spiritual Baptists.

Here is a hint of what goes on in Trinidad in the ecclesiastical night. Psychics and *obeah* practitioners abound; the best-known psychic

nised by V. S. Naipaul in the *Fragment of an Autobiography* section of his book *Finding the Centre*. Naipaul's father, Seepersad, fell foul of a Kali cult while working as a reporter for the *Trinidad Guardian* in the 1940s. He was threat-ened with death unless he performed a blood sacrifice. Naipaul reports: "In the week that fol-lowed my father existed on three planes. He was the reporter who became his own front-page story: 'Next Sunday I am doomed to die'. He was the reformer who would not yield to 'ju-jus': 'I won't sacrifice a goat'. At the same time he was terrified of what he saw as a mur-der threat, and he was preparing to submit. Each role made nonsense of the other".

LEFT: the choir sings out at Sunday service.
ABOVE: a Kartik ceremony on Manzanilla beach.

A bloody coup

No statistics exist for the number of people who avail themselves of extra-religious spiritual help, but the consequences are there in strange anomalies in social discourse. The second, more recent and bloodier attempted coup in the island's history was staged in 1990 by the Jamaat-al-Muslimeen, an Islamic group led by Imam Yasin Abu Bakr. The coup helps to illustrate Trinidadians' perceptions of religion. Things started with a bang when a Muslim "soldier" drove a truck of explosives into the police headquarters in the capital. A group led by Bakr took over the then sole television station, and another stormed

Parliament where the House of Representatives sat in session. They tortured, shot and injured the unpopular prime minister, and waited for the rest of Trinidad to join the revolution. Most people stayed home and shook their heads.

As the siege wore on, the Muslims negotiated to trade hostages for sandwiches, and eventually agreed to release their hostages in exchange for an amnesty. What started with a bang ended with a whimper and became a national joke. Bakr and his sect were charged with treason but freed on a technicality.

The new Muslims make a great show of adopting the garb and customs of orthodox Islam, including polygamy and titles – such as wazir, imam or sheikh – but even this is considered slightly absurd. It has become fashionable for young Islamic women to wear veils, but with them go painted fingernails, bright red lips and ankle bracelets. The rest of the population look upon this with ironic amusement.

It is important to point out, though, that apart from the Jamaat, whose numbers are insignificant, Islam in Trinidad is generally a model of religious co-existence; other Islamic groups tend to be conservative and monogamous, and fit seamlessly into society. Most Trinidadians share the same attitude to religion: an ostensible deference, balanced by a more realistic, not too serious, posture.

A faith less ordinary

Muslims and Hindus in Trinidad are incontrovertibly Indian, blissfully unaware of the Pakistan-India conflicts. Many people who list their religion as Muslim have not visited a mosque for years, but will assert that they remain strong in their faith. Hinduism forbids meat and alcohol, yet for several days before Hindu *pujas* (religious ceremonies) wives and mothers have to cajole and threaten husbands and children to abstain from both.

The Christian season of Lent opens with two days of pagan Carnival, during which many who will kneel in church on Ash Wednesday to be crossed with ashes will parade through the streets in thongs, waists gyrating, and drink any and every form of alcohol yet discovered.

No one sees any conflict between the practice of religion and living their lives uninhibitedly; in fact, many will insist that they are devout Christians, or Muslims, or Hindus.

The Orisa faithful will take you to a feast where you will witness chanting, the invocation of spirits with drums and offerings of food and drink, and perhaps a spirit possession. The Kali worshippers will invite you to temples for a similar festival, but with the invocations made to effigies of garlanded Indian deities and resulting in the possession of the faithful, who will demonstrate fervour by putting live coals on their tongues or, depending on the temple you go to, walking on fire. Some might even offer to take a brave visitor to their psychic. It's all part of life in Trinidad. ❑

LEFT: heating *tassa* drums ready for Hosay.
RIGHT: Hosay decorations are elaborate at St James.

ARTISTIC INFLUENCE

Trinidadians have a unique view of life, which is illustrated in their literature, on canvas, on stage and on the streets at Carnival time

If Trinidadians' attitude to their literature is casual it is because real life is so much more interesting. Two main ethnic groups and several other smaller groups, with overlaid allegiances to class, wealth and social status, all vying for attention in close quarters make fiction quite tame. The newspapers reveal flamboyant characters with lives as complicated as farce, and dialogue as inventive and colourful as any found in literature. With all these stories and real-life intrigues, fiction writers are hard-pressed to keep up.

That is one way of looking at it. Nobel Prize winner Derek Walcott saw it another way in his poem *The Spoiler's Return*: "as for the Creoles, check their house, and look/you bust your brain before you find a book". Or, to elaborate, Trinidad is the richest of the West Indian islands, with the highest literacy rate, an easy familiarity with metropolitan culture, and a campus of the University of the West Indies (St Augustine), in the middle of the densely-populated East-West Corridor, but it has no national plan for artistic matters, no publishing industry, and only one or two decent bookstores.

Literature survives here through sheer determination; aspiring writers know they must be published abroad, and frequently stay in the countries in which their books are published. This culture of exile means that there is little literary activity in Trinidad: no readings, few serious book reviews in the newspapers, and few writers working in the islands.

Indo- and Afro-Trinidadian scribes

Yet such a strange milieu has produced a surprising number of world-class writers, including arguably the finest writer of the English sentence: Sir Vidiadhar Surajprasad (V. S.) Naipaul, winner of the 2001 Nobel Prize for Literature. Trinidad's literature can be most easily grouped into two broad but not exhaustive categories: Indo-Trinidadian and Afro-Trinidadian. V. S. Naipaul's

work provides an excellent starting point. His early novels from the 1960s are comic delights. *Miguel Street*, *The Mystic Masseur* and *The Suffrage of Elvira* all showed a little-seen side of Indian Trinidad. But his undoubted masterpiece, *A House for Mr Biswas*, is a groundbreaking work that illuminates the recesses of the

circumscribed world of clannish Brahmins and transplanted Indian caste prejudice.

The voice of the Indian in literature emerged late. The indentured labourers were brought to the islands from 1845 onwards, and it was not until well into the 20th century that education became widely available to them. Seepersad Naipaul, V. S's father, is credited with bringing the first accounts of rural Indian life to literature in his *Gurudeva* stories and also through his newspaper journalism in the *Trinidad Guardian* in the 1930s.

The focus on Indo-Trinidadian life continued with Vidiadhar and his brother Shiva, and also through Samuel Selvon, whose novel *A Brighter*

LEFT: V. S. Naipaul, acclaimed around the world.
RIGHT: a performance on a Tobago stage.

Sun explored the gritty life of an agricultural labourer, Tiger, entering the new Trinidad of the 20th century.

The Afro-Trinidadian tradition began late in the 19th century. The first novel written by a black Trinidadian was *Emmanuel Appadoca* by Maxwell Phillips, who would convene the first Pan-African conference. The 1930s saw C.L.R. James (who would become famous as a Marxist-Leninist thinker and theorist) and Alfred Mendes examining the life of the urban working-class African and his interactions with the upper classes in novels such as James's *Minty Alley* and Mendes's *Pitch Lake*.

Literary journals like *Trinidad* and *The Beacon* sprang up, and names including Albert Gomes and Ralph de Boissière would establish themselves as novelists and writers of note. An excellent anthology of poetry from this period, *Best Poems of Trinidad* (1943), compiled by A. M. Clarke, including work by several unknown and a few notable writers, was reissued in Trinidad in 1999.

There is another smaller but no less important tradition in Trinidadian (and West Indian) writing: the work of white Trinidadians. Unlike the Africans and Indians, the whites had access to the newspapers and used them to try out their work, which enabled them to start earlier.

Writers in exile...

This was the beginning, but Trinidadian literature and writers would need to travel a long way – usually to England – before it came of age. The exile proved to be a boon, giving writers sufficient distance detachedly to consider and record the uniqueness of West Indianness.

Two writers who made names for themselves from the first migration in the 1950s were Selvon and V. S. Naipaul. They would meet in London other Caribbean exiles: George Lamming, Roger Mais, John Hearne and Jan Carew, producers of the most significant West Indian literature for the next quarter-century. Selvon's *Lonely Londoners* is the most important novel of the period; it introduced the Trinidadian vernacular into the auctorial consciousness – and not just in dialogue – basing reality in a West Indian world-view rather than in the omniscient voice speaking standard English. This mode has been developed since by writers like Ismith Khan and Earl Lovelace.

...and those who stayed put

Lovelace is worth special mention as he was one of the few writers to resist exile. His subjects are the working class and the movement of the people of Trinidad and Tobago through their ethnic and political trials. He has produced three of the most significant Trinidadian novels: *The Dragon Can't Dance* (1979), *The Wine of Astonishment* (1984) and *Salt* (1996). The latter story of a man making his way through the corrupt and ethnically-divided island, won the Commonwealth Writers' Prize for best novel of 1996–7.

His books, particularly *The Dragon Can't Dance*, are among the few that have represented in an artistically satisfying way the ethnic and social complexities of the islands; they gave legitimacy to the notion of Trinidad Carnival as both a form of art and social resistance.

Lovelace, however, and other notable writers such as Michael Anthony and Merle Hodge, remain among the few who refused exile. Still today most promising Trinidadian writers pursue their careers abroad, even if they remain fascinated by their cultural uniqueness.

A litany of literary talent

The Miami-based Robert Antoni's novel *Divina Trace* won the Commonwealth Writers Prize (Caribbean) in 1992–3; this was an ambitious attempt to survey the history of Trinidad through several characters, using magic, mythology and history as his devices.

Kelvin Christopher James, who lives across the pond in the US, has published two books – *Jumping Ship*, a collection of stories, and a novel, *Secrets* – in the past five years. The stories contrast lives in the US and the Caribbean, and the novel returns to a rural Trinidadian setting.

Shani Mootoo, of Irish descent with Trinidadian parentage, writes in her *Cereus Blooms at Midnight* about the sexual dimension of rural Indo-Trinidad life, specifically homosexuality, a subject broached only once before in local literature – by the late Harold Sonny Ladoo in his wonderful novel *Yesterdays*.

Sexual taboo has emerged in the work of another exile, Lawrence Scott, a white Trinidadian who lives and works in London. His two early books, *Witchbroom* and *Ballad for a New World*, address the familiar problems of genealogy: tracing the (fictional) history of a white family in Trinidad. His *Aelred's Sin*, which won the Commonwealth Writers' Prize (Caribbean) in 1999, moved on to more existential concerns, taking homosexuality as a main theme.

Other Trinidadian writers, like Rabindranath Maharaj, whose novel *Homer in Flight* was well received, Ramabai Espinet, Neil Bissondath, Dionne Brand and Claire Harris have migrated to Canada, but write about the ethnic coexistence and quiet miscegenation within the country which defies every other experiment of ethnic coexistence.

Spotlight on social realism

Most of the significant literary pool of talent is abroad, but the local landscape is not completely bereft. Kevin Baldeosingh, a journalist, has published two novels, *The Autobiography of Paras P* and *Virgin's Triangle*: a satire and a romance novel that is somewhat cleverer than the average in that genre. Isaiah Boodhoo, a visual artist, has published one novel,

---

20TH-CENTURY LEGACY

Born in Port of Spain at the beginning of the 20th century, C.L.R. James (1901–89) was a teacher, groundbreaking writer, historian, literary critic and a political activist. He was also a passionate authority on cricket.

Between Two Seasons. V. Ramsamooj Gosine and Sharlow are local writers who have between them published several books, but they are not widely known or appreciated in Trinidad.

The subject matter – social realism mainly – implies that most Trinidadian writers are preoccupied with self-discovery and exploration. The cultural territory is still being mapped, as it were, so there is no opportunity for counter-culture.

Cultural matters are usually the province of essayists, in cultural criticism or theory, but there are few essayists working now, and most of them are academics at UWI St Augustine. Of the small number, one stands out above his peers: Wayne Brown. Brown's *Child of the Sea* (1990) presents slices of contemporary Trinidadian life with a sophistication and an intelligence that few writers from any country can match.

The *Express* newspapers have excellent essayists/columnists, including Lloyd Best and Denis Solomon, both university lecturers, and Keith Smith, whose daily column is a jewel of local journalism.

Poetic licence

Wayne Brown is also one of the few significant Trinidadian poets; the other was Eric Roach, who died in the 1970s. Brown's collection *On the Coast* won the Commonwealth Poetry prize in 1972, and a second volume, *Voyages*, appeared in 1989. There have been few other poets or volumes of such high quality.

Derek Walcott lived in Trinidad for about 20 years from the late 1950s to the late 1970s, and wrote several of his major poetic works here, but strictly speaking the winner of the Nobel Prize for Literature (1992) is St Lucian.

In the 1970s Anson Gonzales launched the journal *New Voices* to promote poetry; it is only half-alive today. Cecil Gray has published about three collections. There are also a few scattered expatriate poets – John Lyons, Faustin Charles and Abdul Malik – but poetry has never really developed in the way that prose fiction has. The reason could be that the poetic urge was subsumed by calypso, a modern-day troubadour tradition.

> **LEGENDS IN PRINT**
>
> Island folk tales come to life in books such as *A Wave in Her Pocket: Stories from Trinidad* by Lynn Joseph and Donna Perrone and *The Mermaid's Twin Sister: More Stories from Trinidad* by Lynn Joseph and Brian Pinkney.

Theatrics on a grand scale

Calypso and Carnival are artistic epicures, deriving more from the theatrical impulse than the fictive. Walcott's poem also has something to say about the theatre: "and as for local art, so it does go/the audience have more talent than the show".

Carnival, which costumes thousands of people and makes the streets of Port of Spain a stage for two days, is a tough act to follow. It is a form of theatre on a huge scale whose major artist, Peter Minshall, has achieved worldwide renown. Then there is the *Ramleela*, a ritual (theatrical) reenactment of the *Ramayana* story that is performed in Hindu villages every year before the festival of Diwali.

Witnessing such spectacles in everyday life makes any other form of theatre pale by comparison. That is perhaps the reason why the only plays that attract a crowd in the commercial theatre are salacious bedroom farces. Three theatre

---

THE CHARACTERS OF TRINIDADIAN FOLKLORE

Papa Bois is the guardian of the forest and all its creatures, also known as the Old Man of the High Woods, Maitre Bois, Hairy Man and Daddy Bouchon. He assumes different guises: an extremely strong, hairy old man with leaves growing from his beard and cloven hooves (similar to Pan, the Greek god of the countryside and fertility); a deer or an old man in ragged clothes.

As protector of animals, he will sound a cowhorn to warn of approaching hunters. He appears as a deer to hunters, leading them astray before assuming his own form to issue a warning or impose a fine on them (married to his hideous consort Mama Glo). Extreme politeness and caution should be exercised in any encounter with Papa Bois.

Mama Glo (or **Dlo**) is the Mother of the Water who assumes different shapes: sometimes a beautiful young mermaid; at others a hideous old woman with the lower half of an anaconda. Bountiful but deadly she is believed to be Papa Bois' lover. Those who have offended the forest (burning trees, killing animals, polluting rivers) may be punished by enforced marriage to her hideous incarnation. To escape from Mama Glo, a man must take off his left shoe, turn it upside down, and walk all the way home, backwards.

companies are able to survive in the market: the Trinidad Theatre Workshop (TTW), Raymond Choo Kong Productions and Ragoo Productions.

Choo Kong and Ragoo are the most successful producers in the country, presenting an average five plays a year between them, but they cannot maintain full-time theatrical companies. The Baggasse Company dabbles in serious drama occasionally, and the Strolling Players, which is about as old as the TTW, also produces local plays, but usually bathetic melodramas.

The third full-time company, the Trinidad Theatre Workshop, is also the oldest. The TTW maintains a full time secretariat and produces

pany. Previously local theatre had consisted of British classics put on by small groups of white Trinidadians or colonial expatriates.

The TTW and Walcott created several classics of Trinidadian (and West Indian) theatre: *Dream on Monkey Mountain, the Joker of Seville* and *Ti Jean and His Brothers*. The TTW toured extensively in the Caribbean, North America and Europe, winning a New York Obie award in 1971 for *Dream*.

From the TTW came a cadre of accomplished actors and directors that continued working after Walcott's departure in the late 1970s. The Tent Theatre was formed in the early 1980s by Helen

serious drama. It has links, thanks to its founder, Derek Walcott, with foreign institutions such as the influential Ford Foundation and Boston University.

The TTW's inception in 1958 marked the beginning of Trinidad and the West Indies' professional theatre. Walcott's intention was to create a company on a par with any playing in the West End in London or on Broadway in New York, or any national performing com-

LEFT: a Tobago folk dancer at Arnos Vale Plantation.
ABOVE: the writer Derek Walcott established the Trinidad Theatre Workshop, the first professional theatre company.

Camps, a TTW alumna, and in its few years of life was responsible for training most of the actors working in the commercial theatre today.

Walcott's drama followed the classical line of Shakespeare and Marlowe, with a little help from Bertholt Brecht, but a separate theatrical stream emanated from a young Trinidadian in the 1980s. Rawle Gibbons, a director and talented playwright, envisioned another kind of theatre: he was more concerned with an indigenous theatre as sophisticated as, say, Wole Soyinka's.

Gibbons's *Sing de Chorus* trilogy marked an exciting turn in Trinidadian theatre: it used calypso lyrics to articulate a vision for the development of Trinidadian society as recorded and shaped by the wholly Trinidadian music.

Gibbons today heads the Creative Arts Centre of the University of the West Indies (St Augustine), which offers a degree in theatre arts and provides training for actors, technicians, playwrights and directors. The Centre produces about two plays per year in St Augustine. A few other companies produce sporadically, but there is nothing like a traditional theatre season.

A promising playwright is Davlin Thomas,

> **KEEPING PATOIS ALIVE**
>
> Paul Keens-Douglas is an award-winning performance artist, poet and writer, founder of the annual Tim Tim Storytelling Show and the Carnival Talk Tent.

but there are three semi-professional spaces: the Little Carib Theatre, the Central Bank Auditorium in Port of Spain and the Naparima Bowl in San Fernando. The Bank is often unavailable, and San Fernando has other uses for the Bowl.

This means that there is in fact only one suitable theatrical venue in the island that is available for the 10 to 15 plays that are staged every year by the commercial companies in Port of Spain. Most productions improvise as best they can for space. Queen's

who directs his own work about once a year. Trinidad's lone self-exiled playwright of note is Mustapha Mathura, who works in London.

Performances on and off stage

There is also a strong oral tradition in Trinidad, which is related to Carnival and embraces quasi-theatrical performances of singing, comic skits and storytelling. This genre and the Carnival absorb a good deal of the funding and support that would otherwise be directed to the other arts by the public, corporate community and government.

There is still no fully-equipped theatrical space in the country for Carnival or formal drama,

Hall, a huge concert hall, is unsuitable for theatre, but is sometimes commandeered into service for shows.

The formal theatre might not be at the centre of the performing arts in Trinidad, but there is never a shortage of shows or performances, and, with few exceptions, Trinidadians are, in general, rarely more at home than when performing, on or off stage.

The visual arts

In an environment where artistic expression is largely focused on Carnival, the visual arts in Trinidad and Tobago have been viewed either as the preserve of a small élite (in terms of both producers and collectors) or merely as expressions of folk art. The lack of a specialist art school underlines the low profile accorded to them, and, apart from some courses at the John S. Donaldson Technical Institute and the UWI Centre for the Creative Arts, aspiring artists must travel to Martinique, Jamaica, Cuba or the metropolitan countries of North America and Europe to study.

However, these insular constraints do not detract from the fact that Trinidad has produced one of the Caribbean's first internationally acclaimed artists in Jean Michel Cazabon, and that some young contemporary artists are highly regarded abroad in cutting-edge postcolonial art circles.

Given its ethnic and cultural diversity (Amerindian, European, African, Indian, Chinese, Middle Eastern) Trinidad and Tobago has a bewildering wealth of artistic traditions to draw on. Sadly, not much remains of the rich Amerindian artistic legacy in either island. Little systematic archaeological research has been undertaken, and in Trinidad the only known Amerindian petroglyphs (rock drawings) are the Caurita drawings of the Amerindians, high on a ridge in the Maracas Valley.

A painting tradition

The first documented artist is Jean Michel Cazabon (1813–88), son of rich, free, coloured Martiniquan planters who settled in the North Naparimas area of south Trinidad in the 1780s. Cazabon's accomplished work (mostly romantic landscapes and some portraits) is important not only for the record of his era but also because he was one of the first Creole or Caribbean-born artists in the region.

Prior to Cazabon the only other artists documenting the landscapes, peoples and customs of the Caribbean were itinerant European painters such as the Italian Agostino Brunias (known for his paintings of the slaves and free coloureds of Dominica and, especially, the Black Caribs of St Vincent). In Trinidad Cazabon was preceded by the English topographical artists W. S. Andrews and Richard Bridgens.

Cazabon was educated in England and then in France, where he studied art under Paul Delaroche. His technique was shaped by the

French landscape schools – Realist and Romantic – the latter dominated by the great landscape artist Camille Corot. Cazabon's preference for working in watercolour, a medium ideally suited to immediate and personal expression, was probably influenced by the Romantic landscape philosophy of the time.

Returning to Trinidad in 1852, Cazabon demonstrated his European training and exercised his skills to great effect in the bright tropical light. His tightly composed luminous watercolour landscapes are still admired today.

The only other artist to have left work from the late 19th and early 20th centuries is

Theodora Walter (1869–1959), who in 1907 migrated to England where, influenced by the Theosophists, she became an early Expressionist painter. Botanical paintings and landscapes are all that survive from her time in Trinidad.

The first signs of the growing current of nationalism affecting the arts was the 1929 foundation of the Society of Independents, a small group of young upper-class artists led by the illustrator Amy Leon Pang and painter Hugh Stollmeyer. Stollmeyer's work reflects international and Caribbean influences, including Gauguin, the Symbolists and Art Nouveau along with the iconography of Shango and other Afro-Caribbean religions.

LEFT: on stage at Carifesta arts festival.
RIGHT: *Madman's Memory,* a charcoal drawing by Jackie Hinkson.

The Independents probably made more impact with their bohemian lifestyle than with their work, but their paintings of nudes were considered equally outrageous by the conservative colonial bourgeoisie. Although the group was disbanded in 1938 it inspired younger artists like the multi-talented Boscoe Holder who, visiting Martinique in the 1940s, was captivated by the elegance of the women in their traditional dress.

Holder's striking exotic studies of black women, both with and without their clothes, became his trademark. Bursting with talent, he left Trinidad for a glittering career as a dancer and musician first in New York and then in Lon-

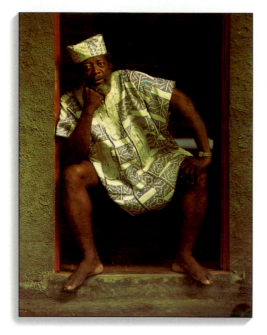

don before returning home in 1962 to assume his role as a popular society painter. His later bold landscapes are considered among his best work.

The 1940s was a period of growing confidence among the islands' intelligentsia and artists, expressed in the formal work of M. P. Alladin, Boscoe Holder, Sybil Atteck and Stollmeyer, the native painting of Leo Basso and the folklore illustrations of Alfred Codallo and Marcelio Hovell.

The Trinidad Art Society founded in 1943 was a conscious attempt to develop a national art movement. Sybil Atteck (1911–75), one of the founding members, trained under the German Expressionist Max Beckman but was also strongly influenced by her study of Inca pottery in Peru. Atteck adventurously combined Abstraction and Stylisation with Trinidadian landscapes and festivals, influencing a whole school of young artists including Carlisle Chang, Nina Lamming and Leo Glasgow throughout the 1950s.

Chang studied painting and ceramics in England and Italy, where he discovered Abstract Expressionism which on his return he developed into an individual style drawing on East Indian and Chinese influences. Chang in turn influenced Willie Chen, Audley Sue Wing and Leo Glasgow.

Art after Independence

With independence in 1962 came unprecedented government support for the arts, which has not been repeated since. Collections were established at the Central Bank and the Hilton Hotel (no longer accessible to the public), and both Atteck and Chang were commissioned to design murals for prominent buildings, including the Hilton, City Hall and the airport.

Several graduates of England's Brighton College of Art returned in the mid-1960s to make their mark on the local art scene. Isaiah James Boodoo initially produced abstracts but after visiting America in 1968 opted for Abstract Expressionist social and political commentary, which captured the mood of Trinidad's 1970 Black Power disturbances and the ensuing State of Emergency. In his later work, still characterised by vibrant Expressionist colour, Boodoo has explored East Indian themes.

Sonnylal Rambissoon, inspired by Cazabon, has produced etchings and paintings of the East Indian heartland, the canefields of Central Trinidad. Ralph Baney and his wife Vera, who worked in sculpture and clay, pioneered the use of local materials to produce glazes.

Foremost among Trinidad's monumental sculptors is Pat Chu Foon (b. 1931), who began as an apprentice to a toymaker and received further training from two legendary craftsmen – copperworker Ken Morris and woodcarver Rafael Samuel. After studying sculpture in Mexico, where Henry Moore's style with its pre-Columbian emphasis predominated, Chu Foon created popular monuments and sculptures such as the statue of Gandhi in San Fernando and "Mother and Child" at Mount Hope Hospital.

The Black Power movement influenced the

Trinidad of the early 1970s and stimulated a rediscovery of African heritage at all levels of socety which found artistic expression in the life work of painter and poet Leroy Clarke (b. 1938). In his continuing series *The Poet* (whose intense imagery recalls the great Cuban Wilfredo Lam) and in a continuing dialectic which owes much to Wilson Harris, Clarke has sought to reaffirm African heritage as a dynamic in self-awareness.

The 1970s also saw a revitalised interest in landscape painting (in the work of water-colourists Noel Vaucrosson, Jackie Hinkson and Sundiata) as well as the emergence of a fine-art tradition in Carnival design, introduced by Peter Minshall (b. 1941). With his Hummingbird design of 1974, Minshall established himself as a kinetic designer, interested in "the living sculpture" of a costume animated by a dancing human rather than just static outfits. Minshall has earned international recognition and commissions to design the opening ceremonies for the Barcelona Olympics and the World Cup football competition.

A new generation of artists

The mid-1980s slump in world oil prices and the ensuing recession in Trinidad and Tobago stimulated new artistic directions and even techniques. Ken Crichlow (b. 1951) stunned the London *Guardian*'s art critic with his "gorgeous abstractions" at the Commonwealth Institute's 1986 exhibition of Caribbean Art. Francisco Cabral (b. 1949) also announced his presence at the show with his series of chair sculptures: assemblages of found and created objects with their trenchant comments on local and global issues. Cabral may have alienated the local audience but he was embraced by the international art scene.

The late 1980s and the 1990s saw the development of a new school of artists led by multimedia artists such as Chris Cozier (b. 1959), Steve Ouditt (b. 1961) and painter Eddie Bowen (b. 1963). Although not a formal group, these three have distanced themselves from the older generation of artists and the limitations of producing safe cultural products for the local gallery circuit. Although their styles differ, all three mix personal statement with provocative satirical analysis of local society, history and culture. Their work is often better appreciated and received in international rather than local circles.

There are several women prominent among the new generation of artists: sculptress Anna Serrao, who works with indigenous images and materials; the figurative painter Irenee Shaw; and Wendy

Nanan, who has explored the ironies and tensions of Trinidad's multi-cultural society. Among the men, Shastri Maharaj's figurative paintings focus on the Indian diaspora, while Rubadiri Victor's celebrate Trinidad and Tobago and regional heroes and elders. The younger multi-media artists Mario Lewis and Dean Arlen are still establishing themselves. Although he has made forays into conceptual art, Robert Yao Ramesar is best known as one of the region's most innovative film makers. With his distinctive camerawork and use of natural light, Yao's documentation of cultural history, including treatments of some of Derek Walcott's poetry, has won international acclaim.

LEFT: Leroy Clarke's work reaffirms African heritage.
RIGHT: the spectacular Carnival costume designed by Peter Minshall is a work of art.

The origins of dance

Dance figures nearly as promininently in Trinidadian and Tobagonian lifestyle as music and, judging from the toddlers who perform in Kiddies' Carnival bands, dancing is learnt in the womb. During Carnival season the whole country to dance, either the sensuous gyrating of hips and pelvis known as "wining" – the national party dance – the ecstatic abandon of the breakaway or the slower chip, a sliding shuffle ideally suited for following a Carnival band through the streets.

Within Carnival there are the specialised dances of traditional characters such as the

King Sailor with his bent-knee sway, pivoting on his walking stick, the graceful flying Bat, the loping Moko Jumbie or the Jab Molassie with menacing pelvic thrusts.

Beyond Carnival there is an enormous range of folk, formal, ritual and popular dance, the legacy of diverse cultures. African, Creole and East Indian forms predominate, but Spanish dances from Venezuela (*joropo*, *castillian* and *paseo*) feature at *parang* festivals, and the Dragon Dance is performed by the Chinese community in Port of Spain for its New Year on Double Ten Day, 10 October.

The limbo, which is possibly the most

famous dance, had humble rural origins before being taken to town and transformed into a spectacular cabaret number in the 1940s, assuming the status of national dance, and then reaching an international audience after exposure in the 1957 Hollywood movie *Fire Down Below* with Robert Mitchum and Rita Hayworth.

Like the *bongo*, funeral dance with African origins, the limbo was originally performed at wakes both as an entertainment for the mourners (and to help keep them awake all night) and as a mark of respect for the departed soul. On the ninth night of a wake, known as Victory or Bongo Night, two family members would sit with a board from the coffin on their knees.

Mourners passed under the board which was gradually raised higher, simulating the passage of the deceased's soul from the lower region of Limbo to Heaven.

When the limbo came to town the coffin board was replaced with a stick, or even a human body, which was lowered rather than raised to change the dance into a spectacular acrobatic feat. Dancers like the great "Stretch" Cox and Julia Edwards popularised the new limbo to the extent that it became synonymous with Trinidad and is a regular feature of tourist revues throughout the Caribbean and beyond. Contemporary dancers such as the current limbo

sticks in a *gayelle* or circle of spectators, were known to have resulted in the deaths of some combatatants from crushed skulls. Nowadays competitions (staged during Carnival season) will stop at the first sign of a bleeding head.

Other African dance retentions have survived in the rituals of African-derived religions, like Yoruban Shango worship or the Rada rites of Dahomey. Immigrants from Grenada and particularly its satellite island of Carriacou, where the Big Drum tradition of African national dances survives, introduced many of these dances to Trinidad. These include the *ibo*, *pique*, *manding*, *coromanti*, *congo*, *juba*, *hallicord* and *banda*.

champion Nidia Byron keep the form alive, although the world record of a 2-metre (6-ft 6in) bar established over 20 years ago remains.

Another ritualistic dance with African origins is the competitive Kalenda, or stick dance, performed to the accompaniment of French *patois* or English songs and intense drumming as a prelude to the stick fight. These competitions, fought with 1.2-metre (4-ft) -long poui

Tobago, with its distinctly Afro-Creole heritage, retains a strong element of ancestor worship in its reel dance. Mainly performed by the descendants of Congo nationals, to the accompaniment of shallow tambourine drums, fiddle and iron triangle, the reel would traditionally be danced to enlist the ancestors' aid at functions like weddings and wakes, or during times of illness or community crisis.

Like the Tobago jig (an Africanised version of the 18th-century French and English dance) and Tobago's version of the *bele* or belle air, the reel is an example of slaves adapting European forms and instruments to their own purposes of cultural survival and resistance.

FAR LEFT: the limbo has African religious origins.
LEFT: dancers at the Carifesta Arts Festival.
ABOVE LEFT: Phagwa boy-drummer.
ABOVE RIGHT: a Tobagonian drummer at Arnos Vale Plantation.

Other European dances which were Creolised were the quadrille, minuet, mazurka, lancers, mazurka and schoteische. In Trinidad, French planters and their slaves introduced Creole dances like the *biguine*, *bele*, *gran bele*, *grenade* and *caribbine*.

The mother of Caribbean dance

Virtually all these dances might well have disappeared had it not been for the pioneering efforts of Beryl McBurnie, the "Mother of Caribbean Dance". From the 1930s onwards, right up to her death in 2000, McBurnie championed the cause of Trinidad and Tobago folk

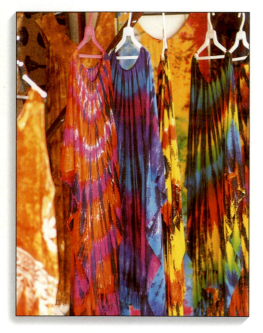

dance and then Caribbean folk dance, starting in an era when indigenous forms from calypso to steelpan were marginalised or even suppressed by the colonial authorities and generally despised by the élite and the bourgeoisie.

McBurnie researched folk forms both at home in Trinidad and throughout South America from Surinam to Cuba and Haiti, choreographing them into stunning stage performances which were instrumental in giving Caribbean folk culture significant international exposure. After training with Martha Graham in New York, where she also introduced Katherine Dunham to West Indian dance, McBurnie returned to set up the prestigious

Little Carib Theatre in Trinidad the first home of Caribbean dance, in 1948.

Although she never succeeded in establishing a national dance company at home, McBurnie was the inspiration behind the Jamaican national dance company. It was her influence that led to the creation of the islands' Best Village Dance Competition in the 1960s, which has been instrumental in keeping folk dance alive. Leading Best Village groups like Malick Folk Performers, North West Laventille and Cocorite Ujaama regularly perform abroad. McBurnie's influence continues in the work of her former students like Heather Gordon-Henderson, Carol La Chapelle and Noble Douglas. In the sphere of modern dance, Astor Johnson, whose company nurtured dancers who have moved on to international companies, was a seminal figure in the 1970s and 1980s.

The East Indian heritage, with its popular, ritual, classical and folk forms, adds another vibrant and colourful dimension to dance in Trinidad. In the early 20th century, dance dramas like the *Rahas Mandal*, *Harischandra* and *Indar Sabha* were extremely popular. The *Ramleela* has survived to become a national institution.

Some of the ritual dances of the Muslim Hosay festival, like the Moon dance, the Gatka and Jharoo stick dances and the broom dance, have also survived, and the Fire Pass of Kali worship, where devotees walk over burning coals is still practised in at least one rural temple.

Exposure to visting Indian classical dancers led to several local schools of classical dance being established. The Indian husband and wife team Pratap and Priya Pawar introduced the classical Kathak, Bharata Natyam and Odissi forms in the 1960s, and local dancer Sat Balkarasingh who studied in India, returned home to found the Nitanjali Dance Theatre, which is flourishing today along with the Sangeet Mahvidyala school.

Popular forms like chutney and "filmi" (based on the hybrid dances of Bollywood movies) have entered the mainstream of Trinidad's culture, frequently appearing at cultural shows and on the ever popular TV talent show *Masatana Bahar*, and popular groups like Shiv Shakti and Desh Premi are in great demand at both the local and the national level. ❏

LEFT: colourful and collectable fashion.
RIGHT: a Tobagonian folk dancer.

ROTI ON THE RUN

The spicy fusion cuisine of the islands reveals a wonderful blend
of flavours from Africa, Europe, the Middle East, China and India

Like Trinidad and Tobago's rhythmic soca music, island food and drink are a sensual blend of many continents and countries. A mouth-watering mélange of African, East Indian, Amerindian, Chinese, Middle Eastern and European flavours combines in recipes that have survived conquest, slavery and indenture-

drop by, and any social event, like playing All Fours – a card game – or watching a video, is a respectable cause for a meal. At parties a full dinner is more the rule than hors d'oeuvres. The style of food you find in private homes depends to a large degree on the ethnic background of your hosts, but a certain blurring of culinary

ship, offering a staggering variety of the most exotic foods in the Caribbean.

The *joie de vivre* that the people of these two islands demand as a birthright is as concentrated in their culinary culture as it is in their Carnival. Good eating is an important part of what Trinidadians and Tobagonians enjoy about living in a part of the world where food is plentiful and fresh, though sometimes expensive. And islanders like to cook and love to eat, so they do both in abundance. The streets of Port of Spain are crowded with food vendors, bars, snack shops and open markets, and every little hamlet has at least a roti stand. T&Ters are quick to have a "cookup" the minute friends

borders has occurred so that Trinidadian cuisine might be said to be made up of unique variations on other people's themes.

Local specialities

The names of local specialities reflect their mixed and exotic sources, encouraging even the jaded to experiment. Who wouldn't be curious about *callaloo, coocoo, pelau, roti, buljol, accra* and "oil down" or *sans coche,* an import from the smaller islands of the Caribbean? And there are unfamiliar and delicious fruit punches – *soursop, shaddock, barbadine* – and rum drinks to cool off the heat.

Creole food – which with Indian, the most

prevalent, is an amalgam of dishes with an African past that incorporates contributions from French settlers who brought slaves here two centuries ago. *Pelau, callaloo* and *coocoo* are all Creole dishes whose likenesses can be found on other Caribbean islands. The country's former Spanish colonists have also left their enduring influence: *pastelles* and *arepas*, spiced corn patties filled with meat or chicken, for example, although Spanish ones taste less of olive oil than do their Latin American counterparts.

A TANGY MIX

Chutney, an Indian-inspired spicy fruit pickle, is a popular accompaniment at meal times. The term is also used to describe Indian-style "chutney" soca music.

Trinidad, for instance, is quickly stir-fried, without the cornstarch that gives it the gooey consistency familiar to so many Westerners.

Like some Indian dishes, many Chinese foods have been "Creolised". Their fried rice borrows spices and flavour from *pelau*, a rice and peas dish, and many Chinese meat and poultry dishes look suspiciously as if they have been "browned down", the Creole process of cooking in caramelised sugar.

The Syrians, Lebanese and Portuguese have

Curries, roti and other exotically spiced dishes brought here by indentured East Indian labourers in the 19th century add to the already singular potpourri. Indian foods, like those of other cultures commingling in Trinidad and Tobago, sometimes take on completly new forms, so that many no longer bear any resemblance to their originals.

The Chinese, who also came under indentureship, brought a crisper, fresher version of their cuisine than that usually found in the Chinatowns of the world. *Chow mein* in

also contributed to the Trinidad and Tobago menu, though to a lesser degree, since their arrival here is more recent. Middle Easterners spread the use of vermicelli and influenced the popular potato salad, augmenting it with beets, carrots and peas.

Whatever the ethnic origins of the range of Trinidad and Tobago cuisine, the common culinary denominator is seasoning and lots of it, which often makes visitors remark on the spiciness of the food; nobody from chef to home cook would dream of cooking without seasoning. Besides salt and black pepper the staples of Trinibagonian seasoning include "cives" (not chives but a local variant of spring onions),

LEFT: delights from the sea: fry fish, prawns and crab.
ABOVE: pumpkin *pelau*.

Spanish thyme, rosemary, *chadon beni* (which East Indians call *bandinya*) and another herb known locally as celery (which bears little resemblance to the European variety). A familiar sight in any market is small bunches of fresh seasoning, which are also sold by street vendors. Garlic and onion can either be added to the seasoning or used separately, by East Indians, to "chonkay" a dish (lightly fry it in oil) before adding the main ingredients. Sometimes dishes are left to marinate overnight.

Rafters on Warner Street in Port of Spain is a small restaurant with a typically Trinidadian atmosphere and menu. It used to be an old rum

Aspara on Queen's Park East and Rasam in Grand Bazaar offer classical Indian cuisine, and Solimar next to the Normandie Hotel has an international menu which changes regularly. Those who hanker for afternoon tea will find a relaxing and very reasonably priced Creole version, complete with panoramic views over the Caroni plains, at the Pax Guesthouse, attached to Mount St Benedict Abbey in the Northern Range.

Roti on the run

One of the most delicious and popular foods to be found anywhere and everywhere is *roti*. A complete meal, *roti* consists of a delicate Indian

shop, and the exterior and interior have been left virtually unchanged. For Creole cuisine there is Veni Mange on Ariapita Avenue, Battimamzelle on Coblentz Avenue, Cascade and D Bocas on Chacon Street or The Breakfast Shed on Wrightson Road.

The best place for Indian food is Curry Marsala in Tragarete Road. For good Chinese (and Polynesian) food and a romantic view, Tiki Village is situated on the roof at the Kapok Hotel. New Shay Shay Tien on Cipriani Boulevard, Singho in Long Circular Mall and The Swan on Maraval Road also offer authentic Chinese cuisine. Joseph's, Rookery Nook, Maraval and Roxan's on Ariapita Avenue specialise in Arab cuisine,

dough wrap filled with curried beef, chicken, goat, shrimp or vegetables. Curried potatoes and chick peas are added, and the wrap is folded over everything to create a portable crêpe. The dough, called *dhalpourri*, is made of two flat thin layers seasoned with ground split peas in between. In many shops the *dhalpourri* is still baked on iron rolling stones heated over coal pots. There are also other doughs and breads used with the curried meats, like *paratha*, *aloopourri* and *dosti*, more common in the homemade varieties.

Rotis are sold from roadside stands, bars and restaurants, and are practically the cheapest food you can buy. They are ideal for lunch, or as an informal dinner. Speciality *roti* shops still do the briskest business of all food sellers, although American-style fast-food restaurants have mushroomed in recent years. In places like the Western Main Road in St James, and Back Chain Street in San Juan, you'll find what might be called "roti rows". Connoisseurs generally agree that Hot Shoppe on Mucurapo Road has the best rotis in Port of Spain. The city centre is full of small, reliable restaurants, each with its own loyal following of gourmets.

A day at the beach should include fried shark

FOOD ON THE HOP

Barbecue (chicken, pork ribs, steak, fish) is just as popular as hotdogs or hamburgers, with cheap street stands competing with the fast-food chains.

buljol, salted codfish, onions, tomatoes and hot pepper, related to the Portuguese dish bacalao; coocoo, a dumpling of cornmeal and okra; callaloo, pureed okra and spinach; and pelau, rice and peas spiced with cinnamon, allspice and any number of secret ingredients such as coconut milk or red wine, depending on the cook.

An unforgettable gourmet experience is eating, fingers only, off a leaf at a traditional Hindu wedding or prayer celebration. One of Trinidad's most delicious dishes, curried duck, can only be truly relished in

and hops, called bake 'n' shark, usual fare at beachside bars and restaurants. The deep-fried roll and thick fish steak are doused with the ever-handy hot pepper sauce, and downed with a number of Carib beers. These hot sauces are usually mustard- or oil-based, and may contain papaya (or pawpaw), lime, onions and plenty of the hot yellow variety of pepper that grows all over the islands.

The hungry visitor must be an adventurous traveller to discover the out-of-the-way (and unassuming) places serving serious local food;

LEFT: eating curried crab.
ABOVE: snow-cones and solo around the Savannah.

its proper setting: beside an icy cold river, cooked over an open fire at a classic river lime, which is as much a social as a culinary ritual, complete with cold beers, plentiful rum and blasting chutney music (see page 152) or soca.

Rumshop society

An aspect of city life that is, sadly, disappearing is the once vibrant rumshop, a liquor bar where working-class men used to gather after work for simple socialising and drinking at a cheap rate. Outside the rumshop, on the pavement, vendors sold black pudding, a sort of blood pudding, and souse or pig's trotters. Akra and float, a salt-fish cake and pancake, and thick slices of fried shark in hop bread were also available. Inside, men (women never entered) sat at tables under ornate ceilings, or lounged against equally ornate bars, and drank their rum and talked. The potent effect of the spirit added considerably to the heat of the arguments about every subject under the sun, voices raised so loudly they could be heard down the street.

Outside, and side by side with the vendors, would be small Salvation Army bands, and groups of Baptist preachers, with lighted candles, ringing bells and conducting services.

There used to be a rumshop in Port of Spain at the corner of Park and Tragarete roads, the walls

still very much a feature of country lifestyle.

Trinidad produces more than 15 million litres (4 million gallons) of rum a year, but grudgingly exports only what the people cannot drink themselves, so Trinidadian brands are less familiar, though no less excellent, than Barbadian and Jamaican brands. Old Oak and Fernandes Black Label are the bestsellers in a country where rum-drinking is a national pastime, approached with even more gusto than eating. Royal Oak aged rum is as smooth as brandy, while overproof Puncheon is strictly for those with hard heads (although it is commonly used mixed with lime, salt and honey,

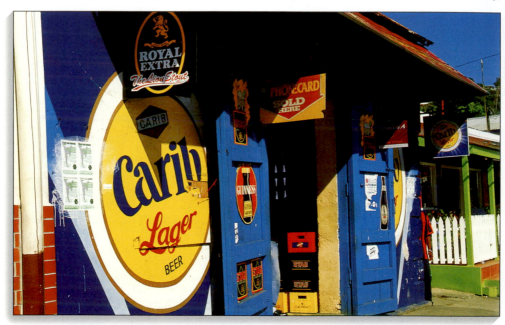

of which were painted green, so the corner became known as Green Corner. It was a terminal for taxis commuting to and from the districts on the western outskirts of the city known as Carenage and Point Cumana, which were close to the US Naval Bases at Chaguaramas during World War II. With foreign servicemen patronising the shop, Green Corner grew notorious.

Today only a few rumshops remain in Port of Spain, but wherever they are found they provide the same familiar atmosphere of friendship and lively conversation. Brooklyn Bar at Roberts Street, Woodbrook and Broadway Bar on South Quay, retain the old character and atmosphere of traditional rumshops which are

as a cold cure). During the Easter, Christmas and Carnival seasons, and for much of the time in between, since there are over a dozen national holidays and at least seven more religious holidays celebrated annually, drinking becomes a national devotion.

Street sweets

During Carnival, food shacks spring up all around Port of Spain's Savannah, and even during the rest of the year street vendors offer a broad choice in one of the safest cities in the Caribbean for buying roadside food.

Doubles, spicy curried chickpeas spread between two lightly flavoured dumplings called

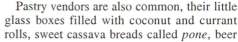

barahs (thus the term "doubles"), is another Indian-influenced street food eaten as a lunch on the run. Indian vendors also carry *aloo* pies, and *katchowrie*, *sahina* and *poolouri*: all seasoned breads eaten with mango or tamarind sauces and, invariably, a touch of pepper sauce.

To cool the hot sauce a nearby vendor will gladly offer coconut water, spilling from the fruit he has just opened with his machete. All around the Savannah in Port of Spain, and by the roadside in more rural areas, the coconut

HEALTH FOODS

Rastafarians use only natural foods, from coconuts to ground provisions. Coconut water is believed to help prevent illnesses of the bladder and kidneys.

Pastry vendors are also common, their little glass boxes filled with coconut and currant rolls, sweet cassava breads called *pone*, beer pies and even vegetable patties. Some vendors have fancier, less ethnic fare, like sponge cake and fruit tarts. In recent years many vendors have begun selling the healthier Rastafarian-inspired meatless "Ital" or vegetarian patty. Other forms of Ital food, sometimes delicious, have gradually found acceptance among the public.

Wherever sugar is produced the "sweet

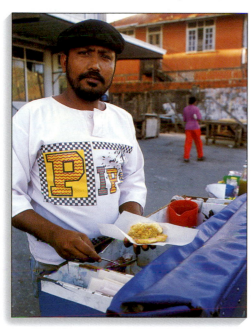

trucks dispense fresh coconuts from the full backs of their flatbed trucks. By merely shaking the fruit the seller knows if it is ready or not, and when he finds a ripe one a few deft, frightening strokes of his blade reveal the milk. This is also an opportunity to savour the jelly that remains after the milk has been drained from the green coconuts, which, after hardening, provides the nut that is grated as flavouring or a main ingredient in numerous dishes.

LEFT: a traditional rumshop in Scarborough, Tobago.
ABOVE LEFT: doubles on sale.
ABOVE RIGHT: gloves are essential for handling the ingredients of spicy hot-pepper sauce.

tooth" is rampant, and in Trinidad and Tobago confectionery is to be found everywhere. The islanders use coconut in a variety of these sweets – mixing it with sugar and baking it into a sugar cake, or grating it into chips to be blended with molasses for *tooloom*, a sweet that was favoured by slaves. The tamarind ball is a wicked idea invented to confuse the tongue. In this candy-like dumpling, sugar and salt collide with the tangy flavour of the tamarind fruit. Indian-inspired sweets include the islands's favourite, *kurma*, a sweet dough dropped in oil and fried until crisp. Other Indian sweets like *jilebi*, *ladoo*, *maleeda* and *sawaine* can only be found on the market stalls on Sunday morning.

Sea moss and sorrel

As you would expect, fruit is everywhere on these two lush islands. An endless variety of mangoes competes for shelf space with more exotic offerings like pomme cythère, guava, sapodilla – the gum of whose bark is used to make *chicle* – soursop, kymet and sugar apple, in addition to vast quantities of bananas and citrus fruits. Mango is curried and used as a side dish, grated and seasoned into chutney as a condiment, and preserved in varying degrees of sweet and sour. Another mango dish popular with children and rural rumshop customers is *chow*, made with slices of green mango mari-nated in lime juice and hot pepper. Tropical plums and cherries are also preserved and sold widely by vendors.

Oysters are another roadside victual, feeding the islanders' belief in their aphrodisiac qualities. The oysters are very small in Trinidad, where they grow on mangrove roots in swamps, and are also more succulent than sea oysters. And while health codes now prevent vendors from selling the molluscs in their shells, oyster cocktails are as popular as the oyster plate that once allowed the aficionado to suck them out. The oysters are dressed in a sauce of hot pepper, tomato ketchup and vinegar.

There are a number of other foods and drinks that islanders claim have aphrodisiac powers. These include *sea moss*, a kelp drink; *bois bande*, made from a tree bark; bush rum or *mountain dew*; and *pachro*, which is sea urchin. Consumption of these and more obscure concoctions never seems to diminish. We offer no guarantees, but do encourage the adventurous to experiment and report back their findings.

The list of non-alcoholic drinks is long. Most popular are sorrel, a tangy, ruby-coloured drink made from the petals of the sorrel flower; ginger beer, the spicy predecessor of ginger ale; mauby, a slightly bitter extract from the bark of the mauby tree; and peanut punch, a peanut butter-flavoured thick shake. Of course, even non-alcoholic drinks are likely to be spiked with a drop of rum and the world-famous Angostura Bitters, whose secret herbal ingredients are under lock and key in the company's offices in Trinidad. Bitters is an important component of *punch-à-crème*, a spiked eggnog that can lay out the weak-headed when really potent. Bitters is also used heavily in a potent mixture of Guinness stout, milk and nutmeg called "the Bomb", said to promote virility.

The ultimate drink on an island that produces some of the finest rums in the world is the rum punch. In Trinidad and Tobago this fruity drink has a flavour more subtle and seductive than that found on the other islands. The best rum punches, needless to say, are more likely to be found in a private home than at the bars. Everyone's uncle or aunt adds some secret ingredients that makes his or her rum punch special – anything from whole spices to fruit slices might appear in homemade punch. The bottled variety put out by Angostura and offered in most restaurants is certainly an acceptable substitute until you can wangle a private invitation.

Trinidad and Tobagoers consume beer like it's going out of style, blaming their thirst on the heat. The sun and the fresh trade winds seem to neutralise the alcoholic content, particularly during Carnival, making it easy to down four or five in a couple of hours. The

ANGOSTURA BITTERS

Only one or two people know the complete recipe for Angostura aromatic bitters. Developed in 1824, it is used in a variety of dishes, drinks, cakes and sweets.

local beers, Carib and Stag, compete vigorously with the other universal favourite, Heineken, and the more recent imports Stella Artois, Beck's and Grolsch. Guinness and Royal Stout are favoured by Rastas and young men, who swear by their alleged strength-giving powers.

A meal at home

As so much on-the-run eating is done during the week, weekends are a time for substantial family meals. Sunday dinner might consist of rice, meat, fish or poultry, and

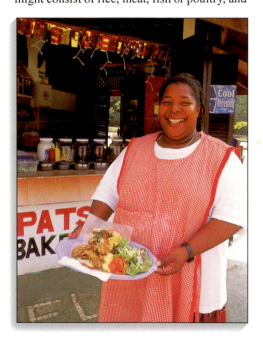

some kind of stewed peas or *callaloo*. Or it could be curried crab, gingered *pak choy* stir-fried with pork or codfish, and roasted aubergine with garlic, or *coocoo* and fish steamed with coconut milk in a thin gravy.

Ground provisions, also known as blue food – root vegetables (yam, cassava, eddoes, dasheen, tannia, sweet potato) – also find their way onto most tables. So, quite often, do a rich macaroni pie and a Lebanese-inspired potato salad.

Preparation for Sunday dinner sometimes begins on Saturday evening, but really gets going with an early Sunday trip to the open market. A Sunday morning market scene begins before full dawn, as knowledgeable housewives

LEFT: oysters for potency.
RIGHT: bake 'n' shark served with a smile.

seize the opportunity of first pick at the offerings. The largest market by far is in Port of Spain, which attracts both wholesalers and retail shoppers, but most medium-sized towns have their own markets. Back at home the entire family is conscripted for odd tasks like shelling pigeon peas, cleaning *callaloo* leaves and okra, or peeling the ground provisions. And by late Sunday morning the entire country is a scented room of seasoned selections.

Callaloo is a mixture of the leaves of the dasheen plant, similar to spinach and called *taro* by the Latins, pureed with chopped okra and flavoured with either crab or salted pork.

Both dasheen and okra were brought here by African slaves and were a big part of the slave diet. *Callaloo* can be cooked with a hot pepper for that little extra kick. Generally it is poured over rice, and served with meat or poultry. Gourmets, however, serve it as a soup, an appetiser for the meal to come. *Callaloo* is such an important part of Trinidad and Tobago that the Carnival designer Peter Minshall named his company after it.

Coocoo is a blend of cornflour and okra, steamed with coconut milk into a cake that hardens after it cools, akin to grits or the Italian *polenta*. The okra moisturises the *coocoo*, although it must still be eaten with lots of gravy to be swallowed smoothly. If you do not know any Trinidadians to invite you for a home-cooked meal, once a week the Port of Spain Hilton puts on by the pool a Creole spread which is surprisingly good and close to homemade, albeit expensive.

Wild meat and seafood

Seafood, not surprisingly, is plentiful and widely consumed. Be on the lookout for beach parties – open to the public – in Tobago, where beachcombers can quickly "season down" something from the day's catch for a peppery fish broth. The cascadura, an oily river fish, has gained almost mythical qualities, allegedly responsible for luring Trinidadians and Tobagonians back home no matter where they roam.

Kingfish usually dominates the day's ocean catch: a meaty fish similar to swordfish, it is often fried, curried a lot, and a favourite in fish broth. Red snapper, shark, grouper, bonito, carite, yellow tuna and salmon also fill the fishermen's nets. There are also good shrimp, chip-chip (a tiny, clam-like crustacean), lobster and oysters. And a beach party is probably the most likely place to find "wild meat", the several varieties of game that more adventurous islanders enjoy. Some people's eyes glaze over when they speak of manicou stew, made with fried iguana or possum. Others love the tender meat of the tatoo, a species of armadillo, or quenk, a wild boar.

More common meats and poultry are likely to be browned down, which has the added effect of making the food a tad sweet. There is also a habit of slipping bits of vegetable into the browned-down meat or poultry, and some people stew beans in the pot, but more often they are done separately, and frequently flavoured with pumpkin.

Pelau is used as either a side dish or a main course. Variations of this dish are infinite, but always the intent is to produce a sweetly spicy mix of rice, pigeon peas and vegetables. Everyone adds this or that little something else for a particular taste – a whole green pepper, coconut milk or a drop of wine.

The proof of the pudding is in the eating. Fortunately there is ample chance to taste these foods wherever T&Ters reside in the world. ❑

LEFT: a Carnival girl takes a snow-cone break.
RIGHT: colourful hot chilli peppers.

TROPICAL FLORA AND FAUNA

Trinidad and Tobago has a rich and fascinating selection of flowers and wildlife, which include mainland, island and imported species

As recently as 15,000 years ago, the islands were both part of the South American mainland; this accounts for an unrivalled diversity of flora and fauna. Besides ranking among the top 10 countries in the world for the number of bird species per square mile, T&T is home to 100 mammals (including 60 different bats, rare ocelots, wild hogs, opossums, armadillos, crab-eating racoons and deer) and 70 reptiles. There are 50 species of snake, including the largest and smallest members of the anaconda family, but only four are poisonous.

FLOWERING PARADISE

The flora is equally impressive, with over 2,300 varieties of flowering shrub and plant, including a staggering 700 orchids. Many ornamental varieties were introduced, including the hibiscus (*rosa-sinensis*) which is so widely planted that it is considered local, although it originated in China. The amaryllis, anthurium, allamanda, passion flower and heliconia came from South America, as did the equally ubiquitous bougainvillea; ginger lily came from Asia, while the bird of paradise hails from South Africa. Trinidad's national flower is the chaconia, a shrub which grows wild and scarlet in the evergreen seasonal forest of the lowlands. This type of forest also supports beautiful flowering trees such as the black poui with its yellow flowers, black fiddlewood with clusters of lilac flowers and bloodwood with its small orange flowers.

▷ **ON HOME TURF**
A gecko protects his domain by presenting a vivid territorial display.

▷ **SNAKE COUNTRY**
The venomous fer-de-lance, known locally as the mapioire balsain, grows up to 2 metres (8 ft) long.

△ **FROM BEAST TO BEAUTY**
Beware of the Swallowtail Butterfly larva: it doesn't look too pretty, and it emits a foul smell if it feels threatened.

▷ **WOODY WONDERLAND**
Teak is one of the most common of the islands' 350 tree species, along with mahogany, cedar, mora, Caribbean pine and balata.

△ **COLOUR OF THE TROPICS**
The brilliant hibiscus (*rosa-sinensis*) is a flowering shrub that originates in Asia. The colours of the delicate petals range from white to red and last for just one day.

SWAMP SANCTUARIES

The Caroni Swamp and Bird Sanctuary, with 4,860 hectares (12,000 acres) of mangrove forest, marsh and tidal lagoons, is the only known roost in Trinidad for the national bird, the scarlet ibis. During the day the ibis flies across the Gulf of Paria to feed in Venezuela, returning to roost at dusk.

The green mangrove turning red against the twilight is undoubtedly one of the best sights in Trinidad and Tobago. Besides the ibis, boat tours of the swamp offer glimpses of the rare red-capped cardinal and the stunning purple gallinule. The mangrove is also home to millions of tree crabs, an essential part of the ibis's diet, while the waters teem with mangrove snapper, snook, salmon and grouper.

The Nariva Swamp, the only sizeable freshwater swamp in the southern Caribbean, is a sanctuary for both visiting migratory birds and the endangered manatee, a herbivorous mammal which grows up to 4 metres (13 ft) long and lives for 50 years. Nariva is also home to red howler and weeping capuchin monkeys. Also look out for caymans (less ferocious relatives of the South American alligator), agouti and lappe (fruit-eating rodents) and more than 20 species of lizard.

△ **WILD MINIATURE**
A young leopard or panther gecko, newly emerged from an egg, displays its distinctive markings.

▽ **FIERY FLOWER**
Flame of the woods *(ixora coccinea)*, a native of Africa and India, has red petals, but cultivated hybrids can be paler.

△ **MAKING A SPECTACLE**
Underwood's spectacled tegu is found in the dense forests of Trinidad. The four poisonous snakes are the fer-de-lance, the bushmaster and two varieties of coral snake.

A MUSICAL NATION

Born of a fusion of African and European influences, the songs of Trinidadian calypsonians pricked the conscience of the people and helped shape public opinion

On a Saturday afternoon walking through the streets of any working-class neighbourhood of Port of Spain, you may well run into a steel band rehearsal under way in one of the many tin-roofed panyards that dot the city. These sessions are a study in discipline and determination. Though the majority are unable to read music, the 30 to 150 members of a steel bank practise for hours, week after week, without pay, until they have memorised an astonishing repertoire. Steel bands pride themselves on being able to play any kind of music – from Mozart to the Mighty Sparrow.

When the rehearsals are through and the band takes the stage, stand back; this is a revolution in sound. The steel drum, evolved as a new musical instrument, first fashioned in Trinidad from cast-off paint cans and oil drums in the 1930s. Only Spree Simon, Ellie Manette and a few other musicians in Port of Spain originally saw their potential as music makers, but now steel bands move young and old, Trinidadians and foreigners, and their sound symbolises Caribbean culture all over the world.

Music in Trinidad is not a spectator sport. Calypsonians and pan (as steel drums are familiarly known) players do not perform for a politely quiet audience. Audience response and involvement are characteristics of black music everywhere, and the ultimate source of this aesthetic is Africa. Though no one ethnic group can claim exclusive credit for Trinidad's musical heritage, it is from Africa that much of the country's music springs, evolving over some 500 years into a spicy international potpourri.

Afro-European synthesis

In Trinidad, as in the rest of the West Indies, music and culture are dominated by an Afro-European synthesis. The first musical result was *parang*, Spanish Christmas carols intro-

duced during Trinidad's days as a Spanish colony (1498–1797). In places like St Joseph, Lopinot, the Maracas Valley and Arima, the descendants of Spanish-speaking peoples in Trinidad maintain the *parang* tradition, and the continual movement between Trinidad and Venezuela, 16 km (10 miles) away, helps rein-

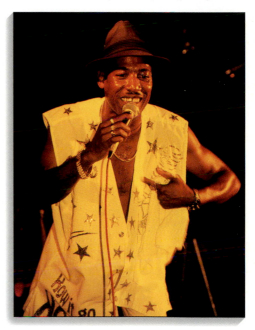

force it. Fusions with other forms have resulted in soca *parang*, chutney *parang* and even reggae *parang*. The lyrics and stringed instruments used in *parang* – guitar, cuatro, mandolin, box bass – are the Spanish contribution, while Africa adds the call-and-response performance style and the incredible rhythms that transform maracas into a solo instrument.

The *parang* season stretches from the last week of November through the first week of January. The house-to-house calls made by *paranderos* of former days have largely been replaced by a national *parang* competition and performances at parties, bars and community events.

Parang is only one of several Afro-European

PRECEDING PAGES: the steelpan band is closely associated with Trinidad.
LEFT: Carnival musician.
RIGHT: Ronnie McIntosh sings.

syntheses in Trinidad, the best known of which hybrids is calypso. Like African folk songs, calypsos are repositories of history, reminders of moral values, and broadcasts of social commentary and news. Calypso combines the African traditions of lively rhythm and an improvised, tell-it-like-it-is attitude sung with European languages, scales and musical instruments.

Steel drums, another Afro-European synthesis, originated when African-style percussion bands, beating brake drums, bottles and other odds and ends, switched to oil drums, which had the potential for sounding more notes. Steel drums are tuned to a chromatic, European scale

have made to Trinidadian music. Its rhythms knock down the walls between Muslim and non-Muslim Afro-Trinidadians, who are drawn to the drumming and join the processions through Port of Spain. Many non-Muslims have become excellent *tassa* drummers, creating an Afro-Indian style of music.

The common point that made such a synthesis possible is the integral nature of drumming to many religious celebrations and social activities, both in Africa and India. The perceived need for drumming is so strong that in the 1880s, when the British banned drumming, Africans and Indians rioted, fighting the police in the streets on

and, from the beginning, their repertoire has included calypso and classical music. A steel band is an orchestra of many moods. It retains its rhythmic punch when playing calypso, but shimmers like steel when tackling Tchaikovsky.

Indian drums

After influences from Africa and Europe, the most important musical traditions come from India. East Indians are now the most populous group in the country, having in the 1970s surpassed those of African descent.

Tassa drumming, which accompanies the street parades of Hosay, a Muslim festival, is one of the most important contributions Indians

several occasions. Even today, drumming is an integral part of many social activities in Trinidad and Tobago, from the rites of the African Shango religion to football and cricket matches.

Calypso's roots

Calypso put Trinidad and Tobago on the world music map, but controversy surrounds its origins and even the word itself. Some argue that the correct name for calypso is *kaiso* – a Hausa word meaning *bravo* – and this name is used in Trinidad today alongside calypso. Some trace the word to the French carrousseaux, a drinking party, the Spanish *caliso*, a topical song, or the Carib *carieto*, also a topical song. The Greek goddess Calypso was " she who conceals, and calypso songs excel in shrouding their point in clever double- or triple-edged lyrics.

The situation is complicated by the fact that several ethnic groups in Trinidad had song forms that merged to create calypso. What is quite clear is that the roots of calypso reach deep into Trinidad's past, and that calypso resulted from a synthesis of the songs of several vastly different ethnic groups, although the dominant elements are most certainly African.

MUSICAL ROOTS

The root of the calypso beat undoubtedly comes from the African drum, brought by the slaves and used in all ceremonies and celebrations.

These songs of self-praise and scorn for others gave rise to the *picong* (or *mépris*) tradition of improvised verbal duelling, which is a respected talent in calypsonians today. Africa – where songs of ridicule are a powerful mechanism of social control and where royalty never appears in public without its praise singers – is the source of the widely practised art of extemporising song texts and music.

In Trinidad these traditions were adapted to local conditions. In the 1780s, a famous French

The African slaves brought by French planters in the 1780s carried with them a tradition of improvised song which is a major ingredient in what we now call calypso. Slaves were assigned land on which they cultivated their own food in a communal fashion. Gangs competed with one another to accomplish the most, led by singers with such names as Elephant, Trumpeter and Thunderer. At night, after the day's work was completed, the lead singer of the most productive group exalted his group's achievements and condemned the inadequacies of other gangs.

slaveholder, Pierre Bergorrat, held court like a king in a cave near Diego Martin, and had slaves sing his praises and damn his enemies in verbal duels. Bergorrat crowned his favourite singer (Gros Jean Master of Kaiso), the first calypso king.

Similar verbal duels were an essential part of the music accompanying the *kalenda*, an acrobatic dance with sticks popular with slaves from Trinidad to New Orleans. The *kalenda* is really a thinly veiled version of the African martial art of stick fighting, and it is always accompanied by singing. The *kalenda* songs became a major force in Trinidad culture, especially after Emancipation.

LEFT: a *parang* group practises.
ABOVE: old folk songs are part of the oral history.

Carnival and *kalenda*

The 1838 Emancipation Act changed the country's cultural life forever. No longer confined by slave society, the creativity of the Africans blossomed. They expropriated Carnival, transforming it from a series of bourgeois balls to a raucous street party, enlivened by African drumming and filled with ribald masqueraders mocking high society. Forced to censor their songs and behaviour during slavery, the freed Africans made songs of praise, scorn and social comment a Carnival institution.

In this period just after Emancipation, Carnival tents of bamboo and thatch were first

erected to provide practice space for the neighbourhood bands at the beginning of the Carnival season. These tents became local night spots where anyone was free to drop in and observe the performances. The Carnival tents and masquerade bands forged a link between calypso and Carnival that is still strong today.

Freed slaves for the most part remained landless, and therefore flocked to the cities in search of employment. At the same time, the colonial government encouraged immigration from other Caribbean islands, and continued to do so until well into the 20th century. The competition for the necessities of life intensified; people divided themselves along ethnic lines and attempted to

hold onto what little they had. Gangs grew out of the need to protect territory to which the inhabitants had no clear title.

The *kalenda* bands institutionalised gang warfare at Carnival. For 40 years, until they were suppressed by the authorities in the 1880s, bands of stick fighters roamed the streets during Carnival. Every band had its chantwell, or lead singer. When two bands met, their chantwells traded insults in song, anticipating the actual battle. Calypso was stigmatised by its association with violence and the cavalier lifestyle of those on the margins of society who did not have steady enough employment to be considered working class. This stigma remained with Trinidad Carnival until well into the 20th century.

The songs of the chantwells were not mere entertainment but powerful and magical talismans that could put a stick fighter into a state of mind where he would not feel the blows of his opponents. Calypso and Carnival were the centrepieces of this synthesised culture, which Trinidadians guarded against any attack.

In one sense, calypso is a poor man's newspaper, one-part *New York Times* and one-part *National Enquirer*, extremely important in the 19th century when literacy was less widespread. Calypso is a cultural record of events as seen from the perspective of the people, and as a result, the whole course of Trinidad's social and political development can be traced through its calypso songs.

Censoring the newspaper

By the mid-19th century, Trinidad had been a British colony for more than 50 years, but its culture was anything but British. Its language was Creole, a French-African mixture. The British were convinced of the need to Anglicise the natives for political stability, and Trinidadians, of course, resolved to resist. The struggle lasted more than 40 years.

Calypso and Carnival came under attack from the press, the police, the church and the courts. The attacks focused on the obscenity and violence associated with them. For years, these aspects of calypso and Carnival had been denounced, but now the full power of the state was brought to bear. In 1884 drumming, the Canboulay processions and *kalenda* bands were outlawed and troops were called out to enforce the ban. In the 1890s various masquerade characters were outlawed. Using police and troops, the government was able to break the back of resistance.

Although masquerade bands continued to be led by calypsonians, the ban on drumming altered the sound of the music itself. Within a few years, tamboo bamboo bands replaced the outlawed drums. Tamboo bamboo consisted of tuned lengths of cured bamboo that when stamped on the ground produced a rhythmic percussion like that of drums, but without their carrying power. The skilled art of these

POOR MAN'S NEWSPAPER

Technically, the calypso was the poor man's newspaper. The songs carried social and political news to the not-so-literate lower classes in the 19th century.

nonetheless ostracised for their ventures into the social milieu of the poor blacks. They fought with sticks (individually, not in gangs), sang calypsos and chased women in poor neighbourhoods; college students, seeking thrills, hired calypsonians for parties. All this activity tended to increase calypso's acceptance by broadening its audience, but, of course, a price had to be paid. Bourgeois taste became much more important.

Soon the Venezuelan string bands, like those associated with *parang*, began to accompany

instruments has a long history in Africa, Venezuela and the Caribbean.

The purge of the drummers cleared the way for the middle and upper classes to participate in both calypso and Carnival. Businessmen sponsored competitions to ensure that bourgeois standards of taste would not be violated. White and mixed-heritage calypsonians appeared in larger numbers than ever before.

Known as jacketmen because they wore jackets as a sign of their true status, they were

LEFT: discarded oil drums were among the first steelpans.
ABOVE: trombones add a soca beat to a Carnival band.

the singing of the middle and upper classes. These string bands were eventually replaced by jazz bands in the 1920s. However, poor blacks continued to accompany their calypsos with tamboo bamboo until the steel drums replaced them in the 1930s and '40s.

In this period of rapid change, one event stands out as a symbol of the transformation of Trinidadian culture. In 1899 the first completely English calypso appeared sung by Norman Le Blanc, a white calypsonian.

Following the tradition of the poor man's newspaper, Le Blanc's song reported on the action of the British Governor, Sir Hubert Jerningham, who disbanded the Port of Spain

Borough Council in a dispute between the Council and the Governor. Jerningham's unpopular and heavy-handed response offended most Trinidadians, who saw it as further evidence of British arrogance.

The almost cryptic quality of the calypso song's lyrics is common in many African-American traditions, from soul to reggae music. A pithy, four-line stanza characterises the single-tone style of calypso, a style rooted in the verbal duels and acerbic comments of the *kalenda* and masquerade bands and work gangs of the 19th century.

The fact that the song was sung in English

marks a milestone in the cultural history of Trinidad. After 100 years of British rule, the English language was finally understood widely enough to be used in a popular song.

Anglophilia

In the early 20th century, the country experienced a wave of Anglophilia inspired by the death of Queen Victoria (widely believed to have abolished slavery). Britain encouraged this feeling as a means to support its involvement in the Boer War and World War I, and the names of many calypsonians of that time – the Duke of Albany and Richard Coeur de Lion, for example – reflect the process of change.

A new style of calypso was also emerging. Known as the double-tone or oratorical style, it featured eight-line stanzas which gave calypsonians more room to present ideas explicitly, leaving much less to interpretation. Chieftain Douglas' "Mourn, Trinidadians, Mourn" is an early example of the new genre.

The oratorical style was preferred by jacketmen such as Atilla the Hun, Lord Executor and Chieftain Douglas, men who tried to elevate calypso by avoiding gossip and scandal in favour of more dignified subjects. These men fought long and hard to change the tastes of the common people, who still preferred the older single-tone style with its implicit meanings and spicy flavour.

In a *picong* battle staged early in the 20th century, Lord Executor explained the requirements for success in oratorical calypso to his opponent, Atilla the Hun, telling him he'd need to study Shakespeare, Byron, Milton and Sir Walter Scott if he wanted to be a *kaiso* king.

By the end of the 1920s, it was clear that the oratorical style would not replace the single-tone style any more than Venezuelan-style string bands would replace tamboo bamboo in street parades. But the style was being converted into a voice for incipient nationalism and opposition to colonial rule. Poor blacks and even the middle class chafed under British dominance and calypsos expressed this discontent. As a result, police spies began to sit in the audiences of calypso performances.

Despite surveillance and repression, the Anglicisation of Trinidadian culture was not a complete success. Instead, Trinidad absorbed some British elements, adding them to a mixture that already contained a number of other ingredients. By the 1920s, calypso had proven that it could adapt and continue, capturing a wider audience by expressing the feelings of a majority. Furthermore, some were just beginning to realise how to cash in on calypso's popularity. The commercialisation of calypso laid the foundation for its golden years.

Commercial calypso

Between the 1920s and World War II calypso enjoyed its heyday, gaining both independence from Carnival and international recognition. Businessmen had long perceived the mass appeal and potential financial value of Trinidad's indigenous culture – especially calypso and

Carnival, which is in part why they were not completely destroyed in the late 19th century. By sponsoring various competitions, the business community was able to reform and influence calypso and Carnival.

Calypsonians themselves began to set up their own tents independent of masquerade bands, and for the first time charge admission. According to Atilla the Hun, King Fanto was the first calypsonian to do so, but others soon followed. By 1929, syndicates or cooperatives of calypsonians were setting up tents and competing for audiences. Frequently, the musicians secured the sponsorship of businessmen in return for advertising. The Toddy Syndicate, for example, took its name from a chocolate malt drink. Their jingle in praise of it seemed to herald the transition from folk songs to professional entertainment.

As fewer and fewer Carnival bands could afford the services of the best calypsonians, mass media – both the radio and records – spread calypso's message at home and abroad, opening up new markets for musicians but changing the nature of their art.

The American band leader Paul Whiteman scored a hit with the calypso "Sly Mongoose" early in the 1920s. In 1929, calypsonian Houdini became the first to emigrate to the United States to perform. And by 1934, when Atilla the Hun and Lion left to record for Decca, the prestigious US record label, Trinidadians were beginning to realise the potential of the international market. A crowd of thousands jammed the docks to see them off, and it was obvious that calypso was something Trinidad could be proud of.

In the United States, calypso became all the rage. Singers Rudy Vallee and Bing Crosby attended Atilla and Lion's recording session, and Vallee included Lion's "Ugly Woman" in a coast-to-coast NBC broadcast. The show was picked up in parts of Trinidad, and thousands of people crowded around radios and public loudspeakers to hear it.

On their return, Atilla and Lion received a heroes' welcome. Crowds filled the streets and speeches were made in their praise. Distributors couldn't keep the stores stocked with the records which they had made abroad.

LEFT: the police band plays.
RIGHT: the strings made an entrance in the 1900s when the music was developed by the middle class.

Lords, kings, lions and dictators

The first wave of professional calypsonians became known as the Old Brigade, and included popular singers such as Growling Tiger, Lord Beginner, Atilla the Hun, King Radio, the Roaring Lion, Lord Pretender and the Mighty Dictator.

King Radio's "Matilda" was a hit in the United States, but the influence of the recording industry was a mixed blessing. Since it required that the ensembles accompanying the songs resemble those current in popular music from the United States, tamboo bamboo bands were out, but string and wind bands, rooted in

Trinidad's Spanish tradition, were in, as were jazz bands featuring trumpets, clarinets and saxophones. Also popular were ensembles derived from minstrel bands, consisting of piano, bass, woodwinds and violin.

Radio and the record industry distributed jazz and other North American popular music in Trinidad as well as calypso, and the calypso folk tradition accommodated itself to the influence of mass media. Masquerade bands parading through the streets at Carnival began to use jazz instruments such as the trumpet, clarinet and trombone which had already proven themselves to have the carrying power necessary for marching bands in the streets of

New Orleans. So the Trinidadian folk tradition absorbed elements of the Afro-American jazz and marching-band tradition in the United States as well.

Though most Trinidadians could not afford these instruments, and tamboo bamboo bands and Venezuelan string and wind ensembles continued to provide music for calypso and masquerade bands in the countryside, these ensembles could not satisfy the tastes of the growing working class. In the urban areas, tamboo bamboo bands were replaced by percussion bands, which transformed the flotsam of industrial society – brake linings, dustbins,

cians discovered that the metal tins they had been beating on could produce more than one tone if the surfaces struck were shaped in certain ways. They began a process of experimentation, heating and pounding out the metal containers to produce several notes.

Gradually, musicians began to use discarded oil drums because their larger surfaces could accommodate more notes than paint cans and biscuit tins. From this process of experimentation, the steel drum was born. International acclaim beckoned, but only at the end of a rocky road, since steel bands were direct descendants of *kalenda*.

paint cans and biscuit tins – into innovative musical instruments.

Tin pan alley

By the late 1930s, the new percussion ensembles were popular with masquerade bands at Carnival. In 1937, newspapers reported on the "terrific din set up by the clanking pieces of tin" in these bands. But in fact this was not an entirely new development, for percussion of one kind or another had been part of Carnival since the emancipation of the slaves.

At first, the metal objects in these new bands produced only rhythm, and bugles were used to provide a melodic line. But by chance musi-

Steel band struggle

Although calypso flourished in the 1930s and '40s, opposition to it had far from disappeared. The Theatre and Dance Halls Ordinance of 1934 gave the British officers within the police the power to censor lyrics, and the Colonial Secretary had the right to ban any record. Furthermore, calypsonians had to obtain licences to sing in tents.

Calypso was still under attack, but it held its own by expressing the experience of a colonised nation. The period between 1920 and World War II had seen disillusionment with British concepts of democracy, the growth of militant trade unionism in response to the Great Depression, and the growth of a Trinidadian middle class anxious to lead the country to independence.

As always, calypso music accurately reflected the feelings of the people and the British could not ignore its ridicule of their continuing failures. Its mass appeal and commercial value made calypso incredibly difficult to suppress, and so the colonial government fought a holding action, muzzling calypsonians to keep them in line. A. A. Cipriani and other nationalist leaders rose to their defence, and the calypsonians' achievements became harder and harder to deny.

The number of calypsonians grew as nightclubs opened to entertain the troops. Steel bands suddenly found themselves in demand to entertain soldiers at the bases, and wartime shortages of imported goods, including musical instruments, increased their popularity.

Soon a boom mentality set in, and for a while everyone was happy. It did not take too long, however, before the presence of so many North American soldiers with money to spend caused an increase in prostitution and promiscuity. Trinidadians of all social classes were shocked by the sudden increase in light-skinned, fatherless children, and Trinidadian men felt that their wives

The Yankee dollar

World War II ushered in a new era – one characterised by the influence of the Yankee dollar. The colonial government signed a 99-year lease granting the US Government land for a major naval base at Chaguaramas, in northwestern Trinidad. The US Airforce and Army also built bases, and work there provided jobs paying 10 or 20 times the 40 cents an hour previously earned by the average labourer. The influx of thousands of soldiers fuelled the economy and in particular the entertainment industry.

LEFT: a calypso performance, *circa* 1940.
ABOVE: homage to musical history in San Fernando.

and daughters had betrayed them. Invader's 1943 classic, "Rum and Coca Cola", perfectly captured the mixed mood of frustration and resentment. But "Rum and Coca Cola" came to symbolise the difficulties faced by Trinidadians in another respect. The song became one of the greatest calypso hits of all time, but Invader had to fight to receive any financial rewards. Americans on the military bases had heard the tune and taken it back to the States, where the calypso craze of the 1930s was not forgotten. The Andrews Sisters then released a cover version of the song, which sold more than four million copies around the world, paying Invader nothing since he had no copyright.

Invader sued and almost lost, but Lion and Atilla had fortunately included the lyrics in a copyrighted booklet of calypso lyrics before the Andrews Sisters released their version. In the end Invader won, narrowly avoiding the plight of many calypsonians: fame and poverty.

The Young Brigade

By 1945 a new challenge faced the Old Brigade. During the war, calypso's foreign audience had grown but, although these fans loved the music, lyrics referring to local Trinidadian events were irrelevant to them. To increase calypso's share of the international

These more commercially oriented calypsonians called themselves the Young Brigade and, although the style was new, in many ways they continued calypso traditions, adopting names symbolising power: Lord Kitchener, Mighty Killer, Mighty Spoiler, Mighty Dictator and Lord Wonder. Lord Melody was one of a few exceptions, and his name may reflect the importance of expanded melodic techniques in the new style.

To defend themselves from the challengers, the Old Brigade began to monopolise the tents, refusing to allow the Young Brigade to sing. But these measures were soon circumvented, as the Young Brigade opened their own tent,

market, calypsonians and their musicians needed to change their lyrics, gain greater technical facility with Western musical instruments, and incorporate more elements of American jazz and popular music. American GIs and Trinidad's middle and upper class, who supported calypso in nightclubs and tents, wanted entertainment, not political satire and news reports.

A new generation of singers rose to meet the demand, de-emphasising *picong*, satire and politics in favour of sex and fantasy, describing events not linked to a particular time or place. Killer's "Green Fowl", which concerns itself with a priapic rooster, is a good example of the prevailing style.

and, having gained a forum, soon became the people's choice. In 1945 Lion released "Mary Ann", which showed his acceptance of the new concern with love and sex.

Calypso's audience broadened, and the music became more of a national art, something with which all classes and ethnic groups identified. It was a creative, experimental period, and musical styles proliferated, as calypsonians incorporated elements of many ethnic styles. Killer sang "Grinding Massala", using Indian rhythms and speech patterns, and Kitchener's "Double Ten" celebrated the founding of Sun Yat Sen's republican China with Chinese rhythms. Like Trinidad itself, these songs represent a synthesis of elements drawn from Africa, Europe and Asia. A new national consciousness had begun to emerge, and the indigenous culture of Trinidad gained new respect.

National recognition

There was such joy after the Allies' victory in Europe that the creativity of the Trinidadian people could hardly be restrained. And as a part of the 1946 Carnival, a special concert was organised to showcase steel drums. In the first solo concert of steel drum

RECYCLING

Poverty was the mother of invention in Trinidad. Would-be musicians made instruments from biscuit tins, dustbins and, of course, the old oil drum.

ever gain final acceptance. As in the clean-up of 19th-century Carnival and calypso, the government took the lead.

In 1948, the Trinidad and Tobago Youth Council asked the government to establish a committee to identify the causes of violence among the steel bands. This committee, chaired by Canon Farquhar, made several landmark recommendations, including the creation of the Trinidad and Tobago Steelbandmen's Association to provide a mechanism for resolving con-

music, Winston Spree Simon demonstrated the versatility of pans, which now featured up to 14 notes apiece. He selected a program which included all kinds of music: a hymn, "I am a Warrior"; Schubert's "Ave Maria"; Kitchener's "Tie Tongue Mopsy"; and "God Save the King." The concert proved to detractors that pans could play classical music, but sceptics were not completely silenced by the applause Simon received. An aura of violence was still associated with steel bands, and this had to be removed before they could hope to

flicts and promoting steel band music. The Association was successful and soon radio stations began to broadcast programmes of steel band music.

Changing attitudes towards steel band and calypso were part of a general shift on the island in support of indigenous culture. The British Government of the day had come to realise that the colony would not be so forever and that it would be best to begin preparing Trinidadians to rule themselves. It had become increasingly clear to middle-class Trinidadians that they could not hope to lead the common people to independence if they didn't respect their culture.

LEFT: a US book taught calypso dance steps.
ABOVE: postwar holidaymakers enjoy their island life.

Acclaim

In 1948, Beryl McBurnie opened the Little Carib Theatre in order to to promote indigenous music and dance. The very first performance by McBurnie's company was attended by prominent people in government, in church, academia and the press. The movers and shakers in Trinidadian society had finally decided that the limbo, bongo, bel air and other local dances were art, along with calypso and steel band. Two years later the government created a new post, director of dance in the Ministry of Education, specifically for Beryl McBurnie. This was the first time that performers had been elected or appointed officials in government.

In 1950, the first national steel band competition was held in Trinidad, and in 1951 the Trinidad and Tobago All Steel Percussion Orchestra, comprising the best musicians from all bands, represented Trinidad at the Festival of Britain. At first, scepticism and sarcasm greeted "the tin can boys from Trinidad" but British audiences went wild when they heard the music. The successful tour opened the door for steel bands at home. They became indispensable at national events, dances, parties, weddings and even church services.

CAN'T STOP THE CALYPSONIAN

In 1950 Atilla the Hun, one of the Old Brigade who never gave up political calypso, was elected to the Trinidad Legislative Council. In true calypso fashion, Atilla ran his political campaign from the calypso tents, and apparently his songs were more eloquent than the speeches of his opponent.

Once elected, Atilla wasted no time making his views plain; he attacked the 1934 Ordinance that required calypsonians to secure licences to sing and forced them to submit their songs to the censors. Never before had the loud and critical voice of the calypsonian been heard in legislative debate.

Calypso campaign

During the 1950s, the bands grew larger and larger, as more pans were added for sound and melodic possibility. Eventually, steel bands rivalled the costumes of the masqueraders as a Carnival attraction. Pan became a national obsession. The tremendous popularity of steel bands during the 1950s created the opportunity for calypsonians to compose specifically for pans.

Calypso tents were now packed with mainly white audiences: Trinidadians, tourists and G.I.s, continuing a trend begun in the mid-1940s. In the United States and England, many nightclubs now featured calypso, and Kitchener, of the Young Brigade, lived and performed in Britain, though he sent a steady stream of records back home. Kitchener was one of several calypsonians who migrated to Britain or the United States to pursue their careers, a trend begun in the 1920s and '30s, reflecting both the international appeal of calypso and the limitations of its Trinidadian market.

Sparrow sings

The most successful Trinidadian calypsonian of the 1950s was a newcomer to the Young Brigade, the Grenadian-born Mighty Sparrow. The record industry was working hard

won the first calypso king competition sponsored by the Carnival Development Committee (CDC), a government agency which meant official recognition.

Fame, no fortune

In 1962, Trinidad finally gained its independence under a government led by Dr Eric Williams. Like most Trinidadians, calypsonians had high hopes for the new government, believing it would reverse years of underdevelopment and colonialism. Specifically, calypsonians and panmen hoped that Williams'

to supply enough records to meet the international demand, and the pressure was on calypsonians to develop greater marketability. Sparrow, with his music talent and business acumen, responded to the challenge more successfully than most.

In the mid 1950s, long-playing records began to compete with 45s, and recording artists needed to produce an LP regularly to remain popular. Sparrow produced a new album every year from 1957.

In 1956, his composition "Jean and Dinah"

new government would actively promote indigenous music and dance. And the government did continue to send calypso and steel bands abroad to represent the country, and to organise competitions like Best Village, a national event that grew from a small craft fair, and Panorama, a competition for steel bands.

But once-a-year competitions and engagements at occasional international festivals are not enough to sustain performers. Too many talented calypsonians and panmen returned home to relative obscurity, after little more than a moment of fame on a foreign stage.

In the 1960s disillusionment set in as Trinidadians begun to realise that, despite

LEFT: a Carnival band brings the music to life.
ABOVE: the great Mighty Sparrow.

independence, pan and calypso were still scrunting – struggling for survival. And dissatisfaction with the results of the cultural policies of the Williams' government paralleled disappointment with economic and social conditions. By the mid-1960s, the CDC's calypso competition had fallen into a predictable pattern. The calypsonian sang a serious song of social commentary and a lighter, catchy tune good for wining (moving your hips) through the streets. Some calypsonians began to complain, among them the Mighty Chalkdust who contended that to win the Calypso monarch title you had to sing about sex.

Steel bands went into decline for a variety of reasons during the 1970s. They lost touch with the masquerade bands, no longer concentrating on providing music for them, and became totally absorbed in the CDC's Panorama competition, becoming so large and so expensive that they priced themselves out of the masquerade market.

They also began to play more and more classical music, perhaps in an effort to legitimise themselves. In any case, classical music does not go over well in the streets of Trinidad at Carnival time.

To recapture their proper place in Carnival, steel bands needed to amplify their sound and ride on flatbed trucks to move through the streets alongside the mas' players. They also needed to expand their repertoire to include more rhythmic music, and in the late 1980s there were indications that many bands were moving in these directions.

From the late 1960s on, while pan has been having its problems, calypso has moved in a very different direction. Absorbing the impact of the Civil Rights and Black Power movements from the United States, it responded to the deteriorating economic conditions of the working class. Out of the social ferment of 1970 and the Black Power movement came a new generation of calypsonians: Mighty Chalkdust, Black Stalin, Explainer and Valentino, who once again concentrated on political calypso. In the 1960s, calypsonians like Sparrow, Kitchener and Terror sang a range of material which included political calypsos as but one aspect of their repertoire.

A schoolteacher speaks

The most important of these new calypsonians was the Mighty Chalkdust, who dominated the 1970s as far as political calypso was concerned, and who continues to be influential. A former teacher and Director of Culture, Chalkie's lyrics are always well-constructed as, in his own words, the calypsonian is " ... not only an articulator of the population, he is a fount of public opinion. He expresses the mood of the people, the beliefs of the people. He is a mouthpiece of the people."

Chalkdust's first album, released on the 10th anniversary of independence, included "We're Ten Years Old" and "Our Cultural Heritage", wherein he wonders why the Port of Spain Hilton serves American, not Trinidadian, food, and "Ah 'Fraid Karl", a reference to the Attorney-General, Karl Hudson-Phillips, who could charge dissidents with sedition and had, in fact, jailed government opponents under the State of Emergency declared after the Black Power rebellion of 1970.

Chalkdust was never indicted, but various attempts were made to muzzle him. In 1969, the Ministry of Education tried to prevent him from singing because, as a Ministry employee, he needed its permission before accepting outside employment. Chalkdust refused to be quieted, or water down his message. He took his case to the people through a calypso which pointed out that other Ministry employees worked part-time in journalism, the military, the theatre and other occupations. The Ministry dropped its case.

In 1989, Chalkdust won his fourth National Calypso Monarch title with, arguably, the most bitingly humorous political critique of his career. "Driver Wanted" casts the leadership of the NAR coalition government in the role of the driver of a fine new Maxi-Taxi – the mid-size vans that transport commuters each day.

Plummer, Shirlaine Hendrickson and Singing Sandra who in 1999 became the second woman to win the calypso crown.

WHAT PROGRESS?

In the 1960s, after Independence, pan and calypso musicians continued to struggle, mirroring the social discontent caused by a lack of black advancement.

Soca fever

While politics gave lyrical focus to calypso, another force, the international pop music industry, was about to change its sound. As entertainers, calypsonians have always had to accommodate changes in the industry. And in the mid-1970s, a new style of calypso emerged which shook the music to its foundations.

LEFT: basic rhythms.
ABOVE: pounding out a pan.

Calypso Rose

The women's movement of the 1970s also had a major effect on calypso. Until then, calypso had been a male bastion but, when women claimed their right to sing, the Calypso King Competition was renamed the Monarch Competition. In 1978, the competition was won by a woman for the first time. Calypso Rose had already won the Road March title in 1977, and then captured it again in 1978. Since Rose's success, the ranks of female calypsonians continue to grow with performers like Singing Francine, Twiggy, Denyse

Called soca, the style is much more than a simple blend of soul music and calypso, as its name seems to suggest; it incorporates technological advances that changed the nature of the US pop music industry as well.

By the mid-1970s, the US was producing dance music heavily dependent on synthesisers and advanced production techniques. The disco craze was only one manifestation of the changes going on. As electronic gadgetry grew in sophistication, musicians depended more and more heavily on arrangers and producers to create the final product. Faced with the need to expand their share of the market, calypsonians began to incorporate the new technology into their recordings. The result was soca – furious tempos, funky bass lines, hot horn sections with plenty of riffs, independent rhythms on bass drum and snare, and assorted percussion to fill out the sound. Soca is an electronic big band assembled in the studio to create sounds nearly impossible to duplicate on stage.

Besides technological developments and the inroads made by US soul and funk, other local and regional influences played a significant role in shaping soca. Among those credited with founding the genre are Maestro, Lord Shorty and Shadow. Shorty, who, after renouncing the pleasures of the flesh in the late 1970s,

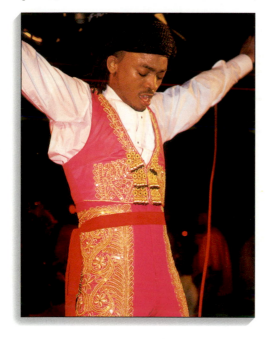

embraced religion and adopted the new sobriquet Ras Shorty I. He was influenced by Dominican *kadans* (cadence-lypso), itself a fusion of popular Haitian *konpa* and calypso, while Tobago-bred Shadow adapted the rhythms of that island's tambrin drums to produce the pounding new basslines that feature on his 1974 classic "Bassman from Hell".

Adding to the cross-fertilisation were the distinctive rhythms of the East Indian community's *tabla* and *jhanji* (cymbals). So while soca may have been catalysed by global musical forces, it developed along indigenous lines much as Jamaican Dancehall evolved out of Roots reggae.

Soca stars

The brass bands of the calypso tents quickly adapted to the new sound, becoming the requisite driving force behind any carnival fete from the 1980s. Bands such as Gemini Brass, Blue Ventures, Roy Cape Kaiso All Stars, Charlie's Roots, Sound Revolution, Shandileer, Traffik and Taxi not only covered the season's hits but started producing their own, with lyrics sung and sometimes penned by their lead singers.

Singers Ronnie McIntosh, Carl and Carol Jacobs, Colin Lucas, Chris "Tambu" Herbert and most notably David Rudder were all products of this era. Rudder went from fronting Charlie's Roots to solo star when in 1986 he won the Road March, Calypso Monarch and Young King competitions with his own songs "The Hammer" and "Bahia Girl". He continues to produce lyrics of local and international interest, refuting the claim that soca lyrics are little more than party chants. Rudder is also one of the few artists expanding soca's musical base, incorporating such disparate influences as zouk, jazz, bhangra and rai.

Ranking alongside Rudder in terms of lyrical output is the people's long time favourite Shadow, one of the few artists on the scene today who comfortably straddle the still controversial divide between calypso and soca music. Although he's penned a number of party songs, Shadow is revered for the deceptively simple William Blake like lyrics of compositions such as "Poverty Is Hell" and "Dingolay", which incisively and often humorously comment on the vagaries of the human condition in its unique Trinidadian setting. After many years of failing to win the judges

---

FROM SOCA TO DUB

Soca music features furious tempos, funky bass lines, hot horn sections with plenty of riffs, independent rhythms on bass drum and snare, and assorted percussion to fill out the sound. Soca is an electronic big band assembled in the studio to create sounds nearly impossible to duplicate on stage.

Today soca artists like Machel Montano of Xtatik and Anslem Douglas dominate the scene, and in recent years the Road March has been won by soca artists.

There is also a growing passion among the young for reggae music – Dancehall known as dub – produced by Jamaican artists such as Capleton and Buju Banton.

approval, Shadow was finally crowned Calypso Monarch in 2000.

If Rudder and Shadow are the voices of "conscious" soca, there are others such as Superblue, Iwer George, Ajala, Anslem Douglas, Machel Montano, Sanelle Dempster and Destra Garcia, who favour party lyrics.

Just as calypso evolved into soca, so soca itself developed through the 1990s, producing new fusions such as ragga soca and chutney soca; both have their own carnival competitions. Ragga soca, a blend of Jamaican Dancehall and soca, was the product of a generation raised on rap and dub music. Leading proponents include Machel Montano (the youngest Road March winner with "Big Truck" in 1997), and his band Xtatik, Bunji Garlin, KMC, Shurawyne Winchester, Naya George, Maximus Dan and Onika Bostic, who died tragically young in a car accident in 2004. Meanwhile, Sharlene Boodram, whose version of "Joe, le Taxi" was a hit in the French Antilles in 1997, ranked as the princess of chutney soca before heading to Miami to study music.

The birth of rapso

Contemporary soca and its fusions, in attempting to cross over into the global market unashamedly borrow from rock, hip hop, techno or whatever form is fashionable, yet there is another branch of Trinidadian music, rapso, which has been gestating since the 1970s and looks to Trinidad Carnival as well as the African oral tradition for inspiration.

Lancelot Layne's 1970 song "Blow Away", is regarded as the first rapso recording. His drum-driven chants were inspired by the bombastically loquacious "Midnight Robber" character, from old-time Carnival and other folk traditions. In the 1980s Brother Resistance and the Network Riddum Band, and Karega Mandela developed their own style of dub poetry.

In the 1990s a new generation of rapso artists emerged, including Kindred, 3 Canal, Ataklan and the short lived Homefront. Ataklan has the quirky inventiveness and humour of the calypso greats, while 3 Canal surprised themselves with their runaway Jouvert hit "Blue" in 1995. Originally formed by three actors, the group has

successfully developed rapso as Jouvert (the official start of Carnival) performance art, a reaction against the increasing commercialisation of Carnival.

A welcome spin-off from the rediscovery of Jouvert has been the emergence of formal rhythm sections such as The Laventille and Point Fortin. They are based on the impromptu groups that traditionally provided the percussive accompaniment to Carnival's Jouvert "jump-up", with an assortment of biscuit tins, bottles, pieces of iron and anything else that came to hand. The groups can trace their roots back to the kalenda stick fighting bands and the Canboulay proces-

sions of flambeaux and drums which were such an important feature of the riotous Jamette Carnival from the 1840s to '80s, which did so much to offend both the colonial authorities and middle class sensibility (see page 44).

Tambrin and chutney

Although the main focus and limitation for the Trinidad's music has been Carnival, other forms, besides calypso and its derivatives, add to the musical soundscape. Tobago's unique tambrin folk music, made with the tambourine-like goatskin drum, swooping violin melodies and Afro beats is virtually unknown outside that island.

LEFT: Machel Montano of Xtatik represents the modern breed of Trinidadian musician.
RIGHT: Sanelle Dempster is one popular face of soca.

The chutney music of Trinidad's East Indian community however, has travelled to New York, Toronto and London. Chutney's roots lie in the Bhojpuri folk and women's spicy wedding songs imported by the Indian indentured labourers who arrived between 1845 and 1917. Both the music – produced by harmonium, occasionally the *sitar*, *dholak* double-headed drum and *dhantal*, an iron rod held upright and struck with an iron beater – and the song in chutney are accompaniment for the

> ### HISTORY MAKER
>
> David Rudder made Trinidadian musical history when, in 1986, he won the Calypso Monarch and Young King titles, and the Road March too, with his song "Bahia Girl".

dancing, a steamy mix of pelvic winding and delicate hand movements, derived from Bhojpuri folk music.

It was the late Sundar Popo who gave the first public chutney performances in the mid-1970s, quickly endearing himself to Afro as well as Indo Creoles with his sometimes risquè lyrics, part Hindi, part English.

By the 1980s, chutney had a lucrative market, even crossing over into the soca domain, utilising keyboards, guitars and drum machines, as in the Drupatee Ramgoonai composition in 1989, "Indian Soca", in which she sang of the blend of Indian and African rhythms, which had first inspired Ras Shorty

I's (then known as Lord Shorty), "Soka Music" in the 1970s.

Following the election of Basdeo Panday as Trinidad's, and the Caribbean's, first prime minister of Indian origin in 1995, chutney entered the Trinidadian mainstream, playing a significant part in the Carnival of 1996, when the Chutney Monarch competition was established. Sonny Mann's winning "Lotay La" figured prominently on the airwaves alongside the season's soca hits. Chutney soca, whether sung by Indo Creoles like Rikki Jai, Drupatee Ramgoonai or Afro Creoles such as Brother Marvin, or the calypsonian, Crazy, is a vital element of the island's musical heritage.

Kaiso jazz

Although jazz doesn't have a high profile compared to other popular musical forms, Trinidad occupies a special place in the development of Caribbean jazz. Veteran guitarist Fitzroy Coleman was a star on the London jazz scene in the 1940s and '50s, and was voted one of the world's top five jazz guitarists by *Downbeat* magazine. After accompanying such vocalists as Mahalia Jackson, Tony Bennett and Lena Horne while in London, he was re-discovered by Eddy Grant in the early 1990s and emerged from semi-retirement to record an album of classics with Roaring Lion.

During the 1960s, Scofield Pilgrim and composer and pianist Clive "Zanda" Alexander initiated a series of calypso jazz workshops at Queen's Royal College in Port of Spain, resulting in the development of the indigenous *kaiso* jazz. The music they created has inspired subsequent generations of Caribbean jazz musicians, most notably St Lucian Luther Francois, who after attending the workshops went on to become director of the West Indies Jazz Band, and who ranks among the region's top jazz composers.

Zanda's approach is to break from the tradition of combining jazz standards with Caribbean rhythms, and instead he delves into the country's unique musical heritage as a basis for improvisation. His original compositions "Fancy Sailor" and "Chip Down" are Caribbean jazz favourites, along with his rearrangements of folk songs and classic calypsos such as Lord Kitchener's "Old Lady Walk A Mile and a Half" and Mighty Sparrow's "Mr Walker".

A younger generation of musicians including the small pan ensemble Panazz Players, drummer Sean Thomas, guitarists Mike Boothman and Theron Shaw, the Ruiz brothers on brass, and reeds player Dawud Orr, are all building on Zanda's foundation. Opportunities to perform in Trinidad are limited, especially after the demise of the excellent Panjazz festival in 1996.

Pannists such as Len "Boogsie" Sharpe, Robbie Greenidge, Ken "Professor" Philmore and Liam Teague are a few of the virtuoso panmen who are respected for their work in the wider world of jazz.

From Patasar to Tanker

Mungal Patasar, an Indian-trained sitarist, is another pioneer who benefited from the *kaiso* jazz experimentation. His Pantar group combines steelpan, *sitar*, *tabla*, drums, keyboard and sax to produce Indo calypso jazz, and his improvisations range from classical Indian ragas to reggae and classic calypso. In the late 1990s, Patasar released "Dreadlocks", a composition rearranged for the European dance market in two versions: the first with gifted British-Asian composer Nitin Sawhney and another with the seminal Jamaican rhythm section of Lowell "Sly" Dunbar and Robert Shakespeare, more commonly known as Sly and Robbie.

One of Patasar's collaborators, and probably the greatest unsung musician of 20th-century Trinidad, was composer, guitarist, flutist and blues harp player, Andre Tanker. Born in Woodbrook in the 1940s, within earshot of several steelbands, Tanker taught himself the *cuatro* before graduating to guitar. Working on musical arrangements for the Little Carib Theatre, he encountered Carriacou master drummer Andrew Beddeau, a meeting which began a lifetime's reverence for the Afro rhythms of the Orisha faith, which pervaded his music. Tanker was also influenced by the polyrhythmic Latin music, which was a regular feature on Trinidadian radio in the 1950s and '60s before American and British pop took over.

With his pan-Caribbean ear and generosity of spirit, Tanker forged the prototype Caribbean world music long before the music industry invented the term. Moving easily between the idioms of jazz, calypso, reggae, zouk, blues and R&B, Tanker's compositions such as "Sayamanda", "Basement Party" and "I Went Away" have become Caribbean anthems.

Another artist who draws inspiration from Orisha traditions and faith is the singer Ella Andall, whose powerful voice and music reflect an African influence.

The country also has a healthy crop of musicians producing alternative forms, not

traditionally associated with the Caribbean music scene: there is rock from the Orange Sky and the lyrically gifted Joint Pop; New Age chanteuse Gillian Moor uses elements of rapso, blues and folk, and the Love Circle, (a group formed by the children of the late Ras Shorty I), continue to perform the Jamoo (Jah music), which their father initiated.

Trinidad and Tobago may be geographically small, but musically the twin island republic is massive and is constantly evolving. While legends such as Roaring Lion, Lord Kitchener, Ras Shorty and Andre Tanker have made their mark and gone ahead to the Big Yard in the sky, the music continues to move forward. ❑

LEFT: David Rudder.
RIGHT: Andre Tanker, a Trinidadian musical icon.

FESTIVALS

An intermingling of African, European and Indian cultures means that the islands have lots of lively festivals and celebrations throughout the year

To the casual onlooker at a Trinidadian Hosay (or Hussein) festival it may seem incredible that what is being celebrated is a procession of deep mourning observed by Shi'ite Muslims in places such as Iran, Iraq, Lebanon and India. To Muslims of the Eastern hemisphere, Hosay in Trinidad would seem a travesty of what in essence should reflect the grief, pain and martyrdom of Hussein and his brother Hassan, grandsons of the Prophet Mohammed, at Kerbela in long-ago Persia during the famous Jihad (Holy War). But in the 150 years since Indian Muslims first arrived on these islands there has been much intermingling of European, African and Indian cultures.

Hosay

What the hundreds of onlookers see in the present-day procession, then, is the effect of a century of indigenisation. Since its arrival with the Indian indentured labourers in 1845, there has been a painstaking attempt to keep the tradition alive, and until about 50 years ago Hosay, retained its aura of mourning, with austere rituals brought over intact from the Indian subcontinent.

Now the holy men who used to walk on beds of fire (some Hindus and Africans among them) no longer perform their daring feats, and gone also are the old women who sang the *maseehahs*, wailing dirges, behind the *tadjahs* (Ta'ziyeh), the elaborate and beautiful replicas of Hussein's tomb. But fire-eating is still seen on occasion, as is *banaithi*, the dance where whirling sticks of fire make eerie patterns against the night sky.

The massacre of Hussein and his party was said to have taken place on Ashura, the 10th day of the Muharram month, in AD 680. The modern celebration takes place around the month of Muharram, and could occur twice within the Roman calendar year, with different areas observing each occasion. The most popular processions are between February and March in towns such as St James, Curepe, Tunapuna, Couva and Cedros.

After 40 days of fasting, abstinence and prayers, devotees begin the festival with Flag Night. Flags of various sizes and colours are carried through the streets to symbolise the

beginning of the Battle of Kerbela, and are then ceremoniously placed on a mud and wattle dais amidst burning incense.

The following night two small *tadjahs*, miniaretted tombs made of bamboo and decorated with brightly-coloured tissue, tinfoil, crêpe paper, mirrors and coconut leis, are carried on the heads of the dancers through the streets, accompanied by drums. At midnight there is symbolic contact, with dancers gently touching *tadjahs* with their heads and against each other.

The highlight, however, is on the third night, when the large *tadjahs* are produced to gasps of delight. These incredible works of art have

LEFT: a Hosay procession in 1904.
RIGHT: modern Hosay, with *tassa* drummers.

borrowed from the Carnival tradition over the years, with a lavish flair blending Eastern designs with local innovations. Anything up to 6 metres (20 ft) tall, and covered with glitter and colour, the *tadjahs* emerge from different yards to pass through streets bearing great significance for the descendants of those who brought the tradition. In the area of St James, for example, in close proximity are Lucknow, Hyderabad and Delhi streets, named after main centres of Muslim observance in India.

In addition to the *tadjahs*, the two moons representing Hussein and Hassan are carried by specially trained dancers. These large

together with great ceremony and allow the moons to meet as if in brotherly embrace. This brings cheers of delight from the onlookers, and perhaps twinges of pain for devotees.

The excitement of the festival is further enhanced by the pulsating drums of the *tassa* players. These drummers are quite famous, and attract great crowds who follow behind them dancing. Among the drummers are some of African descent, drawn to *tassa* as they are to the African tamboo bamboo and steel drum. The younger generation of this Carnival-orientated society sees this later part of the procession as a time to jump up and make

crescent-shaped structures, 2 metres across and 1 metre at their highest point (6 ft by 3 ft), are usually red, to represent the decapitation of Hussein, and green or blue, for the poisoning of Hassan. Sharp blades are inserted between the thickly ruched material, projecting upward for the spiked effect that is a symbol of battle.

The dancers whirl in a stately dance of the brothers' triumph over death as they move with one foot raised onto its ball and the other flat. The moons are placed over one shoulder, with the pole end stuck in the *shamotee* at the waist. The dancers appear mesmerised, and they enthral the crowd. At midnight there is a ritual kissing of the two moons, as the dancers come

merry. The West African attitude of jovial celebration of life at funeral rites surely influences these actions.

Another attraction is the performance of the *ghadka*, a stick fight/dance between two men, each holding in one hand a stick about 1 metre (3 ft) long and in the other a small leather pouch as a shield. They perform in a circle drawn around them in the street, and go through their symbolic battle.

The climax of Hosay comes as the *tadjahs* and moons are wheeled into the streets the following day for their last procession to the sea, into which they are ceremonially cast after prayers and offerings have been made.

Phagwa

Spring is not known as a season in Trinidad and Tobago, but the vernal equinox does not go unnoticed among people whose traditions are based in lands far away. The Hindu festival of Phagwa celebrates this event here as it does in India each year, heralding the Hindu New Year with gay abandon.

At the time of the full moon in March, elaborate rituals celebrate the triumph of light over darkness and good over evil. As with other religious festivals in Trinidad, a Carnival spirit has gradually pervaded the festivities as a wider population becomes involved. Phagwa is not confined to Hindus, but includes anyone wishing to participate.

Bonfires are lit to symbolise the destruction of Holika, the evil sister of King Hiranya Kashipu, and before the actual day of Phagwa, there are *chowtal* singing competitions. *Chowtal* is a mixture of the religious and the secular, and the competitions display the skills of singers who perform both devotional songs and local compositions, the latter being influenced by calypso, borrowing from its extemporaneous artistry. Special instruments such as the *dholak* (a small skin drum), *kartals*, *mageeras* (a pair of brass cups joined by a cord) and *janji* (cymbals) accompany the Hindu singing and dancing.

One of the more popular rituals is the spraying of *abeer* powder, a red vegetable dye made into a bright fuchsia-coloured liquid and sprayed over observer and devotee alike. It creates a messy but colourful scene as clothes take on a tie-dyed effect and skin and hair are drenched. Recently other colours have been introduced as the festival becomes more secular, including the innovations of other ethnic and religious groups.

Dancing is a central part of Phagwa, and it varies in style, tending toward the suggestive dances of Carnival but with a good admixture of East Indian movements.

There are re-enactments of the legend of Holika during the day as bands similar to those of Carnival participate in competitions set up at several locations throughout the island. All

---

> **CHAGUANAS RITUALS**
>
> Some of the best and liveliest Phagwa events are held in central Trinidad. One of the biggest is the Kendra Phagwa Festival in Chaguanas.

manner of Oriental costumes, many of them white, are worn with crowns, garlands, jewellery and flowers, and various characters from the epic drama are portrayed. The plays are more or less light-hearted, as befitting a celebration of rebirth.

A recent innovation has been the use of trucks as floats on which pretty girls are paraded as queens in fine vestments, accompanied by drummers and dancing revellers who blend African, calypso and East Indian rhythms and fashions.

Diwali

On one October night Trinidad sparkles with the light of thousands of tiny flames and electric bulbs strung through trees and across buildings, wherever a light can be affixed. The festival of Deepa Diwali (pronounced "Duwali") is a national religious holiday celebrated by hundreds of thousands of Hindus. This they do to honour Lakshmi, goddess of light, beauty, riches and love, who was the wife of Vishnu and was born out of the churning of the great ocean. For her they make elaborate advance preparations, offering *pujas* – sacrifices and prayers – in her name.

Weeks before the actual event, men cut long

LEFT: Phagwa celebrants covered in *abeer* powder.
RIGHT: *deyas* lit for Diwali.

bamboo poles to build structures in village parks, school and *mandir* (temple) grounds, and their own yards. On these structures are placed tiny clay pots called *deyas*, filled with coconut oil, each with a cotton wick. The *deyas* are also placed along the walls of verandahs and fences, on the ground and an all vantage points.

Patna Village in the Diego Martin valley has become famous for its elaborate Diwali decorations and celebrations. A ceremonial gate at the village entrance leads to the main street, which is carefully festooned with lights and lined with complex bamboo sculptures, highlighted with *deyas*. Diwali night itself is the

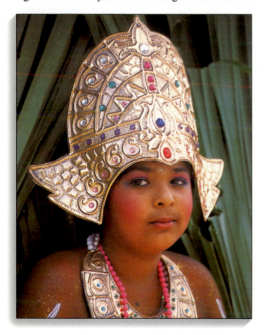

occasion for a major village fête, to which visitors are most welcome.

Another Diwali tradition especially popular with young boys is "bussin' (bursting) bamboo". In rural areas and small villages the nights preceding the festival are punctuated by the sound of the booming of bamboo cannons, scaring dogs and unwary humans alike. A 2- metre (6 ft) length of sturdy bamboo is required for the cannon, and a small hole is made in one section, into which pitch oil is poured. A lighted taper held over the hole eventually ignites the gas building up inside the hollow section with a resultant explosion, causing jubilation or consternation depending on the listener.

On the evening of Diwali the *deyas* are lit, and are tended during the night. They illuminate the way for the visitation of Lakshmi, and must not be allowed to go out before the appointed hour. Modern embellishments have also made their mark on this festival as, more and more, electricity is used to augment the lights of the *deyas*. Strings of coloured bulbs are used in the manner of Christmas lights, and, needless to say, this phenomenon brings thousands of non-Hindus out to visit the various well-illuminated public places.

Prior to the night of lights there are shows and pageants where Diwali Queens are chosen amidst Indian dancing and singing. Special song competitions highlight local composers and feature star Indian musicians. It is a joyous occasion, and everyone tries to emulate the qualities of Lakshmi, spreading peace and goodwill. Greetings and gifts are exchanged, with food being the traditional gift, and there is the usual abundance provided in private homes, shared liberally with non-Indian neighbours and friends and the less fortunate in the vicinity. A special sacrificial meal of *parsad*, a doughy concoction of flour, sugar, milk and raisins, provides an offering to the gods.

The importance of Diwali, the triumph of good over evil, has meaning on a national scale, and so public prayer services are held for thousands of people, with the leaders including clergy from other religions who come together with their Hindu brothers and sisters to celebrate a shared ideal.

Indian Arrival Day

Traditional Arrival Day was re-named Indian Arrival Day; it is observed on 30 May and replaced the Christian holiday of Whitsun (Pentecost). Arrival Day was initially inspired by the 150th anniversary of the coming of East Indian indentured labourers to Trinidad. The concept was broadened to include all races, since none of the diverse ethnic groups (except the near extinct Caribs) in Trinidad and Tobago is indigenous to the country. But this was changed in 1995 to celebrate the 150th anniversary of Indian arrival, and became a specifically Asian event.

Spiritual (Shouter) Baptist Liberation Day on 30 March has been added to the calendar of public holidays. African forms of Christianity are rarely acknowledged, so the day is celebrated with verve and jubilation. Religious rituals at the Hasely Crawford National Stadium in Port of Spain include bell-ringing and enthusiastic hand-clapping.

The Tobago Heritage Festival is held from mid-July to early August; it attempts to keep alive Tobago's indigenous traditions, such as folk tales and superstitions, courtship codes, old-time weddings, the *saraka* feast and wakes. This is Tobago's version of Trinidad's Best Village event *(see page 161)*, and it attracts many visitors.

Eid-ul-Fitr

The new moon of Ramadan marks the observance of Eid-ul-Fitr, the Muslim New Year (any time from January to June). It is a national holiday, but cannot be predicted exactly as the actual day depends on the sighting of the new moon by a holy *imam*. The official announcement comes after this sighting, and what follows is an obligatory day of feasting to break the month-long daylight fast. The usual visit to the *masjids* (mosques) for prayers and thanksgiving is followed by almsgiving to the poor in the form of money, food and clothing.

Observers prepare sumptuous dinners, and large gatherings of all ethnic groups are invited to celebrate the occasion with Muslim friends. The traditional dish of *sawaine* is a requisite on the menu. A rich tantalising concoction of fine vermicelli boiled in milk, it contains raisins, sugar and chopped almonds.Throughout the country there is an air of spiritual renewal as Muslims and non-Muslims alike honour Allah, wishing each other *Assalam O Alaikum*.

Emancipation Day

For those of African descent – the second largest group in Trinidad and Tobago's population – the designated Emancipation Day on 1 August is of special significance.

The day commences with an all-night vigil and includes church services, street processions past historical landmarks, addresses by dignitaries and an evening of shows, with a torchlight procession to the National Stadium.

LEFT: a young boy celebrates Indian Arrival Day.
RIGHT: the groom at the Heritage Festival old-time wedding, Tobago.

The event marks the achievements of the sons and daughters of slavery; it also reflects on sobering thoughts of man's inhumanity to man, and honours the contributions of the black people to Trinidad and Tobago's rich culture.

Ramleela

In his acceptance speech for the 1992 Nobel Prize for Literature, Derek Walcott spoke in awe of a visit to Felicity, a small village in central Trinidad, to witness preparations for the *Ramleela*, a ritualistic reenactment of the Hindu

SPIRITUAL BAPTIST DAY
Membership of the Spiritual or Shouter Baptist sect was banned by law in 1917. Spiritual Baptist Liberation Day in March celebrates the lifting of the ban in 1951.

epic, the *Ramayana*. The activity awed the poet because of the drama and the revered memories of one of the ancient civilisations that had contributed to making the West Indies. But to the participants it is something very serious and holy that takes place in several villages in central and south Trinidad in the lead-up to the Diwali festivities.

Weeks beforehand, a giant effigy of Ravana, (whose abduction of Queen Sita sparked the war), is constructed, and in the villages the characters of the play – Rama the king, Hanuman his adjutant and Lakshman his brother – are assigned according to the personalities of the villagers or the priests.

On the evenings before Diwali, the Festival of Lights, spectators turn out to witness the mimed re-enactment of various stages of the battle. The men are dressed in colourful costumes, with bows and arrows, and enact the battles told in Valmiki's epic. They shoot arrows and feign hand-to-hand combat in slow motion to the accompaniment of the *tassa* drummers, who are also colourfully attired for the occasion, while (in more recent times) a narration of the events is broadcast to the spectators over a public address system. The festival culminates with the burning of the effigy of Ravana.

Independence Day

In August and September, Trinidad and Tobago celebrates two patriotic milestones. On 31 August 1962 the country gained its independence from Britain, and on 24 September 1976 it became a republic. The fact that both these events were achieved in a peaceful and civilised manner is enough to warrant enthusiastic revelry and thanksgiving. Republic Day on 24 September has been officially replaced by Spiritual (Shouter) Baptist Liberation Day, celebrated on 30 March *(see page 158)*.

Independence Day is celebrated throughout the country as various villages and towns host

PARTY ISLAND

Apart from the Carnival music competitions, such as Panorama for the steel pan and the Road March for the most played soca or calypso song, there are a number of other extremely popular music festivals. The national instrument, the steel pan, is featured in both May's Pan Ramajay, for small pan ensembles and jazz musicians, and October's biennial World Steel Band Festival "Pan is Beautiful", for larger bands. Also held in October, Pan Royale is a notable event on the steelpan calendar, while Pan Parang is a traditional folk festival, which celebrates the influence of Spanish Creole music. Parang is most popular in the east of the island.

sporting events, dances, concerts, exhibitions and seaside activities. Among the highlights is the military parade at the Queen's Park Savannah on the morning of 31 August.

The emphasis here is on pomp, tradition and ceremony, without the ominous overtones of military might. The Regiment, Coast Guard, Police and Fire Services lead a host of voluntary organisations in an impressive parade observed by thousands.

The police and regiment bands arrange popular calypsos into military marches, and at the end of the parade everyone traditionally follows the band through the streets to the Barracks, like children behind the legendary

Pied Piper of Hamelin, only this time in Carnival style.

The same evening the National Awards Ceremony is held, when local awards like Chaconia, Hummingbird and the highest, Trinity Cross, are bestowed on recipients who have made some kind of outstanding contribution to the nation.

Before the secular observances take place, official and unofficial church services are arranged. A great achievement in this multi-ethnic, multi-religious country is the

CELEBRATING FREEDOM

In 1985 Discovery Day was replaced by Emancipation Day, which celebrates the end of slavery rather than the Spanish colonist Columbus.

The emphasis is on family participation in art and food displays, lectures and nightly shows. On the Sunday nearest the 24th a parade of historical floats climaxes the weeks of celebration.

Best Village

The prime minister's Best Village trophy competition began in 1963 as a small handicrafts fair, and has since expanded to five categories involving numerous towns and villages and hundreds of participants.

An effort to encourage and record old folk

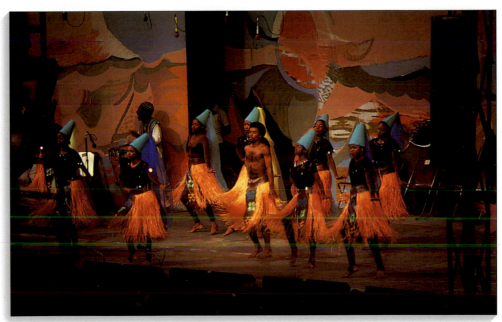

meeting of the various religions as a mark of national unity.

During the first week of September the annual Folk Fair brings a big taste of rural life and customs to the capital, Port of Spain. Over a hundred booths are established to display and sell handcrafted items, locally made works of art and colourful clothing, and traditional cuisine, sweetmeats and beverages. Traditional music and dance performances encourage the air of festivity. One week later, around 15 September, the Family Fair opens for a 10-day run.

LEFT: traditional dance on the beach.
ABOVE: a Best Village dance performance.

arts and local pride, Best Village is a month-long series of small contests culminating in a feast of music, dance, drama and song. Under the guidance of elders, young people create shows on various themes relating to life in the village, using traditional dances, music, storytelling and song.

It is in this setting that the Afro-French *bele* and *pique* are seen alongside the Hispanic *parang* and the African-derived *bongo* and *saraka* dances. Stick fighters are in full cry as they dance the *kalenda*, while others choose to excite their audiences with spectacular dances like the limbo.

Rich folk music is sung by choirs which include grandparents, grandchildren and everyone in between. Whole families participate in some villages. Around 32 villages reach the finals, presenting their shows at the grandstand of the Queen's Park Savannah, where at other times Carnival Kings and Queens display their musical arts.

In addition to the theatrical presentations, in the autumn there are also craft shows, concerts and a beauty pageant called "La Reine Rivée", *patois* for "The Queen Arrives", with costumes approaching the elaborateness of Carnival. In October the Trinidad and Tobago Steelpan and Jazz Festival is a week-long event, with pan, Latin jazz, reggae and local choirs.

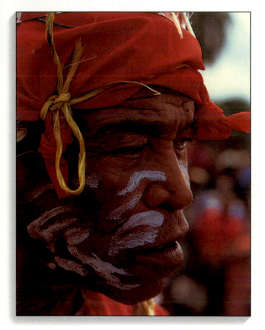

One of the more significant regional celebrations is Arima's Santa Rosa festival, held during the last week in August. Organised by descendants of the Caribs, the island's indigenous people, the festival celebrates Amerindian traditions and culture.

La Divina Pastora, held in Siparia on the second Sunday after Easter, is another example of Trinidad's Creolising synthesis of cultures. The statue of the Black Virgin which is paraded through the streets is worshipped by Roman Catholics and East Indian Hindus alike.

Another religious thanksgiving feast celebrated islandwide in fishing communities is St Peter's Day, 29 June (or the closest weekend).

The limbo

Along with steel band music, visitors to the Caribbean associate the limbo with the sexy abandon of a tropical island. But the limbo as we know it today – exhibitionist, glittery, sensual – is not the limbo of a bygone era, when men (and women) symbolically passed below the bar of the underworld to rise towards light and deliverance, representing the path which the soul of the deceased takes in its journey to the next world. The limbo was originally danced on the ninth night of a wake, before the funeral and burial, and the bar was gradually raised not lowered.

The limbo was a way of assisting, encouraging and guiding the soul into the world of the ancestors. With much singing, clapping, drumming and ribald taunts, each dancer shimmied under the length of wood, held by two supporters who allowed the dancers to go no lower than hip level. Now, expert limbo dancers compete to beat the world record of 15 cm (6 inches), with a soda bottle as the standard measure, and the dance is more a display of athletic prowess than an acknowledgement of another world.

Easter sports events

The Tobago Easter Goat and Crab Races are among the more bizarre traditions that are maintained in Trinidad and Tobago. During the long Easter weekend Tobago is flooded with vacationers from abroad and from the bigger island, and when people are not on the beaches they go to the races.

The goat races, featuring large sanaan goats, are serious yet comic affairs. Introduced from Barbados in 1925, these races are unique in the Caribbean. The goats are bred and trained specifically to race. Swimming in the sea and a special diet build stamina. The jockeys, who hold their charges by short lengths of rope, have to be robust sprinters to keep pace.

The Easter goat races climax at Buccoo on Easter Tuesday in front of a crowd of spectators, especially children, who delight in the butting antics of some furious and rebellious goats.

The crab races are a riot of fun as the owners spur their crustaceans on to the finish line. But crabs are wont to be wayward, and gamblers take their losses seriously as the crabs make their usual sideways movements.   ❏

LEFT: old timer celebrates.
RIGHT: the pomp of Independence Day celebrations.

CARIBBEAN CARNIVAL

Nothing can quite match Trinidad's bacchanal – everything closes down as the islanders and thousands of visitors join in spectacular street parties

Each year, two days before Ash Wednesday, the citizens of Trinidad and Tobago pay homage to the gods of antiquity and their ancestors, follow their muses and the promptings of the flesh, and celebrate life in an explosive and beautiful two-day bacchanal. The climax to a year-long build up of energy, creativity and ingenuity, Carnival is the ultimate expression of the spirit of Trinidad and Tobago. A kaleidoscopic display of musical and artistic creativity, of high-spirited camaraderie and hedonistic beauty, it opens the floodgates to unbridled self-expression in a spectacle of colour, movement, music, sensuality and of course the lavish joy in life which is the hallmark of Trinidad and Tobago.

In many ways the epitome of the country, and certainly the primary attraction for most visitors, Carnival meshes all fibres of Trinidadian life – the histories of Europe, Africa, Asia and oppression, calypso and steel band, imaginative and applied artistry – into a dazzling parade. Every year, race, colour and idea bind together without prejudice, united in the potent force of a truly universal festival.

A national party

Carnival in Trinidad and Tobago – or, more specifically, in the capital, Port of Spain – is different from and better than any other major pre-Lenten celebration. An integral part of both black and white communities for more than 200 years, Carnival today knows no boundaries, as children and grandmothers, rich and poor, Indian, black, white and Creole merge in bands and at fêtes in a warm-hearted, exuberant national party.

Even a stranger is drawn in, if willing to soca and wine with the Trinis, and there is nothing that makes a Trinidadian prouder or more hospitable than a foreigner eager to immerse himself in Carnival. It is a feast for the eyes that can be thoroughly enjoyed as a spectator

sport, but for an unforgettable cultural experience you must "play mas'" – masquerade – with the locals.

Carnival is a highly organised festivity: no one just takes to the streets in last year's costume – except perhaps during Jouvert, popularly known as "joovay". There are about 15

or 20 carnival bands based in their workshop headquarters, known as mas' camps, whose sole purpose is to plan, execute and display Carnival costumes.

Called by the names of their main costume designers – Peter Minshall, Wayne Berkeley, Harts, Stephen Derek and Ivan Kallicharan are a few of the better known – or simply by the name of the carnival band (Poison, Legends, Barbarossa), these carnival bands are open to all for a price, but contain a foundation of loyal members who every year wear the costumes of their band, marching together through the streets. Each band has a king and queen representing that year's theme – Callaloo, Wonders

---

LEFT: the hard-to-miss face of a reveller.
RIGHT: a Carnival queen.

of Buccoo Reef, Rat Race, Bright Africa, Ye Saga of Merrie England and M2K are a few – and each band of 500 to 9,000 people is divided into smaller groups called sections, dressed as variations on the theme.

The best way to join a band is to know a local who will help you buy one of his band's costumes, which generally cost about US$150. If you do not know anyone in a band, check with your hotel or TIDCO (tourist office): they often reserve costumes in certain bands.

Wrongly condemned as an excuse for public drunkenness and sensuality, Carnival is, in fact, an exhibition and a competition of the best in

ical and ethnic themes require authenticity, and every idea needs multiple inspiration. Libraries, encyclopedias and the internet provide information, and are consulted for period and regional costumes. Some leaders explore the structures of the society to be portrayed, and elements of their customs and lifestyle are selected after careful consideration.

There are brainstorming meetings, supplemented by liberal supplies of food and drink, and quiet moments of introspection and imagination, yielding fantastic ideas for the drawing board. The designers then start to produce the enticing drawings displayed as adver-

music and design. Its influence is felt in the country throughout the following year.

Months in the making

Preparation for the next Carnival commences on Ash Wednesday, right after Shrove Tuesday, the last day of the current year's Carnival. Even as band leaders relax from the physical and mental exhaustion of the months before, they engage in a post mortem of the recent past. What is done is done, but of vital importance is the theme for next year. Should they play on a historical, fantastical, social, natural, traditional, or cultural one?

Subject decided, the research begins. Histor-

tisements and blueprints later on. Starting in January, the drawings are hung at the mas' camp of each band, to be gazed at and discussed by potential masqueraders.

Raw materials must be decided upon, and trips are made abroad for bulk purchases of brilliant lamés, velvets, satins, imitation fabrics of animal prints, plastic materials, beads, sequins, mirrors, rhinestones, feathers and the many other components of elaborate costume making. Several band organisers and designers choose to use local materials like wood, seeds, leaves, straw and shells, and locally manufactured cottons, wire, foam, steel, fibreglass and other articles for the construction.

Years ago, before the advent of now commonplace mechanical devices – such as plastic-moulding machines – and the numerous ready-made articles of decoration, there was the laborious task of making clay moulds for papier-mâché forms. Today this has given way to mass production of lightweight forms for head pieces and props, and of moulded parts for the bases of large costumes. The costume-making commences many months before Carnival, and each step requires ingenuity and meticulousness, as motorised. Devices such as small wheels and ball bearings placed to take the peripheral weight are used to facilitate easy carrying by the wearers.

BIKINI MAS'

Modern Carnival has seen the rise of "pretty mas'" bikini bands whose members replace traditional and elaborate costumes with adorned and decorated bikinis.

Numerous man-hours are dedicated to the production of these masterpieces *(see page 230)*, and the end result is fussed over, admired and treated just like a birth experience by those who laboured. During the first appearance on stage during the week preceding Carnival, when the costumes are judged in their categories, thousands crowd

the final result can be a complete failure if there is a lack of engineering and construction skills to turn ideas into practical reality.

For the large and often cumbersome costumes of the kings, queens and principal characters in the bands, a great deal of experience is necessary to construct one which is light, mobile and theatrically effective. Some costumes could indeed be called floats, except for the facts that they are carried by one individual and are not permitted to be pushed, pulled or

Queen's Park Savannah in Port of Spain to get a preview of the splendour of the mas'.

As the kings and queens prepare to cross the open stage in front of the grandstands crammed with party-goers, members of rival bands – aficionados not content to sit in the stands and await the presentations and the direct supporters of the contestants – crowd the holding bay where all the real-life drama takes place. Excitement mounts as they line up, and speculation as to the finalists and eventual winners runs rampant. Light-hearted banter is often exchanged, with some comments building confidence while others, even proffered in jest, make for uncertainty.

LEFT: careful preparation and attention to detail are important for the art of Carnival.
ABOVE: jumping up in glitter, feathers and beads.

The determination to win, and the excitement of living the fantasy, inspire each character to take to the stage with zest and flourish. The sight of these magnificent structures, animated by their human bearers glittering under the lights as their movements synchronise with calypso or soca is overwhelming.

On the night of Dimanche Gras, the Sunday before the actual days of Carnival, the much anticipated finals are held, and the King and Queen of Carnival are chosen amidst great fanfare and boisterous applause. The new monarchs will lead their respective bands with great pride and prestige.

Saturnalia and slaves

Carnival traces its origin to ancient times, to the Phoenician celebrations of Dionysus, god of wine, vegetation, new growth and survival, and to the Roman Saturnalias honouring the god of birth and renewal. The Latin *carne levare*, to take away flesh, is said to be the root of the word carnival, which is an orgy of the senses preceding the Lenten period in Christianity when the things of the flesh are prohibited.

While Rome ruled Europe, these pagan rituals underwent several changes in order to survive, and ended by being the exclusive province of the aristocracy. In this way, the pantheistic customs survived the rigid decrees of the Middle Ages, when all celebrations that could be termed bacchanalian or saturnalian were considered licentious abominations akin to devilry. By 1783, when Trinidad and Tobago experienced an influx of French settlers, Carnival was well established among the French as an aristocratic celebration.

With the French settlers came slaves acquired in other Caribbean islands, especially the French-speaking lands of Martinique, Guadeloupe and Haiti. The slaves brought the custom of celebrating Christmas, with a mixture of Christianity and African rites and traditions, up until Shrove Tuesday.

At first the slaves' festivals were modest, but although there was fragmentation among the slaves as a result of the variety of African "nations", the similarity of their belief systems, secret societies and rites of passage allowed for shared celebration of ancestral dramas.

The slaves' fervour in music and dancing made up for the rusticity and makeshift quality of their disguises, and they ventured outside their areas grouped in bands accompanied by *batonniers* – stick men – ritual protectors and champions of their bands. In 18th- and 19th-century Trinidad and Tobago, Carnival masquerade became an occasion where the slaves could relieve their frustration with their lot, as within the confines of Carnival they could mimic and mock the styles and habits of their masters.

Meanwhile, the grand balls of masqueing (dressing up) and revelry continued on a more sumptuous scale in the plantation houses. By the early 19th century the élite had taken their masqueing into the streets in their own fashion, travelling in carriages from estate party to estate party.

After Emancipation, the days of Carnival became days of protest as ex-slave revellers threatened the ruling class and its towns in a number of ways. The lit torches of the Canboulay procession (from the French *cannes brûlées*, burning canes) endangered the wooden buildings of Port of Spain as much as the lascivious play-acting compromised the morality of the aristocracy, and the government feared the violence of the *batonniers* who accompanied every band. Attempts were made to outlaw Carnival, but the French aristocracy, also at odds with the now-British government, intervened to protect its own right to revelry.

In the years since, each new group of immigrants has added to the festival, and old traditions – that of *jamet*, or the "underworld" carnival, of throwing powder and streamers, of Canboulay and Kalenda – have faded. The nightly parties at friends' homes have given way to enormous public fêtes, and the steel band and calypso competitions are as much a focus of attention as the masqueing. Carnival is now a thoroughly modern event, but one with a deep underpinning of history and ritual.

DUTTY MAS'

St James, Port of Spain, is the location of "dutty mas'" on joovay. People parade through the streets covered in mud. The action does not begin until around 3am.

islandwide fêtes. As the season progresses, the number and frequency of the fêtes increases: the calypso tents (Spektakula, Revue, Kaiso House and new additions like Kaiso Karavan and Maljo Kaiso) open, steelpan yards reverberate till the early hours of the morning as steel bands practise for Panorama, and carnival fever builds to a crescendo.

In the last two weeks, excitement is further fuelled by various calypso, soca, ragga soca, chutney soca and steel band competitions. The new calypsos and soca party

Fêtes and finals

Carnival officially begins at about 4am on the Monday before Shrove Tuesday, and the Sunday night before, Dimanche Gras, is one of great anticipation and revelry. Fêtes are held everywhere in Port of Spain: in private homes, hotels, bars, clubs and restaurants.

Most parties are huge, with hundreds of people dancing en masse. Though Jouvert (joovay) is the official start to Carnival, it is by no means the beginning of the fun. The Carnival season now starts on Boxing Day night with a series of

songs for the year have been introduced at shows and on the radio; by Carnival all are thoroughly familiar, and music lovers have chosen their personal favourites for the Road March (the song most played on the streets over Carnival Monday and Tuesday) and Calypso Monarch.

Starting on the Friday before Carnival, huge fêtes with live and taped music are held at the big hotels, open to all for a small entrance fee, and are as full of locals as they are of foreign guests. The pounding music begins around 5pm on both Friday and Saturday, and plays without a let-up until 3am, and with the exuberant fun of Kiddies' Carnival on Saturday, followed by

LEFT: marching with the band.
ABOVE: at "dutty mas" on joovay.

the finals of Panorama, the national steel band competition, by Sunday evening the mood is already one of joyful exhaustion.

But there is definitely something about rum punch, beer and the rhythmic soca that gives a second wind, and by midnight on Sunday the city is ready to explode. As the great countdown begins, players gather in costume at special band headquarters.

BLUE DEVILS

Blue devils run amok in Paramin on Carnival Monday. The traditional carnival character offers the opportunity to behave outrageously on the street.

Sunday night marks the formal start of Carnival proper with the extensive Dimanche Gras

many will not hear them through the din of music and shouts of laughter as players spill out into the streets, thronging behind their favourite steel band, or more traditional brass bands and drums accompanied by folk instruments.

The costumes of joovay are at once less elaborate and more satirical than the colourful masquerades of Monday and Tuesday. For joovay morning revellers don homemade costumes either satirising the political and social scene or illustrating grotesque

show at Queen's Park Savannah in Port of Spain. The show, which can run until 2am on Monday, features the finals of both the King and Queen of the Carnival bands competition and the eagerly awaited Calypso Monarch competition, in which 12 of the island's best calypsonians who have made it through the preliminary stages sing it out to partisan support.

Joovay jump-up

At around 4am, strong coffee and tea, coconut sweet bread, sandwiches and other goodies counteract the aching heads and provide sustenance for the next few hours. The cocks crow to herald the break of the day – Jouvert – but

historical figures who have been a part of Carnival since its beginnings. The music makers are more rhythmical and more primitive than the amplified electrified groups who lead mainstream Carnival, beating tin cans, brake pans and glass bottles with spoons and knives. Human rivers move slowly through the crepuscular light, jumping, gyrating and shuffling along in varying states of consciousness, all driven by the relentless drumming.

In this parade, traditionally called "Ole Mas'" (short for Old Masquerade), anything goes, as costumes are personal statements ranging from the horrendous and bizarre to the lewd and jocular. There are grown men in oversized nappies sucking babies' bottles full of rum, male politicians with a penchant for their aunts' underwear, caricatures of prominent figures and, most popular, those who have smeared their bodies with mud, paint and axle grease from head to toe. These last delight in hugging onlookers, especially those dressed in white. Some people refer to this as "dutty mas'".

Although many of the traditional costumes of sweepers, tailors, doctors and *pai banan* (banana straw) characters rarely appear in the city, some, like the pierrot grenades, are making a comeback, particularly at the Carnival Sunday traditional mas'. These familiar figures of days gone by used

Jams and judges

Around 10 or 11am the larger bands begin to converge in costume at their mas' camps to prepare for the street parade – the heart of modern Carnival. There are four judging stands throughout the city, including Independence Square and the main and final one at the Savannah, and each of the bands must pass by each judging area. Routes have been set long in advance to prevent, as far as possible, traffic jams, but the main streets are packed from noon until dusk with parading bands. The bands are simply enormous parties, led and inspired by the ear-splitting soca music coming from accompanying flatbed

to rouse sleeping families with their falsetto speeches as they rushed into open yards offering their services for a small fee. The traditional players have given way to organised bands similar to the fancy-dress bands, with well-thought-out themes and more colourful costumes than players of earlier days. The masqueraders and observers dance through the streets until morning, when it's time to get ready for the first Road March "jump up". Do try to get some sleep between 7am and 11am, because the Road March is seven or eight hours of feverish dancing and singing.

trucks full of musicians and huge speakers.

When bands cross paths there are battles, with each group of musicians trying to drown the other out with its favourite tune. Eventually one or two songs win out, and one is chosen as Road March, People's Choice. Until then a variety of songs inspires the revellers to dance for hours on end in the blistering sun.

Though Port of Spain is the centre of Carnival activity and the locus for all the big competitions, San Fernando, Chaguanas, Arouca, Arima, Scarborough and other smaller towns have their own parades and fêtes, often preferred by veterans who can no longer stomach the incessant music and crowds of Port of Spain. ❑

LEFT: a costume with an Amerindian theme.
ABOVE: masqueraders and spectators fill the streets.

LIMING AND LEISURE

The Trinidadian pastime of liming – doing nothing in particular – is as important as sports such as cricket, athletics and table tennis and the card game All Fours

In Dickens's *Pickwick Papers* Quanka Samba, a Jamaican slave, bowled himself to death on behalf of his master in a cricket match. It is unlikely that a Trinidadian would have done that. Life may be hard, but in the Trinidadian psyche it is always sweet. It is certain, though, that throughout the Caribbean slaves were often used in the game by their masters, very probably as fast bowlers.

Name any sport, apart from baseball and American football, and it is played with passion in Trinidad and Tobago, but cricket is the national sport of each West Indian island. Historians have argued that the "gay abandon" style of the Caribbean cricketer, so unlike that of the text-book correct Englishman, is a direct retaliation for the shackles of slavery. It has been suggested that when pioneers like Clifford Roach and Learie Constantine repeatedly risked getting out in an effort to hit the ball out of the ground, they were in fact hitting out "to prove they were free" and not under the control of the Englishman's approach to the game.

In spite of its origins, cricket has given the Caribbean people a sense of identity and pride. Like the calypso and the steel band, it is rooted in Trinidadian culture. It is a way of life. Surgeons have been known to take transistor radios into operating theatres during a match – there is even a story of one who, in his zeal to complete an operation to rush down to the cricket ground, inadvertently left an instrument inside his patient's stomach.

Victory over an English or Australian team at the Queen's Park Oval in Port of Spain could mean an impromptu jump up, and a soccer match can precipitate a similar Carnival-style celebration. Defeat has the reverse effect. When the West Indies were "whitewashed" (massacred 5–0) by South Africa in Africa and later by New Zealand in New Zealand, hundreds met at their "liming" spots at Pelican Inn (close to the

Trinidad Hilton) and Smokey & Bunty, a roadside bar in St James, to roast the "delinquents" of the team alive.

Trinidad became a British Colony in 1797, when a force under General Ralph Abercromby took it from the Spanish governor Don José Mariá Chacon. Before that it had been French. And while it

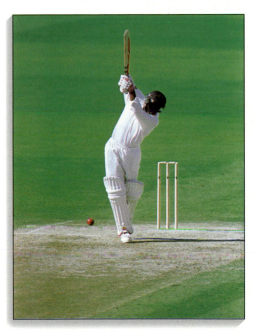

COMMANDING CRICKETER

Brian Lara ranks among the world's top batsmen. He holds the world record for the highest individual score in first-class cricket – 501 not out, amassed over seven hours 54 minutes while playing for an English team, Warwickshire, against Durham at Edgbaston in June 1994. His innings included the most runs in a day (390) and the most runs worth four or more from one innings (308) made up from 62 fours and 10 sixes.

Lara also holds the world record for the highest individual Test innings: 400 not out for the West Indies, against England at the Recreation Ground in St John's, Antigua in April 2004.

LEFT: the Trini Olympian Ato Boldon.
RIGHT: Brian Lara carries the cricketing torch into the 21st century.

was the British who introduced their favourite game (cricket) to the islanders, there have been a few who maintain that "cricket" was a derivation of an ancient French diversion called "criquet". Cricket was unknown in France while it was gaining popularity in England in the 12th and 13th century. Some historians suggest that the first reference to cricket actually did not appear until the 16th century. Nobody, it seems, knows for certain the date or place where it was first played, or how it gained its name.

Trinidad is about 80 km (50 miles) long and

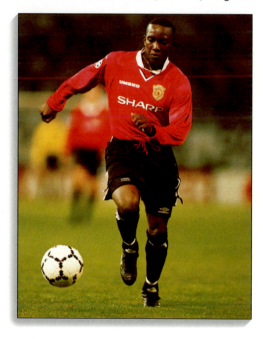

48 km (30 miles) wide; there is hardly a village or town without a cricket pitch. There is also tense rivalry among village teams and primary school, college, weekend and minor leagues.

The country has produced world-class cricketers such as Sir Learie Constantine, Clifford Roach, Jeffrey Stollmeyer and Brian Lara, all household names in the island. Lara ranks supreme in the quartet. In the eyes of the Trini the world record-holding sportsman can do no wrong, and for good reason. When he achieved the highest test cricket score of 375 in 1994, he was lauded by his countrymen who gave him a parade and gifts based on the number 375.

On the ball

While the origins of cricket are probably lost in the mists of antiquity, there is no doubt that football (soccer) was brought here by the British. The ambition of every young player is to emulate the success of the Tobago-born footballer Dwight Yorke, who was bought from Aston Villa by Manchester United for £12 million (US$18 million) and later played for Blackburn Rovers and Birmingham. Yorke is a product of the vigorous Colleges Football League, which gave birth to stars such as Russell Latapy, and internationals like Stern John, Shaka Hislop, Silvio Spann, Ansil Elcock and Arnold Dwarika.

Today the Trinidad and Tobago team is regularly ranked in the top 80 by FIFA (Fédération Internationale de Football Association), the world governing body of the sport – truly remarkable in a country with a population of just 1¼ million. The names of the top players from Brazil and Europe are always on the lips of the local soccer fans, who follow their progress match after match.

The national team competes in the hectic World Cup qualifiers. In 1989, though, Trinidad was in soccer shock. It needed only a draw to reach the World Cup finals in Italy, but hopes were dashed when it was defeated 1–0 by the US. Dozens wept openly on the streets, and the following day – already declared a public holiday, in anticipation of victory – was a day of mourning.

The Olympians

That Trinidad and Tobago with its tiny population could produce an array of awesome athletes has baffled sports officials. Its prowess was evident in the 1964 Olympic Games in Tokyo, Japan, from which it returned with four medals. Quarter miler Wendell Mottley, a Cambridge Blue, took silver in the 400 metres; Edwin Roberts was a bronze medallist in the 200 metres; and the relay quartet of Mottley, Roberts, Edwin Skinner and Kent Bernard made up the 4x400 metres relay team which finished third.

There was euphoria throughout the country in 1976 when in Montreal, Canada, the brilliant sprinter Hasely Crawford rocked the Games, clocking 10.06 seconds in the 100 metres final to win the gold medal. The National Stadium in

Port of Spain was renamed the Hasely Crawford Stadium in his honour. Several calypsos were composed to commemorate his victory; a BWIA jet was named after him; and his popularity was such that United National Congress (UNC) the political party later presented him with a house for his services to sport.

Trinidad and Tobago sprinter, Ato Boldon, retired in 2004. A 200-metre world champion, and a bronze medallist in both sprint events (100 metres and 200 metres) at the 1996 Atlanta

WINNERS

A Japanese newspaper, which compiled a computerised breakdown of medal standings compared to size of country, suggested that Trinidad and Tobago had in fact won the 1964 Tokyo Olympics.

Ray Robinson, Muhammad Ali, Archie Moore, "Jersey" Joe Walcott, Rocky Marciano, Gene Tunney, Joe Frazier and Evander Holyfield have visited the island. Two World champions, lightweight Claude Noel and light heavyweight Leslie "Tiger" Stewart, have emerged from local boxing clubs. Trinidadian fighters such as Yolande Pompey, who fought from his London base for two decades, Matt Donovan, Fitzroy Guisseppi and Nick Rupa have challenged for world titles.

Olympics, US-based Boldon was born in the valley of Santa Cruz, 13 km (8 miles) from Port of Spain. He completed more sub-10-second runs than any other sprinter in modern history. The nation's contribution to track athletics continues with Darrel Brown, the World Junior 100 metres record holder in 2003, and Marc Burns.

Stars of the ring

Boxing has a high profile in the local sporting landscape. Great fighters like Joe Louis, Sugar

Only in Trinidad & Tobago

The truth is that there is a sport in Trinidad and Tobago for everybody. The range is enormous: from the goat and crab races in Tobago, to the annual 127-km (79-mile) powerboat classic – known as the Great Race (from Port of Spain, Trinidad to Store Bay, Tobago) – to race walking.

Though tennis is widely played on public courts, with regular age group zonal and open tournaments, it is table tennis that is the more popular game. Although fans are waning as a result of expensive hi-tech equipment used to speed up the game and make it more exciting. In fact the game is now so fast that spectators – especially TV viewers – cannot see the ball and

LEFT: Dwight Yorke.
ABOVE: Trinidadian football fans show their support for the national team at a match in St James.

therefore find it hard to follow the game. It is also a difficult sport to play. The introduction of bigger balls aimed at slowing down the speed of the game should create more interest.

Sport for all

Canada-based Stephen Ames registered his first American PGA tour victory in 2004, winning in a field that included Tiger Woods. This success catapulted the San Fernando-born golfer to 18th in the world rankings.

Though there are approximately 8,000 golfers and four golf courses on the island, it is argued in some quarters that golf is an élitist

key to longevity and maintaining a vibrant youthful appearance. There is standing room only in gyms in the afternoon, especially around the Carnival season. Scant attention is paid to rest and proper diet as a result of the belief in "a regular good sweat".

Wappie

Trinidad and Tobago has also created its own little world of sport – games which will not be found in any booklet. Number one is Wappie, an addictive indoor gambling game, which started during World War II (1939–45) when the Yankees were flaunting their money.

game for white men. Ironically, more black than white people play it.

Basketball is played year-round and with intensity. Top players dream of becoming a Michael Jordan, a Scottie Pippen or a Magic Johnson. The bad news is that all the visiting American coaches have warned that the fast-food diet and the size of the average Trini – well under two metres (barely 6ft) – are not conducive to the rigours of the NBA.

Sports such as aerobics, weightlifting, karate, swimming and women's boxing are becoming increasingly popular. It is widely believed that a good sweat – achieved via walking, jogging, aerobics and even swimming – could be the

Wappie is based on sheer luck. All the gambler has to do is pick a card, invest anything from TT$1 up and hope that the chosen card turns up. The *casa* (house) is always the big winner since it starts with nothing and keeps on raking in 25 cents in house tax from each dollar on all the night's takings.

Addicted wappie players, and there are thousands, have been known to wager their pay packets on one night of heavy playing. Rules are strict and intense. To minimise the chance of cheating, cards are changed regularly and shuffled and reshuffled. This has not, however, prevented a string of brutal murders over the years as a result of arguments over the gaming tables.

The novice, unaware of the dirty tricks, could lose almost all the time. Unscrupulous wappie players have been caught marking cards with blood – deliberately puncturing their hands with a pin or scratching them with their fingernails.

Three-card game

Another game considered to be a rip-off, which has fooled many tourists, is the three-card game played on street corners. Roaming the city with a cardboard box and a pack of cards, hustlers run the game which tempts onlookers

A CONTACT SPORT

Rugby is developing into a major sport on the island. There are regular matches in Port of Spain at Queen's Park Savannah and the President's Grounds in St Ann's.

All Fours

All Fours is considered the most popular of all Trinidadian games. It is a corruption of the ancient Indian card game *toroop chaal* (meaning to pull from one's hand and play in four). In a way it is similar to bridge. It is played wherever and whenever Trinis converge for a "lime and ole talk" – at a wake, or even at a Test cricket match. The game creates friendships and brings people closer through healthy rivalry. More than 50,000 people play it at weekends.

with the prospect of making quick cash. Three cards, usually a two, a jack and an ace, are placed on top of a box. The headman begins to switch the three cards around, before dropping and promising to double up to the person who finds the jack, while two associates are on the lookout for the police.

Once the slightest interest is shown, the casual spectator is cajoled into taking a chance. The chances of winning are nil, since the jack is palmed at the last second or switched with blinding hand speed.

Chinese traditions

If you are walking around town and hear an incessant sound, "pax, pax, pax" – like objects smashing on marbled tables – from any one of the Chinese Association buildings, it will be dozens of Chinese businessmen indulging in their favourite gambling games of *pai kow* and *mah-jong*. The playing tiles used are almost identical to those used in dominoes.

Thousands of dollars change hands as stern-faced Chinese men sip tea and soup while engrossed for hours. There are stories told about men who have been known to lose not only their homes, cars and businesses over a game of *pai kow*, but also their wives. ❑

LEFT: gaming tables at the "Sunday School" beach party, Tobago. **ABOVE:** *mah-jong* is a Chinese import.

ABOVE AND BELOW THE WATER

*The islands have abundant birds, butterflies, wildlife and marine life,
combining the best of both the Caribbean and neighbouring South America*

Its native Indian inhabitants called it Ieri, "Land of the Hummingbird", and even today Trinidad and Tobago is home to about 15 different species of these brilliant fluttering creatures, among over 420 species of bird. There are also 617 species of butterfly, and a wealth of flora and fauna matched only by the South American continent itself.

Unlike other Caribbean islands, which are volcanic in origin, as recently as 11,000 years ago Trinidad and Tobago were a part of the coast of Venezuela. Thus, despite their small sizes, the two islands are graced with a diversity of environment which includes four mountain ranges, four major rivers, mangrove swamps, tropical savannahs and numerous streams and small rivers, plus a marine environment influenced by Venezuela's Orinoco River as well as the Atlantic and Caribbean.

The rich rainforest

The Northern Range of Trinidad is only minutes away from the centre of Port of Spain, yet is almost primeval in its unspoiled richness of life *(see page 235)*. In the dry season, December to March, the cultivated valleys and slopes glow with the deep orange blossoms of the tall mountain immortelle tree, *erythrina micropteryx*, introduced to the islands over 150 years ago as shade for cocoa and coffee trees.

At the end of the dry season, around the beginning of April, the yellow poui tree blooms spectacularly, its leaves dropping to present the yellow flowers in solitary splendour. It is a popular belief that the rains arrive with the third burst of blooms.

In the early months of the year, when forest trees are in flower, honeycreepers and hummingbirds, as well as other nectar feeders, are visible in profusion. This is nesting time for many of these birds. With the coming of the rains in April and May, bringing the seeding of

the numerous grasses, finches and other seed-eaters bring forth their young while there is an abundance of food.

In August the hundreds of butterflies that have lain dormant during the dry season emerge to paint the islands in vibrant colours. In short, there is no bad time for nature-watching in

Trinidad and Tobago, and every season offers its particular beauties and wonders.

Victorian nature retreat

There is perhaps no better place to begin than at the Asa Wright Nature Centre and Lodge *(see page 248)*, in the Northern Range's Arima Valley 370 metres (1,200 ft) above sea level. The winding, mountainous drive from Port of Spain to the Asa Wright Centre climbs through a tropical rain forest which has several tiers of lush vegetation.

The uppermost tier is that of the spreading branches of trees growing up to 50 metres (160 ft). Orchids, bromeliads called "wild pines"

LEFT: oilbirds roosting in a Northern Range cave.
RIGHT: a mountain immortelle in the Northern Range is garlanded with epiphytes.

and liana vines grow in profusion on their trunks and limbs, even on telephone wires. Various species of fern, heliconia and philodendrons are common below, and huge stands of bamboo and small mossy waterfalls line the road.

Along the way are glimpses of sliding-roofed sheds used for drying cocoa and coffee on the big estates; Asa Wright was originally a private cocoa, coffee and citrus plantation, and is surrounded by working estates.

The centre still retains the aura of a civilised country retreat. At the end of a bumpy drive is the "Great House" or lodge, constructed in 1906–1908 as a Victorian estate house, and

were being hosts to visiting naturalists and bird-watchers who wished to take advantage of the rich flora and fauna of the valley.

Among these early visitors was Donald Eckelberry, an American bird artist and naturalist who came to paint the species of the Arima Valley. It was Eckelberry who, after the death of Dr Wright, persuaded his widow Asa to sell the property in order that a non-profit-making trust might be established to preserve that part of the valley in perpetuity as a conservation, study and recreation area.

And thus in October 1967 the Asa Wright Nature Centre, the first of its kind in the

perched over a forest valley alive with birds and butterflies.

After the turn of the century the 80-hectare (200-acre) estate changed hands a couple of times, ending up in 1947 in the possession of Dr Newcome Wright and his Icelandic-born wife Asa, who came to Trinidad from England.

In 1950 Dr William Beebe, a famous explorer and naturalist, established the Tropical Research Station of the New York Zoological Society in the Arima Valley, close to the Wrights' property. Dr Beebe and many of the research staff at Simla, as it was called after a sister station in India, became friends with the Wrights, and it was not long before the latter

Caribbean, was established. Following the closing of Simla in 1970, the New York Zoological Society passed its property – 93 hectares (230 acres) and several small buildings – to the Asa Wright Centre as a gift. Today researchers and students of natural history are housed at Simla, while amateur naturalists can stay in the colonial comfort of the Great House and enjoy nature hikes guided by experts.

Little devils of eternal darkness

One of the most renowned species to be observed at Asa Wright is the *steatornis caripensis*, the nocturnal oilbird. In hiking distance of the world's most accessible colony of these birds, Asa Wright offers a rare opportunity to see them in their strange natural habitat.

Guacharos – "he who cries", to the Spanish-speaking people of South America – oilbirds are known in French *patois* as *diablotins*, or "little devils", and Jon Lindblad, the famous nature photographer, described them as "the bird of eternal darkness". The medium-brown oilbird can be as much as 38 cm (15 inches) long, with a wing span of 1 metre (3 ft), and lives deep in caves, leaving only at night to forage for food

PROTECTING THE OILBIRD

Dunston Cave at the Asa Wright Nature Centre is a breeding colony of the nocturnal oilbird. In its protected environment the rare birds' numbers remain stable.

oil, which never went rancid – hence the name. They ate the flesh and used the oil for lamps and torches.

In Trinidad there are eight known nesting colonies of oilbirds: some in the limestone caves of the Northern Range, and some on Huevos, an offshore island. The colony at Asa Wright increased from 22 birds in 1967 to 170 in 1980, but after that there was some migration to a more remote cave. In December 1985, during the annual Christmas bird count, only 48 birds

in the forest. The only known nocturnal fruit-eating birds, oilbirds prefer the fruit of the palm, laurel and incense trees, which they pull off in flight.

The young birds become very fat on this diet, and at about 70 days are approximately 1 kg (2 lbs), one and a half times the weight of the adult bird. The Amerindians and other inhabitants of the Caribbean chose this time – mid June – to collect the fat young nestlings, which they then boiled and rendered for their

were recorded at the cave near the Centre. However, after limits were placed on the number of visitors to the interior of the cave, the population stabilised at about 100 birds in 1989, gradually increasing to 142 adult birds and 33 chicks by the summer of 1999. A cave about 16 km (10 miles) east of the Arima Valley, at Cumaca, also supports a large colony.

High-level birds

For a chance to see such birds as the yellow-legged thrush, the nightingale thrush and the blue-capped tanager, which only appear at elevations above 650 metres (2,000 ft), the intrepid must make an all-day trip to the heights

LEFT: the tangled roots of mangrove trees in Nariva Swamp, near Manzanilla.
ABOVE: scarlet ibises roosting at dusk, Caroni Swamp.

of Aripo, slightly south and east of Asa Wright. With luck, you might also see a pawi or piping guan, a bird endemic to Trinidad and Tobago but very rarely seen even here.

A less strenuous trip is one to the Aripo Savannah and the Arima Forest, which may provide sightings of up to 70 species. A short stop at the government cattle farm on the road to the savannah can yield a glimpse of the savannah hawk, the southern lapwing and flocks of jacanas. In the savannah are many colourful and easily

FOREST FRUIT

The papaya sits at the top of a palm-like trunk, in a cluster of large green fruit from which extend deeply lobed leaves at the end of long stems. It looks a little like a windmill.

spotted species, including red-bellied macaws and orange-winged parrots which feed on the fruit of the moriche palms growing abundantly at the fringes of the grasslands. The drooping fronds of that palm also provide a home for the uncommon fork-tailed palm swift; and during the rainy season the rare white-tailed golden-throated hummingbird may be found nesting in the shrubbery of the savannah.

The area is interesting for its plant life as well. Sundew, or *drossera capilaris*, a kind of Venus-flytrap, covers the surface of the grasslands, waiting for insects upon which to feed. These plants have little competition here because a layer of impervious clay just beneath the surface keeps the soil very dry in the dry season and water-logged when the rains come. Because the soil is therefore very poor in nutrients, many of the plants found there must capture insects for food.

Flying sunset

Another fertile area for bird-watching is the Caroni Swamp Bird Sanctuary, just South of Port of Spain, where the white, red and black mangrove trees sink their spidery support roots into the brackish water. The entire swamp comprises over 4,800 hectares (12,000 acres) of mangrove forests, tidal lagoons and marshlands which are subject to daily tidal fluctuations. It is here that the beautiful scarlet ibis, one of Trinidad and Tobago's national birds, makes its home.

In flocks that number up to 100, the scarlet birds which Trinidadians call flamingos fly in from all directions and perch on the top branches of the mangrove islands. During the rainy season as many as 12,000 birds will arrive in the twilight hours, but in the earlier part of the year there are fewer, as most migrate to the mainland to nest.

While you are waiting to see the birds you might want to let down a line, as the swamp waters are thick with fish, including tarpon, grouper, snook, salmon and mangrove snapper; 45-kg (100-lb) groupers are not a rarity. The blue crabs often used in *callaloo*, a popular souplike dish, and in curried crab and dumplings, traditional in Tobago, are also caught in the mangrove swamps of both

TWITCHER'S TIPS

Trinidad and Tobago are good places to see a rich variety of birds; there is something for everyone, from the beginner to the experienced birder. It is easy to combine a few days' bird-watching with time spent exploring Trinidad's lush forests or relaxing on Tobago's beaches. There are many places to choose from, including Mount St Benedict, the Caroni Swamp, the mudflats around Waterloo and the northern hill area surrounding the Asa Wright Nature Centre. Also worth an excursion are Little Tobago and Buccoo; the latter is also ideal for diving.

Essential items to pack include binoculars, a field guide and a notebook.

islands. During their egg-laying season hundreds of crabs leave the mangroves and appear to "run" to the sea to release their eggs.

Tobago's tropical pheasant

For most of Trinidad and Tobago's wildlife, life has not changed for thousands of years. This was the case with the cocrico, or rufous-vented chachalaca, a turkey or pheasant-like bird indigenous to Tobago and one of the republic's national birds. But Hurricane Flora struck Tobago in September 1963, inflicting severe damage on the elevated forests. With their original habitats destroyed, many birds and beasts,

of cheese from the fingers of visitors as well.

The verandah of the Grafton Great House became a popular rendezvous for visitors to Tobago, who joined the birds at teatime. Nowhere else could cocricos, motmots, red-crowned woodpeckers, blue-gray tanagers and many more species be seen and photographed at such short range and such leisure. Since the death of Mrs Alefounder the great house has fallen into disrepair and the bird feedings have been reduced becoming less of a tradition. Today the grand property is known as the Grafton Caledonia Sanctuary, and it is still possible to see a goodly number of birds hovering around the estate.

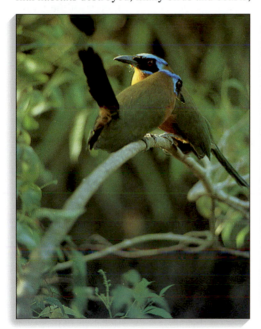

including the cocrico, had to seek food in the lowlands close to human areas of habitation.

Aware of the birds' predicament, Eleanor Alefounder, the owner of the 160-hectare (400-acre) Grafton Estate on Tobago's north shore, along with a number of other residents, began to feed the birds regularly. By 1970 the cocricos at the Grafton feeding tables were so tame that they could be fed from the hand, and in a short while, racquet-tailed blue-crowned motmots began to swoop from their perches to take bits

Sea birds and sanctuaries

In 1968 Charles Turpin, the proprietor of Charlotteville Estate in northeast Tobago, presented a group of islands known as the Melvilles to the Government of Trinidad and Tobago for the establishment of a wildlife sanctuary. The largest of these islands, which are situated about a kilometre (half a mile) off the northeast coast of Tobago, is the 30-hectare (72-acre) St Giles Island. Thick masses of cacti, low shrubs and deciduous trees cover the steep slopes which rise from the water to a height of 107 metres (350 ft).

Largely because of their inaccessibility to humans and animals, these islands are able to

LEFT: the cocrico.
ABOVE LEFT: the blue-crowned motmot.
ABOVE RIGHT: a purple honeycreeper at feeding time.

Local Flora

It would be virtually impossible to list all the species of plant and tree the visiting naturalist is likely to see while on a tour through the Trinidad and Tobago, and even the simple beach-loving traveller is certain to notice dozens of colourful and fragrant tropical plants. But certain ones crop up over and over again, either for their ubiquity or for their beauty, and the following is a list of some of those species, with a brief, unscientific description of each, designed to make it easy to name those trees and shrubs the visitors notice.

COCONUT PALMS

The groves of tall, graceful palms with smooth trunks and fronds emanating in a circle from the top which line the beaches of Trinidad and Tobago are money-spinning coconut palms.

ROYAL PALMS

Similar to the common coconut trees, but their trunks are white and tend to be straight, and with a few feet of green trunk below the frond ball at the top.

BANANA PALMS

The banana tree is not really a palm but rather the largest member of the herb family. Low, squat plants about 2 metres (6 ft) high, banana trees are also planted in groves, though not usually along the beach. They look like miniature palm trees, with trunks with thick pieces of peeling bark, and wide flat fronds whose edges look as though they have been ripped, unevenly, by hand. There are numerous groves on the Arnos Vale Road towards Les Coteaux and near the Turtle Beach Hotel, both in Tobago.

TRAVELLER'S PALM

A grey trunk holds long stems standing straight up and ending in regular fronds. It grows two-dimensionally, and looks like a wonderfully huge fan.

ALMOND

On resort beaches you will notice low trees with dark green rubbery circular leaves, often trained into umbrella shapes. These are almond trees, though not the kind that produce nuts – their fruit just looks like almonds. The flat leaves turn red before they fall, and the branches grow horizontally from the trunk.

BANYAN

The banyan is hard to mistake; its enormous trunk looks like hundreds of woody vines growing down from the upper branches.

BREADFRUIT

This evergreen tree has dark glossy leaves with deep lobes, and its round fruits are yellowish and covered with small pointed bumps. The breadnut tree can be distinguished by its fruit, which is similar but covered with sharp points.

COCOA

With their deep red pods and ovoid leaves in various shades of green, these low trees have a bush look. They grow in groves, and are often shaded by the rusty-blossomed immortelle. There are numerous groves in the Northern Range, and one small one on the path to the King's Bay waterfall in Tobago.

FLAMBOYANT

This umbrella-shaped tree is covered all over with bright red flowers from February to August, or even longer. It can be distinguished from the immortelle because it retains its leaves when it is in flower.

MANGO

Tall and glossy, it has slender, waxy dark-green leaves. The fruits are purply-brown and round, and are ripe from March to October. When broken, the leaves smell like turpentine. ❑

support one of the most important seabird breeding grounds in the southern West Indies. Noddy terns, brown boobies, the beautiful red-billed white tropic birds, red-footed boobies, magnificent frigate birds and other species feed and nest on the rocky shores.

Little Tobago, or Bird of Paradise Island, is another fertile place for bird-watchers, situated about one mile off the northeast coast of Tobago near the village of Speyside. In 1909 Sir William Ingram, a former owner of the island, became concerned about the threat

ACCIDENTAL TOURISTS

The Venezuelan coastguard patrols the country's territorial waters around Soldado rock and has arrested uninvited guests, so beware if you go fishing there.

nature photographer an opportunity to see at least 58 other species, including brown boobies, brown noddies, sooty and bridled terns, laughing gulls, Audubon shearwaters and red-billed tropic birds.

From March to July, sooty terns and brown noddies nest in considerable numbers on the 1-hectare (2-acre) rock called Soldado. Ten kilometres (6 miles) west of the extreme western point of Trinidad, only 11 km (7 miles) from Venezuela, Soldado was declared a sanctuary in 1934. Brown pelicans, royal terns, sandwich

posed to birds of paradise in their native New Guinea by trade in their plumes, and so he arranged to have 48 greater birds of paradise captured in the Aru Islands, off the coast of New Guinea, and released on Little Tobago. The birds and their new home, were presented to the government by Sir William Ingram's heirs in 1928 as a sanctuary.

Hurricane Flora ravished this smaller island as well, and since then there has been a constant decline in the number of birds of paradise. Nevertheless Little Tobago offers the naturalist and

A GILDED CAGE

In rural areas it is not uncommon to see birds in cages hanging from the eaves of houses during the hunting season. Songbirds especially are enticed into cages with decoys and "laglue" or "laglee", a honey-like substance made from the sap of the breadfruit tree.

As a result, there has been a steady decline in the islands' songbird population, and the twa-twa, or large-billed seed finch, the chickichong, or lesser seed finch, and the Tobago picoplat, or variable seedeater, are in great peril. Yet Trinidad and Tobago still ranks among the world's top bird-watching destinations because of its rich birdlife.

LEFT: cocoa pods.
ABOVE: a tufted coquette hummingbird sipping nectar.

terns and brown boobies are also to be found there, attracted by the abundant fish around the island. Boats may be hired for fishing around Soldado, but take care not to pass the rock and go into Venezuela's territorial waters.

Elusive forest dwellers

The forests of Trinidad and Tobago also abound in mammals, the most beautiful of which is arguably the ocelot, *felis pardalis*. Although fully protected by law, ocelots are often shot by farmers who consider them pests, and consequently are confined to forested areas, and rarely seen.

Below the water

The swamps, rivers and streams of Trinidad and Tobago support over 70 species of fish. Perhaps the most familiar is *Lebistes reticulatus*, or the guppy. Locals called the prolific wild guppies "millions": they appear everywhere, even in roadside drains, and provide the welcome service of eating mosquitoes. Selective breeding has also produced the beautiful delta-tailed varieties so popular for aquariums.

Many streams and rivers are replete with the South American plated catfish, *hoplosternum littorale*, dubbed cascadura or cascadoo. It is considered a delicacy despite its external

Relatively more common are brocket deer, white-collared peccary or quenk, tattoo or nine-banded armadillo, manicou or opossum, and two members of the rodent family – the agouti and the lappe or paca.

Aficionados maintain packs of well-trained beagle hounds to hunt with, but mongrels can be trained too. Though protected by law, manicou, tamandua, ocelot and other mammals are much sought-after by gourmets and are sold for as much as twice the price of the best tenderloin steak. From October to March these delicacies are all in season; they can only be hunted with a permit. Hiking in the forest reserves is another good way to see wild animals.

covering of bony plates, and legend has it that anyone who eats of the cascadoo will eventually return to Trinidad.

Another common freshwater fish is *tilapia mossambica*, a species of the cichlid family, which was imported from Africa with a view to being farmed in ponds and rice paddies. While experiments were being conducted in the government fish farms at Valsayn, several slippery specimens escaped into the nearby St Joseph River and found their way to Caroni Swamp.

Now, more than 35 years later, *tilapia* is so plentiful in the shallower parts of the swamp that it has become a popular sport to catch up to

1-kg (1–1½lb) fish with bare hands. Unfortunately, however, *tilapia* has destroyed the feeding grounds of the thousands of migratory ducks which used to visit Trinidad every year.

But the swamp still provides much food for man and beast. Tree oysters, sold on the street in oyster cocktails, grow on the roots of the red mangrove, just below high water mark. Embedded in the muddy bottom one can find Trinidad's indigenous mussels, which, steamed in garlic sauce, make their way onto the menus

DIVING

Tobago has some of the best dive sites: Arnos Vale has a rich eel population, and Buccoo Reef, a protected marine park, is a favourite of snorkellers.

any major coral growth on Trinidad's coast. Tobago, on the other hand, is relatively free from the Orinoco's influence, and its marine fauna are more like those of an oceanic island.

Reef life

The turquoise waters of Buccoo Reef lie just off the southwestern corner of Tobago. A fringing reef made up primarily of stag and elkhorn coral, Buccoo swarms with electric-coloured French angels, grunts, trigger, butterfly, surgeon and parrot fish, all of

of local restaurants. And although manatee are not common, a boat trip up the Ortoire or into Nariva Swamp may provide sightings of these charmingly ugly sea mammals.

Rarer still are the otters which live in the Paria and Madamas rivers on Trinidad's north coast. These rivers teem with life and, through the swamps, affect the life in the ocean as well.

But the river that most greatly affects Trinidad's marine life is the Orinoco in Venezuela. Its fresh, turbid floodwaters prevent

which are accustomed enough to snorkellers to remain unconcerned with their investigations. The Buccoo Reef ecosystem is complex, and includes not only the reef crest and flats, where the tourist boats anchor, but also the Nylon Pool, an area where the white sand of broken coral fragments has settled into an offshore sandbar, creating a swimming-pool-like area. The mangrove-fringed Bon Accord Lagoon, which is home to the vohites or cone shells so prized by collectors, serves as the nursery for many of the reef-dwelling fish.

Buccoo Reef and the Nylon Pool first gained popularity as sister attractions during World War II (1939–45) after Dillon and Cecil

LEFT: a rock beauty underwater.
ABOVE: a leatherback turtle lays its eggs on the beach while observers look on, a bit too closely.

Anthony, two Buccoo village residents, located the more beautiful areas and identified the channels which led to the reef crest. But over the years the popularity of the area has resulted in serious destruction of the coral heads; boats, anchors, people walking on the coral heads and the removal of the corals, conch, lobsters and fish by visitors and boatmen have all contributed to the reef's demise.

Under the Marine Preservation Act, Buccoo was declared a protected area, but unfortunately this legislation is not as strictly enforced as it could be. The destruction continues and has resulted in a reef which is a poor cousin to the

less spoiled environments of some other Caribbean tourist islands.

A deep area of the reef called the Marine Gardens is still undamaged and supports a variety of coral formations. It is alive with star, fire, brain, staghorn, elkhorn and soft corals, as well as sea fans, sea ferns and sea whips. This area and the less popular reefs of Tobago's northeast coast can provide a memorable experience for the scuba diver, protected as they are from the heavier waves of visitors. Professional Association of Diving Instructors (PADI) certified instructors are available to conduct tours, and can be found through the major hotels.

Tobago also provides variety in abundance

for the fisherman. Spanish mackerel, locally known as carite, is the most abundant fish food, with king mackerel and red snapper present in lesser numbers. Crevalle and bluefish, or ancho, are plentiful during their breeding season, as is albacore.

Professional fishing expeditions will supply comfortable motorboats, rods and reels, and knowledgeable guides at a price. The impecunious might try to persuade a local fisherman to take them out some early morning, for a fraction of the cost. Tobagonian fisherman, though, tend to use small outboard motorboats and heavy handlines with massive hooks, but they can read the waters as if their lives depended on it. And they often do.

On Turtle Beach

Perhaps the most mysterious marine phenomenon is the nesting ritual of the leatherback turtle. This is the largest – up to about 2 metres long (6 ft 6 ins) and weighing up to 544 kg (1,200 lbs) – of the five species of sea turtle (of seven in the world) which nest on the beaches of Trinidad and Tobago. The green, the loggerhead, the hawksbill and the Olive Ridley turtle – the smallest, at around 1 metre (3 ft) – all also visit the beaches at Matura on the east coast of Trinidad, and Toco, Tacarib and Las Cuevas on the north coast; on Tobago they are at Courland (or Turtle), Grafton, Bloody, Speyside and Charlotteville bays. The leatherback females climb up on the beach to lay anything from 100 to 150 eggs at a time. They dig relatively deep holes, lay the eggs within and cover them with sand, and then return to the sea to continue their annual far-flung migrations, sometimes swimming as far as Australia. The turtles do not seem concerned about the humans who observe them at their labours.

Legislation protects turtles during their nesting season, from March to July, but from September to February, when they are at sea, the season is open, and turtle steak is a delicacy and local favourite. Each year since 1965 the Trinidad and Tobago Field Naturalists' Club has organised regular night trips to see the turtles nesting. Inquire at your hotel reception or the tourist information office about how to join one of these trips. ❑

LEFT: a crab blends into the coral polyps.
RIGHT: a scuba diver encounters a scorpion fish.

THE SISTER ISLANDS

A detailed guide to Trinidad and Tobago, with principal sites
clearly cross-referenced by number to the maps

Trinidad and Tobago is like one of those married couples one sometimes meets where the spouses are so different from one another as to be almost incompatible, but who in successfully joining so many opposing qualities create a union that is unusually dynamic and all-encompassing. Within this small country are the cosmopolitan enticements of one of the most fascinating and sophisticated cities in the Caribbean and the serenity of a pastoral tropical island; the exuberant bacchanalia of Carnival and the quiet of deserted beaches; the wildlife of a mainland jungle and the beauties of a Caribbean coral reef; East Indians and Africans, Europeans and Asians; a tumultuous past and a wealthy and literate present; the elegance of international hotels and the intimacy of seaside bungalows.

In short, there are the worldliness, ethnicity, industry and commerce of Trinidad and the friendliness, languor, natural beauty and beaches of Tobago.

The travel section that follows has been divided into six chapters that tour Trinidad: Port of Spain, the Northern Range, Chaguaramas Peninsula, Northwest Peninsula, Central Trinidad, the South; and two on Tobago. The most rewarding visit would include a bit of each island. Many visitors come to Port of Spain first, so our tour begins there, with a short history of Port of Spain and how the city grew as well as an introduction to major sites and excitements. The capital offers a bustling, colourful cross-section of the history, culture and population of the whole country.

Next, a series of trips, starting from Port of Spain, provides a more in-depth look at a nation unique in its geography and combination of cultural influences. Indian towns of sugar-cane farmers and Creole fishing villages, mangrove swamps and mountain savannahs, the heavy industries and the balmy beaches offer everything a visitor could want.

Tobago is a perfect foil for the complications of Trinidad. It is more typically Caribbean, or at least more what vacationers have come to expect: endless sun, clear blue sea and sparkling sands. Many Trinidadians holiday there after the exhaustion of Carnival. In Tobago you can do nothing or a little bit of something, but you can't help but relax.

Finally, one of the country's primary natural resources and attractions is its people. Outgoing and sincerely friendly, Trinidadians are notoriously talkative, and their eagerness to make friends turns a sightseeing trip into a cultural introduction. And once you've been introduced, don't be surprised if you fall in love. ❏

PRECEDING PAGES: tie-dye and palm trees at Pigeon Point, Tobago; Paramin musicians entertain; Port of Spain and the Gulf of Paria from Fort George.
LEFT: relaxing at Pigeon Point, Tobago.

WELCOME TO TRINIDAD

The larger of the two islands has a modern capital, outside of which are country hamlets and rugged mountains

While Port of Spain is the administrative and tourist hub of Trinidad, much of the country's character and wealth emanate from its provincial towns, industries and countryside. It would be difficult to get a true picture of Trinidad without visiting some of the rest of the island: the sharp cliffs of the north coast and flat palm-fringed beaches of the east, the Caroni Swamp and Bird Sanctuary and mountain rainforests, the 44-hectare (109-acre) Pitch Lake and oil and sugar industries of the south are all as essential to Trinidad and Tobago as Carnival, calypso and steel band.

Trinidad, the most southernly of the Caribbean islands, is just 11 km (7 miles) off the coast of Venezuela, across the Gulf of Paria, and lies 10 degrees north of the Equator. Its size – 4,828 sq. km (1,864 sq. miles) – makes it very accessible by car.

You can tour the island by driving yourself or hiring a car with driver, and taxi drivers who serve the major hotels are often glad to sign on for a day's tour, providing an insider's view of the sights. Even the furthest points are only three hours or so from Port of Spain, and a number of tours can be made in a half-day, if necessary. Primary roads are in excellent condition – though often crowded – and even secondary roads tend to be easily negotiable, if a little bumpy. However, there are still some areas that are not easy to access and may require an experienced local driver.

Since most visitors to Trinidad stay in Port of Spain, this section is organised as a series of day (or two- or three-day) trips most often starting in Port of Spain, unless otherwise stated. When heading out of the capital be aware that all tours begin from Stollmeyer's Castle, west on Queen's Park Savannah.

If you want to tour the island from coast to coast, stopping off here and there for a bite to eat or to overnight, then each chapter provides a self-contained tour pointing out the historical sites, the hot spots at Carnival time and after, and also the tranquil getaway-from-it all places. ❑

LEFT: Trinidad's highway system.

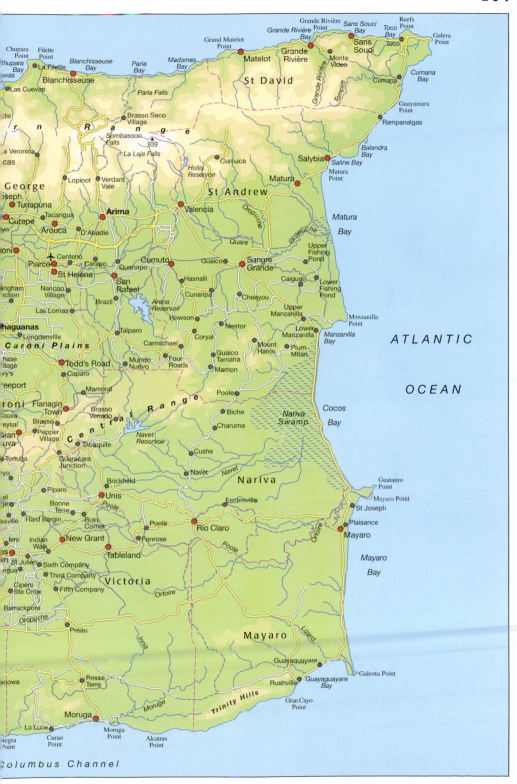

St David

St Andrew

George

ATLANTIC

OCEAN

Central Range

Caroni Plains

Nariva Swamp

Cocos Bay

Mayaro Bay

Matura Bay

Victoria

Nariva

Mayaro

Trinity Hills

Columbus Channel

Chupara Point
Filette Point
La Filette
Blanchisseuse Bay
Blanchisseuse
Las Cuevas
Chupara Point
evas
La Veronica
cas

Paria Bay
Madamas Bay
Paria Falls
Brasso Seco Village
Sombasson Falls
▲939
La Laja Falls
Hollis Reservoir
Cumaca

Grand Matelot Point
Matelot
Grande Rivière
Monte Video
Grande Rivière Point
Grande Rivière Bay
Sans Souci Bay
Sans Souci
Toco Bay
Toco
Reefs Point
Galera Point

Cumana
Cumana Bay
Guayamara Point
Rampanalgas
Balandra Bay

Salybia
Saline Bay
Matura
Matura Point

Lopinot
Verdant Vale
Joseph
Tunapuna
Tacarigua
Curepe
Arouca
D'Abadie
Centeno
Carapo
Piarco
St Helena
Guanapo
San Rafael
Nancoo Village
Brazil
Las Lomas
Arena Reservoir
Howson
Coryal
Nestor

Arima
Valencia
Quare
Oropuche
Cumuto
Guaico
Sangre Grande
Hasnalli
Cunaripa
Cheeyou
Caigual
Oropuche

Matura Bay

Upper Fishing Pond
Lower Fishing Pond
Upper Manzanilla
Lower Manzanilla
Manzanilla Bay
Manzanilla Point

haguanas
hase
illage
ry's
reepot
Todd's Road
Caparo
Mamoral
Flanagin Town
Brasso
Pepper Village
Brasso Venado
Tabaquite
Guaracara Junction
Mundo Nuevo
Four Roads
Carmichael
Talparo
Guaico Tamana
Mamon
Mount Harris
Plum Mitan
Lower Manzanilla

roni
ouva
eysal
ran
uva
Tortuga
yo

Navet Reservoir
Navet
Cushe
Navet
Brickfield
Poole
Biche
Charuma

Piparo
Bonne Terre
Hard Bargin
Busy Corner
Unis
Poole
Ecclesville
Poole
Fonrose
Rio Claro
Poole
Guatauro Point
Mayaro Point
St Joseph
Plaisance
Mayaro

el
je
asville
iere
St Julien
igua
New Grant
Indian Walk
Tableland
Sixth Company
Third Company
Fifth Company
Cipero
Ste Croix
Barrackpore
Oropuche
idowa
Preau

Ortoire
Ortoire

Innis
Rasso Terre
Moruga
La Lune
Moruga
Moruga Point
Curao Point
Alcatras Point
Negra
Point

Guayaguayare
Rushville
Guayaguayare Bay
Gran Cayo Point
Galeota Point

A COLOURFUL CAPITAL

*Port of Spain is a city that pulsates with life. The friendly banter
and vibrant music on the busy streets reach a crescendo at Carnival.
In contrast, the wide-open parks offer a peaceful haven*

Map
on page
207

Sprawling eastward from the Gulf of Paria, for the past two centuries **Port of Spain** has been spreading itself freely, nestling into the curves of the Northern Range which rises immediately behind it. In the rainy season the verdant foliage of these hills, that stretch from east to west across the island, crowns the city with an emerald coronet studded with the brilliant red of the flamboyant flowers and the gold of the yellow poui tree. In the dry season, as the sun dazzles against galvanised roofs and concrete buildings, Port of Spain is as brown and crisp as toast, its hills at times alive with brushfires that ignite and explode the bamboo and turn the undergrowth into black soot.

Nature, however, is on the city's side. The rainy season lasts much longer than the dry, and it takes only a few showers to effect a miraculous change from brown to green. Port of Spain is almost always green, its many parks and gardens living testimony of a tropical land on which nature has bestowed its bounty.

The lush and decaying confusion of the surrounding hills has a subtle correspondence in the nature of the city. The streets of Port of Spain are well laid out, but there the orderliness ends – it is in many respects an unruly place, a characteristic deriving from its peculiar history. Port of Spain became the capital of Trinidad and Tobago almost by accident, a fact that gave it a sort of frontier beginning, as people of different races and cultures flocked here seeking new horizons.

The Spanish choose a new capital

In 1757 Puerto de España was a mere fishing village of mud huts and a few wooden thatched-roof houses, surrounded by hills and swamps. Its residents then were mainly Amerindian and Spanish mestizos, most of whom earned their livelihood by fishing and occasional trade with the Venezuelan mainland. It was hardly an appropriate choice for a governor's residence, particularly a Spanish governor representing the grandees of his country.

Since the 16th century the capital had been St Joseph *(see page 242)*, 19 km (12 miles) inland. Surrounded by cocoa and sugar estates, St Joseph was often affected by various tropical diseases and, in the mid-18th century, by a serious shortage of workers. But as Trinidad had neither gold nor silver, it was of little interest to the authorities in Spain, and they allowed the capital to go to rack and ruin. The situation was such that when in 1757 a new governor, Don Pedro de la Moneda, arrived he found his house uninhabitable, and no money for repairs.

So he decided to set up residence elsewhere. Being a seaport, Port of Spain had a definite advantage. The *cabildo* (council) resisted the move, but Governor de la Moneda ignored it and rented a small house in the

LEFT: festival fever.
BELOW: tropical fruit
and veg for sale.

The red, green and gold colours symbolising Rastafarianism are evident everywhere in the city.

vicinity of present-day Piccadilly Street. Eventually the cabildo followed him to Port of Spain, which then consisted of only Nelson Street and Duncan Street, and was surrounded by mangrove swamps, hills and high woods.

Around 1780 the arrival of the French started an agrarian revolution, giving rise to commerce and trade, which in turn made expansion of the city inevitable and urgent. The surrounding mangrove swamps were filled in, land was reclaimed from the sea, and woods were cut down to make room for more streets.

An important diversion

In 1787 the last Spanish governor before the British took over, Don José María Chacon (after whom Trinidad and Tobago's national flower, the chaconia, is named), facilitated the city's expansion by solving a problem of flooding: the Río Santa Ana (St Ann's River) then ran from the hills in the north through the area now known as St Ann's and straight through the centre of Port of Spain, its course travelling along what is now Woodford Square, down Chacon Street and Independence Square to the sea. During the rainy season, the growing population suffered the effects of regular flooding, so Chacon diverted the river to run along the foot of the Laventille Hills and to the sea that way. The old river bed was filled in, and the city continued to develop.

Within a few years Port of Spain had grown to 11 streets, seven running from south to north – Duncan, Nelson, George, Charlotte, Henry, Frederick and Chacon – and four from east to west – King, Queen, Prince and Duke. Around the same time, with the demands of a burgeoning population, the city began to spread towards the valleys and slopes of what are now the suburbs of Belmont, Laventille, St Ann's, St James and Maraval.

BELOW: an old plan of the capital.

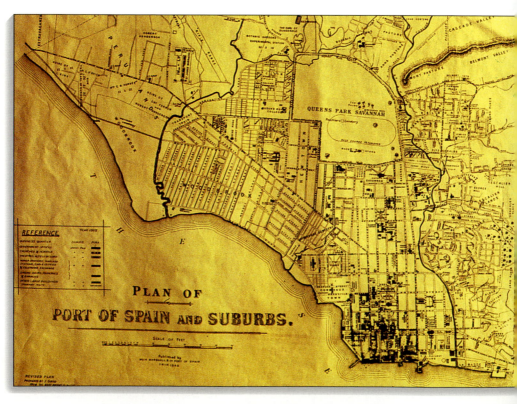

PLAN OF
PORT OF SPAIN AND SUBURBS.

The extent of Port of Spain's spread across the hills of the Northern Range is obvious today, particularly when darkness falls. Then the city is illuminated by twinkling lights from houses stretching from Laventille in the east, beyond the boundaries of Port of Spain proper to the western districts of Carenage and Diego Martin. Many of these present-day hill residents are immigrants who came from neighbouring islands and began squatting here, much as the earlier inhabitants had. To a large extent, though, the crudely constructed wooden huts have been replaced by more solid concrete buildings, and to the west the many hill dwellers are wealthy citizens who have built themselves mansions with views. And it is a breathtaking view of a city at once international, modern, provincial and seedy: both an old colonial town and the capital of one of the most progressive nations in the Caribbean.

An architectural mélange

Today Port of Spain is a city of modern skyscrapers, old-fashioned gingerbread houses, neo-Gothic cathedrals, Hindu temples and Muslim mosques, all existing happily side by side. There are modern apartments, department stores, oriental bazaars, cinemas, Indian, Creole, Chinese, French and Italian restaurants, and sports bars. It is a city of informal malls and pavement stalls blaring calypso and soca music, where vendors weave through traffic selling nuts, and carts peddle coconut water, chicken and chips, Chinese fried rice and Indian *roti*. It is a city of men with Rasta locks in brightly coloured woollen hats, burning incense and selling home-made jewellery. It is also a city of stray dogs and vagrants.

The latest figures show that half of the country's population of 1¼ million lives in what is known as the east-west corridor, which stretches straight across the

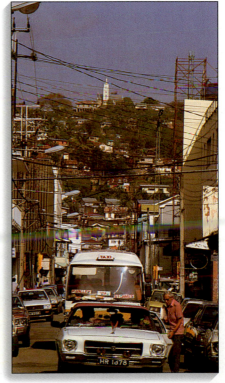

LEFT:
modern designs.
RIGHT:
view of Our Lady of
Laventille Shrine
from Duke Street.

Map on page 207

foothills of the Northern Range, from Chaguaramas in the west and eastwards to Arima. A great percentage of this half is centred in Port of Spain itself and its surrounding districts.

A melting pot

As the inner city developed into a business and administrative centre, the majority of people have settled in the outlying suburbs of Laventille, Belmont, Woodbrook, New Town, St Clair, St James, Cascade, St Ann's, Federation Park and Maraval.

More than anywhere else in the Caribbean, the capital shows evidence of the great and unusual variety of races, religions and cultures that make up the country. In a lunch-hour "lime" *(see below)* in the centre, a panorama of race walks by: people from west, central and east Europe, from Africa and India, Asia and the Middle East. Intermarriage has brought variations on the theme, and this blending of races is endemic to Port of Spain. A serendipitous side effect is some of the loveliest women and handsomest men in the Caribbean.

As the city centre is usually crowded during the day with office workers, shoppers, limers and traffic, it is perhaps better to park at one of the car parks and walk around. Route taxis to any suburb are very easy to hire.

Stylish Port of Spain

In such a cosmopolitan city, residents are accustomed to a wide choice of modern goods. It is a fashion-conscious city, as a result of the money flying around during the oil boom of the 1970s and early 1980s, and weekend shopping trips to Miami, Curaçao and Caracas have become the norm, as have holidays to New York, Toronto and London. In these days of free markets, with a floating exchange rate and no restrictions on imports, the range of goods available to the consumer in Trinidad is even greater now, although the shopping trips are still popular.

A great inspiration to style is the Port of Spain pastime of "liming": shooting

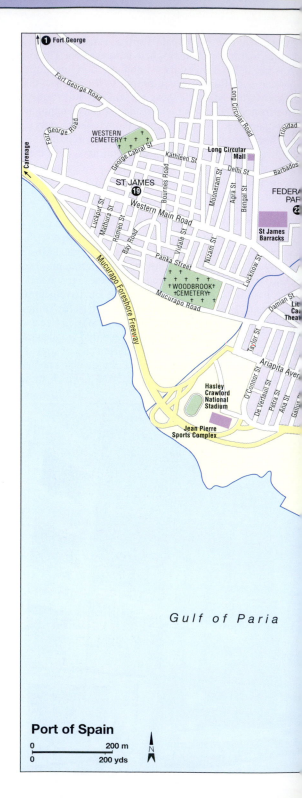

Maraval

ST ANN'S
26

Prime Minister's
Residence
Normandie
Hotel

CASCADE
25

BOTANIC
GARDENS
11

Cascade Road

Lady Young Road

Emperor
Valley Zoo
12

President's
House

WILD FLOWER
PARK

HOLLOWS
ROCK GARDEN

Circular Road

Queen's
Hall

Pelican
Inn

Belmont Valley Road

Stollmeyer's Castle
13

Whitehall
14

Hilton
Hotel

Lady Young Road

Layan Hill

Jackson
Square

Archbishop's House
15

Belmont Circular Road

ST CLAIR
24

Roomor
16

QUEEN'S PARK

Mille Fleurs
Hayes Court

Hayes Street

SAVANNAH

Archer St

Cadiz Road

Norfolk St

Pelham St

St Francois Valley Road

Queens Royal
College
17

Meyler St

St Clair Avenue

Queen's Park

10

BELMONT
18

St Barbs Road

Sweet Briar Rd

Harts Mas
Camp

Alcazar St

Jerningham Ave

101 Tragarete Rd
Art Gallery

Marli St

All Saints
Church

Tragarete Road

Queen's Park West

Hermitage Road

Quarry Circular Road

DBROOK

NEW TOWN
23

Knowsley House

MEMORIAL
PARK

Oxford St

National Museum
& Art Gallery
9

Wayne Berkeley
Mas Camp

Keate Street

Belgrade St

Laventille Road

Fort Chacon

3

Gordon Street

Lord
Harris
Square

New Street

Observatory Street

Plaisance Quarry Road

Mas Camp
Pub

The Mas
Factory

LAPEYROUSE
CEMETERY

Park Street

LAVENTILLE
20

Fort Picton
2

Mahatma
Ghandi
Square

Duke Street

City
Hall

Lodge Place

Victoria
Square

National
Library

Knox St
Woodford
Square
7

Prince St

Nelson St

Riverside
Plaza

8

Red
House

Picton Road

Sackville Street

Trinity
Cathedral

Queen St

People's Mall

King's Wharf

Cruise Ship
Complex

Independence Square North

Brian Lara Promenade
5

Independence Square South

Columbus
Square

Cathedral of
the Immaculate
Conception
6

Financial
Complex

Tower

South Quay

Central
Market

Fort
San Andres

City
Gate
4

Queen's Wharf

Beetham Highway

El Socorro

the breeze on street corners, outside cinemas and bars, appreciating the minu-tiae of daily life. These days the pace of city life has quickened: around Brian Lara Promenade you will be treated to a selection of pirated music thanks to young men selling bootleg cassettes and CDs and advertising their wares at full volume. The attitude is aggressive, borrowing from the Jamaican "Rudeboy" culture, but it is mostly show. Rarely are there any incidents in the city, but caution should be exercised there, as anywhere else.

An irritating aspect of Trinidadian culture will assert itself almost immedi-ately if you are a woman walking through the city. Trinidadian men, especially those who spend a good deal of their time in the streets, think it is their duty to heckle women and inform them of their prowess in manly matters. Sometimes it is amusing, sometimes graphic, but it is more annoying than dangerous; smile sweetly if you are so inclined and walk on, as stopping to argue is a waste of time.

The **City Gate**, a transportation hub, is about 90 metres (100 yds) to the south of the Promenade, and you can get buses and maxi-taxis (minibuses) to any part of the island from here. This has eased congestion, but there has been a dras-tic increase in the number of cars in recent years, so lower Port of Spain is always lively. There are taxi stands here from which route taxis will take passengers to any part of north west. *(See the Tip opposite and Travel Tips on page 348 for more taxi information.)*

Fabulous forts

For a panorama that challenges the beauty of the population, the hills of the North-ern Range surrounding Port of Spain offer an excellent vantage point from which to get a sense of the sweep and size of the capital. Four forts define the original

All PTSC buses start from City Gate, although they are not always reliable.

BELOW: view of Fort George above the Gulf of Paria.

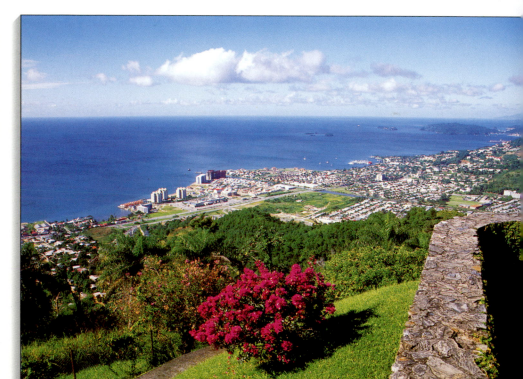

Map
on page
207

boundaries, and two, Fort George and Fort Picton, afford particularly good views.

Fort George ❶ is situated in the hills overlooking St James, northwest of the city. To get there take Tragarete Road, which runs into the Western Main Road after the Roxy Roundabout, and at the Cocorite Junction turn right to reach Fort George Road. The winding, bumpy road climbs uphill steadily for about 3 km (2 miles). In some places it is so narrow that only one car can pass, but there is not much traffic.

Fort George was built by Governor Sir Thomas Hislop in 1805, eight years after the island had been conquered by the British. Fears continued that the Spaniards would try to retake Trinidad, and war had just broken out between Britain and its arch-enemy France. Hislop knew that the French fleet was in the Caribbean, and built the fort within shooting distance of the Gulf of Paria.

The fort has been well renovated, and one can see the original dungeons, cannon balls and implements used by the soldiers. Above all, it has a breathtaking view of Port of Spain and far out to sea. Also at the fort is a **Signal Station** designed by Prince Kofi Nti, son of King Kofi Calcali of Ashanti, West Africa.

Fort Picton ❷, in the hills of Laventille southwest of the city, is one of the oldest fortifications in Trinidad. To get there take the Eastern Main Road to Picton Hill Road. Picton *(see page 30)* was a member of Sir Ralph Abercromby's victorious expedition in 1797 in which Trinidad passed from Spanish to British rule. Abercromby left Picton in charge as governor, and he built the fort to protect shipping in the harbour as well as the small settlement of Port of Spain.

A little further on from Fort Picton are the fenced-off ruins of **Fort Chacon ❸** – a misnomer, since it was more of an observatory than a fort. It was from here that the astronomer Don Cosmo Damien Churruca fixed an accurate meridian

TIP

Taxis for St Ann's and St James are south of Woodford Square; for Diego Martin, on South Quay; for Carenage, on the corner of St Vincent and Park streets; for Maraval, on Duke and Charlotte streets, and for Laventille and forts, on Prince Street.

BELOW: strategically positioned and sturdy: Fort Picton.

Port of Spain's lighthouse was originally built to keep boats away from the rocks, but owing to land reclamation it is now stranded – and leaning slightly – on an island surrounded by concrete in the middle of Wrightson Road, behind City Gate.

in the New World in 1792: hence the name Observatory Street for the road that runs from the site.

Fort San Andres ❹, built in 1887, is an innocuous looking building located on South Quay, overlooking the sea, but is a good example of a Spanish wooden fortification. There are murmurs of making it into a museum, but it is used as an art gallery at the moment, and has recently been restored. The gates are open only if an art exhibition is being held.

A classic way to view the city is from the sea, or at least from the seaside, down along the docks of the port to the west of Brian Lara Promenade. From this vantage point the white ziggurat of the National Library, the tinted glass of the Issa Nicholas skyscraper, the twin towers of the Financial Complex, the revolving Crowne Plaza Hotel sky restaurant, the slim chimneys of PowerGen Electricity Company and the hood-shaped roofs of the National Stadium stand out from an ocean of red and green roofs of smaller businesses and homes, punctuated by treetops and the mountains behind.

Creating a working harbour

Until the mid-1930s, **King's Wharf** had no facilities for docking deep draught ships. Cargo and passengers were off-loaded as the ships lay at anchor, and were brought by launches to the docks. In 1935 work began on a deepwater harbour with an expanded quay frontage which was created by building up almost 162 hectares (400 acres) of the shore with the earth that was dredged out.

Today the harbour handles an annual average of 1½ million tonnes of cargo. Several cruise ships dock at the **Cruise Ship Complex** on their journeys through the Caribbean, and the ferry for Tobago also leaves from here, but overall the

BELOW: the Financial Complex reaches for the sky.

port is an industrial forest of cranes and not picturesque at all. In the high season about 10 ships per week stop off for a day or so, and in the off season perhaps one. Then the duty-free shops in the complex open, and an expensive craft market materialises, only to close down again when the ships sail on.

To return to Brian Lara Promenade you cross **Wrightson Road**, which stretches from west to east in a straight line. A section of this road was known during World War II as the "Gaza Strip". Numerous notorious nightclubs, which were frequented by US servicemen stationed at naval and other bases in Trinidad at the time, were located along here, and part of the evening's entertainment usually included a raid by the vice squad and the arrest of striptease dancers. Now the nightclubs are gone, and the Gaza Strip is a respectable part of the road.

A cricketing tribute

A pleasant place to sit in the shade of the trees, **Brian Lara Promenade** ❺, down the centre of Independence Square, was named after the world-class Trinidadian cricketer when he broke the record for the number of runs in a single innings in 1994. The promenade was laid out on reclaimed swampland in 1816 by Baron Shack, who planted it with trees imported from Venezuela. Really an avenue of trees with double traffic lanes on either side, this area has been

Map on page 207

ne holder of many titles. It was originally known as King Street, later changed o Marine Square and then became Independence Square in 1962, when Trinidad nd Tobago ended colonial rule. The promenade has been landscaped with seats nd tables for games of chess and dominoes, and a stage has been installed for ree concerts during festivals. Stalls and street food vendors are kept busy in the venings as more and more people choose to meet here after work.

In the centre of the square stands a life-size statue of Captain Arthur Andrew Cipriani *(see page 50)*, the country's first national hero, mayor of the city for nany years, a member of the Legislative Council – a forerunner of today's Par-ament – and a defender of workers' rights. Cipriani campaigned as early as 914 for unity in the West Indies, self-government, an end to child labour on the ugar cane fields and compulsory education. He died in Port of Spain in 1945 nd is buried at Lapeyrouse cemetery in Woodbrook.

Along the southern side of the square are some of the most important build-gs in the country, notably the **Financial Complex** and the TSTT building, its adio antennae proclaiming its function, as well as the offices of the media ompany, the Caribbean Communications Network (CCN) and banks. The strik-ng twin towers of the Financial Complex appear on the newer Trinidad and obago currency notes – appropriately, as the complex houses the Central Bank f Trinidad and Tobago and the Ministry of Finance. Designed by a Trinidad rchitectural firm at a cost of TT$400 million, it opened in March 1985. The two 2-storey towers, the highest in the country, are clad in solar-insulated glass trong enough to withstand earthquakes, and inside the walls are decorated with vorks by local artists and sculptors. While excavating the site before building the omplex, the diggers revealed many exciting archaeological remains, including

Taxis to St James run regularly from Independence Square.

BELOW: a statue of the heroic Captain Cipriani.

*Hand-made leather
sandals – made to
your own design if
you prefer – and
Rastafarian arts and
crafts can be bought
east of Captain
Arthur Cipriani's
statue on Brian Lara
Promenade.*

the old sea wall, ships' anchors, cannon balls and some Amerindian pottery

On the northern side of Independence Square stand the large Treasury Build ing, which was the previous home of the Central Bank, and the head office o Customs and Excise, as well as more banks and other offices.

Governor Woodford – a man with insight

The Roman Catholic **Cathedral of the Immaculate Conception** ❻ sits in the cen tre of the eastern end of the promenade, and is one of two imposing neo-Gothi cathedrals erected through the enterprise of Governor Sir Ralph Woodford (1813–28). From the time of his arrival, in 1813, Governor Woodford began t make improvements in the city, which had been mostly destroyed in the grea fire of 1808. A man with insight, he recognised that a city was not only a col lection of large buildings and streets, commercial and residential houses, but als a place that needed open spaces where people could enjoy leisure time. Queen' Park Savannah *(see page 218)*, the green heart of the capital, was developed a a result of Woodford's initiative, along with a number of other parks and squares

Woodford was an Anglican, but, for historical reasons dating back to the tim of Spanish rule, many state occasions were marked by services in the Roma Catholic church, at the time a small and unremarkable structure. Woodford con sidered that Port of Spain should have cathedrals in keeping with the status o a growing capital, and so in March 1816 he laid the foundation stone for th Cathedral of the Immaculate Conception. Designed in the shape of a Lati cross, it is built of blue metal stone from the Laventille quarries.

It took 16 years to build owing to a shortage of funds and delays with mate rials from abroad, such as the iron framework from England and the Florentin

BELOW: Cathedral of the Immaculate Conception.

marble used for the high altar and the communion rail. But once completed, the new cathedral was able to accommodate 1,200 worshippers at the first service on 1 April 1832. At that time the sea came right up to its eastern wall.

In 1984 the cathedral underwent extensive renovations, and 16 stained-glass windows from Ireland were added, along with a set of Italian marble Stations of the Cross. One of the magnificent stained-glass windows depicts the apparition of the Blessed Virgin at Lourdes in France. The other windows portray children of Trinidad and Tobago, representing the various ethnic groups that make up the population of the country. The inner pillars were also adorned with heraldic shields of the archdiocesan and national coats of arms, as well as the coat of arms of the city of Port of Spain and those of the various religious orders of nuns and priests who have worked here.

Immediately behind the cathedral a statue of Christopher Columbus stands in **Columbus Square**. Beyond is Piccadilly Street, running alongside St Ann's River, where Port of Spain began, and where today stands the imposing **Riverside Plaza**, which houses government ministries and departments. Back in Independence Square in front of the cathedral you could stop for lunch at one of the many Chinese and Indian restaurants that cater to the thousands of people working in the city.

A bustling thoroughfare

The intersection of **Frederick Street**, the main shopping boulevard, and Independence Square, where the statue of Captain Cipriani stands, is an excellent point to set out northwards on a tour of the city, keeping the Northern Range in view as a reference point. Frederick Street is a bustling thoroughfare of shops, malls and street vendors selling everything from clothes to home-made jewellery. More international shops are springing up, and the department stores have been making way for malls like Colsort and Excellent City Centre.

The **People's Mall**, a dense warren of vendors' huts on the corner of Frederick and Queen streets, burnt down in 2005, instantly ending the life of businesses. However, there is talk of rebuilding in the future. The site was originally a large variety store destroyed by fire many years ago, and individual vendors who previously sold from suitcases and barrows on the pavements around the city were relocated to this spot.

The mall was once the centre of the "suitcase trade" – when imports were severely restricted, prohibited shoes and clothing were brought in suitcases and sold at exorbitant prices – but import rules have long disappeared, and with it the mall's niche.

For visitors interested in Rasta jewellery, local craftwork and imported clothing, there's a mall on the southeast side of Independence Square, and the small variety stores on Charlotte Street are ideal for bargain hunters.

On the block north of Queen Street is the multistorey National Library, which opened in 2003, it was designed by the local firm of architects Colin Laird and Associates. Internet-ready with computers available to the public, the library offers all citizens, including school children, 21st-century resources.

Map on page 207

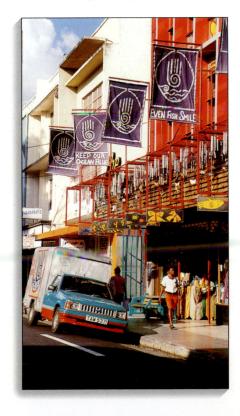

BELOW: busy Frederick Street.

The national flag flies high above the coat of arms.

BELOW: cast-iron water fountain in Woodford Square.

Woodford Square – a political hub

Halfway up Frederick Street lies **Woodford Square ❼**. Sir Ralph Woodford laid out the large square in the heart of the city and named it Brunswick Square; it was changed to its present name after his death in 1828. Woodford planted the area with many trees, which continue to provide beauty and shade today. The fetchingly painted cast-iron water fountain supported by mermaids and mermen was a gift to the city in 1866 from the local merchant George Turnbull.

A focal point of life in Port of Spain, Woodford Square provides a thoroughfare between the east and west sections of the city as well as a meeting place and forum for all sorts of people. Baptist preachers with lighted candles ring bells, would-be politicians harangue all comers, and at almost any hour of the day small groups can be found vigorously debating religion, politics and sport. Even before the square was created, the area was a hub of the city: after the great fire of 1808 the homeless were accommodated in tents here. Later that year, following a slave uprising on one of the sugar-cane estates, the leaders of the rebellion were hanged here, and their bodies left on display as a deterrent to others.

Right through the 20th century the square was the scene of much political activity. In 1903 a mammoth protest meeting against new water rates took place here, developing into a riot which cost 17 lives when the crowd surrounded the Red House, the seat of government, and burnt it down. And in 1956, at the birth of the national independence movement, the square was unofficially renamed the University of Woodford Square because of the lectures delivered here by Dr Eric Williams (*see pages 60–61*).

In the 1970s it was again a political focal point, this time of a Black Power prising, when the square was referred to as the People's Parliament. The largest uneral ever seen in the city, for a member of the Black Power movement shot y police, took place here in 1970.

On the south side of the square sits the Anglican **Cathedral of the Holy Trinity**, which owes its existence to Governor Woodford. The original church vas destroyed in the 1808 fire and rebuilding of the present one began in 1816, ight in the middle of the square. However, the local residents protested at its osition, and Woodford stopped construction and laid a new cornerstone at the resent site. The roof of Holy Trinity is copied from London's Westminster Iall, and is supported by hammer beams of mahogany carved in England. There re six stained-glass windows, and inside stands a marble figure of Sir Ralph.

he Red House of Parliament

'o the west of the cathedral stands the unmissable **Red House** ❽, where Parliament sits. It got its colourful name in 1897 when the original building was given a coat of red paint in preparation for the diamond jubilee of Queen Victoria. After it was burnt down during the water riots, rebuilding began soon fterwards, in 1904, and it was up and running again in 1907. The next time the Red House came under attack was in 1990, this time from a rebel Muslim group, he Jamaat-al-Muslimeen, in an attempt to unseat the then prime minister, A.N.R. Robinson. An eternal flame, on the Abercromby Street side of the Red Iouse, commemorates the 24 victims of the coup. West along Sackville Street re the Police Headquarters, across the road from the ruins of the Old Police Station, which the Muslimeen rebels fire-bombed during their insurrection.

TIP

The Friday afternoon parliament session is open to the public from 1.30pm; enter via Knox Street.

LEFT: the Victorian façade of the Red House. **RIGHT:** the old-time cost of birth, death and marriage.

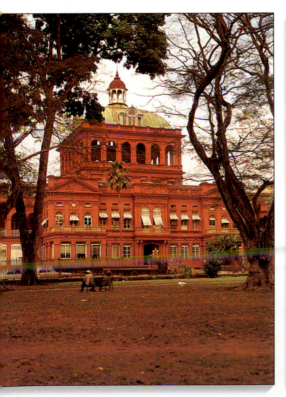

The **City Hall** at the corner of Frederick Street and Knox Street, on the nort side of the square, is the administrative heart of the capital. The present build ing was opened in 1961, replacing the original town hall destroyed by fire in th 1940s. The front is decorated with a mural entitled *Conquerabia*, the Amerindia name for Port of Spain. The mayor, aldermen and city councillors all have thei offices here, along with a large auditorium for lectures, plays and other function

A missionary remembered

Next to the City Hall is the century-old **National Heritage Public Library**, buil in 1900, and behind that the small **church of St John the Baptist**, built in 185 by George Sherman Cowan, a missionary sent to Trinidad from England b the Lady Mico Charity to provide education for the children of former slaves

Cowan arrived in 1840, shortly after Emancipation, and this small church wit a flat triangular-shaped façade of natural stone and two small turrets is a memo rial of his work. One of its walls is the last remaining relic of the old Spanis cabildo building, forerunner of today's City Council. An outstanding feature is beautiful stained-glass window, a replica of Holman Hunt's *The Light of the Worl*

Across Pembroke Street the **Hall of Justice**, which opened in Decembe 1985, takes up the entire block and fronts onto Woodford Square. To select it design a competition was held among local architects, but none of the submis sions achieved the desired effect of a modern building that blended with the Vic torian architecture of the Red House and the Cathedral of the Holy Trinity. I the end a design by Anthony Lewis Associates (who also designed the Financia Complex) came closest to the concept and, working in collaboration with British firm of architects, they created the existing building.

BELOW: some cheerful city youngsters.

Map on page 207

Traditional values

Northwards along Pembroke Street are several very old buildings, of various architectural styles, standing side by side with modern buildings. Further up the street is the country's first secondary school, **St Joseph's Convent**, which celebrated its 150th anniversary in 1986. The school was run by St Joseph de Cluny nuns, who came to Trinidad from France in 1835. The original French nuns were succeeded by Irish sisters, and control has now passed to Trinidadians. Today the convent is one of the leading girls' schools in the country.

Opposite looms **St Mary's College**, a successful boys' school, which was established in 1863 by the Holy Ghost Fathers of Ireland. The school has several prominent former pupils, including the first president of the Republic, Sir Ellis Clarke.

Pembroke Street ends at Keate Street, where a right turn brings you to the **National Museum and Art Gallery ❾** (open Mon–Fri 10am–6pm, Sat 10am–3pm, Sunday 2–6pm; free). It was built as a science and art museum in 1892, to commemorate the jubilee of Queen Victoria, and was then called the Victoria Institute. Destroyed by fire in 1920, it was rebuilt three years later. The National Museum houses a disparate collection of Amerindian artefacts, an exhibition of the petroleum industry in Trinidad, lithographs and paintings of old Port of Spain by Jean Michel Cazabon, alongside the work of contemporary Trinidadian artists *(see page 115)* and internationally acclaimed ones such as Carlisle Chang, Leroy Clarke, Dermot Lousion, Ralph and Vera Baney and Nina Squires. The **Museum Annex** has been opened to the public only recently, and art and photography exhibitions, the occasional literary reading, and lectures are sometimes held here in the evenings. Across from the museum is the

The history of the steel pan and its music is charted in the National Museum and Art Gallery in Keate Street.

BELOW: the rambling National Museum and Art Gallery.

At the Emperor Valley Zoo the animals live in an environment as close as possible to their natural habitats.

BELOW:
taking a break
on the Savannah.

Memorial Park, with a cenotaph in memory of the Trinidadian servicemen who died in World Wars I and II. The park is planted with many beautiful flowering trees such as the red flamboyant and the yellow, pink and purple poui.

On the corner of Keate and Abercromby streets is **Zen**, a hot nightclub and sushi restaurant, which is also a venue for live Soca and visiting dancehall acts.

Gorgeous Queen's Park Savannah

Of all the parks in the city, the most beautiful is **Queen's Park Savannah** ❿, across from the north end of Memorial Park. The Savannah and its surroundings, which include the Botanic Gardens and the Emperor Valley Zoo to the north, are in many ways the city's centre.

In the early days Queen's Park Savannah was part of a sugar plantation known as St Ann's Estate, and belonged to the Peschier family. In 1817 Governor Woodford bought 94 hectares (232 acres) of it for the city. The Peschiers' small family cemetery in the middle of the Savannah was enclosed by a high wall, with arrangements that it remained their responsibility, and today it is still used by their descendants. To begin with, the Savannah was mainly used as pastureland for cows, but was also a place where the public could stroll and play games among the many beautiful samaan trees.

In 1890 attempts were made to use part of the Savannah for housing. This was vigorously opposed by city residents, as have been all similar attempts over the years to reduce the size of the park for one reason or another. The most recent was the successful tarmacing of a section of the turf in 1999. The deed drew immediate condemnation and protests from a good section of the population, but the hard surface remains.

The dominating species of tree in the Savannah is the samaan, which spreads out like a giant umbrella. There are also some beautiful yellow poui trees and flaming flamboyants around the 3.5-km (2-mile) perimeter of the park. Horse-racing has been relocated to Arima in the east. However, the grandstand remains and is used for cultural events, such as large-scale concerts and shows.

The grandstand's most popular use is in February, when various events and competitions of Carnival culminate in a week-long series of shows on its huge stage. On Carnival Monday and Tuesday the bands pass across the stage in a few minutes of abandon that thousands of masquerade players look forward to every year. During Carnival the park is ringed with makeshift food and beverage stalls, and everyone in the city seems to be liming in the park or attending the shows.

The Botanic Gardens

The northern end of the Savannah forms a natural declivity which has been converted into a rock garden known as the **Hollows** and is landscaped with shrubs and flowers around small fishponds. Across the road is the **Botanic Gardens** ⓫ (open daily, free), laid out in 1820 by Governor Woodford and David Lockhart, the first curator, who lies buried in the small cemetery in the gardens. Called "God's Acre", the cemetery is a final resting place for many former governors, including Sir Solomon Hochoy, the first Governor-General of an independent Trinidad and Tobago.

The gardens flourish over undulating land, and the collection of native and imported trees is extremely impressive. Trinidadians have created their own sobriquets for the flora. There is, for example, a tree known as "Raw Beef" owing to a reddish sap that flows when the bark is cut. A fence had to be

Map on page 207

BELOW: a samaan tree is reflected in a pond in the Hollows.

*Hummingbirds are
lured to the sweet
honey-flavoured
liquid left for them in
brightly coloured
plastic feeders.*

LEFT: corn on
the cob for sale
on the Savannah.
RIGHT: red and
yellow canna in the
Botanic Gardens.

erected around it to protect it from visitors who wanted to keep cutting the bark to witness this strange phenomenon for themselves. The "Hat Stand" tree has branches reminiscent of an old-fashioned hat stand, and the "Boot Lace" tree is so called because its flowers and fruit hang down from stems that are sometimes as long as 900 cm (3 ft). There are also many beautiful specimens of palms, and a tree called "Napoleon's Hat" because its flowers have three corner points. All the plants are labelled with their botanical names and, Trinidadians often offer their services as unofficial guides for a small fee.

Both the president of the Republic of Trinidad and Tobago and the prime minister have the good fortune to have their official residences in these beautiful surroundings. The president's house dates back to 1875, and is clearly visible from the walkways in the gardens and from the road, but the prime minister's residence, built in the 1960s, is hidden from view; it can only really be seen from the back of the Hilton Hotel.

The nearby **Emperor Valley Zoo ⓬** (open daily, last ticket at 5.30pm; entrance fee), in the southwestern corner of the gardens, was established in 1952, and is today the best zoo in the Caribbean. It houses both native and foreign animals, birds, reptiles and fish, and includes Trinidad's beautiful wild deer, plus a collection of tropical snakes.

At night, mobile food vendors gather around the periphery of the Savannah, selling various snacks, such as corn on the cob, either roasted over a charcoal grill or boiled in spicy stock with salted meat; or oysters in the shell, which are cracked open expertly and doused with peppery condiments while you wait. Vendors with trucks laden with green coconuts, still in bunches, do a good business selling delicious and refreshing coconut water.

The Magnificent Seven

The buildings that surround the Savannah are remarkable, their architecture ranging from a Scottish castle to a Moorish house. They offer a fascinating cross-section of cultural influences and prevailing fashions in the 19th century. On Maraval Road are seven of these amazing buildings, known as the **Magnificent Seven**. Six were built in 1904 at a time when cocoa was king and there were many wealthy estate owners in Trinidad. The seventh, Hayes Court, dates from 1910. The mansions are in various states of repair, and none is open to the public without arrangement with the owner. For a look at the exteriors, a good starting point is the St Clair Roundabout at the northwestern end of the Savannah.

As you stand on the "Pitch", the walkway around the periphery, the first is **Stollmeyer's Castle 13**, also known as Killarney. A copy of Balmoral Castle in Scotland, it was built by the Scottish architect Robert Giles for the Stollmeyer family, who were estate owners and whose home it was until the government bought it in 1979. Constructed in imported brick, the house is trimmed with local limestone. The interior panelling is of local woods, and the floors are of Guyana purpleheart, as are the beautiful staircase, with its harp-like design on the landing, and the elegant balustrade of the minstrel gallery. A spiral staircase leads to a typically Scottish-looking tower.

The second magnificent building is **Whitehall 14**, Venetian in style, and undergoing major refurbishment. It was home to a wealthy cocoa estate owner, J.L. Agostini, who had Barbados coral brought by sloop to be cut locally. After Agostini's death his widow sold it to Robert Henderson, who took up residence there with his family. It was the Hendersons who gave the house its name. At the beginning of World War II Whitehall was commandeered by the US Armed

Map on page 207

"A German built a bit of an untypical Scottish castle in Trinidad and called it by an Irish name. He must have been by that time a Trinidadian, because only Trinidadians do these things."
–JOHN NEWEL LEWIS, architectural historian, on Killarney.

BELOW: Stollmeyer's Castle, one of the Magnificent Seven.

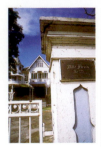

Mille Fleurs is on Maraval Road.

BELOW: beautiful Hayes Court is the home of the head of the Anglican Church in Trinidad.

Forces in Trinidad, who occupied it from 1940 to 1944. It was purchased by the Trinidad Government in 1954, and became the prime minister's domain for many years following Independence until it fell into disrepair. Restored in the late 1990s it has again become the prime minister's office.

Next comes **Archbishop's House** ⓯, home of the Roman Catholic Archbishop of Port of Spain. The architect was an Irishman, but the style has been described as Romanesque, reminiscent of a monastery. The marble and red granite were imported from Ireland, and the roof was covered with copper sheeting and slates. Native hardwood was used for the interior wood panelling, floors and beautiful Y-shaped staircase.

Flood Street, named after the archbishop responsible for the building of the house, separates it from the next elaborate edifice, **Roomor** ⓰, also known as Ambard House after Lucien F. Ambard, the French planter who commissioned it. It was built in the French Baroque colonial style; materials used included marble imported from Italy and tiles from France, and it has an outstanding roof of towers, pinnacles, dormers, elaborate galleries and a cupola of unusual proportions. Renaissance ironwork is incorporated in its elongated columns. Bought by Timothy Roodal in 1940, it is still the family residence.

Mille Fleurs is next, formerly the home of one of the city's mayors, Dr Henrique Prada. He was a prominent medical practitioner before he entered politics, serving as mayor of Port of Spain for three consecutive terms from 1914 to 1917. This flamboyant gingerbread house is distinguished by its considerable and detailed wooden fretwork. It was bought by the government and is now the headquarters of the Law Association.

Next is **Hayes Court**, home of the Anglican Bishop of Trinidad. A typical

Map on page 207

grand country house, it is a pleasant mixture of French and English architectural styles, and inside is a mahogany staircase and wood panelling.

The last of the Magnificent Seven is **Queen's Royal College** ⓱, a secondary school for boys. This building is in German Renaissance style, built of concrete with facings of blue limestone and coloured with reddish tint to contrast with the limestone. A clock was installed in the tower in 1913 and chimes on the quarter hour. This is where Trinidad and Tobago's most famous novelist, V .S. Naipaul, went to school before winning the Island Scholarship and going to Oxford *(see page 42)*. It is also the *alma mater* of the country's first prime minister, Dr Eric Williams, who was himself a distinguished academic, having also won the Island Scholarship and gone to Oxford from here *(see page 59)*.

Wealthy suburbs

To some degree the Savannah marks the northern end of the city proper and the beginning of the residential areas, called the suburbs by the locals though most are within walking distance of the city centre.

Above the zoo lies the smart residential area of **Chancellor Hill**, where cricketer Brian Lara – among other wealthy residents – lives in a house given to him by the government for his sporting achievements and for breaking Barbadian Sir Garfield Sobers's world record for the most runs in an innings in 1994.

Just off to the northwest is the suburb of Maraval *(see page 236)* which follows after the Kapok Roundabout. The **Ellerslie Plaza** is about a few hundred metres beyond the Kapok Hotel favoured by business travellers, offering upmarket goods to the residents of Ellerslie Park and Federation Park. Further up, a right turn at the intersection brings you to Maraval proper.

BELOW: two little girls from school.

BEAUTIFUL GINGERBREAD

The Savannah has many other outstanding buildings not referred to as part of the Magnificent Seven, and several of them were built in the West Indian "gingerbread" style by the Glaswegian architect George Brown, who perfected a way of mass-producing the distinctive intricate wooden fretwork. The ornate Knowsley House, now the Ministry of Foreign Affairs, south of the Savannah on Queen's Park West, was built in 1904 for William Gordon, a prominent city merchant. Its grounds take up an entire block, and among its spectacular features are a marble gallery on the ground floor, a beautiful staircase crafted from Guyana purpleheart wood, and ceilings of plaster of Paris. It was purchased by the government in 1956.

The George Brown House, a little further round to the east on Cipriani Boulevard, is not quite as elaborate, but is still trimmed with a large amount of fancy fretwork. A few steps onwards is Boissière House, which is such a wonderful example of the gingerbread style, with a small pagoda-like roof and copious wooden fretwork and bargeboards, that the locals call it the Gingerbread House.

The oldest building in the Savannah area is All Saints' Church on Marli Street nearby. Built in 1846, it is one of the oldest Anglican churches in the country.

On the corner is the **Trinidad Country Club**, catering mainly but not exclusively for the French Creole and local white population. Maraval is an enclave of the French Creole community, and many of the street names are reminders of this. Trinidad's only bagel shop, **Adam's**, is a little way up the road. In typical Trinidadian confusion, this Jewish bread is baked and sold by a Syrian. The Royal Palm Suite Hotel is about a half mile from the intersection, and is one of the less expensive hotels on the island.

The Maraval route leads to the Maracas pillars, passing the St Andrew's Golf Course in Moka and various smart residential areas. Maraval also leads to **Paramin** *(see page 237)*, up in the hills, which is renowned for both *parang* at Christmas and its Spanish Amerindian heritage. The Paramin Hill is extremely steep, and should not be attempted unless you are sure of your car and have a guide.

Belmont – a traditional African community

Back at the Savannah, if you travel east on the Circular Road past the President's House and St Ann's Road you come to **Belmont** ⓲, which has the distinction of being the first suburb of the city and is a densely populated mass of higgledy piggledy lanes. Situated to the northeast of Port of Spain, it rises up the slopes of the Northern Range and used to be a sugar plantation until it was converted into a settlement for a number of African tribes.

These Africans had been able to escape a life of slavery as a result of the anti-slave trade patrols along Africa's west coast. Brought to Trinidad, they were given land in various parts of Belmont, stretching from Belmont Circular Road, near Observatory Street, to Belmont Valley Road. Some of the original leading members of the community are commemorated in place names such as Zampty Lane

BELOW: a serious game of chess.

and Maycock Place. Later on, liberated slaves came to Trinidad from other islands, and they also settled in Belmont. The early community was a well-organised one, complete with priests, chiefs, leaders and close-knit family units, enabling the African cultural traditions to survive, as they still do even today. For example, the African Rada Community holds religious ceremonials according to African custom, accompanied by drumming, dancing, food and the sacrifice of feathered animals.

Belmont was never laid out in the conventional sense of the word. Houses were built willy-nilly, and it was only later that new streets were laid out to a plan. The result is a labyrinth of narrow, winding lanes. The records show that it has more lanes than anywhere else in the city, and it also has more people, more churches and more schools, in addition it has produced many leading citizens, such as Sir Ellis Clarke, who was born in Myler Street.

Though many of the houses today are still old wooden constructions, or a strange mixture of part wood, part concrete, the suburb has witnessed considerable progress over the years. Because originally the house sites were so small, expansion has largely been upwards. Today there are many narrow two and three-storey houses and commercial properties, solidly built, some looking down on the tiniest of houses next door.

Belmont has an exquisite Gothic church, **St Francis of Assisi** on Belmont Circular Road, and a rumshop with the unusual name of the **Tiger Cat Bar**. The country's first "lunatic asylum" was here, until it was re-sited in St Ann's, and promptly took on the more respectable name of a mental hospital. The **Pan Vibes** and **Pandemonium** steel bands have their yards in St Francois Valley Road and Norfolk Street.

Across from Belmont on the other side of Lady Young Road stands the **Trinidad Hilton**, set in the foothills of the Northern Range. It is built down the side of a hill; you descend from the lobby to the other floors, and the balconies hang over extravagantly verdant surroundings.

St James – an East Indian influence

Where Belmont's settlement is African in origin, in **St James** ⓳, the city's most westerly suburb, the influence is decidedly East Indian. St James too was once a sugar plantation, and the workers there were largely East Indians who arrived as indentured labourers after Emancipation. The streets bear witness to its earliest inhabitants with names such as Delhi, Bombay, Madras, Calcutta, Benares and Ganges.

Much of the city's nightlife is centred around St James. The Western Main Road, which passes through the area, is littered with fast food joints, bars, betting shops and music emporia. The activity spills out onto the pavement, particularly at weekends, creating a carnival-like atmosphere. St James's most celebrated bar, **Smokey and Bunty**, is a popular stopping-off point after a hard day's work. The mood changes for the annual Muslim festival of Hosay *(see Festivals chapter, page 155)*, when *tassa* drummers replace loud commercial music. Around Carnival the **Hummingbirds Pan Groove** on the Fort George Road provide yet another kind of sound.

At the entrance to the suburb is **St James Barracks,**

Map
on page
207

TIP

You can visit the Pashimtaashi Hindu Mandir (temple), off the Mucurapo Road in St James. If someone is there, they will probably be happy to show you around. Tel: 622 4949.

BELOW: the Pashimtaashi Hindu Mandir.

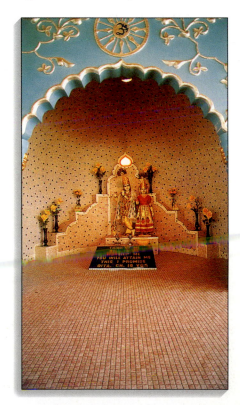

Angostura bitters is a blend of herbs and spices, first concocted in 1824 to combat stomach upsets in troops liberating Venezuela from Spain, and has been produced in Trinidad from a secret recipe ever since.

BELOW: Laventille houses crammed on the hillside.

an important building housing the Police Training College. Dating from 1827, when it was built by Governor Woodford to provide a barrack for His Majesty's Forces in the Windward and Leeward Islands, it is in fact the oldest government building still in use in Trinidad today. A little way from the police college is the T&TEC **Power Stars Panyard**, which is active around Carnival time.

Characterful Laventille

Laventille ⓴, to the east, is a suburb second only to Belmont in character. The hills are lined with houses roof to roof, some solidly constructed, others makeshift shanties. The two roads into the area are Duke Street Extension via Piccadilly Street, and Picton Road, a turning off the Eastern Main Road near the Central Market and the Beetham Highway Roundabout. Both roads are winding and narrow, and require considerable driving skill, particularly when overtaking, an activity which taxi drivers have down to a fine art. The unwary, however, run the risk of crashing off the road and, as has often happened, straight onto the roof of someone's living room, as many of the houses are built a foot or two below the level of the street on the slope.

Laventille is a highly depressed area, with much unemployment and thousands of suspected illegal immigrants from the neighbouring islands. As a result, there is a lack of running water and sanitation, though there is no shortage of cars, televisions and DVD players.

Present-day Laventille revolves around its steel band, the famous **Desperadoes**, whose leader Rudolph Charles was a legend even before he died in 1985. He was carried to his cremation site on a *shariot*, a casket made of steel drums. This larger-than-life character was immortalised by David Rudder in the 1986 Carnival

calypso entitled *The Hammer*, which won both the national calypso contest for the best song and the Carnival Road March for the song that is most popular with the bands. *The Hammer* eulogised Charles as he lived, always dressed in army fatigues and tall boots, marching across the hills of Laventille with a hammer in his hand, a hammer he used not only for tuning musical notes out of the steel drums but also for keeping wayward Laventilleans and "badjohns" in check. The Desperadoes, as their name implies, were once noted for street fights and general rowdiness.

There are many accounts as to exactly where the steel band started in Port of Spain. Some say it was in a yard in **East Dry River**, when a man called "Fish Eye" experimented on an old oil drum and beat out the tune of "Mary had a Little Lamb". Others state that the first sounds of the steel band emerged from a yard in Woodbrook, while others argue that it originated in Laventille.

What is not in dispute is that when World War II ended in 1945, VE Day was marked by an impromptu carnival on the streets of Port of Spain, accompanied, for the first time in the history of Carnival, by the music of the steel band. Now every town and neighbourhood has its own band, and around Carnival time, they are all out practising in the panyards. *(See Travel Tips pages 361 for a list of bands.)*

Woodbrook – a traditional stronghold

To the west of the city, **Woodbrook** ㉑ was settled in 1911. Originally another sugar estate, it belonged to the Siegert family, creators of Trinidad's famous Angostura Bitters. For the ensuing decades Woodbrook was largely residential, with comfortable medium-sized dwellings, and became the traditional suburb of the middle classes, which included Syrian/Lebanese families who came here in the 1930s and 1940s. Since the 1960s the district has gradually become commercialised, although great efforts have been made to preserve the old gingerbread-style houses, and it is still a pleasant place to stay.

On the corner of Ariapita Avenue and French Street is the **Mas' Camp Pub**, where calypsonians and comedians often perform, and which was once the home of Peter Minshall's Callaloo mas' camp *(see page 261)*. In the other direction is the **Veni Mange** restaurant, which serves Creole food and has a colourful ambience.

Posher parts

To the north, across Tragerete Road, is the popular suburb of **Federation Park** ㉒, commemorating the period when Port of Spain was the capital of the short-lived West Indies Federation *(see page 64)*. Here the curving roads bear the names of Caribbean islands, and house spacious buildings that could have been embassies but are instead gracious private homes.

Federation Park's main street intersects with the Long Circular Road, which runs from St James to Maraval. A little way up the road is the **Long Circular Mall**, which is one of the best shopping malls in the country. Further up is the **Ambassador Hotel**.

A little way west are the districts of New Town and St Clair. **New Town** ㉓ begins at the top of Richmond Street and Tragerete Road and extends up to Maraval Road Boulevard, but the borders are not rigid. On Cipriani Boulevard, next to Nipdec House, the

---

Map on page 207

Atop Laventille Hill sits the white stone chapel of Our Lady of Laventille Shrine that can be seen from all over the city. The statue came from France in 1876, and today pilgrims of several religious denominations from around the country visit it on the Feast of the Assumption.

BELOW: practising on the steelpan.

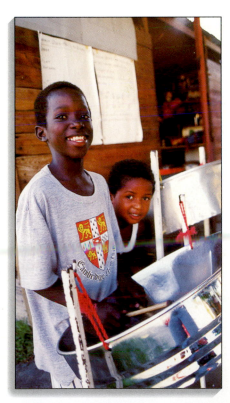

Map on page 207

Mas' camps are dotted all over the western suburbs of Woodbrook, New Town and St Clair.

BELOW: kitted out for Kiddies' Carnival.
RIGHT: Queen's Royal College – a prestigious school.

magistrates' court, is **Jenny's on the Boulevard**, a converted Victorian house which is now a restaurant and bar. Higher up on the opposite side are two more wateringholes: the American-style restaurant **Tony Roma's** and **Fifty-One Degrees**, which features both live music and comedy. Nearby, on Maraval Road, is **Trotters**, a popular sports bar. From Wednesday evening through Sunday it is almost impossible to find a parking space on the boulevard, and around Carnival time the situation is made worse since **Wayne Berkeley's mas' camp** is just up the road.

St Clair ㉔, a little way west of New Town, was laid out in very large lots at the turn of the 20th century, and today is still a highly prized neighbourhood with many elegant houses and gardens, several occupied by foreign ambassadors. However, in the middle of all this gentility, in Alcazar Street, the **Harts' mas' camp** can be found.

On Gray Street the **Kisskadee Cultural Laboratory** occasionally functions as an art gallery, or as a space for lectures on artistic and cultural matters. The annex of the laboratory now houses the **Trinidad Theatre Workshop** (TTW), which was formed by Nobel laureate Derek Walcott in 1958 in Beryl McBurnie's Little Carib Theatre in Roberts Street close by, and is the closest thing to a national performing company *(see page 111)*.

Further west and obliquely opposite the well known Cricket Wicket bar is the **Queen's Park Oval**, where international cricket is played.

Up in the hills

On the northeastern outskirts of Port of Spain, on the slopes of the Northern Range, lie the suburbs of St Ann's and Cascade. **Cascade** ㉕ began in 1794 as a sugar plantation owned by a French royalist from Martinique. At that time it comprised 558 hectares (1,395 acres) and included the Fondes Amandes Valley. These days it is mainly a residential area for the middle and upper classes. There is a school for the deaf a few kilometres up the valley.

St Ann's ㉖ is much more exciting. On St Ann's Road, skirting the Botanic Gardens, is **Queen's Hall**, a large space used for concerts and recitals, it has been refurbished and is now equipped with state-of-the-art acoustics. The hall borders the official addresses of both the president and the prime minister. Just across the street from the prime minister's residence is the **Pelican**, an English-style pub with lots of Trini flavour and occasional live music, packed every night. Further along St Ann's Road the **Normandie Hotel** has a bookshop, a performance space called "Under the Trees" and the **Cascade Club**, a small bar.

Continuing into St Ann's, you reach the high walls of the cloister of the **Rosary Monastery** of the nuns of the Order of St Dominic. The monastery was founded here in the 19th century by nuns fleeing political troubles in Venezuela. Entirely self-sufficient, the nuns grow their own food and make the bread for their communion services, as well as doing the artistic decorative work for statues and altar vestments. The monastery has its own chapel, and the only time the nuns leave the cloisters is when they die. ❑

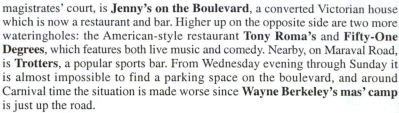

CARNIVAL COSTUME AND MAS' CAMP

As one Carnival ends, work begins on the next.
Designers and steel bands must be ready for the
festival's climax three days before Ash Wednesday

The creation of the thousands of costumes that dazzle, delight, mystify or horrify spectators on the streets during Carnival Monday and Tuesday is a multi-million-dollar, year-round, labour-intensive industry, particularly for designers who also work at other carnivals. Some of the mas' camps, like Peter Minshall's *(above)*, are factory size, others make do with converted houses.

Although a simple joovay costume (a pair of shorts with some mud, paint or grease) can be created quickly for a minimal sum, it is an entirely different story when it comes to the costumes of the major Carnival bands, some of which have grown to nearly 10,000 strong. The costume for the king and queen of the band can take months to construct (some are so large that they have to be supported on wheels) and can cost up to US$20,000.

MAS' DESIGN

Along with Peter Minshall, the doyen of mas' design as kinetic art and street theatre, other well-known designers are Wayne Berkeley, Stephen Derek, Richard Affong and Jason Griffith.

◁ **QUEEN OF THE BAND**
The elaborate and carefully constructed costumes of the king and queen of the band are magnificent and also an engineering accomplishment.

◁ **DEVILISH BEHAVIOUR**
The joovay blue devil is a traditional terrifying character, particularly popular in the mountain village of Paramin where the devils run amok.

◁ **A JUNIOR EVENT**

Kiddies' Carnival is celebrated with as much fervour as the adult version. See the bright, fun Junior Carnival costumes in parades in St James a week before the main event.

△ **EARTH MAN**

A character from Peter Minshall's Song of the Earth band. Minshall has established himself as the most creative and controversial Carnival designer.

PAN, SWEET PANORAMA MUSIC

The energy that fires Carnival and sustains it through the long season from January until Ash Wednesday is music. There is the thumping turbo drive of soca and rapso, which keeps fêtes of thousands on their feet all night; the subtleties of calypso to be savoured in the comfort of a tent, and then there's pan, sweet pan, the primal musical voice of T&T.

For the big steel bands – and there are more than 200, with up to 150 players – Carnival and the national steel band competition Panorama are synonymous. This is their time to shine, to battle their way through the regional preliminary stages and win a coveted place in the finals the weekend before Carnival. The bands – Despers, Renegades, Exodus, Phase II, Nu-Tones, Angel Harps, Fonclaire – are partisanly supported, and as Panorama finals draw close the nation goes into a fever of discussion and even bets as to the coming champions.

For weeks the panyards echo to the sounds of the tune being learnt, largely by repetition.

▷ **JOINING IN**

Joining a Carnival band requires a bit of forward planning and money to buy a costume. The bigger bands have thousands of members.

△ **BIKINI BAND**

"Pretty mas'" has been dominated by bikini bands in recent years – one way of beating the tropical heat.

◁ **ACCESSORIES**

Accessories are an important part of Kiddies' Carnival costumes. There is also a Junior Parade of Bands.

NOTICE ONLY PLAYERS BEYOND THIS POINT

AROUND AND ABOUT THE NORTHERN RANGE

The dramatic scenery of the mountain rainforests in the north is teeming with birdlife, and slopes down to the fertile Santa Cruz Valley and some of the best beaches in Trinidad

T he mountains of the Northern Range stretch for 65 km (40 miles) across the top of Trinidad and are covered in rainforests which provide a home for an abundance of birds and wildlife but very few humans. Not many roads penetrate this rugged barrier to the sea, sliced by rivers and the verdant Santa Cruz Valley and punctuated by magnificent waterfalls with pools you can swim in, caves to explore and the highest peaks on the island – El Cerro del Aripo (940 metres/3,084ft) and El Tucuche 936 metres/3,072ft) – and those that do are steep and winding and should be negotiated with care. Only one carves its way across the range from Blanchisseuse on the coast to Arima on the Eastern Main Road to the south. The northern coast, from the lovely beaches of Maracas Bay to Blanchisseuse, is popular with the residents of Port of Spain at weekends and holidays, so be prepared for some traffic, but after that the road turns into a donkey track, and it is another 30 km (19 miles) before the tarmac reappears at Matelot. You can hike along this undeveloped part of the coastline to some beautiful beaches where leatherback turtles come up to nest.

Along the southern side of the Northern Range the busy bustling Eastern Main Road runs through some interesting towns and villages, paralleling the faster Churchill Roosevelt Highway to the south. Often a scene of pandemonium and hair-raising driving between Port of Spain and Arima, the Main Road continues more peacefully to the remote east coast and up to Toco on the spectacular windswept northeast tip.

Most of the attractions and activities of northern Trinidad can be tackled in a day trip from Port of Spain, although you might prefer to spend a night or two around Toco (about two and a half hours away) where there are some guesthouses and private holiday homes to rent *(see Travel Tips on page 349).*

The Saddle

The Saddle Road, or the Saddle as it is referred to locally, leads out of **Port of Spain ❶**, passing through some of the more popular suburbs of the city before forking to the right through a tight gorge into the Santa Cruz Valley. The left fork becomes the North Coast Road, continuing up to the popular beaches and providing lovely vistas of valley and sea. Landslides occasionally block the coast road so it is worth checking the situation before setting out.

Leaving from Stollmeyer's Castle on Queen's Park Savannah *(see page 221)* you come to a small roundabout by the Ministry of Agriculture, Lands and Food Production, where you should turn left onto Long

PRECEDING PAGES: football fun on Las Cuevas beach. **LEFT:** an eastern view of the northern coast. **BELOW:** deserted Blanchisseuse Bay.

St Andrew's Golf Course in Moka, outside Maraval, is the best course on the island. Built on the old Moka Estate, it was originally owned by William Hardin Burnley, an Anglo-American who moved here in 1802. Visitors can become temporary members through their hotels.

Circular Road. After the third service station in Boissière Village turn right onto the Saddle Road. At the left corner is the **Trinidad Country Club**, first the estate of Rosa de Gannes (de Charras), daughter of Simon de Gannes de la Chancellerie and later the home of the de Boissières, after whom Boissière Village is named.

Made into a club by the Canning family, it was used exclusively by whites until about 20 years ago. Today membership policy is more liberal, and a visit here, which you can arrange through your hotel, is a way to meet and mingle with a variety of Trinidadians at the bar. It has tennis courts, a swimming pool and other facilities, and is well known for its wonderful Christmas and Carnival dances.

In the upmarket suburb of **Maraval** *(see pages 223–4)*, about 5 km (3 miles) out of the city, the Saddle passes through the former sugar estates of **St Andrew's** and **La Seiva** which are now sought-after residential areas. On the right is the vine-covered **Chaconia Inn**, whose restaurant and club are a weekend haunt for the younger generation. **Andalucia**, another residential area, is on the left, and immediately after it you will see the Maraval Reservoir, built in 1854. Still in perfect condition, it supplies the area with water from the Maraval River, which in fact is not much more than a stream.

The Roman Catholic church of **Our Lady of Lourdes**, on high ground on the right, is typical of most churches in Trinidad – a bit of history, an abundance of pride. This one was built in 1879 and enlarged in 1934. The grotto behind the church was built by Spanish missionaries of the Augustinian Order who were in Trinidad until 1950. The marble altar was donated in 1872 by J. A. Cipriani, father of Captain Arthur Andrew Cipriani, wartime hero and trade unionist *(see page 50)*. Next to the church is an old tomb which has the inscription *Es Sacerdos in aeternum* [*sic*]: "You are a priest for eternity".

BELOW: St Andrew's Golf Course in a tropical setting.

Parang in Paramin

Perched high above Maraval is the mountain village of **Paramin** ❷, known as "the herb basket of Trinidad" and best reached by taking one of the four-wheel-drive jeeps which operate as taxis from Maraval itself. Its steep slopes are used to cultivate popular local seasonings like French and Spanish thyme, peppermint and *chadon beni* as well as vegetables.

Paramin is also famous for *parang* and *patois*, legacies of colonial settlement. This is one of the few places where *patois*, introduced by an influx of French planters at the end of the 18th century, is still spoken. *Parang*, the exuberant Christmas carol and folk-music tradition, was brought here by Venezuelan peons or *cocoa payols*, who came to work on the cocoa estates of the Northern Range during the 19th century *(see pages 43 and 135)*.

Back on the Saddle, Haleland Park, a former nutmeg plantation, is another residential area noted for its gracious homes and landscaped gardens. Further on the road continues left into Santa Cruz Valley. On the left, large pillars signal the start of the **North Coast Road** to Maracas Bay, the first seaside village you come to. The vegetation here is abundantly tropical, with balisier shrubs (heliconia), the flower of the People's National Movement party, bamboo, samaan – the enormous canopied trees – and other tropical trees and plants lining the road.

In the dry season, January to May, when the immortelles and poui are in bloom, the hills are a carpet of red, pink and yellow. The flora and fauna of the Northern Range are relics of the Venezuelan jungle, proving that Trinidad is a continental island, unlike the volcanic oceanic islands in the rest of the Caribbean. Drive up and around curve after curve, but take care, this mountainous trip alongside drops of up to 300 metres (1,000 ft) is not for drivers with vertigo. There are two official

Map on pages 240–41

The North Coast Road was built by the Americans in 1944 to compensate for their occupation of Chaguaramas.

BELOW:
a north-coast beach.

The Silver Suspension Bridge crosses the Marianne River at Blanchisseuse and you can wade along the riverbed to Three Pools and Avocat Falls. A village guide will show you the way and the wildlife.

BELOW: on the beach at Las Cuevas Bay.

lookout stops on the road, both breathtaking. The first looks down on La Vache Bay, the second on Maracas. At both stops local vendors will try to tempt you with delicacies such as pineapple chow, sweet prunes and tamarind balls.

Maracas Bay – a Trinidadian favourite

On the road to wide, sheltered **Maracas Bay** ❸, 16 km (10 miles) from Port of Spain, after La Vache lookout, you can experience a phenomenon known as "the magnetic road". On an incline just before you start to descend to Maracas Bay, if you stop and take off the handbrake, instead of rolling backwards you roll upwards, it is said. There have been many explanations, one of which is that the road has magnetic powers, but according to locals this is simply an illusion. The beach below is a favourite with picnickers on sunny weekends, when Trinidadians bring hampers of food, floats and games and make a day of it. The length of the beach lends itself to cricket and soccer, and pick-up games abound. Where the sea on shore is marked with a red flag, beware of strong currents; lifeguards are on duty at peak times. Usually the sea is warm and pleasant with gentle waves.

Behind the beach, among the booths selling snacks, crafts and souvenirs, you should sample the Maracas delicacy – bake 'n' shark – fresh fried shark garnished in pepper sauce and seasoning, served in a fried batter "bake". At the left end of the beach, in a cove, is the sleepy fishing village of Maracas. The villagers here are of Spanish-Amerindian descent, and there are still a few who speak a Spanish *patois*. Seines (nets) dry on the beach next to overturned boats, and pirogues drift at anchor in the bay. Late afternoon is the best time to buy fish; carite and kingfish are plentiful in these waters, and the locals are happy to share their recipes. The small chapel is dedicated to St Peter, and on his feast-day 29 June, it holds a small festival in his honour.

Night trips with the fishermen

For those keen on fishing, the fishermen here and at the village of La Filette further on might take you with them. The best time to go is on the evening tide around 5pm, returning before dawn. A night out in the wind in a small boat, with only a lantern and the moon for light, is not everyone's idea of a good time, but if you do go, on your return you might see vultures, locally called corbeaux, standing on the posts in the cove like sentinels, waiting to catch the first rays of the sun. They prefer fish for food, and so can be seen at most fishing villages and ports in Trinidad.

On the outskirts of the village is the new **Maracas Bay Hotel**, whose air-conditioned rooms provide a more comfortable alternative to camping on the beach, as many Trinidadians are wont to do.

The next beach along the coast is **Tyrico Bay**, favoured by those wishing to escape the crowds at Maracas. The road then cuts inland with views of **El Tucuche**, Trinidad's second highest peak, looming on the right and returns seawards to **Las Cuevas**, which is also more secluded and less crowded than Maracas. The beach restaurant serves fresh fish dishes and a variety of tasty local specialities.

Las Cuevas is Spanish for caves, and into this sheltered horseshoe bay with its long sweep of sand

flows the **Curaguate River**, creating sandy hollows in the low banks ideal for picnics and barbecues. Although its long expanse of sand and gentle surf make Las Cuevas the second most popular beach in Trinidad, sandflies can be an irritant, particularly in the rainy season, so insect repellant is advisable. Just beyond Las Cuevas is **Rincon Trace**, the start of the two-and-a-half-hour trail up to the breathtaking **Rincon Waterfall** ❹.

The North Coast Road continues through the delightfully pretty fishing village of **La Filette** and the hamlet of Yarra, ending at the village of Blanchisseuse. Along the way are many small beaches, some quiet, some with heavy surf, and most accessible by footpaths down the rocky cliffs.

Blanchisseuse ❺ (named in *patois* after the washerwomen of the local Marianne River) was originally Trinidad's most isolated settlement, accessible only by boat until 1931, when the road over the mountains to Arima was cut, followed by the extension of the road from Maracas in the late 1970s. Although the population has grown it retains its character as a quiet village, with little besides a church and an old bell for announcing masses, funerals, weddings and the like, a dry goods store, a bar and the school at the top of a hill. There are many families who live year-round in the village, leading by and large quiet rural existences, as well as city dwellers who own holiday homes.

The coastal road ends beyond the **Silver Suspension Bridge** over the Marianne River, but the old donkey or bench trail 30 km (19 miles) to Matelot makes a splendid two-day hike. An easier day trip is the 6-km (4-mile) hike to **Paria Bay** and the waterfall along the trail, past beaches where turtles nest. The locals tend to travel the coast by boat, however, and some of them have found marriage partners in Las Cuevas.

Map on pages 240–41

For a jungle experience stay a few days at Petit Tacaribe in the beautiful bay of the same name. The simple guesthouse is only accessible by boat or by a day-long hike. Contact Petit Tacaribe, c/o 5 Moore Avenue, St Ann's, Port of Spain; tel: 624 1774; e-mail: tacaribe@wow.net

BELOW: farming in Santa Cruz Valley.

TIP

The 8-km (5-mile) La
Sagesse to Maracas
Bay trail is a popular
half-day hike through
forest and over hills.
It is best to go in a
group or with a guide,
starting in Santa Cruz
at the end of
Gasparillo Road past
the quarry there.

The Santa Cruz valley

Return from Blanchisseuse the way you came, to the pillars marking the
entrance to the North Coast Road, and take a sharp left over the Saddle, a narrow
pass between two slabs of the hill. **Santa Cruz Valley ❻** used to be an enormous citrus plantation but is now dotted with small settlements. Although it
can no longer be described as "the country" it retains its calm aura.

You will come to the church dedicated to the Holy Cross, behind which lies
the **La Pastora Estate** and estate house. Owned by Antonio Gomez, a senior
judge when Sir Ralph Woodford was governor of Trinidad (1813–28), it later
belonged to Hippolyte Borde, who wrote the first history of Trinidad, covering
events on the island from the late 15th century to the late 18th.

On a small rise to the right stands the estate house of Dr John Stollmeyer's
family, which once owned Stollmeyer's Castle in Port of Spain *(see page 221)*.
They came from America to make their fortune in citrus and cocoa plantations.

The many clear, cool pools of **La Canoa River** a little further down provide
a refreshing swim. The main village of the valley is called **Cantaro** (where the
cricketing hero Brian Lara grew up), consisting of the hamlets Petial, Gasparillo and La Pastora. The name La Pastora (the Shepherdess) crops up again and
again in Trinidad because of Trinidadians' devotion to the Virgin of Shepherds,
taught to them by Capuchin monks, the first missionaries to this new world
(see pages 287–8).

Branching off from the Saddle, the old road on the left takes you to some Spanish ruins. There is also a monument to the Amerindians here, a statue of an Arawak
wearing a loin cloth and painted in naturalistic colours. Legend has it that wherever
a treasure is buried an Indian was killed and buried next to it: hence this monument.

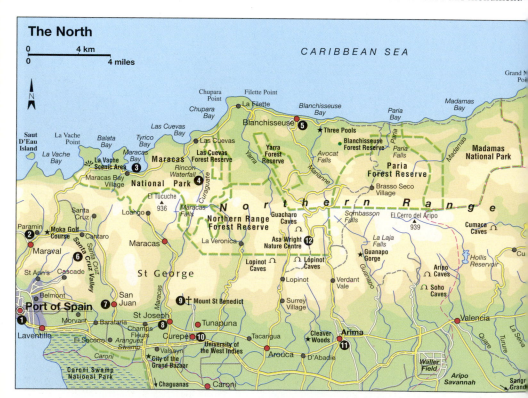

However, digging is not recommended. Also here are a consecrated chapel and an old cemetery whose tombstones provide a documentation of Trinidad's past.

Backtrack to the Saddle and continue a little further. **Croisee** (pronounced "Quasay"), meaning crossroads, is the heart of activity in **San Juan ❼**. Inhabitants of this area were once noted for speaking a French *patois*, hence the distinctive pronunciation of certain words. Today the community is a mixture of descendants of Africans and East Indians, and the *patois* is rarely heard. The Croisee is a lively junction of stallholders and traffic by day and food-and-drink vendors and party goers by night.

In days gone by (*circa* 1876), San Juan was the first stop for the train, and so it became highly commercialised, with a market every day. Just south of San Juan the Saddle meets the Eastern Main Road, which if you turn right will take you back into Port of Spain via Laventille *(see page 226)*. Should you prefer another route into town, at Barataria turn right at the traffic lights onto Lady Young Road, named after the wife of a former governor. As you drive over the hill, Morvant, a poor housing area, is on the left. After several turns and bends you come to Belmont, then the Hilton Hotel on the right, and finally the Savannah.

On the Eastern Main Road

The Eastern Main Road is a colourful thoroughfare lined with shops, stalls, businesses and restaurants. All the different types of taxi are jostling for space with lorries and cars. Without warning, one driver may stop dead for a chat with another. Do not expect to go anywhere fast. The road leads out of Port of Spain for about 60 km (38 miles), all the way across Trinidad to the Manzanilla coast at Matura Point, and passes several roads into the Northern Range, where

Map on pages 240–41

Coconut water straight from the coconut makes a refreshing drink.

BELOW: a street vendor waiting for customers.

A fine example of gingerbread fretwork on an old house in St Joseph.

BELOW: floral views from the mountains. **RIGHT:** a St Joseph farmer tending his crops.

there are some interesting places to visit. Mount St Benedict, the Asa Wright Nature Centre, the University of the West Indies and the Aripo Savannah are all accessible via the Eastern Main Road, and you may choose to linger for picnics or hikes in the woods.

An example of an afternoon's tour would be a drive to the St Augustine Campus of the University of the West Indies, followed by tea at the monastery of Mount St Benedict. On the way back you could stop off at the **City of Grand Bazaar**, Trinidad's biggest shopping mall, which has several restaurants and bars.

For a faster journey, but just as colourful, the Churchill Roosevelt Highway which runs parallel to the south of the Eastern Main Road, may be a better bet. Leave from Stollmeyer's Castle, taking the Lady Young Road to the highway. The third set of traffic lights is **Aranguez Junction**. This region was once called the food basket of the country, and today beautifully decorated fruit stalls stand at the junction; just before the rainy season begins in June there are mountains of watermelons lining the roadside. The highway passes through **Valsayn**, a residential area where the Spanish handed the island over to the British on 18 February 1787. **Valpark Plaza** offers a number of restaurants and a cocktail bar.

St Joseph – Trinidad's first capital

Once San José de Oruña, then St Josef, and finally its present Anglicised name, **St Joseph ⑧** is about 15 km (9 miles) east of Port of Spain. It was the first capital of Trinidad during Spanish rule, founded in 1592, but after years of disasters and neglect – Sir Walter Raleigh ransacked the town in 1595; the Dutch destroyed it in 1637, followed by the Caribs three years later, and there was a major earthquake in 1766 – the Spanish abandoned it in favour of Port of Spain in 1784, although

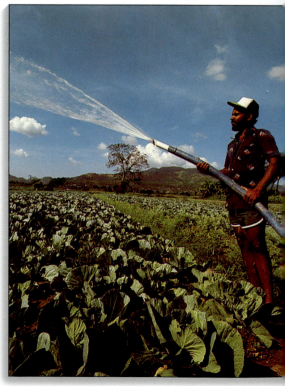

when the English arrived in 1797 they found a small town bustling with sugar, coffee and cotton mills. Now a rambling village St Joseph no longer bustles, unless with students from one of its many schools. The past lives on in the tombstones of the Roman Catholic Church, the oldest in Trinidad, dated 1682, and the memorial in the park to Makandal Daaga, leader of the 1837 mutiny *(see page 34)*.

From St Joseph the Maracas Royal Road plunges northwards into the mountains along the Maracas Valley, providing a delightful drive through thick green vegetation, past small privately-owned estates, new housing developments and the old villages of Acono, Maracas and Loango at the end of the valley: the beginning of a three-hour trek over the mountains to Maracas Bay.

You can bathe in the **Maracas River**, visit the modest Maracas waterfalls, or climb **El Tucuche**, at 936 metres (3,072 ft) high, the second highest peak in Trinidad. If you do choose to hike up the mountain, find an experienced guide before setting out as trails can be precarious and poorly marked, and at some points skirt a 600-metre (2,000-ft) cliff. For the falls, follow the Waterfall Road and then walk for 20 minutes through the forest.

Tea and birds at Mount St Benedict

Back on the Eastern Main Road heading east, take another left turn into St John's Road, the well-paved entrance up to **Mount St Benedict** ❾, 244 metres (795 ft) above sea level, a monastery with an excellent view of the Caroni Plains and the Piarco Savannah. The white-walled red-roofed collection of buildings was first home to Benedictine monks in 1912, when civil unrest in Brazil forced them to flee temporarily. Later, communication with Brazil became difficult, and the monks affiliated themselves to the Belgian Congregation.

Map
on pages
240–41

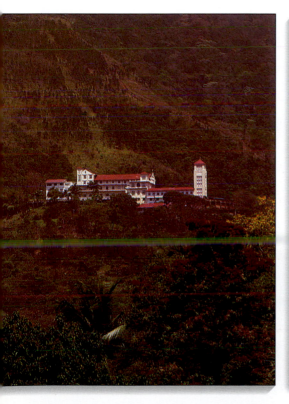

Look out for hummingbirds if you are near any heavily scented flowers.

LEFT: Mount St Benedict is popular with birdwatchers. **BELOW:** poui blooms litter the hillside.

*The St Augustine
Campus of UWI was
once a sugar
plantation. The
principal now lives
in what was the
estate's Great House.*

BELOW: gleaming
minarets of the
Mohammed Al
Jinnah Mosque.

Since then the monastery has expanded, and now includes a seminary where most Roman Catholic priests for the English-speaking Caribbean are trained, and a school where practical skills are taught to local teenagers. A guesthouse is available for retreats, where visitors can stay overnight or just for tea and delicious cakes (open daily from 3pm), awaiting the ringing of the bells for the Angelus at 6pm. Birdwatchers stay at the guesthouse to take advantage of the excellent nature trails, and to watch the birds of prey gliding high above **Mount Tabor**. The vista over the plains is spell-binding, in both bright sunshine and hazy weather, and even at dusk when the variable light provides an entirely different scene.

Caribbean seat of learning

Returning to the Eastern Main Road, to the west you will see towering the impressive minarets of the **Mohammed Al Jinnah Mosque**. At **Curepe**, a teeming traffic-snarled junction, the island's best doubles, pudding and souse *(see page 126)* are sold at the side of the road. The Eastern Main Road continues past a campus of the **University of the West Indies ❿** on the right. Spread over more than 81 hectares (200 acres), UWI was first established in 1948 in Mona, Jamaica. In 1960 the Imperial College of Tropical Agriculture at St Augustine, founded in 1923 as an agricultural college for the British Commonwealth, was incorporated as the Faculty of Agriculture of the UWI, heralding the opening of the St Augustine Campus. There is a third campus in Barbados, with extramural offices in other Eastern Caribbean islands.

In 1963 the first chancellor, Princess Alice, Countess of Athlone, opened the new buildings for the Faculty of Engineering and, later on, the John F. Kennedy College of Arts and Sciences and the Faculty of Agriculture building. In that same

year the library, notable for its collection of material relating to the West Indies, was moved to new premises in the JFK complex. The library's slide collection of Trinidad's flora and fauna was assembled by Professor Julian Kenny in honour of UWI's 25th anniversary and the UWI Herbarium displays a variety of dried plants.

Map on pages 240–41

Caura Valley and the doomed dam

Beyond the St John's Road junction, on the left of the main road is the **Exodus** panyard, where visitors are welcome to go to hear this band of champions practising. After endlessly busy Tunapuna, just after the El Dorado Consumer Cooperative and the impressive Hindu mandir, is the turn-off onto the **Caura Royal Road** which follows the Tacarigua River into the heart of the **Northern Range Forest Reserve**, where there are a number of cool, breezy picnic areas. Several dirt nature trails crisscross the region, including a beautiful one linking the Caura Valley to Maracas. Check at the Forest Division Recreation Centre, 8 km (5 miles) up the Caura Royal Road, for advice and directions.

In the 1950s a dam was partially built in Caura, and a Roman Catholic Church had to be torn down to accommodate it. Residents, many of Amerindian descent, were resettled in Arouca and Lopinot. The dam could not be completed because of sandy soil, and a scandal ensued. Village gossip has it that the Catholic priest's resistance to the whole idea doomed the project from its inception.

On the Eastern Main Road, continue east over the bridge past the Tacarigua Orphanage and on through Tacarigua, Five Rivers and Arouca. Before Arouca take the left turn off for the Trincity Shopping Mall and the American-style cineplex, Caribbean Cinemas 8. A few hundred metres after **Arouca Junction** the sign to **Lopinot**, a restored 19th-century agricultural estate 8 km (5 miles) up the road (open daily 6am–6pm), is clearly marked on the left. Charles Josef, Comte de Lopinot, left Haiti (then St Domingue) after the slave uprising in 1791. He went to Jamaica, heard about land grants in Trinidad, and came here in 1799 with his wife and 100 slaves. The land grants came about because Roume de Saint Laurent, a French Grenadian, visited Trinidad in the late 1770s, and he was so impressed with the rich soil and flourishing crops that he advised the King of Spain to grant lands to French settlers.

As a result, in 1783 the Royal Cedula of Population was passed, the conditions for grants being that settlers were Roman Catholics and observed allegiance to the King of Spain. Lopinot's first land grant was in Tacarigua, but after his sugar crop failed he moved here and planted cocoa.

Craftsmen in Lopinot still make the cuatro, the small four-string type of guitar which is the lead instrument of parang.

BELOW: part of the restored Lopinot estate house.

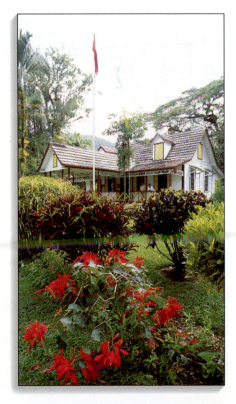

Home of *parang*

The road to Lopinot is narrow and winding, climbing gradually through the lush forest and passing through **Surrey Village**, the home of the celebrated steelpan arranger Jit Samaroo. In Lopinot is a well-kept savannah with tables for picnickers and a bar near the car park. The inhabitants of the village, resettled here from Caura Valley, are mostly the descendants of Venezuelan *peons* and, besides the old estate, Lopinot is best known as the home of *parang*, the music they brought with them (*see page 135*).

At the foot of El Cerro del Aripo are the Aripo Caves, the island's largest network of caverns, home to a colony of oilbirds (see pages 180–81). From Aripo village, where you can hire a guide, it is a difficult two- to three-hour hike (best in the dry season) to the caves' mouth. Only experienced and equipped cavers should consider entering.

Over the ravine is the restored portion of the original Great House. The few pieces of furniture within are said to have belonged to Colonel Thomas Picton, the first and not very pleasant British governor of Trinidad *(see page 30)*. In 1803 the Comte de Lopinot completed the residence on the estate he named La Reconnaissance, and he died there in 1819 after playing an important part in the history of Trinidad as a successful cocoa estate owner and an eschater – a sort of tribunal head and judge. Both he and his wife are buried on the banks of the river named after him on this beautiful fertile plateau in the mountains. There are no Lopinots left in Trinidad today, but the founders of the village have been honoured by a photographic exhibition on permanent display at the house.

In **Arouca**, back on the Eastern Main Road, the Spanish-style church in the square is dedicated to San Rafael, and across from it used to be the town hall. The Amerindian heritage of many Aroucans is immediately apparent in their features.

Three kilometres (2 miles) further on the town of **D'Abadie** is an area of small crop and livestock farms. At the fir forest look for Cleaver Trace, which leads to the **Cleaver Woods**. The **Ajoupa Hut** (open daily 7am–6pm) is a reconstruction of an Amerindian shelter, with copies of original pottery and other artefacts on sale. Modified versions of the clay oven are still used in many parts of the country-side. It is heated with wood or dry coconut shells and housed in a small outdoor shed; the baking pans are placed on long wooden pallets and inserted in to it. The track leads to a small ravine and clean stream, a pleasant short walk.

Arima – gateway to the Northern Range

Arima ⑪ was once the third largest town in Trinidad, but has now given way in importance to such towns as Chaguanas, nearer the heavy industries down south.

BELOW:
at the open-air market in Arima.

Situated 26 km (16 miles) east of Port of Spain, it began as a large Amerindian settlement and then became popular with French planters. In the late 19th century it expanded rapidly as the centre of the cocoa boom. Today the population is predominantly a mixture of African and Spanish blood, but those who claim to be descended from the Amerindians still celebrate their heritage at the end of August and crown a "Queen of the Caribs" on the feast of Santa Rosa, their patron saint.

Arima has a certain old-world charm, and there is plenty of architectural evidence of the French and Spanish presences. The **Arima dial** (clocktower) in the town centre is a familiar landmark, donated by a former mayor in 1898. It was damaged by a truck in 2000 and later restored. The town is also famous as the birthplace and home of the late **Lord Kitchener**, the grand master of calypso, who died on 11 February 2000 at the age of 77, and there is a statue of him in Hollis Road.

A road through the mountains

Just outside Arima, the 47-km (29-mile) long Blanchisseuse Road cuts into the Northern Range and over the other side to the north coast, twisting and turning alongside the Arima River through stands of all sorts of jungle vegetation, and passing a mostly abandoned government estate called Mount Pleasant which once produced cocoa and coffee. Much of this area of the Northern Range was used for cocoa and coffee farming, and there are still the sliding-roofed drying houses dotted across the hills. The panoramic views of rain-forested peaks and valleys, with enormous bamboo plants and exotic wild flowers are a pleasure not found elsewhere in the Caribbean islands.

In the forests towering nutmeg trees, bearing brown and red nuts, compete in height with the mighty mahogany and cedar and the odd teak. Vines and mosses

Map on pages 240–41

TIP

The Santa Rosa Carib Community Association (tel: 667 0210) on Paul Mitchell Street in Arima provides information on Carib culture and sells traditional Amerindian craftwork.

BELOW: a butterfly in the bush of the Northern Range.

hang from their limbs in the steamy depths of the jungle, and the abundantly flowering poui and immortelles splash the verdant surroundings with colour.

Look out for the dramatic pendulous blooms of the balisier palm, popular in hotel floral arrangements, but also be cautious as the leaves are a noted hiding place for snakes. In fact there are several venomous species of snake in the Northern Range. In the 19th century the English introduced the mongoose from India to eat them, but instead the mongoose is near extinct and the snakes are thriving.

Birdwatching and hiking in the jungle

The Asa Wright Nature Centre is committed to conservation.

BELOW: a guide at the Asa Wright Nature Centre makes bird calls.

The **Asa Wright Nature Centre** ⑫ (open daily; entrance fee; tel: 667 4655) 366 metres (1,200 ft) up in the Northern Range, 12 km (8 miles) along the Blanchisseuse Road is an ideal starting point for nature hikes, not least because the centre provides expert guided tours. Go early and have lunch at the centre, which was once a coffee, cocoa and citrus plantation *(see pages 179–80)*, or spend the night in the old colonial Great House and take part in the night and dawn birdwatching hikes, which include a visit to one of the world's most accessible colonies of nocturnal fruit-eating oilbirds. Other rare species to look out for are the white-necked jacobin hummingbird, the manakin lek and the blue-crowned motmot, along with black-throated mangos, rufous-browed peppershrikes and chestnut woodpeckers. Regarded as a model of sustainable development and eco-tourism, the centre offers a variety of field trips to all the other major birding sites in the country as well.

A few kilometres after Asa Wright, as you continue northwards, is a right turn leading to **Brasso Seco**, one of the few settlements in the Northern Range, which provides another good starting point for nature hikes to waterfalls and

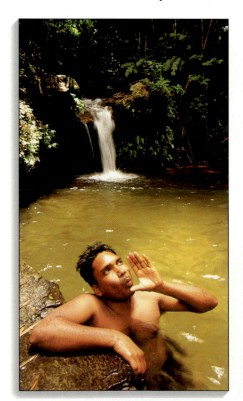

HIKING IN THE JUNGLE

Tours of the mountain rainforest of the Northern Range with its abundant bird and wildlife offer some of the most memorable tropical delights. There are organised birdwatching tours around Aripo Savannah and to the Asa Wright Nature Centre, or follow traditional Amerindian trails along the northern ridges and valleys. Several tour companies organise short and extended guided tours for all fitness levels, from the fit adventure seekers to visitors wanting a gentle walk in the countryside.

Caribbean Discovery Tours (tel: 624 7281; www.caribbeandiscoverytours.com) can organise trips that combine a drive in the mountains and a rainforest hike. Others offer the best sights in one or both of the islands.

Fit birdwatchers and naturalists can try the Iron Man Trekker 7-day hike, a challenging trail which passes by old cocoa plantations, rising into montane forest and includes camping on quiet beaches along the way. The highlight of the tour is a final ascent to El Tucuche – one of Trinidad's highest peaks – which rewards hikers with spectacular panoramic views of the area.

Alternatively, you can walk through the Arena Forest, with its historical Amerindian sites, or choose a 3-hour hike to Paria Waterfall along the rugged north coast.

Map on pages 240–41

birdwatching expeditions. Ask in the village for a guide *(see Travel Tips on page 362)*. The rest of the drive to Blanchisseuse is awe-inspiring as it climbs up, and then descends gently to the sea. The round trip tour to Asa Wright via Arima and back by the North Coast Road is a good day's outing.

There are more opportunities for forest hikes in the mountains on the eastern side of Arima. The Eastern Main Road quietens down to a country road, and soon afterwards meets another left turn that leads up to the **Heights of Guanapo** where you can explore the magnificent **Guanapo Gorge** – you must be fit, and bring a guide – and, even further still, the falls of **La Laja** and **Sombasson**. Three high-level species of bird, the blue-capped tanager, the orange-billed nightingale-thrush and the yellow-legged thrush, inhabit these upper heights.

A further 5 km (3 miles) along the main road is the turning on the right to **Waller Field**, an old American base, now a farming area. The Cumuto Road crosses the broad and lovely **Aripo Savannah** and **Arena Forest**, which are prime birdwatching spots *(see page 182)*. Allow a day to birdwatch or hike here. Follow the Cumuto Road over the river and past a small pumphouse where at once there is a track into this natural grassland dotted with trees.

Northeast to Toco

The county of St David, on the northeast coast, is Trinidad's closest point to its sister isle of Tobago and, edged by secluded beaches, is sparsely populated. At **Valencia**, 11 km (7 miles) after Arima, you pass through the Valencia Forest and over the river of the same name. Trinidadians often light wood fires and cook on the banks of the river here. Up the Cumaca Road to the left are hiking trails leading to the **Oropouche Caves**, home to another colony of oilbirds.

Up in the mountains the Paria Springs Eco-Community project is unfolding near Brasso Seco. Here nature lovers can stay in villagers' homes and explore the rainforest with knowledgeable guides, and by the end of 2001 they will also be able to stay in Amerindian-style huts (tel: 622 8826; email: rooks@ pariasprings.com).

BELOW: a tropical sunset in Toco.

Map on pages 240–41

Turtle-watching trips require a permit; ask at your hotel or call Nature Seekers in Matura (tel: 667 9075; 668 0171).

BELOW: foothills of the Northern Range.
RIGHT: secluded Maracas Bay.

Turtles on Matura Beach

Continuing on through fir and pine forest on the Valencia Road, after about 10 km (6 miles) you reach a left turn to Toco which is sometimes difficult to see. The side roads are tracks and trails into farming estates, and after the small town of **Matura** you eventually arrive at **Matura Bay**, where leatherback turtles come to lay their eggs. Between the months of March and July they go to open or exposed beaches with both heavy surf and coarse sand as at Matura, to lay their eggs under the cover of darkness (*see page 188*).

Leaving sleepy Matura, the road follows the splendid rugged coastline to the new bridge at Salybia. An inland track leads to the **Salybia Waterfall** ⓭, an excellent bathing spot in the **Matura Forest Reserve**. The next settlement back on the road is **Balandra** fishing village, a popular spot for city-dwellers to have holiday homes, some of which can be rented for a weekend. In fact, with the sheltered bay providing wonderful swimming and body surfing, a visit to this part of the island should ideally be for not less than that. Houses to rent are advertised in the newspapers. Bear in mind not to park under any coconut trees.

Awe-inspiring Toco

After Balandra you reach the eastern part of the **Toco Coast**; its sharp, sheer cliffs and sheltered bays and coves grow more awe-inspiring as you travel north past Breakfast River, the name the locals have given it. Here is a lovely bay, where you can enjoy a swim, pass the tiny, friendly villages of **Rampanalgas** and **Cumana**, and eventually you reach the northern coastline and the weather-beaten village of **Toco** itself and its tumbledown gingerbread houses. The folk museum at **Toco Composite School** provides insight into the area's history and distinctive culture. A road to the right takes you to a marvellous bay, also called **Salybia**, where snacks are available under shady trees. At **Galera Point**, on the northwest tip, stands an old lighthouse warning shipping of the extremely dangerous sea conditions below in what fishermen call the "graveyard".

On the other side of Toco village around **Sans Souci Bay**, about 8 km (5 miles) away, you will find some excellent surfing beaches. The road then veers inland and uphill, and then back down again across the **Grande Rivière**, another beautiful swimming spot. This river flows on both sides of the road and is lined by huge trees. The village of the same name has become a centre for ecotourism with the opening of the delightful **Mount Plaisir Hotel** and guesthouses. The sheltered beach is one of the best sites for watching turtles.

From there go on to **Shark River**, where in days gone by there used to be a tub race; today it is popular with hunters, swimmers, fishermen and artists.

Matelot is a small coastal fishing village on a beautiful safe bay. To get to it head for the Roman Catholic Church where the metal road joins the donkey track to Blanchisseuse (*see page 239*). A left turn leads through the village to the river; you will have to walk part of the way. Cross the bridge some 10 metres (30 ft) above the river and walk to the playground, and from there to the bay. This is a very quiet spot and worth an hour's stay in good weather. ❏

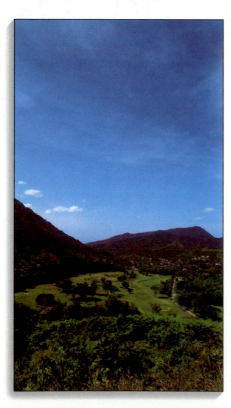

BIRDLIFE AND BUTTERFLIES

Trinidad & Tobago is awash with beautiful birds. The tiny iridescent natural jewels fill the tropical skies, offering birdwatchers unforgettable sights

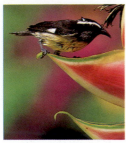

Even Trinidad Carnival pales in comparison with the sister islands' paradise of birds and butterflies whose names are as spectacular as their colours: purple honeycreeper, ruby-topaz hummingbird, silver-beaked tanager, flambeau, donkey eye or coco mort bleu.

Its diverse habitats (mangrove swamps, fresh and saltwater lakes, tropical rainforest, mudflats, grasslands) and South American flora and fauna make Trinidad and Tobago the southern Caribbean's most unique birding destination. With over 420 bird species and 617 butterfly species, Trinidad has the world's highest density of birds (and probably butterflies) per square mile. It is not unusual to spot up to 65 species in a day or up to 200 in a week. Tobago has 210 bird species, some not found in Trinidad. Besides rare species like oilbird, white-tail sabre wing hummingbird and blue-backed manakin, Trinidad is home to 16 of the rarest South American hummingbirds, living up to its Amerindian name Iere – Land of the Hummingbird.

BIRDING SITES

Unforgettable sights include the roosting flight of the scarlet ibis to its home in the Caroni Swamp, and the macaws flying through the silhouettes of the royal palms at Manzanilla. Trinidad's endangered indigenous pawi (piping guan) can be found on the north coast. There are rainforest species, raptors and seabirds (especially on Tobago's offshore islands) as well as migratory birds from North and South America. Some of the best birding sites are in the Northern Range at the Pax Guesthouse and Nature Lodge and the Asa Wright Nature Centre. Others include the Caroni Swamp Bird sanctuary, the Nariva freshwater swamp, the Waterloo mudflats and the Pointe-à-Pierre Wildfowl Trust, unique for its setting in an oil refinery compound.

▷ **IT'S IN THE SCENT**
The small postman or crimson-patched longwing is similar to its close relative the postman, but the postman smells of fried rice and the longwing of witch hazel.

△ **MOTMOT**
The blue-crowned motmot is a rare sight in Trinidad but very common in Tobago. This fearless little bird will feed from the hand.

△ **BRILLIANT RED IBIS**
The scarlet ibis, one of the national birds, owes its distinctive brilliant colour to its carotene diet of crustaceans and small crabs

◁ **PARROT ISLAND**
The blue-headed is one of three species of parrot found T&T. The others are the yellow headed (often kept as pets) a the common orange wing.

ASA WRIGHT: A BIRDING HOT SPOT

The Asa Wright Nature Centre, situated 13 km (8 miles) up Trinidad's Arima Valley, in the heart of the Northern Range, is one of the Caribbean's most important conservation areas and wildlife sanctuaries, frequented by the world's leading ornithologists and naturalists like British film maker David Attenborough. Originally a cocoa, coffee and citrus estate, the centre now comprises 300 hectares (750 acres) of unspoilt tropical rainforest, complete with the original house and outlying guest rooms. The verandah makes for leisurely birdspotting as successive flights of hummingbirds, bananquits, honeybirds and cowbirds hover at feeders suspended from the eaves, or the feeding trays below. More than 170 bird species have been spotted in the Arima Valley, making the centre a birding hot spot. Overnight guests can look forward to a visit to one of the world's most accessible colonies of rare nocturnal fruit-eating oilbirds.

WHITE BEARD
The white-bearded manakin is known for its elaborate courtship displays, including the popping sound of its carotene encrusted wingtips.

FOREST DWELLER
Butterflies from the fragrant postman family are frequent visitors to Trinidad and Tobago's forests and shaded tracks.

▷ FRUITY TOUCAN
The channel-billed toucan which despite its dangerous looking beak is largely a fruit eater. There is much to choose from in the fertile forests.

CHAGUARAMAS AND THE DRAGON'S ISLANDS

You can take a boat trip "down de islands", drop anchor in the sheltered harbours of the northwest peninsula and enjoy the nightlife just a dragon's breath away from South America

The rainforested hills of the Northern Range continue west of Port of Spain, reaching out to Venezuela across the Dragon's Mouth like a pointed finger, broken up at the tip into tiny islands; the city rambles along the Western Main Road, on the southern coast of the northwestern peninsula, as suburbs littered with high-rise apartments. Few roads branch off into the mountains, which hide pretty waterfalls and refreshing clear pools to swim in. At Chaguaramas, the western half of the peninsula and once an US wartime base, rural Trinidad splays out in a wide strip of grassland along the south coast, fringed by shallow beaches and backed by acres of untouched rainforest, protected as a national park. Owing to the industrial nature of parts of this coast, swimming is not usually recommended in the sea here, although lots of the locals do swim.

Once joining Trinidad to the South American continent during the Ice Age, the far western islands of Gaspar Grande, Monos, Huevos and Chacachacare are little gems which have become the domain of the well-to-do, sailors and yachtsmen who anchor in the waters between Trinidad and Venezuela to enjoy the fine north-coast beaches and rural scenery. The residents of Port of Spain go "down de islands" for day trips or weekend jaunts to enjoy their natural beauty, beaches, good swimming and rich fishing waters.

Because the network of roads in Trinidad is built for getting into Port of Spain, exploring the peninsula means using the same route time and again. One way of making a change is by going "down de islands" across the sea, on a boat trip *(see pages 259 and 263).*

Procuring the island links

In 1791, Don Gaspar Antonio de la Guardia, the procurator syndic, in charge of state lands in Port of Spain, presented Governor Don José María Chacon with a petition that the northwestern islands be ceded to the *cabildo* (council) of Port of Spain to increase revenue. The petition was passed on to the first commissary of population, Don Pedro Ybarrate, who replied that the King of Spain had no occasion for the islands of Monos, Huevos and Patos (belonging to Venezuela) and was pleased to cede them to the *cabildo.* Chacachacare had already been given to Gerald Fitzpatrick Carry, an Irishman, for services rendered to the King of Spain, though it had to be returned if the king needed it. Carry grew cotton and sugar apples there for a while, and later whaling stations were set up. Chaca, as it is fondly called by Trinidadians, is now a solid part of "down de islands". Although Patos has remained outside Trinidadian

PRECEDING PAGES: sunset down the islands **LEFT:** isolated Saut d'Eau Island off the northern coast. **BELOW:** soaking up the sun.

The Western Main Road along the Chaguaramas Peninsula is a riot of colour and a prime spot to do business. Stalls selling fruit, vegetables and fish line the road, and ramshackle rum shops offer respite.

ownership, the island was leased in 1876 to one L. Dennis O'Connor for 30 years, to raise stock and catch fish for salting. But it soon grew too lonely for him; the land reverted to Spain, and in 1940 was ceded to Venezuela in connection with establishing boundaries. When you are near Patos you are in Venezuelan territorial waters, so do not visit it as travel between the two countries is not entirely free.

Heading out to Chaguaramas

Before the American forces arrived during World War II, Chaguaramas peninsula was a popular weekend haunt with the residents of Port of Spain, but in 1941 that all came to an end with the establishment of the US naval base at the town of Chaguaramas: the region's inhabitants were resettled in places like Carenage, and the peninsula was designated out of bounds. Fifteen years after the end of the war, the Americans were still there and it took a large demonstration in 1960 to make them relinquish the lease in 1967.

To reach the peninsula from **Port of Spain** ❶, head out along the **Western Main Road**, which continues on from Tragarete Road, and drive through **St James** *(see page 225)*. Alternatively, start off on Wrightson Road at South Quay and join the Audrey Jeffers Highway heading west. On your right are the **National Stadium** and the **Jean Pierre Sports Complex**. Jean Pierre was captain of the national netball team that won the world championship jointly with New Zealand in 1979 in this stadium. After the end of a successful sporting career Jean Pierre became an MP and minister of sport for Trinidad. Past the stadium, on the left, is a huge area called the **foreshore** looking out over the sea where the MovieTowne entertainment and shopping complex opened in 2002.

BELOW: an old portrayal of the whale-filled waters around Trinidad.

With its 10 luxury cinemas, upmarket shopping and bars, MovieTowne is in keeping with the Miami style of development of the western peninsula and a truly 21st-century liming venue.

Map on page 262

The coastal highway meets Western Main Road in **Cocorite** where you will find the pastel-coloured, high-rise apartment complex, Bayside Towers, which was once considered to be a sign of a property boom on the island owing to high demand from international companies coming to the island to cash in on the oil and natural gas discoveries. More tower blocks fracture the skyline as you approach **West Mall**, which offers classy shopping facilities. Here are the modern, mirrored façade of the Guardian Life Insurance Company building and the obligatory Kentucky Fried Chicken food outlet.

A right fork leads to the genteel suburb of Diego Martin and the Blue Basin Falls *(see pages 265–6)*, but the Western Main Road continues along the coast through more upmarket residential estates reposing on reclaimed swampland and abutting the fishing village of **Carenage**, 8 km (5 miles) outside Port of Spain. Just after the supermarket in Glencoe, on the left, is the entrance to the **Trinidad and Tobago Yacht Club** (TTYC), from where you can take deep-sea fishing trips and boat excursions to the islands. (Other boat trips to the islands are described on page 263.)

Carenage goes back to the days of the Spaniards in the 18th century when they used to bring their ships into the protected harbour to be careened (have the barnacles scraped off their hulls). The population burgeoned during World War II when people were relocated here to make room for the US forces. The town then developed into a popular nightspot for the American sailors and prostitution became a thriving business.

A baptism in the sea, practised by both Seventh Day Adventists and Baptists, is a common sight.

BELOW: yachts at anchor in a natural marina.

The Chaguaramas Development Authority (CDA) was set up in the 1960s to look after Chaguaramas National Park. As well as providing guides for treks in the park and elsewhere in the Northern Range, the CDA (tel: 634 4312) organises all types of eco-friendly tours, runs nature camps for children and arranges diving, swimming and sightseeing trips to the islands.

BELOW: industrial activity at Chaguaramas.

Today Carenage is famous for being the home town of Bernard Julien, one of Trinidad's former leading cricketers. Julien played for the county of Kent in England in the 1970s, and was blacklisted, along with several other sportsmen, when he toured South Africa in 1983 with a rebel team of West Indian cricketers. He remains involved in the sport, as a cricket coach. On the sea front stands the wooden church of **St Peter** whose day is celebrated on 29 June in grand style and includes a ceremony in which the fishing boats are blessed.

The US military base – converted

The region of **Chaguaramas** ❷ starts about a kilometre (half a mile) or so from Carenage, around the winding Western Main Road, backed by hills on one side and the sea on the other, and after silos and a dock belonging to the National Flour Mills. It continues for about 7 km (4 miles), edged by a series of beaches which are not always suitable for swimming, owing to pollution, although the locals do not seem to mind. Not a pretty place, with no one really living here, it is a great spot for socialising, with plenty of nightclubs and restaurants *(see Travel Tips on page 363)*.

At the beginning of Chaguaramas stands **Pier 1**, a smart nightclub by night and a restaurant by day. Just across the street is **The Base**, another nightclub, painted in naval camouflage colours, which is adjacent to a huge complex, originally the US military base, containing the **Convention Centre**, the offices of the **Chaguaramas Development Authority** (open Mon–Fri, 8am–3.45pm; tel: 634 4312 or 634 4364), an army base and the **Chaguaramas Military and Aviation Museum** (open daily; entrance fee; tel: 634 4391). Chronicling the country's military history from 1498 until today, the

museum also has an exhibition portraying soldiers in the two world wars and a photographic exhibition of Trinidad's VE Day celebrations.

Remnants of the Americans' tenure are to be found all along the stretch, including aircraft hangars, most of which lie deserted. One such hangar, opposite the helicopter port of the National Security Services, is used by Bowen Marine, owned by a former Trinidadian Miss Universe, Janelle Chow. Another is the workshop of **Peter Minshall's Callaloo Company**.

Natural shelter from the storms

Trinidad is a safe harbour, rarely hit by hurricanes, so increasingly pleasure craft and yachts are choosing to dock here. The coast at Chaguaramas forms a natural harbour in Williams Bay, the crook of the protective arm connecting **Point Gourd** with the main land, and the place is packed with boats on land and sea. At one time fishermen and sailors were able to take a short cut across Point Gourd to Chaguaramas Bay through Hart's Cut, just 5 metres (16 ft) wide and 1 metre (3 ft) deep. The idea of a police superintendent named Hart in 1856, the cut saved a lot of hard work pulling around the point, but it has been filled in for many years now. Yachting businesses offering their services to the yachties abound along the shore. The **Trinidad and Tobago Yachting Association** (TTYA) is the first one on Williams Bay, just after the Callaloo mas' camp.

Further round on Point Gourd is the smart new marina and **Crews Inn** (tel: 634 4384), which has an excellent restaurant with waterfront dining. Close by are The Anchorage (*see Tip in margin*) and **MOBS 2** (Moon Over Bourbon Street 2 – MOBS 1 was at West Mall for many years before it closed down), an open-

Map on page 262

TIP

The Anchorage is an open-air nightspot near Crews Inn on Point Gourd at the weekends, with a restaurant open daily overlooking the harbour and the rainforest behind. Call 634 4334 for more information.

BELOW: one of Peter Minshall's Carnival mas' bands takes to the streets.

COSTUME THE CALLALOO WAY

The high ceilings of the hangar in Chaguaramas, which is home to Peter Minshall's Callaloo mas' camp, are perfect for the huge area needed to create the works of art parading on the streets of Port of Spain every year. Minshall is the leading Carnival costume designer in Trinidad, and one of the leading designers of large-scale spectacles in the world.

His Callaloo Company produces something like 2,000 costumes each year for the Trinidad Carnival. The spectacular theatrical costumes include large-scale puppets for the King and Queen of Carnival show, which are sometimes 6–9 metres (20–30 ft) tall. The creations "Saga Boy" and "Tan Tan" are just two of his more popular puppets, and they have performed in events all over the world, from the Bastille Day celebrations in Paris to West Indian carnivals in the United States and Europe.

Minshall and his team have also produced costumes for the opening ceremonies of major events such as the 1992 Barcelona Olympics and the 1994 Los Angeles World Cup. You may be able to watch his team at work at the mas' camp, although bear in mind that the months running up to Carnival are very hectic, with little time for talk. To ask if this is possible phone 634 4491.

The Chaguaramas beaches are always alive with music, dancing and laughter.

air bar which hosts medium-scale musical events for select crowds, such as jazz, Caribbean and alternative music or calypso (tel: 634 2255). Still further around the point is the **Point Gourd Marina**, opened in 1996.

Back on the Western Main Road alongside Chaguaramas Bay you come to the Aluminum Company (Alcoa), which is also the docking point for boat trips to the Gasparee Caves on the island of Gaspar Grande *(see page 263)*. More yachting facilities are provided at **Peakes** (tel: 634 4533), before Alcoa, and IMS, which also offers a boat maintenance and repair service.

Near the end of the peninsula the main road stops at **The Cove**, a restaurant and hotel with a well-kept private beach (entrance fee). The barrier with a uniformed guard marks the entrance to Trinidad's defence force headquarters.

Exploring Chaguaramas National Park

Returning to the Chaguaramas base the Western Main Road forks left onto the Back Road, and the first left turn takes you deep into the rainforest of **Chaguaramas National Park ❸**. The area has been developed by the CDA *(see page 260)* into a recreation centre, and everything above the 90-metre (300-ft) contour line in the hills has been designated a wildlife reserve. No one is allowed to enter the reserve without a CDA-approved guide, but the nature tours that the CDA organises are interesting and varied, and feature sights such as cayman (an indigenous relative of the crocodile), rare birds, howler monkeys, water fowl and perhaps a scarlet ibis in the late afternoon amongst vegetation which is virtually unchanged from the time the first Amerindians to the island walked through it. Other eco-educational tours go along a river through a winding gorge to a waterfall with a small pool that you can swim in, or up Mount Catherine for birdwatching. A

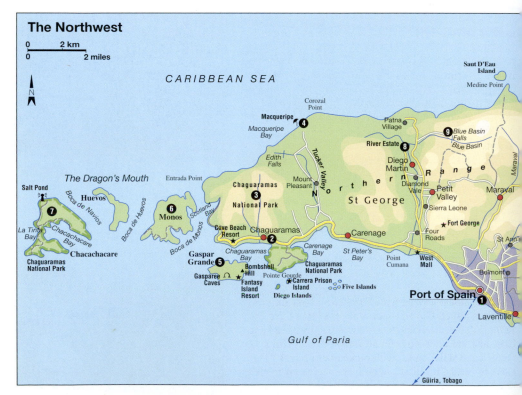

tour by bus takes groups through the kind of natural landscapes which Trinidad's leading 19th-century artist, Jean Michel Cazabon, painted *(see page 113)*.

Macqueripe Beach – a sheltered cove

Just at the entrance to Chaguaramas, at The Base nightclub on the Western Main Road, the Tucker Valley Road heads north across the peninsula to Macqueripe Beach 4 km (2½ miles) away. Or from Port of Spain, after the major bend in the western Main Road, take a right turn after the first bridge. About 3 km (2 miles) along the road a sign points left to **Edith Falls**, and a little further on, just before the golf course, a trail plunges left into the thick undergrowth of jungle. The sparkling 180-metre (590-ft) falls are at the end of a magical 30-minute hike through the rainforest which is dripping with tropical flowers, draped with lianas and alive with the sounds of monkeys, parrots and birds. It is best to be guided by the CDA here as it is not a well used path.

Macqueripe Beach ❹ is maintained by the CDA and the tourist authority, so there is secure parking available, but the route to the sea is down a steep stone stairway so it is not accessible to everyone. The beach is in a small cove with a jetty that you can swim out to, but only if you are a strong swimmer as the water is quite deep. Triathalon athletes train here and regularly swim across the bay – a distance of almost 1 km (about half a mile) – where American submarines used to dock during World War II.

Going down de islands

You can go several ways "down de islands" to Gaspar Grande and the **Bocas**, or mouths – the channels of water separating the rugged islands of Monos, Huevos and Chacachacare from each other and linking the sheltered Gulf of Paria to the Caribbean Sea in the north. By boat from Port of Spain harbour is one way; either ask at your hotel or contact the CDA *(see page 260)*. Other alternatives are from the Chaguaramas coast through the TTYC *(see page 259)*, and in Chaguaramas itself the TTYA (tel: 634 4519) and the **Island Property Owners' Association** (tel: 634 4331) at The Cove offer trips, shuttle services and boat rental. The CDA also arranges an assortment of tours to the islands, including birdwatching.

Gaspar Grande ❺, also known as Gasparee, is a 25-minute boat trip from Port of Spain or 15 minutes from Chaguaramas *(see page 260)*, and originally belonged to a Don Gaspar de Percin. When the Spaniards capitulated to the British in 1797, there was lengthy litigation concerning to whom and to which country the islands around Trinidad belonged.

In the 18th century two whaling stations were established at **Point Baleine** (Whale Point), and cotton was grown. Noël Coward used to stay at a guesthouse at Point Baleine where he wrote the novel *Point Valeine*. The **Gasparee Caves** (open daily; entrance fee) at Point Baleine, are home to a colony of squeaking fruit bats, and are adorned with an array of colourful stalactites and stalagmites, with nicknames such as "The Lovers" and "Buddha", which are reflected in the deep, clear pool. You enter down steps now, not a rope

Map on page 262

TIP

The US forces left behind the 18-hole Chaguaramas Golf Course (tel: 634 4349) near Macqueripe Beach. Open to the public at reasonable rates, the club hires out equipment and provides caddies.

BELOW: a northwestern view.

ladder as children did long ago. Around 7 am every Sunday you can see little boats making their way across the sea to the island's Roman Catholic chapel, and several holiday homes are dotted over the hillside.

On your return to the mainland you pass a small island inhabited by centipedes. Three of the five smaller islands to the east are **Caldeonia**, **Lenegan's** and **Nelson**, originally the Diego Martin islands. The East Indians who arrived as indentured labourers from 1848 were kept here until they were assigned to estates. The other two, **Pelican** and **Rock**, were quarantine stations. The two larger islands, once called Long Islands, were Trinidad's first holiday resorts: **Creteau**, sometimes known as Begorrat, is now a stone quarry, and **Carrera** has been a prison since 1877. Prisoners are still sent here for hard labour, and the strong currents prevent any thought of escape.

Monos and the first Boca

The first of the islands in the Bocas is **Monos** ❻. On the way you pass by **Staubles Bay** at Teteron at the tip of the peninsula. It was from Staubles Bay that the hills of the Northern Range were shelled by government forces during the Black Power uprising in Trinidad in 1970. There are many derelict houses here which were once Trinidadians' holiday refuges; they became the homes of senior officers of the US armed forces during World War II. The house on the tip of the point belonged to the Canning family, and later the US armed forces turned it into a club called the Crow's Nest. Later still, Prime Minister Dr Eric Williams made it a holiday home for himself and his young daughter Erica.

The open channel of water between the peninsula and Monos, around the tip after Gaspar Grande, is the first Boca, or mouth, and the small rock jutting out of the churning sea is the Dent Ma Tetron. There is a strong and tricky current here called Remous (pronounced *ray-moo*) which inspired the old Trinidadian caution: "Don't row your boat if Remous is running." If you are fishing you will feel Remous pulling your line. Tucked into the mainland on the right, sheltered **Scotland Bay**'s calm shallow waters make it easy to anchor for a swim, followed by a picnic on the white sandy beach.

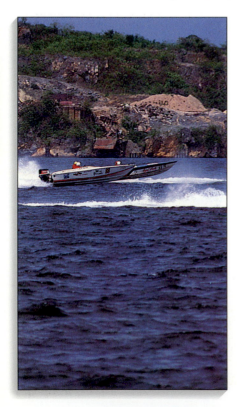

All the bays or points on Monos have names. The first one, **Maria Elba**, is owned by the Gatcliffe family. Tommy Gatcliffe is said to be one of the two people alive who know the secret formula for the world-famous Angostura Bitters (*see page 127*). The second point is known as **Gittens**; the third is **Copperhole** in Turtle's Bay and was originally a whaling station. You can see the copper cauldrons in which the whale blubber was boiled partly submerged in the shallow waters at this point. On the western side of the island a sharp drop of sheer rocks into the tempestuous sea below creates a spectacular sight. This, the second Boca, divides Monos from **Huevos**, which is privately owned by the Boos family.

Chaca – island of adventure

The largest island of the link and the most westerly, **Chacachacare** ❼, an hour away from the mainland, supposedly got its name from the sound of the chat-

Map on page 262

tering of monkeys. In Venezuela it is called the Island of the Deer, and the Spanish called it El Caracol. Nevertheless, it has been Chaca to the Trinis as far back as most can recall.

The third Boca separates Chacachacare from Huevos, and on the other side the **Dragon's Mouth** yawns across to the Venezuelan mainland. Spanish sailors used to pray to their favourite saints to get them through the Dragon's Mouth safely. Sometimes it is calm like a lake, but on other occasions it truly earns its name. A boat larger than a pirogue should be used for a visit to Chaca; the best time is mid-afternoon, around 4.30pm.

Swimming and fishing are excellent in Chaca – and so was smuggling once, when smugglers from Venezuela, and there were many, used to bring their boats into Trinidad territorial waters via the island. In 1877 the British established a leper colony here, building extraordinary red-brick Victorian houses: the doctors' residence, the home for the nuns who cared for the lepers, a hospital and a chapel. With the departure of the last patients in 1984 the island was left uninhabited, except for the two lighthouse keepers who look after the small white lighthouse, dating from 1885. You can join a Lighthouse Trail tour, which includes the boat trip, a five-hour hike – with the possibility of seeing giant iguanas, which can grow to 2 metres (7 ft) long, and a salt lagoon – to the lighthouse, which has spectacular views of Trinidad.

River Estate and the waterwheel

For a pleasant day trip inland you can visit the **Blue Basin Falls** (north of Port of Spain) in the Northern Range, via **Diego Martin** and the River Estate. If you are without transport you will need to hire a taxi specially to get to the

Deep-sea fishing "down de islands" is renowned: Franklin D. Roosevelt came here to fish during World War II. There are good grouper banks behind Monos and Huevos, and if you would like to try your luck contact the Trinidad and Tobago Game Fishing Association on 624 5304.

BELOW: the wild and empty north coast.

falls, as no taxi routes pass nearby and do not forget to make arrangements to be picked up afterwards. Otherwise, bear right on the Western Main Road at West Mall and head north to Diego Martin and a former sugar and cocoa plantation called River Estate in a gentle, fertile valley.

When the British took over Trinidad at the end of the 18th century, 26 French families had already settled into the parish of Diego Martin, and 900 slaves were growing coffee and sugar on the plantation. By 1812 the population had increased to 1,655, and a number of distilleries had been set up to produce rum. With the abolition of slavery and the arrival of East Indian indentured servants, the distribution of the various racial groups helped to shape Diego Martin's character as villages such as **Petit Valley** to the east – now one of the main middle-class areas – popped up.

Even though little concentrated pockets do exist, today Diego Martin is ethnically integrated, with several intriguing variations of ethnic mixture apparent in the residents. **Diamond Vale**, one of the more recently established middle-class areas in Diego Martin, is the home of Wendy Fitzwilliam, Miss Universe 1998, a law student who entered the pageant for a joke.

At the northern end of Diego Martin parish lies **River Estate ❽**, where inside the restored wooden plantation house is a small unscintillating museum which gives a glimpse of parish history, and illustrates cocoa production when Cadbury's owned it. An old restored **waterwheel**, which was once an integral part of sugar production, stands close by. Dating from 1845, it was powered by water brought along an aqueduct from the Diego Martin River and drove the cane crushers.

Across from the museum is the **Panatics** panyard. If you are visiting around Carnival time, you can drop in to listen to them practise in the evenings.

Cane juice is crushed and dispensed from trucks parked at the side of the road.

BELOW: farmworkers taking a break.

At the waterwheel, take the first right turn and proceed down the road, which leads to Blue Basin Road; turn into the road. (Alternatively, proceed down the main road until you come to the sign announcing the waterfall, but the "waterwheel road" is a short cut and should save time).

A dip in the Blue Basin Falls

The drive to the **Blue Basin Falls** ❾ is a few kilometres along the road, and the final 46 metres (50 yards) of hillside leading to them are very steep. Once you reach the sign it is about a five-minute walk to the falls. Be aware that there used to be a concrete path skirting the hillside, but there have been landslips in recent times. The way is still accessible, and not considered to be too dangerous, but it is best not to carry too much in the way of food or drink; a backpack will be fine. The waterfall is not very high, about 11 metres (35 ft), and not quite as powerful as it was even a few years ago. Depending on the time you go, you might see on the rocks which line the way, or among the high trees and vegetation of the surrounding rainforest, coloured flags and the remains of coloured candles – signs of rituals by Orisa and Shouter Baptists. There is even a statue of the Madonna nestled in a natural cave at the base of the falls.

The pool at the bottom is good for bathing, and there are a few more downriver. The rocks are not precarious, but caution should be exercised, in more ways than one. As in any other isolated place, it is advisable to travel with a group, and do not let the rainforest and sounds of nature lull you into a false sense of security. The River Estate area has a high number of unemployed young men, and some are not picky about how they acquire money to purchase their designer clothes. ❑

Map on page 262

TIP

The pools at the Blue Basin Falls are usually busy with children after school, at weekends and during the holidays. The best time to go is during the week.

LEFT: Blue Basin Falls deep in the rainforest.
BELOW: a splash of of bright colour from a poui tree.

Map on page 274

COAST TO COAST

Trips across central Trinidad reveal swamps teeming with water birds, wide expanses of cane-covered plains, more rainforested hills and a never-ending coastline of sand and coconut groves

Central Trinidad is around 80 km (50 miles) from west to east and spreads from the foothills of the Northern Range into the vast rolling greenery of the Caroni Plains, swaying and rustling with sugar cane. The cane arrows, or flowers, are a beautiful sight just before harvest. A cane field then looks like a green wall with white tops stretching into the distance. To the south the Montserrat Hills and the Central Range cut across the island, covered in lush rainforest and alive with a colourful array of bird and animal life. More birds can be seen in the coastal swamps and their sanctuaries – Caroni in the west, which is best visited in the late afternoon, and Nariva in the east – and around the two large reservoirs of Arena and Navet.

Along the western side of the island industrial pockets feed the population in the small towns such as Chaguanas and Couva. There is a strong sense of India in this region, which is mostly peopled by descendants of the East Indian indentured labourers who arrived in their thousands in the middle of the 19th century to work on the plantations. The further inland you go the fewer people there are, with only a few villages dotted here and there right over to the palm-fringed, sandy Manzanilla coast. Public transport is minimal in these parts, so it is best to organise a taxi for the day or hire a car, although finding your way around the narrow winding roads in the countryside can present quite a challenge. You can make a round tour to the east coast, or several shorter trips.

Chaguanas – a bustling market town

A visit to **Chaguanas ❶**, 30 km (19 miles) south of Port of Spain, starts the tour of Trinidad's central region. It is easy to get a taxi there from Port of Spain or San Fernando, and because the city is not very large: it can be traversed on foot in under an hour, but there is plenty to see.

You leave the capital on the Churchill Roosevelt Highway and after about 13 km (8 miles) take a right turn southwards down the Uriah Butler Highway. Trinidadians consider the Caroni River to be the dividing line between north and south Trinidad, and until you get to Chaguanas, about 10 minutes after the shopping mall called **City of the Grand Bazaar**, the highway is bordered by scattered houses and the odd commercial enterprise such as a car dealership. Otherwise the landscape is mainly flat and green, with only the Caroni Swamp *(see pages 280–1)* between you and the Gulf of Paria to the west.

When you reach Chaguanas, the route to the east coast is left through Montrose and past **Longdenville**, a former convict depot named after James Longden, governor from 1870–74. The right turn will take you in less than a minute into one of the

*Just outside
Chaguanas is the
National Council for
Indian Culture, a
focal point at festivals
such as Diwali.*

BELOW:

Shivetha Verma in
traditional dress.

important cities in the island. At its heart Chaguanas is a market town providing commerce to the small towns along the sugar-cane belt.

Three large shopping malls, **Centre Pointe**, **Mid Centre** and **Centre City**, are within walking distance of each other. The island's banks are represented here, along with shops offering clothing, electrical goods, dry goods, industrial goods and toys, and supermarkets. In the middle of it all is the old **marketplace**, an agricultural market where vendors have sold homegrown produce since the 19th century. People from all over the island come for the low-cost shopping, so there is always a steady traffic flow into the town. On market day, Saturday, the traffic is thick and slow from early morning to late afternoon.

Birthplace of a literary lion

On Chaguanas Main Road, a little way west of the Catholic church, stands **Lion House**, a large and imposing building in the style of northern India, dating from 1926, where the Nobel Laureate and controversial writer V. S. Naipaul and his brother Shiva *(see page 107)*, were born and brought up. However, the house is not open to the public.

Although Chaguanas can be garrulous and brassy, it has become one of the most desirable places to live through both its central position and the low cost of living in comparison with Port of Spain and San Fernando. The influx of people has contributed to the growth of commerce in the town, apparent on the Caroni Savannah Road, which intersects the main road just after the Catholic church, where every other house for nearly 2 km (1 mile) has a storefront.

Around 1950 the residents were mainly descendants of East Indian indentured labourers; these days the city's composition has evened out, but you still see signs

TEMPLE IN THE SEA

Until around the 1950s the Hindu religion was considered by the colonials to be barbaric and heathen: something to be tolerated but not encouraged. So when a *mandir* built on the beach in 1947 by an Indian labourer called Siewdas Sadhu came to the attention of the sugar company that owned the land in 1952, the temple was bulldozed. Siewdas was imprisoned for two years for not having building permission.

But Siewdas was not going to be beaten, and on the premise that if the sugar company owned the land it did not own the sea he decided to build a platform about 90 metres (100 yards) into the Gulf of Paria, and place his shrine there. The undertaking took most of his life; he persevered singlehandedly, carrying rocks out at low tide for the foundations, and battling against a sea that was no more accommodating than the sugar company. Eventually, in 1995, the 150th anniversary of the arrival of the East Indians in Trinidad, the National Council for Indian Culture stepped in and replaced the original structure.

Today services are held on Sunday mornings in the elaborate octagonal temple at Waterloo, and on land there is a Hindu cremation site, decorated with *jandhis*, or prayer flags, to mark the ceremonies honouring the departed.

Map on page 274

of the Indian presence: the Hindu prayer flags in the yards, the brown faces in the crowded streets, the outlandish colours of some of the houses. East Indians were brought here after the abolition of slavery *(see page 34)*, first arriving on the *Fatel Rozack* (a corruption of *Fath Al Razak*, Arabic for "victory of Allah the generous"), a boat owned by a Bombay merchant, Ebrahim bin Yoosuf, in 1845. Their descendants have hung on to their customs, cooking, dress, music, religion and even some forms of speech. This cultural retention has been helped by "Bollywood", which provides a constant diet of Indian movies, popular in Trinidad, but the Western and African influences have also mingled freely with the Indian, creating a culture similar to its origins in some respects but vastly different in others.

Just 3 km (2 miles) to the south of Chaguanas on the Southern Main Road, opposite the residential area of Edinburgh Gardens, is **Carlsen Field**, the site of a US Armed Forces Airbase during World War II. Still called "The Base" even though many people have forgotten about the wartime activities, Carlsen Field provides a collection of Indian potters with clay from the soil here which they fashion into pots and lamps, called *deyas*, for Diwali *(see page 158)*. The potters sell them from their workshops strung along the road just before Chase Village.

A shrine built with blood, toil, sweat and tears

A right turn soon after Chase Village brings you onto a road bordered by sugar cane and palm trees that ends on the coast at **Waterloo**, 8 km (5 miles) away. En route, look out for the 12-metre (40-ft) statue of the Hindu god Hanuman in Carapichaima, which towers above a yoga centre and ashram. Jutting out into the bay at Waterloo is the magnificent **Temple in the Sea ❷**, the forerunner of which was largely built by the blood, toil, sweat and tears of Siewdass Sadhu, an Indian

Lion House in Chaguanas was featured in V.S. Naipaul's novel A House For Mr Biswas (1961) as the enclave of the domineering Tulsi family. Biswas was modelled on Naipaul's father, Seepersad.

BELOW:
the Temple in the Sea at Waterloo.

labourer. Today this sparkling white Hindu *mandir* stands proudly at the end of a pier in the sea as if cocking a snook at the sugar company that would not allow it to be built on land. Hindus come from miles around to worship here, and visitors are welcome too provided that they remove their shoes before entering the temple.

Returning to the Southern Main Road and continuing south, you pass through several kilometres of cane fields which, depending on the time of year and the state of maturity of the canes, will either form a high wall on both sides of the road or provide a panorama of green carpet. Further along you see in front of you **Brechin Castle**, once the main factory area of Caroni (1975) Ltd, the former state-owned sugar company purchased from British firm Tate & Lyle in 1977, which was closed in 2004, after many years of running at a loss. Sevilla House, once occupied by members of the company's senior management, is perched up on the hill. The road leading to this former estate house is lined by royal palms, giving it a very colonial air, and the grounds have been converted into an 18-hole golf course for the use of the occupants. Caroni Ltd owns another factory at Usine Ste Madeleine near San Fernando.

Couva's industrial awakening

Smaller than Chaguanas, **Couva** ❸ was once a sleepy little town, but it has livened up in the last few years through the commerce of the Point Lisas Industrial Estate, a few kilometres away on the coast. Chemical and industrial processing plants set up by a number of multinational companies have brought a flood of expatriates, high-income executives and well-paid workers to the area. Restaurants are numerous along the Main Road, and so are industrial support services like welding and machine shops, and of course, consumer goods. In the

own is the **Convent of the Holy Faith**, a school in the grounds of the great house of a former plantation overseer. The old house is beautiful, though the school is merely a collection of new buildings spread across large areas of land.

The massive **Point Lisas Estate** industrial complex has been built up over the past 15 years to encourage use of the country's high natural gas and oil reserves and to diversify the economy away from oil dependency. The steel company Caribbean Ispat, Arcadian, the PowerGen power station, the Methanol company PCS Nitrogen, Farmland Miss Chemicals and other heavy industries are situated here. To get to it, after leaving Couva keep driving west to **Carli Bay**, a small fishing village on the Gulf Coast. Then turn left for San Fernando at the Anglican Church (the signs are clearly marked). About a kilometre or so (½ mile) along, past residential neighbourhood, you come to the Point Lisas Roundabout which leads into the estate.

Tours of the different enterprises are available to those who have a special interest in industry, or for potential investors interested in downstream industries. Contact the Point Lisas Port Industrial Development Corporation (PLIPDECO) on 636 2201 or TIDCO (Tourism and Industrial Development Company of Trinidad and Tobago) on 675 7034/5 *(see Travel Tips on page 343).*

Into the depths of the countryside

Continue south along the coastal road to dusty **Claxton Bay**, where there is a cement factory, and head inland directly west until after about 5 km (3 miles) you reach the main Solomon Hochoy Highway to San Fernando. Turn left onto this road and return north, passing vast undulating fields, many full of sugar cane, to Chaguanas and the **Caroni Plains** ❹ which form a broad belt across

Map on page 274

Farrell House (tel: 659 2271), at the southern end of Claxton Bay, is a hotel on a hill with a wonderful view of the Gulf of Paria. Used mainly by businessmen, the hotel has a pool and offers excellent lunches. Or you could stay here overnight and witness the beautiful sunset.

BELOW: a tour of a sugar factory.

The Arena Reservoir and Dam is another of Trinidad's wonderful wildlife and birdwatching spots and, in the middle of the Caroni Plains, heralds the start of the Central Range Wildlife Sanctuary. Open daily; tickets must be bought in advance from WASA (Water and Sewerage Authority) in Port of Spain or St Joseph (tel: 662 2302).

BELOW: walls of sugar cane border the road south.

the middle of the island. The cane industry, once the economic mainstay of the island, is now heavily subsidised by the government. Leave the Highway by the Chaguanas exit, and hang a sharp right at Longdenville junction *(see page 271)*; it is a 10-minute drive to Longdenville. (Traffic arrangements can change regularly in Chaguanas.) The Brasso Caparo Road, runs southeastwards through the middle of the cane belt towards the Central Range and the Montserrat Hills

This smooth but long and winding road travels through vast plantations of sugar cane once owned by Tate & Lyle*. Every now and then the monotony of the waving green cane is broken by several kilometres of citrus plantations or by small villages. Some of the villages are not much more than a couple of houses at the side of the road, with a few secondary roads, a petrol station and a couple of stores to sustain day-to-day needs. Life is slow here, but it has its pleasures. Crime in these areas is almost non-existent, and a rural folksiness pervades. Sometimes you will see little wooden roadside stalls with old women or restless youths vending whatever is in season: mangoes, *pomme aracs* (a small red fruit similar to an apple, but softer), oranges, homemade pepper sauce or leather and wooden crafts. Stop and have a look, and you could become involved in the colourful world of haggling, with perhaps a historical fact or social observation thrown in by the vendor for good measure.

Down on the farm in the Central Range

After a 30-minute drive from Longdenville junction along the Brasso Caparo Road, turn right at the Brasso Police Station into the Central Range, towards **Tabaquite**. Perched on a hill on the right a little further on, about 10 minutes from the police station, is **Lakeside Farm** (daily; free), a luxurious round house

Map on page 274

flanked by two smaller houses. At the rear is an area for picnicking, and if you feel adventurous enough you can swim in the lake here. A side road to the right plunges downhill, a few metres after the farm, into the village of **Gran Couva** in the Montserrat Hills. The beauty of this region was glowingly mentioned in the book *At Last, a Christmas in the West Indies* by the 19th-century English writer Charles Kingsley, who visited Trinidad in 1869.

From here you can reach the small towns of Mayo and Tortuga to the southwest, and get back onto the Solomon Hochoy Highway just 15 minutes away. After Emancipation and their ensuing apprenticeships *(see page 37)*, many exslaves came to these hills, clearing away patches of forest to grow their ground provisions, but the government was looking for taxes and established the towns as a means of procuring them. More than two centuries earlier, a mission to convert the Amerindians had been set up in Tortuga, and the wooden gingerbread-style Catholic church of **Our Lady of Montserrat** stands as a reminder of those times. Inside is a shrine to the Black Virgin, a legacy of the missionaries.

About 10 km (6½ miles) off the Solomon Hochoy Highway and a 10-minute drive down the twisty roads from Lakeside Farm, west of Gran Couva you arrive at **La Vega Estate ❺** (daily; free; tel: 679 9522), a large nature retreat where you can have lunch and a swim, canoe in the small lakes or go on a guided nature trail to see the many different types of tropical plant growing in the estate nursery – a selection of which are for sale – and perhaps spot an agouti or wild deer.

Birdwatching at Navet

East of the Montserrat Hills and hidden in a valley on the southern slopes of the Central Range lies the **Navet Reservoir and Dam** (tours of the waterworks

TIP

If you want to buy plants and flowers during a trip to the nature reserve, be sure to check with Customs in your home country that you can safely transport them back without having them confiscated.

BELOW: village cricket in the Montserrat Hills.

The deserted east coast has little to offer in the way of restaurants, so people tend to bring barbecues and have a cook-up on the beach.

BELOW: a coconut grove at Mayaro.

and dam by appointment; entrance fee; tel: 662 2302), home to many species of bird, including wildfowl. To reach the reservoir turn left at the Tabaquite Composite school onto the Guaracara Tabaquite Road, which leads to the east coast via Río Claro. The reservoir turn-off, a few kilometres up the road on the left, is clearly marked, but the final turn is not. After you come off the main road you reach a four-way intersection; turn right for the reservoir. To visit the water works or tour the 320-metre (1,050-ft) long dam you need a pass, available from the Water and Sewerage Authority (WASA) in Port of Spain or its outlet in the Southland Mall in San Fernando *(see page 289–91)*.

Río Claro – a town with a Spanish touch

The road from Navet Dam to **Río Claro ❻**, one hour's drive away, cuts through a teak forest said to be the largest in the western hemisphere. Along here the settlements become increasingly sparse until finally the houses stand in isolated splendour, framed by the dark forest. The scenery is idyllic, and so it comes as something of a shock to hit built-up Río Claro, 80 km (50 miles) from Port of Spain, the seat of local government for the surrounding Nariva County. The Spanish influence is heavily marked here, and the town is surprisingly well equipped with internet cafés, fast-food outlets and branches of the larger banks and stores – it is also home to a good *parang* group.

A musical form which took hold of the country in Spanish colonial times, *parang (see pages 135–6)* was kept alive by the free movement of adventure-seeking men and women between Trinidad and Venezuela in the early 1900s. The lyrics are mainly in Spanish and accompanied on a four-stringed mini guitar called a *cuatro (see page 245)*. The *paranderos (parang* singers) come to

Map on page 274

he fore around Christmas time to sing of the Virgin, St Joseph and the birth of Christ. *Parang* was also practised by the island's population of Amerindians, who were taught by the Capuchin monks to make and play Spanish stringed instruments, to sing and to venerate important Catholic feasts.

Swamps, coconut groves and beaches

Turn left at Río Claro onto the Mayaro Road, and soon wide expanses of coconut trees come into view, indicating that you are approaching **Mayaro**, 17 km (11 miles) away on the east coast. On a lovely bay with a beautiful clean beach, Mayaro is similar to Río Claro in that it is equipped with all the usual amenities, but is slower and smaller. Turning left at Mayaro will take you north to **Manzanilla Beach** ❼, which stretches for 22 sandy kilometres (14 miles) and is edged by acres of coconut groves. The trade winds keep this coast refreshed all year and across from here, as the crow flies, lies Africa, and according to the 18th-century planter Roume de Saint Laurent the first coconuts arrived here when an African ship transporting the nuts ran aground.

Manzanilla is divided into two coconut estates, or *cocals*. The first, on your way north, has many grazing buffalypsoes (a cross between a buffalo and a cow bred for its high-quality beef). The road hugs the eastern coast, and several tracks cut through the *cocals*, allowing cars access to the beach. On a weekday you can choose any spot along this stretch and be assured of relative privacy; your only company might be some trysting lovers. Swimming along this coast is pleasant, and late afternoon at sunset is delightful, but the waters can be rough and there are some dangerous undercurrents, so a degree of caution is required. On moonlit nights, the beach shimmers a silvery white.

TIP

A kayak trip into the Nariva Swamp National Park will enable you to observe the wildlife and birds quietly without disturbing them. Contact Caribbean Discovery Tours, tel: 633 5614.

LEFT: sneaking up on the wildlife in Nariva Swamp.
BELOW: hiking on Bush Bush Island.

Just behind the coconut groves lies the **Nariva Swamp National Park**, a mangrove freshwater wetland, with the large **Bush Bush Wildlife Sanctuary** ➑ (tel: 662 5114) on a 15-sq. km (6-sq. mile) island in the middle. The swamp is an internationally recognised nature reserve under the 1996 Ramsar Convention, which means that the government is obliged to protect it. It is home to more than 200 species of bird and animal, the most famous being the manatee, a sea cow indigenous to Trinidad. Red howler monkeys swing between the hardwood trees and the massive silk cotton trees, which are also the habitat of colourful parrots, the red-breasted blackbird and an array of beautiful butterflies. The swamp waters, edged by a tangle of mangrove roots and covered with large lily pads, hide cayman and many species of fish. Mosquitos are rampant, so come armed with repellent. To visit the reserve, a pass is needed from the Forestry Department in St Joseph, which also provides information on tour guides, who are essential as the sanctuary is not easily accessible.

If you are taking a tour strictly to visit the Manzanilla coast and you have not brought a picnic, the **Calypso Inn** (tel: 668 5113) at the northern end of the beach by Manzanilla Village provides a reasonable lunch. You then have a straight drive through **Sangre Grande** on the Eastern Main Road back to Port of Spain.

Caroni Swamp – home of the scarlet ibis

The huge flocks of scarlet ibises coming home to roost at dusk across the flat deep-green of the **Caroni Swamp and Bird Sanctuary** ➒ (open daily; entrance fee; tel: 646 1305), just south of Port of Spain, are perhaps one of the most unforgettable sights in Trinidad. A visit to the bird sanctuary is an afternoon's tour, best taken at the weekend when traffic on the Uriah Butler Highway is

BELOW: scarlet ibises roost in the Caroni Swamp.

lighter. You can book a boat with a guide (tel: 645 1305), in advance to take you around the sanctuary, or set off without a reservation and make arrangements upon arrival. Binoculars, mosquito repellent and a sweater are recommended.

Leave Port of Spain on the Churchill Roosevelt Highway and turn right onto the Uriah Butler Highway after Aranguez junction. The highway was named after Princess Margaret when it was first opened, in 1955, but was renamed in honour of Uriah "Buzz" Butler, an oilfield worker and trade unionist who led the labour uprisings in 1937 *(see page 54)*.

The highway takes you through County Caroni. The Caroni River can be seen on both sides of the road. Take the first left turning onto the flyover bridge and turn sharp right into the swamp, where you will see the jetty from which boats depart. It is best to arrive around 4.30pm. Flat-bottomed outboard motorboats ply narrow mangrove waterways where the trees are entangled with undergrowth, and thick roots show above the water level. There are 157 species of bird to be found here, spread over 6,000 hectares (15,000 acres) of protected land.

Tell the boatman that you wish to await the arrival of the egrets and the scarlet ibises or he will only take you through the waterways. The birds travel in squadron formation, transforming the drab landscape with movement and colour, just as the sunset lends its own brilliance to the scene. It is said that the ibises feed on the Venezuelan coast and fly to the swamp for the night, a distance of about 64 km (40 miles) across the Dragon's Mouths. No one seems to see them during the day.

Returning to the city at dusk, between 6 and 7pm, you can stop for a drink and a bite to eat at the City of the Grand Bazaar or at **Valsayn** on the Churchill Roosevelt Highway *(see page 242).* ❑

Map on page 274

The scarlet ibis is one of the national birds, and the Caroni Swamp is the only place where it can be seen in Trinidad.

BELOW: birdwatchers on the lookout.

DOWN IN THE SOUTH

*Barely touched by tourism, the south of the island offers
one of only three pitch lakes in the world, mud volcanoes, wildlife,
oil wells and even more empty palm-fringed beaches*

Map
on pages
286–7

lthough the sights of the south are not always among Trinidad's most picturesque, to know the country it is essential to see that part of island, which to Trinidadians seems to be anything below the latitude of Port of Spain. Almost matching the north in shape – like a child's wet painting folded in half and opened out again – the Deep South, as the southwest peninsula is known, reaches out to Venezuela across the narrow Serpent's Mouth. The remarkable Pitch Lake at La Brea, the curious mud volcanoes and the nodding presence of oil pumps in these parts present a stark contrast to the sandy beaches backed by red cliffs, the dense forests and tiny fishing villages.

Some parts of the southeast are hard to access, and the Trinity Hills, with the three peaks that inspired Columbus to call the island Trinidad, bear lush evergreen forests which have been long designated a protected wildlife reserve. Not many people visit this rich ecological haven, but with a guide you can experience the sights, sounds and smells of untouched rainforest at first hand. Further on the southeastern coastline presents another kind of marine beauty from that of the rocky northern coast, as beaches here lie beside flat coconut groves which stretch for miles to the sea and link up with the never-ending Manzanilla Beach *(see page 279)*.

A new highway linking the southeast coast with San Fernando in the southwest is scheduled for the future and the easier access it will give is likely to mean more development in this remote region, along with the recent discoveries of more oil and gas reserves here. The island's second biggest city, and mostly driven by the oil industry, San Fernando is only about an hour's drive from Port of Spain, and many people commute daily between the two. Transport is developed, but mainly by private rather than public agencies. The route taxis run according to demand, and are not concerned with providing continuous service; this means that there are many taxis during rush hours, but not at other times. So for touring it is advisable to hire a car.

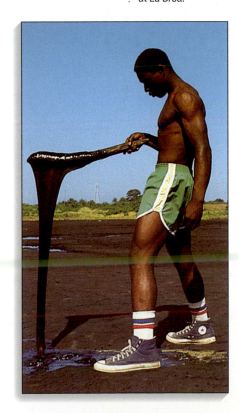

PRECEDING PAGES:
an elusive parrot.
LEFT: oil pipes line
a southern road.
BELOW: black gold
in the Pitch Lake
at La Brea.

Pointe-à-Pierre Wild Fowl Trust

An oasis of nature surrounded by industrial development, the **Pointe-à-Pierre Wild Fowl Trust** ❶ (open daily by appointment; entrance fee; contact Molly Gaskin, tel: 637 5145 or 658 4200, ext. 2512) occupies two lakes in beautifully landscaped grounds within the complex of the towering Petrotrin Oil Refinery. It takes nearly an hour's drive to get there from Port of Spain on the Uriah Butler and Solomon Hochoy Highways via Claxton Bay *(see page 291)*, just north of San Fernando.

After Claxton Bay you enter Victoria County. The entrance to the town of Pointe-à-Pierre was heavily

With the motto "To know is to love, to love is to preserve", the Pointe-à-Pierre Wild Fowl Trust, a voluntary organisation funded by donations, has successfully bred, and released into the wild, endangered wetland birds such as the scarlet ibis, white-cheeked pintail, wild muscovy duck and three species of whistling duck.

guarded during World War II, protecting the strategic industries. Once owned by Texaco, the oil refinery was acquired by the Trinidad and Tobago Government in 1984.

This is a beautiful hilly area covering 25 hectares (62 acres), and the natural scenery provides a stark contrast to the abundant man-made surroundings. Driving through you will see the Augustus Long Hospital and Club House. The bungalows and the bachelors' quarters are located on the high ground looking down on the rigs and tanks.

Pointe-à-Pierre's lakes, covered with lotus flowers and waterlilies, are in the hands of the Wild Fowl Trust, a non-profit making and non-governmental organisation set up in 1966 to ensure the survival of the hundreds of species of bird that alight here, such as the muscovy duck and the white-cheeked pintail. A learning centre is housed in a small wooden building, like an enlarged version of a bird house, next to one of the lakes, providing literature on the various species, displaying a unique mollusc collection and including a small Amerindian museum. Contact members of the committee or Molly Gaskin, who heads the Trust, to organise a visit to this nature centre.

Pointe-à-Pierre has the sulphurous smell of any refinery area. **Guaracara Park**, owned by the oil company, is a good sporting centre and was formerly the scene of the popular Southern Games, with leading international track and field stars; its use has been expanded to include football games, territorial cricket matches and night cricket under floodlights.

Head towards **Marabella**, an urbanised, commercialised suburb of San Fernando with a daily roadside market, on the Southern Main Road, and continue around the outskirts of the city past St Joseph Village, a middle-class housing area.

The oil-rich south

The sugar crop begins in January and ends in June, and during this time buffalo-drawn carts traverse the southern outskirts of San Fernando. Turn right towards Siparia and you enter the Philippines Estate, once owned by Sir Norman Lamont, a Scotsman who was gored by a bull on his own plantation. Part of the estate has been developed into Bryan's Gate, a residential area, after being turned down for agricultural development by the government and the Imperial College of Tropical Agriculture.

The days when sugar was king are long over, and for about 50 years now, it has been oil driving the engine of commerce. Pass from the residential areas into Penal or Moruga, and down any of the side roads, and you will see pumps draining the oil wells. **Debe**, a few kilometres further on, provides a good pit stop with a Quik Stop convenience store attached to a modern service station. The shop provides snacks and drinks on a Sunday, when most of the restaurants and shops are closed. Proceed through **Penal**, where most of the Indian indentured labourers settled in the 1840s *(see pages 40–1)*. It was also a goldmine for the Presbyterian missionaries who found many converts here, opening their primary school in 1907. Today Penal's power plant serves the entire southwest.

The Black Virgin of Siparia

Another 8 km (5 miles) to the west lies the small town of **Siparia ❷**, which has become famous for its statue the **Black Virgin of Siparia** at the main Catholic church. This devotion to La Divina Pastora, the Divine Shepherdess, was introduced by the sheep-rearing community of Andalucia in southern Spain in the 18th century. The Capuchin monks were the first missionaries to come from

Map
below

Around the neck of the Black Virgin of Siparia are many necklaces that are offerings from devotees, and she is illuminated by perpetual lights.

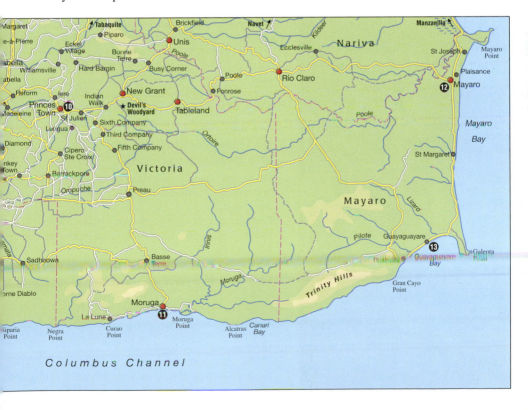

TIP

Los Iros, down a turn-off about 2 km (just over a mile) before Erin, is a secluded beach which has excellent swimming and a few bars. You will need to bring food with you.

Spain to convert the Amerindians, and they instilled in them their traditional devotion to La Divina Pastora. In 1759 the last mission was founded in Siparia, and according to legend the statue was brought from Venezuela by the Capuchins when fleeing an Amerindian revolt. Over the years Hindus and other non-Catholic groups have been attracted to the statue, believing it to have miraculous powers, and the East Indians call it Soparee Kay Mai, meaning Mother from Siparia. The feast of La Divina Pastora is on the second Sunday after Easter, when the statue is carried in procession down the main street of the town: a big day in the life of the Siparians, when they adorn themselves with new clothes, and feasting and celebrating are the order of the day.

After Siparia is Santa Flora and then Palo Seco, meaning dry wood. This is now oil territory. Just past is Rancho Quemado, meaning burning hut.

Fyzabad – centre of the labour movement

Named after a district in India from where most of its settlers came in the 19th century, **Fyzabad** ❸, 7 km (4 miles) to the north of Siparia, won notoriety in June 1937 when the trade-union activist and Moravian preacher Uriah "Buzz" Butler staged an oilworkers' strike here which turned into a riot *(see page 54)*. Today Butler's statue, complete with bowler hat and black suit, marks the spot, and 19 June (Labour Day) is celebrated every year with rallies and fiery speeches.

Directly south of Siparia, about 11 km (7 miles) away on the Coora Road running through teak forest, you reach **Quinam Beach** (it is clearly signposted). Quinam is maintained by the tourist authority, which runs a small visitors' centre here with information on local flora and fauna. Popular with Trinidadians, the beach has several huts with earthen firesides which you can use to cook.

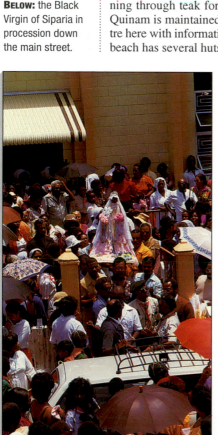

BELOW: the Black Virgin of Siparia in procession down the main street.

Southwest of Siparia, about 14 km (9 miles) along the Siparia–Erin road, you come to **Erin** ❹ (pronounced *Ay-reene* by the locals), a fishing village with liming fishermen and a generally slow pace. You can drive straight down to the beach into the fishing depot, where you can buy fresh fish. However, you will have to park in the depot yard, which can get quite crowded, and walk to the beach to swim. Venezuelan parrots and pretty hammocks are sold in this village, and occasionally whales are washed up on the shore here.

The Oropuche Lagoon

On the way back to San Fernando, bypassing Fyzabad and going on to Mosquito Creek, you pass the mouth of the Oropuche River which runs into the **Oropuche Lagoon**, a tidal mangrove swamp and an unspoilt sanctuary for many species of water bird, where the Pointe-à-Pierre Wild Fowl Trust releases birds into the wild. Tour companies such as Avifauna (tel: 633 5614) and Caribbean Discovery (tel: 624 7281) can organise kayak trips into the lagoon. On a tributary further on is a crematorium aptly called the Shore of Peace. On its journey to the sea the Oropuche passes through La Fortune and Woodland, where there is a mixture of both sugar and rice plantations.

The coast road runs straight into San Fernando through La Romain, a residential district with a new middle-class development called Gulf View. Turn into

Lady Hailes Avenue, with San Fernando's main thoroughfare on your right, and turn off onto the Rienzi Kirton Highway. This short link road was named after Gertrude Kirton, mayor of San Fernando in the 1980s, and Adrian Cola Rienzi, a former member of the Legislative Council who was responsible for both extending adult suffrage to the Indians and founding two trade unions – the Oilfield Workers' Trade Union (OWTU) and the All Trinidad Sugar Estates and Factory Workers' Trade Union (FWTU) – in the 1930s *(see page 55).*

Map on pages 286–7

San Fernando – Trinidad's second city

By entering **San Fernando ❺**, Trinidad's second most important city, from the coast, you pass the Gulf City Mall and **Skinner Park**, a major Carnival venue where the southern leg of the Carnival Monarch and the Young Kings competitions are held. You also pass Naparima College, a prestigious boys' school. Close by the college are the hospital and the **Naparima Bowl**, a space used for dramatic performances and other shows. Officially decreed a city in 1988, the settlement was named San Fernando de Naparima, after the Spanish King Carlos III's son, in 1784. Naparima was the Amerindian name for the hill that the city has grown up around, endowing it with some steep and narrow streets. To begin with, San Fernando flourished as a sugar town and was fuelled by the arrival of the railway in the late 1880s. By the 1930s, the oil industry had become the town's main driving force.

San Fernando differs from Port of Spain in that it still retains a residential character just a short walk away from the commercial centre, and there are still some signs of the past in of the remaining old colonial houses. You can get to San Fernando easily via route taxi or maxi taxi from City Gate in Port of Spain.

LEFT: the church of Our Lady of Perpetual Help. **BELOW:** San Fernando Town Council building.

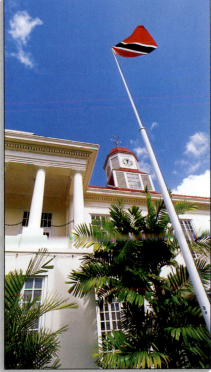

This statue of Mahatma Gandhi on Harris Promenade was brought from India in 1952. A service is held beneath it on his birthday (2 October), on the anniversary of his death (30 January), and at Diwali.

BELOW: the quarried San Fernando Hill, now a park.

In the centre **Harris Promenade**, commemorating Lord Harris, Governor of Trinidad from 1846 to 1854, is laid out similarly to Port of Spain's Brian Lara Promenade *(see page 210)*. The Roman Catholic Church, **Our Lady of Perpetual Help**, was consecrated on 29 May 1849. The Town Council building was rebuilt in 1930, and Council was established in 1846, and the wharf opened in 1842, increasing San Fernando's importance. Several churches of other denominations, Methodist and Anglican, also line the promenade, and in the centre stands a statue of Mahatma Gandhi.

Nearby is an old steam engine of the last train which left Port of Spain for San Fernando, marking the end of railway service in Trinidad in 1965. Lord Kitchener sang in his famous calypso *Last Train to San Fernando* that if you don't get this one, you'll never get another one, so on its last journey people were crammed into the carriages, with heads sticking out, and some even managed to get onto the roof of the train, just to be on that last ride.

High Street and Harris Promenade join at the **Library Corner**, a popular meeting point – "meet me at the Library Corner" – in San Fernando with its non-functioning clock. The library is a well-appointed red brick building recently restored. On the **High Street**, the main business and shopping street, ask for "Ali's doubles". Doubles are an Indian delicacy, with a bite in the taste. Try them with a cold drink.

The Coffee and steelpan

Several metres south of Library Corner is **Carib Street**, a remnant of the colonial past of the city, lined with dilapidated colonial buildings, evidence of the indifference of most Trinidadians to their heritage. Coffee and Cipero streets

intersect with Carib. The statue of the pan player at the intersection gives a good indication of the area's preoccupation with steelpan. **Coffee Street**, known as The Coffee, was immortalised by the American pannist Andy Narrell in his composition *Coffee Street* for a local steelband in 1999. The Coffee is also the home of the panyards of TCL Skiffle Bunch and Vat 19 Fonclaire. The shed that contains the Skiffle Bunch pans is surrounded by walls with a mural of pan players and old-time Carnival characters in a scene from old-time Carnival called the Dancing Walls. From November until Carnival, when the bands are practising, the area livens up, and it is worth going along for the atmosphere.

Rising up behind is the oddly shaped **San Fernando Hill** (200 metres/655 ft). At one time the hill was privately owned and quarried, providing house builders with high-grade gravel until quarrying was stopped by the government. Today it is a park, with a wonderful view over San Fernando and Paria Bay, and has been beautified with benches and trees. The entrance (open daily; closed at night) is near **Soong's Great Wall Restaurant** on the Circular Road.

Return to Port of Spain through Marabella past the old **Union Park Race Course** and onto the Solomon Hochoy Highway. Sir Solomon was the first Trinidad and Tobago citizen to be Governor of Trinidad and Tobago in 1959 and later became the first Governer-General after Independence. Turn off at the **Claxton Bay** exit. On the second hill after the bridge there is a statue of a headless woman, which is surrounded by countless stories. The most popular is that the daughter of an overseer had been romantically linked with a labourer on the estate. One day the father tried to keep his daughter at home and placed a snake at the meeting point to scare away her lover. The girl ran away to meet him and was bitten by the snake. The father built this statue for her. Motorists swear

Map on pages 286–7

Coffee Street was named after the coffee plantations that were once established there.

BELOW: a store at the side of the road.

The hard crust of asphalt that covers the Pitch Lake at La Brea makes it easy to walk on.

BELOW:
swimming in the sulphurous water of the Pitch Lake.

that on some nights they have seen the young girl walking along the highway or standing in front of their cars. There certainly have been many accidents in this area. Others say that the statue is just one of the Virgin Mary.

To the Deep South and the Pitch Lake

The southwest peninsula, like a bigger shadow of the northwest peninsula, is known as the Deep South, and it takes about three to four hours to drive from Port of Spain to the furthest point, at Icacos at the end of the Southern Main Road. So if you plan to stop off for a while at the Pitch Lake in La Brea, look around the fishing villages, take in the views and return the same evening, start your journey early. Also keep in mind that on a weekday the traffic can build up into jams as early as 7am on the highways around the capital.

Bypass San Fernando on the Southern Main Road, past Gulf City to Mosquito Creek, and follow the signs to the Pitch Lake. Continue on through the fishing village of **Otaheite** and Rousillac on the edge of a coastal swamp, signalled by the bothersome mosquitoes and sandflies.

Around the village of **La Brea**, 20 km (13 miles) from San Fernando, the road is very bumpy and potholed, making fast driving impossible and good car suspension a necessity. This is due to the underground eruptions which keep the 44-hectare (109-acre) **Pitch Lake ❻** (open daily) supplied with asphalt. One of three pitch (tar) lakes in the world, the others being in Los Angeles (Rancho La Brea) and Venezuela (Guanaco), the lake is big and black and you can walk on it, although at times you may feel yourself sinking – do not wear high-heeled shoes. Ignore the people on the road who pester you to hire them as guides and go to the visitors' centre for an official one. A good guide, and perhaps a witty

Map on pages 286–7

one, will tell you where on the lake you can find a cure for your ailments, most probably your sinus or aching joints. He might even explain how you can bathe in the sulphurous waters in different parts of the lake, but not how you might sail on it, as a popular publisher of British romance once claimed.

In the late 16th century, Sir Walter Raleigh came to the south of Trinidad and wrote that he used some tar from the lake to caulk his ships. He claimed it was better than anything else he had used. A century later José María Chacon opened a factory to prepare tar for export at a rate of 700 barrels a year – the first shipment went to the Royal Arsenal in Spain – but the British did not invest in it until the 1860s. Today tar is exported to Europe and most of the Caribbean, and is used to pave roads in New York City and Paris, among other places.

The village – which is how La Brea should be described – the court house and post office seem to relate closely to the surrounding tar. When the sun is very hot, the street and the houses seem to move in the shimmering light. The French planter Roume de St Laurent, who came to Trinidad in the late 18th century, refers to two pitch (tar) lakes at La Brea, so perhaps the village was built on one.

Oil wells that once produced but have since been capped are called ghosts. Several ghost towns (old oil towns) litter the south; they are quite difficult to spot, as a disused oil rig may be overgrown with vines.

The oil town of Point Fortin

A little further west along the coast road is **Vessigny**, a small beach with changing facilities. It is generally calm but in the rainy season the water is quite dirty. **TJ's By the Sea**, a guesthouse off the main road, is a good place to stop for a meal.

Keep travelling along the main road to a roundabout which gives you the option of going to **Point Fortin**, a small fishing port: a town said to be able to breathe as its wide streets permit sea breezes to blow freely around it. Built around the oil industry, the town's growth has been closely linked to the refinery,

BELOW: making a broom with stripped palm leaves.

At the end of the 19th
century the tiny
region of Cedros was
famous for its rum,
and a grand total of
seven distilleries
was squeezed into
the island's
southwest tip.

originally owned by Shell, nationalised in the mid-1970s and now called Petrotrin. The old part of the town, Teschier Village, is occupied by the semi-skilled workers of the refinery who live in semi-detached houses. Petrotrin's senior staff are housed at Clifton Hill, a beautifully landscaped area with a golf course. Borough Day celebrations are the high point of the Point Fortin year, and take the form of a mini Carnival.

The playground at Mahaica saw the birth of some fine national footballers and one of the country's leading football teams, Point Fortin Civic Centre, has its home ground here.

Isolated Icacos Point

There is a helpful sign at the Point Fortin roundabout, which begins the final leg of the journey. Once you have passed through a densely wooded area you come to the Chatham Junction (misspelt on the signs as Chatam). The ward of **Cedros** begins here and covers the tip of the peninsula, which is edged by attractive deserted beaches. One of them is **Granville Beach**, which has a bar. Towards the furthest point, through some forested areas, lies the delightful village of **Bonasse** ❼, with a palm-lined park bordered by the sea and the road, where the locals sit in the evenings enjoying the sun and each other's company. This is a "ribbon-line village", as are most of the villages in Cedros, where the houses are strung out along either side of the road.

Villagers going between Bonasse and the neighbouring village of **Fullarton**, often prefer to walk along the beach rather than the road.

The two main means of livelihood in this area are fishing and coconuts, but the coconut industry is much scaled down these days. Ask for Kelman, who owns the **Star Trek bar** in Fullarton; he can tell you everything you need, or want, to know about the village. You can order a meal here, go to the beach, and come back and find it waiting.

Leaving Fullarton bear right at a fork in the road to **Columbus Bay**, driving through never-ending coconut groves, and through the village of **Los Gallos**. It is believed that Columbus dropped anchor here on his third voyage to the West Indies. **Columbus Bay** is a crowded beach at public holidays and most weekends, but if the tide is low you can drive another 3 km (2 miles) along the secluded beach or walk all the way to **Icacos Point** ❽. Icacos is a fishing village, the furthest point on the southwestern peninsula and only 11 km (7 miles) across the **Serpent's Mouth** from Venezuela. An old lighthouse for fishermen is fast receding into the sea through erosion.

From Columbus Bay or anywhere along that beach you can see **Soldado Rock** ❾ and three other small rocks. The negotiations with Venezuela in 1940 over the island of Patos, concerning the boundaries, landed Trinidad with Soldado. That was all the importance attached to the very small rock until the 1970s, when the zealous coastguard from Venezuela (La Guardia Nacionale) began patrolling the waters around Soldado and roping in fishermen for the Venezuelan jails near the Orinoco. If any fisherman offers you a boat ride, as they are wont to

BELOW: a "straw man" basket seller.

Map on pages 286–7

do, insist that he does not go past Soldado or hope that your Spanish is adequate enough for a contretemps with a Venezuelan coastguard.

Moruga and Guayaguayare

To visit Moruga, in the middle of the south coast in the county of Victoria, and Guayaguayare, in the extreme southeast in the county of Mayaro, from Port of Spain, you need to set aside an entire day. Alternatively, for a less hurried trip, you could stay overnight around San Fernando or Mayaro Bay, although there is still little accommodation to choose from *(see Travel Tips on page 350)*.

Take the route out of the capital to San Fernando *(see page 289)*. Just before you reach the city, leave the highway at the Princes Town exit and bear left; drive along till you come to the Naparima Mayaro Road intersection; turn right for the Manahambre Road, and drive for just over a kilometre (1 mile) to the National Petroleum (NP) station; turn left here on to the Manahambre road towards Princes Town. A little further on you will see the sugar refinery of **Usine Ste Madeleine**, its beauty surpassing that of the rolling fields of Brechin Castle in Caroni. The road to the refinery is lined with royal palms just like its counterpart's.

Continue along the Manahambre Road past other sugar villages – Jordan Hill, Cedar Hill and Manahambre – into **Princes Town** ⑩, the birthplace of former Prime Minister Basdeo Panday. As you enter you will see the Anglican church where two poui trees were planted by Prince Albert and his brother Prince George, who later became King George V. They visited Trinidad in 1880, arriving on HMS *Bacchante*, and were guests of Governor Sir Henry

The seas south of the island, especially off Mayaro and Guayaguayare, are peppered with oil rigs. Oil and industry are the mainstays of the south, providing employment and commerce to the benefit of the locals.

BELOW: a fisherman sorting out his nets at Icacos.

Turner Irving. When they visited the south, what was known as "the Mission" was renamed Princes Town in their honour.

From here take the southern Moruga Road past villages called **First**, **Third**, **Fourth**, **Fifth** and **Sixth Company**. These villages housed demobilised black American soldiers who had fought for the British in the British-American War of 1812. The Second Company was lost at sea, hence no mention of its name. Each company village has its own cemetery and church.

A village of many beliefs

The countryside from here to the coast about 24 km (15 miles) away is flat – hence the French name of **Basse Terre** – with rolling savannah, dotted with typical old houses. The road goes straight into the fishing village of **Moruga** ⑪ which has only one main street. Many villagers are Spiritual Baptists, and numerous houses on Indian Walk Road are Baptist shrines.

The most striking thing about this village is its Roman Catholic **church**. The sight of the white-painted Gothic structure with a tower topped with what looks like a green Byzantine dome is quite startling after the pastoral and ad hoc architecture of the region. Ironically, Moruga is also a centre for *obeah*, West Indian black magic brought to the region by African slaves. People from all over Trinidad come to the small villages around Moruga to visit the *obeah* men and women. *Obeah* folk practice uses the "bush bath" to wash out evil or affliction; candles can be used to do evil or cast spells. For the bush bath herbs are selected and boiled according to the problem, but it is difficult to say what these selections are.

The beach in Moruga, backed by sheer cliffs, is extraordinary at low tide.

BELOW: a shop by the roadside in Princes Town.

THE COMPANY VILLAGES

The villages of First, Third, Fourth, Fifth and Sixth Company, which lie in a cluster in the far south of the island on the road to Moruga, are the legacies of black American soldiers who settled in Trinidad after the end of the British-American War of 1812. The men were ex-slaves who had fought for the British and, since they could not remain in America, Sir Ralph Woodford, the governor of Trinidad from 1813, took advantage of their plight and, seeing the underdeveloped state of the island, particularly the south, petitioned for the soldiers to be resettled here. Slavery still operated in Trinidad at the time, so it is possible that Woodford wanted them far away from plantations and the imaginations of the African slaves still working on them.

The companies, without Second Company, which was lost at sea, numbered 574 men on arrival, and were settled in areas the Amerindians were supposed to have cleared long ago, but which were in fact closer to forest. However, the ex-soldiers duly cleared the land themselves, and land grants were awarded (6.5 hectares/16 acres per family). But the lack of roads would plague the settlement until the turn of the century. Today the villagers have lost all traces of their American legacy but one: like the soldiers, they are Baptists.

Map on pages 286–7

You have to walk over 2 km (1½ miles) on the seabed of sand before you reach the water, passing a delightful scene of fishing boats stuck high and dry, waiting to rise again when the tide comes in. Looking back towards land you will also see the church, the old plantation house on high ground, and this beach extending as far as the eye can see to both left and right. This is where Christopher Columbus spotted the three hills (those of the Southern Range) which led him to call the island Trinidad. To have a clear view of the three hills you need to be out on a boat like Columbus, closer to the Guayaguayare area.

The villagers love to celebrate, and their main festival is **Discovery Day** (the first Monday in August) which everywhere else on the island has been renamed Emancipation Day. However, here they continue to celebrate the grand occasion of Christopher Columbus's short stopover in Trinidad all those centuries ago, and each year they re-enact the explorer's arrival with some embellishment. Dressed in 15th-century garb, the person playing Columbus arrives with his fleet, disembarks onto dry land and lying flat, as Roman Catholic priests do on ordination, kisses the sand and claims it in the name of the king and queen of Spain. If you are near on this day, do not miss the opportunity to join in the fun.

Mud volcanoes at Devil's Woodyard

Return to the Manahambre-Mayaro Road via the Company villages and turn right towards New Grant a little way along. Just off the road to the south is the **Devil's Woodyard**, an active mud volcano. The route there is very scenic, featuring a road on the edge of steep-sided green hills with cattle grazing, but the actual road is in a bad state. The Woodyard itself may be an anticlimax: just

BELOW: low tide at Moruga Bay.

The Devil's Woodyard mud volcano is one of many dotted around southern Trinidad.

a circle of dry earth with a few bubbling mounds of foul-smelling mud; but it erupted in 1996, caking most of the village in mud, and you never know when it will happen again.

The long sandy beaches of the southeast

Back on the road, Río Claro *(see page 278)* looms; continue eastwards, and once you get to the town of **Mayaro** ⓬ (also called Pierreville) after another 17 km (10 miles), if you are not stopping for a snack or a swim here, turn right at the market and head towards the long palm-tree-lined coast for Guayaguayare. By the beach front, Atlantic Shores is a new development of houses which are second homes for affluent city dwellers; you also pass a luxurious built-up residential area where employees of BP Amoco (the British-American oil company) live. A number of local families have beach houses here, and there are two coconut plantations owned by the de Meillacs, a Trindadian French family.

As you drive south the beach is always on your left, and you can stop anywhere for a good refreshing swim. Two major currents meet here, creating a crisscross effect in the waves. If you are not in any real hurry, you may want to stay here a while, taking in the fresh sea breeze from the Atlantic. If you are hungry, the **South Sea Port** restaurant and lounge, a few kilometres from Mayaro, serves a reasonable lunch.

As you continue to skirt this beautiful shoreline you pass through the villages of Radix, St Margaret, Grand Lagoon, New Lands and Cal Mapas to **Guayaguayare** ⓭, an Indian-sounding name like Chacachacare. In the same manner, people fondly refer to it as "Guaya". Along the road you will see a

BELOW: busy on Mayaro Beach.

Map on pages 286–7

sign for **Galeota Point**: ignore it; that peninsula, which hangs off the end of Trinidad like an appendix is given over to the oil company operations. But all along the south coast the beach is visible, and so are the oil rigs out at sea.

There are a few more houses along this coast in villages such as Rushville, La Brea (not to be confused with the Pitch Lake) and Guayaguayare Village. A little way before the end of the road is the **Sea Wall Boat Club**, a bar and restaurant where you can sit and have a drink, or a meal, and use the beach.

Hiking in the Trinity Hills

The road ends where the Petrotrin oil company compound begins; it harbours the **Trinity Hills Wildlife Sanctuary**, covering 64 sq. km (25 sq. miles) of a fairly rugged part of the Central Range, a treasure trove of unspoilt vegetation and wildlife such as howler monkeys, parrots and toucan. The hills are an essential catchment area for the Trinidadian water supply, and the region has been protected since 1934.

The reserve attracts birders and is also an excellent hiking ground, with trails for novices and experienced hikers. A permit from Petrotrin is required to enter the grounds (tel: 658 1291), and tour companies such as South East Eco Tours (tel: 644 1072), Caribbean Discovery Tours (tel: 624 7281) will arrange guided excursions.

From Rushville in Guaya to Upper Manzanilla in the north is about 73 km (44 miles) of flat sandy beach lined by endless tall straight coconut trees. Return to Port of Spain along the Mayaro Road into **Manzanilla** *(see page 279)* over the Ortoire River. Then head for Sangre Grande and Valencia. From there, the Churchill Roosevelt Highway will take you straight back into Port of Spain. ❑

BELOW: a sugar worker's home in Guayaguayare.

WELCOME TO TOBAGO

*A detailed guide to the entire island, with principal sites
clearly cross-referenced by number to the maps*

Like a Caribbean island of 50 years ago, Tobago stands relatively unmarked by international tourism. Though this is changing, picturesque bumpy roads still wind past palm groves, tiny hamlets with locals waiting for a "drop," and small hotels frequented by Trinidadian holidaymakers; it is a place where an outsider can still be an interesting anomaly and not simply an oppressive necessity. The traditional Tobago of unspoiled beaches and friendly fishermen will remain for some time, but the question is: for how long?

From the cosmopolitan snap of Port of Spain to the rural languor of Tobago seems a far longer distance than the mere 20-minute flight. Though Trinidad and Tobago are indeed united in more than just economic and political ways, there are subtle (and not so subtle) differences between them. Where Trinidad presents a surprising mixture of African, East Indian, Oriental and European cultures and peoples, almost 90 percent of Tobagonians are of black African descent. And while Trinis tend to be a cosmopolitan bunch, even Scarborough, Tobago's largest town, is more of an enlarged market village than a real city.

But Trinidad and Tobago were of the same piece of South American land, and so Tobago offers the same diverse geography and plant and animal life. Forty-two kilometres (26 miles) long but only 11 km (7 miles) wide, Tobago is a constant feast for the eyes, as even interior roads are usually only 15 or so minutes from glimpses of the sea, and a route through the mountainous interior passes stands of enormous creaking bamboo and dense jungly growth before suddenly giving way to vistas of sparkling white palm-fringed beach, or open pastures grazed by placid cattle and scruffy goats.

The fish-shaped island is circumnavigated by two main coastal roads. However, the "head" and "tail" are beyond the reach of this circle, and north of Charlotteville there are only paths. As small as the island is, access is not always easy, but any point on Tobago is reachable in a few hours' drive at most, and most drives are a good day trip, with as much to see along the way as there is at the final destination. ❏

Tobago

0 ——— 2 km
0 ——— 2 miles

N

CARIBBEAN SEA

Englishman's

Castara
Castara Bay   **8**

Mount
Dillon

King Peter's Bay

Woodlands   Runnemede

Moriah   Indian Walk

Culloden Bay   Golden Lane

Arnos Vale Bay   Mount Thomas   Les   **St David**
    Coteaux   Courtland   Nutmeg
    Arnos Vale   Grove

Plymouth **5**   **7** *Arnos Vale*   Mason   East
6 Fort James   *Water Wheel*   Highland   Hall
Great Courland Bay   Adventure Farm   *Falls*   Adelphi   Belmont
    and Nature Reserve   **French Fort**
    Turtle Beach   Franklyn   *Craig Hall*
    Hotel   *Waterfall*
    Courland   Providence   **St George**
Black Rock   *The Whim*   Mesopotamia
Fort Bennett   Lower Quarter   Mount St G
Grafton Beach   or Roselle   Harmony Hall   Calder Hall   Hope
Resort   Orange Hill   *Hillsborough*
    Grafton Caledonia   Rockly Vale   *Bay*
Mount Irvine Bay   Wildlife Sanctuary
Buccoo Reef   **Mount Irvine**   Patience Hill
Buccoo Reef National Park   National Fine   **Scarborough**
1   Booby   Arts Centre   **12**   Fort   **Bacolet**
    Point   Kimme   Bethal   King George
Nylon Pool **2**   *Buccoo Bay*   Museum   **St Andrew**   *Rockly Bay*   *Bacolet Bay*
Pigeon   Buccoo   Prospect   Old Donkey   Minister
Point   **3**   **St Patrick**   Diamond   Cart House   *Bacolet Point*   Point
Bon Accord Lagoon   Carnbee   Lambeau
Store Bay   **Shirvan**   Village   *Little Rockly Bay*
Sandy   Canaan   Mount
Point   **Fort Milford**   Pleasant
    Bon Accord   Lowlands   ★ **Tobago Plantations**
Crown   Robinson   Friendship   Wildfowl
Point   Crusoe's   Cove   Sanctuary
    Cave   *Canoe Bay*   *Petit Trou Lagoon*

Columbus
Point

Trinidad

Marble
Island
London
Bridge
Rock
Bird
Sanctuary
St Giles
Island

The Sisters

North Point

Man O' War
Bay
Corvo Point
Pirate's
Bay
Flagstaff Hill
★ Navigational Beacon
Starwood

Booby
Island
Black
Rock

Brother's
Rock

L' Anse Fourmi
Cambleton
Charlotteville

St John
Belmont
Blue
Waters Inn
Bateaux
Bay
Bird
Sanctuary

Bloody
Bay
Speyside
Water Wheel ★
Eastern Tobago
National Park

Goat
Island

uvier Bay
Bloody
Bay
Bloody Bay
Tyrrel's
Bay

Parlatuvier
Speyside

Little Tobago
(Bird of Paradise
Island)

Parrot
Hall

Tobago
Pigeon Peak
576

Forest
Trois Rivieres

Reserve

South
Rock

Main Ridge
594

Forest
Reserve

Merchiston

St Paul
King's
Bay
Cape
Gracias-a-Dios

Argyle
Waterfall
St Mary
Delaford
King's
Bay

Cardiff
Roxborough
Shore Park
Pedro
Point

Pembroke Glamorgan
Hill Waterfall
Goldsborough
Belle Garden
Richmond
Prince's
Bay
Queen's
Bay
Louis D'or

Glamorgan
Hillsborough
Dam
Pembroke
Queen's Island

sborough
Goodwood
Carapuse
Bay

Montrose
Goldsborough
Bay
Richmond
Island

Studley
Park
Fort Granby
Pinfold Bay
Granby
Point
Smith's
Island

ATLANTIC   OCEAN

THE SOUTH, WEST AND THE CARIBBEAN COAST

Map on pages 306–7

Visitors can enjoy great diving and pretty beaches, plus lively nightlife tempered by the relaxed pace of life in the fishing villages in the west and north of the island – also called the Leeward side

Scarborough

From the air, Tobago appears like a travel brochure picture, with bright blue water sparkling around a rolling green land, stretches of pale beach and frothy waves defining the perimeter. The mountains of the interior loom deep green and dusky purple.

Tobago is rumoured to be Robinson Crusoe's island, and some local guides would happily show you his exact cave, though the caves of the southeast tip of the island could have been formed by wave action or man. More important than the verifiability of this claim, though, is the truth that Crusoe could have subsisted happily here. Tobago is a self-contained paradise, a verdant island where the visitor could well imagine himself housed in a palm-frond cottage, sustained on the fruits of land and ocean, eternally entertained by the changing beauty of the landscape of sand, sea, sky and mountain.

Most place names reflect the recent European history of the island – Studley Park, Les Coteaux, Roxborough, Aukenskeoch, Courland – and the ubiquitous bright orange immortelle, imported as shade for cocoa trees, is as much a reminder of the colonial past as are the crumbling sugar mills hidden here and there in the forests. This is still an agricultural place where almost everyone makes at least a part, if not all, of their living from farming or fishing.

An increasing number of tourists, from Europe in particular, are discovering Tobago. More hotels are being built, and accommodation is becoming more exclusive and all-inclusive. But there remains an easy relationship between Tobagonians and visitors. The individualism of the island still survives, and each beach has its own personality, with fishermen's nets drying on one and goats grazing the edges of another.

Crown Point and Crusoe

Most visitors to Tobago fly into **Crown Point Airport**, at the southwestern tip of the island, though some still take the ferry from Port of Spain direct to Scarborough, the island's capital. The airport is a comfortable blend of the modern, the tropical and the touristy. A warm gusty wind blows scents of the sea through the hangar-like building, and across the driveway is a pleasant, inviting open-air snack bar where travellers can take a moment to unwind before moving on to their hotels.

At the front, taxi drivers jostle for passengers, but do not choose one until you have investigated the options. A number of hotels provide minibus transport to and from the airport, and if you are staying at one of the nearby hotels, like Sandy Point or Kariwak

LEFT: a solitary catamaran near Grafton beach.
BELOW: Scarborough schoolboys at break time.

Village, you can pretty well walk there. Car rentals are also available at the airport. Taxis are expensive, particularly for journeys to the further ends of the island *(see Travel Tips, page 348)*, but a taxi driver can be your best guide. But be sure to agree on the charge before you begin; the rates drivers quote often depend on whether they can expect to benefit from your custom again in the future.

Hotel haven

Kariwak Village Hotel is a unique eco-friendly place with holistic health facilities, beautiful herb gardens and Amerindian-style ajoupas (dwellings); tel: 639 8442 (see Travel Tips section, page 353).

Right next to Crown Point are a number of modern hotels; the first is the large luxurious Coco Reef Resort. Air traffic noise does not seem to be a major problem, and the hotels are conveniently located for the major tourist attraction of Buccoo Reef, but this corner of the island is basically flatlands, so do not miss the rest of the island even if you do stay here.

Sandy Point Village and Crown Point Beach Hotel offer inexpensive apartment-type accommodation in modern air-conditioned buildings, as do the Tropikist Beach Hotel and the smaller Belleviste Apartments. The choice in quality and price can appear to be endless, with Arthur's By The Sea, Coconut Inn, Golden Thistle, James Resort, Jimmy's Holiday Resort, Jetway Holiday Resort, Store Bay Holiday Resort, Surfside Hotel, Toucan Inn and Conrado Beach Resort, the closest to Pigeon Point *(see Travel Tips page 352)*.

Also nearby is Kariwak Village, and even if you do not stay here it is worth a trip for dinner and drinks just to see what owner/manager Allan Clovis is up to. One of the most knowledgeable and helpful hoteliers on Tobago, he presents art and photography shows of local artists, can find you a good taxi driver/guide, or point you towards a secluded beach where pre-Columbian arrowheads and potsherds can still be found. He is a storehouse of local intelligence and tourist advice.

BELOW: an aerial view of an island paradise.

Though Bon Accord Road to the airport is little used past the airport turn-off, it does lead to some quiet shallow bays. This is the area which Robinson Crusoe is said to have inhabited. Continue around the runway, past Sandy Point Village and all the way to the end of the road, and you will have completed a horseshoe. Through the low-growing sea grapes is a lovely half-mile double curve of sand, a flat, narrow and deserted beach only occasionally disturbed by the planes landing at the airport nearby.

A little off the beaten track and further around the coast from the airport, but worth the detour, **Canoe Bay**'s waters are clear, shallow and calm; it is seldom visited by more than the infrequent local fisherman or jogger. There is a fee to enter the beach, but there are toilets and other facilities. You can poke around in the clay banks for relics of the earlier, Amerindian, inhabitants.

Buccoo boat ride

Return along the airport road to reach **Store Bay**, whose name is an Anglicisation of its first Dutch settler, Jan Stoer. This is a starting point for trips to Buccoo Reef. It is also the finish line of the annual Great Race powerboat race from Trinidad, held in August and the occasion for a massive weekend beach party. The Bay can be approached by Pigeon Point Road further along, or more quickly by a small side road across from the airport.

The beach itself is very pleasant, a sheltered cove nestling against low rocky ledges. On the right is the modern **Coco Reef Resort**, formerly the Crown Reef Hotel, which underwent a multi-million dollar refurbishment and reopened in 1995. The bathing facilities are extensive here, with changing rooms, showers and toilets, and a number of red-roofed cement pagodas with picnic tables and

Map on pages 306–7

Little eateries dot Store Bay serving the Tobago staple of curried crab and dumpling and a host of tasty dishes. Try Miss Jean, Miss Trim, Silvia's (above) or any of the others.

Cooking up barbecue chicken and other tasty Tobagonian dishes.

benches. The Trinidad and Tobago Tourist Board has built extensive beach facilities throughout the island, which can be used for a small charge.

Some of the best food shacks on the island have taken advantage of the tourist trade here, and delicious curried crab and dumpling, the Tobago speciality, as well as generous portions of stewed or fried fish, ground provisions, macaroni pie, callaloo soup and fresh fruit, is for sale at little stands, many adorned with colourful paintings and slogans. A number of craft shops also offer some of the best local souvenirs.

An excursion to nearby **Buccoo Reef ❶**, off Pigeon Point, is worth it just to satisfy your curiosity. Boat tours leave from Store Bay, Buccoo and Pigeon Point. The price can vary, depending on the length of the trip, from 2 to 3 hours to a whole day, and whether food and drink is provided, and the trip's success depends on the quality of the glass-bottomed boat you charter. Unfortunately it is hard to know beforehand what a boat will be like, since tickets are bought onshore and boats rest offshore until the moment they must pick up passengers. Most of the "glass" consists of a central plexiglass panel in varying stages of cloudiness, so check with your hotel reception about the best boatmen.

It takes 20 minutes to reach Buccoo Reef, but 10 minutes out is the equally renowned **Nylon Pool ❷**: basically an offshore sandbar whose thigh-high pale turquoise waters and soft clean sand provide a sybaritic bath. Floating in the still lagoon, with the deep ocean on one side and palm-fringed beaches on the other, is an entrancing experience.

BELOW: fun at the Nylon Pool, with a glass-bottomed boat in the background.

Out beyond the pool lies the reef, a coral fringe much destroyed by pollution, boats and both thoughtless tourists and locals *(see Above and Below the Water, page 179)*. Boats remain here for half an hour or more before returning to shore.

The boat may stop at **Pigeon Point** ❸ (daily, 8am–6.30pm; entrance fee) to let passengers off. This is the beach used in almost all of Trinidad and Tobago's travel advertisements for its intense aquamarine waters, graceful palms and picturesque thatch-roofed dock. But do not disembark here unless you want to pay for a taxi back, because it is a long (half-hour) walk back to Store Bay.

Pigeon Point is the only private beach on Tobago and lies at the end of Pigeon Point Road (also known as Milford Extension Road). When driving keep to the left at the major fork, and at the end of the pavement continue down the dirt road to the ticket booth and guard.

The beach is a long idyllic stretch, the holidaymaker Platonic ideal of a Caribbean seashore. Along the way, food shacks and picnic tables are shaded by royal palms, while beyond, cattle graze the soft green grass of a coconut grove, like something out of a Rousseau painting.

All over the island there are areas reserved for grazing cattle. Until the 1960s, when labour became expensive and scarce, these were generally coconut estates. The beach curves around into the **Bon Accord Lagoon**, a fisherman's harbour perfect for strolling and beachcombing.

This is probably the best place on the island for shells, lying as it does off the reef. The classic conch shells with their sunny pink and apricot insides are scattered here and there where fishermen have left them after removing the meat. At mid-morning or late afternoon a fisherman might return with his catch of yellow and pink snapper, hog fish or conch. Not as perfectly groomed as Pigeon Point, this beach is scattered with palm fronds, coconut hulls and the more mundane rubbish of bottles and cans, but it is often uncrowded even when Pigeon Point is overrun.

Map on pages 306–7

BELOW: windsurfing at Pigeon Point.

The Art Gallery (Mon–Fri, 9am–5pm) on All-fields Crown Trace, off Milford Road, is a good place to buy work produced by local artists.

Like Buccoo Reef, Pigeon Point is a necessity for most visitors, but do try to avoid it during the weekend, when it is likely to be crowded with visitors from one of the cruise ships which regularly dock offshore, eager to make the most of their two-hour taste of Tobago.

Surf and turf

Heading inland along Milford Road are the villages of **Bon Accord** and **Canaan** (home of football star Dwight Yorke), small settlements named after the Christian missions which originally occupied these sites. There are small shops serving the concrete-block homes. Further along, near Shirvan Road, are government-funded housing areas of neatly similar concrete-block houses.

Continue down Milford Road, which joins the Claude Noel Highway at Lowlands. A few miles down the highway, on your right, is the entrance to Tobago's latest and largest upmarket development, the **Tobago Plantations** (tel: 637 1030). This 300-hectare (750-acre) nature resort is built around the **Petit Trou Lagoon**, and also has a 24-hectare (60-acre) mangrove forest and wetland area and a 1,500-metre (5,000-ft) -long beach. Tobago's very own 200-room Hilton Hotel fronts the beach, while the rest of the resort offers accommodation in bungalows, condominiums and luxurious Caribbean villas. An 18-hole golf course and a PADI dive centre add to the resort's attractions.

Return along the highway the way you came and take a right turning off Milford Road up Shirvan Road, which is quietly pretty and runs near the water through pale-green groves of tall palms and squat bananas. At Buccoo Junction turn left and head down to **Buccoo** fishing village, famous on several counts. Besides the beautiful sheltered bay, Buccoo is home to the

BELOW: surfing near Mount Irvine.

Tobago institutions of **Sunday School** and the **Easter Goat** and **Crab Races**.

Sunday School is the weekly Sunday-night beach party, with live steelpan followed by booming sound systems playing the latest Caribbean party hits. This is one of the best spots for visitors to socialise with islanders and learn the art of partying. Vendors' stalls crowd the roadside, offering barbecued chicken, fish and drinks. The Goat and Crab Races held on Easter Tuesday are unique. The goat races are serious affairs *(see page 162)* with betting and prizes, whereas the crab races are strictly for fun.

Shirvan Road turns into Grafton Road, with **Mount Irvine Bay Hotel** (tel: 639 8871) marked by the pink, orange and purple bougainvillea that fringes its cottages and by the neatly clipped greens and towering palms of its famed international championship 18-hole golf course. Mount Irvine is built on the site of an old sugar plantation owned by Charles Irvine in the latter half of the 18th century. The golf course is open to anyone for a fee, and there is a restaurant built around the old stone sugar mill.

Now closed, the Museum of Tobago History was originally set up by Edward Hernandez in the grounds of Mount Irvine Bay Hotel. He was so passionate and learned about the history of his island that he started the museum with a one-room collection of artefacts. In 1989 the museum was integrated into the Tobago Museum, and the exhibits were moved to larger premises in the Barrack Guard House at Fort King George in Scarborough *(see page 330)*.

The public beach just northeast of the hotel has some of the nicest and most complete facilities. A favoured spot for surfers, it has good waves breaking about 400 metres (¼ mile) offshore. Catch the strongest ones from December to March. The changing-room building is next to the old site of the Mount Irvine

Map
on pages
306–7

The Tobago Pro-Am tournament is held at Mount Irvine golf course in January.

LEFT: archaeological finds at the former Museum of Tobago. **BELOW:** a monument to the first European settlers.

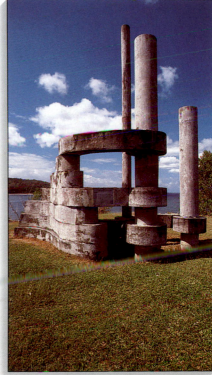

Estate sugar depot, where ships from many places deposited their ballast of slate and bricks in exchange for sugar and, later, cocoa cultivated on the estate.

Today there are the usual locker rooms and showers, as well as a small bar where you can sit at a concrete table and drink a cold Carib beer with a bake 'n' shark. This is also the venue for local parties sometimes held here at night, featuring plates of wild game and wild music. The deep, clean beach is dotted with sea-grape trees whose leafy canopy has been trained into sun umbrellas. The sea floor is rocky in places, and at low tide there are wonderful little pools caught in the declivities, swarming with sea roaches, crabs and tiny fish. The safest bathing spots are marked by yellow and red flags.

Inland and close to the Mount Irvine golf course up Orange Hill Road is an intriguing museum belonging to the German sculptor Luise Kimme, who has been a resident since 1979. In the **Kimme Museum** the artist's larger-than-life painted woodcarvings of local dancers and folklore characters perfectly capture the robust Tobagonian spirit. Further examples of her work can be seen at the museum at Fort King George *(see page 330)* and elsewhere on the island.

Secluded sun spots

For a really secluded beach, walk a short way down the main highway to a rusted, rickety gate leading into a palm grove. Walk across the grove to the sea, past benign cattle to the cliff, and it should be easy to find a spot to climb down to deserted **Back Bay**. This is a popular beach for nude sunbathing, but is usually deserted, and the waves can be quite good for body surfing.

Continuing along the road towards **Black Rock** ❹ and Plymouth, keep to the main road to the right, or take a turning a little beyond the Back Bay entrance

TIP

Viewing at the Kimme Museum is restricted to Sunday (11am–2pm). Otherwise call ahead and book an appointment, tel: 639 0257.

BELOW: schoolboys at Black Rock.

and take the shore road along **Grafton Beach**. This long, wide, usually empty stretch of beach is easily accessible from the road. It might be totally deserted, or there could be a couple of people running dogs and fishing for sea roaches, the tiny sand-coloured crustaceans which look exactly like their namesakes and are used for bait for offshore fishing. It is a nice place for a swim as well, as there are often gentle waves, but there can be strong currents at times.

Le Grand Courland Resort and Spa, right next door to its sister resort Grafton Beach, is an example of Tobago's trend towards upmarket development. Italian marble floors, jacuzzis and a health club combine to offer tropical luxury.

Grafton Beach Resort – considered by some to be one of Tobago's best hotels – dominates this area, and offers its guests a lovely view of Grafton Bay and a quiet beach. Grafton beach is located just across the road from the hotel which stands on the old Grafton estate, which was once owned by the Smith family, who had a long history on the island. Although the house fell into disrepair, part of the estate is now the **Grafton Caledonia Wildlife Sanctuary** (free) where many Tobago birds like cocricos and motmots can be seen feeding.

Just outside the small village of Black Rock is the unassuming **Black Rock Café** *(see Travel Tips, page 358)* which often looks closed. Try it anyway, for the wonderful kingfish pelau and other inexpensive Creole dishes.

Of turtles and kings

Northeast of Black Rock is **Turtle Beach Hotel** on **Great Courland Bay**, once the site of an early settlement and now famous for the immense sea turtles which come up on the beach at night to lay their eggs. Courlanders, more commonly known as Latvians, were some of the first Europeans to settle on

Grafton Caledonia Bird Sanctuary was set up after the death of the owner of the Grafton estate, who began feeding the birds after Hurricane Flora devastated their woodland habitat in 1963. Feeding time is around 4pm, and the sanctuary is open daily 6am–6pm.

BELOW: baby turtles on Turtle Beach.

The ruins of Fort Bennett (circa 1680) lie just outside Black Rock village. The views over the area around Grafton and Black Rock from the Fort are spectacular, especially at sunrise and sunset.

Tobago, Lutherans looking for a place to emigrate after the Thirty Years' War. The settlement was begun around 1659 by Duke Jekabs, a godson of James I of England. Eventually the Courlanders sent to Tobago by Jekabs were absorbed into other colonies on the island, some at Mount Irvine, or at Little Courland Bay.

The bar at Turtle Beach is popular on the nights that the hotel hosts its weekly steel band show. During the egg-laying season, in April and May, organised tours and groups meet at night to observe the turtles on the beach, who seem unperturbed by the presence of humans. Turtle-watch tours can be arranged through local hotels (*see Travel Tips page 363*).

Beyond Black Rock is **Plymouth** ❺, the biggest town on the north side, but do not look for a town centre. Plymouth is mostly a small residential village on a promontory overlooking Great Courland Bay, with small shops for local needs, a gas station and one tourist attraction: **Fort James** ❻.

The fort was built by the British in 1768 as a barracks, and named after King James II. Now all that remains is a neat low stone edifice, set amid clipped lawns and a few botanical plantings. Peering in through the window you see the fort's present usage: a tool shed. The view from the escarpment is pleasant, with vistas of curving Turtle Beach to the left and fishing boats at rest closer by.

The approach road to the fort passes a small concrete block School for the Deaf, the local grandstand and field, and another attraction mentioned in every guidebook. In the courtyard of a small stone church is the **mysterious tombstone**, whose inscription reads: "She was a mother without knowing it and a wife without letting her husband know it except by her kind indulgences to him." (Betty Stiven 1783). One can only imagine Betty's domestic situation. Descendants of the early Latvian settlers (Courlanders) make pilgrimages to

BELOW: fishing boats at rest at Plymouth.

the area near the tomb to see the **Courland Monument**, a sculpture by Janis Mintks honouring the 17th-century arrivals. Continue on Jager Road to the ocean, and if you can get around the fence you might find Carib and Arawak tear-drop axes in the freshwater rivers where they meet the sea.

The walk from Fort James provides a delightful, superficial picture of village life, with cocks crowing and schoolchildren in neat blue uniforms running about, and pastel houses with neat yards against wooden shacks overgrown with hibiscus, banana palms and other tropical plants.

North Road, one of the main streets in the town, turns into a track and then ends in a narrow stretch of rough beach – good for a quick dip only, but refreshing if you are both hot and a half-hour's drive from the next beach.

The Motmot Trail

The gently curving road out of Plymouth leads inland for some time, with **Arnos Vale Hotel** about a mile away. Terraced along a small hillside with winding paths through botanical gardens, Arnos Vale offers some of the best snorkelling and birdwatching on Tobago. Even if you do not stay there, it is worth the trip for those attractions.

The original English owners covered the hillside with scarlet ixora, pink oleander, pastel bougainvillea, rosy hibiscus, multicoloured foliage bushes, many flamboyant trees with their deep-green leaves and orange flowers, and other sweet-scented tropical plants. The stunted trees with rubbery leaves on the beach are Indian almonds. Take the Motmot Trail early in the morning for birdwatching, or follow other little paths to their summits overlooking the bay.

Because the cove is so protected, with sharp rocky outcroppings stepping

Map on pages 306–7

Look out for the blue-crowned motmot along the birdwatching and nature trails.

BELOW: cannon stand guard at Fort James, Plymouth.

Gang Gang Sara, a witch in folk tales, is believed to be buried in Golden Lane. She flew from Africa to Les Coteaux, in search of her family who had been transported. Finding them in Golden Lane, she stayed and married her sweetheart Tom. On his death she climbed a silk-cotton tree, ready to fly back to Africa, but found she had lost the art of flight through eating salt.

BELOW: a fisherman brings in his seine.

down into the water, there are myriad places for brilliant tropical fish to live and hide. Hire snorkelling equipment from the hotel, and swim out to see barracuda, brain coral, sea fans, the blue-green parrot fish, male stoplights, the multicoloured angelfish with their pendant "whiskers", yellow and black rock beauties, hawkfish, electric-blue tangs and surgeonfish, rays, trumpetfish and the waves of small silver-blue grunts which miraculously surround you in shallow water. Fishing off the rocks can yield Caribbean salmon, kingfish, bonito or albacore, though offshore your chances are improved. To the left of the main beach, a short hike over the rocks or a brief swim, is a secluded triangle of sand; to the right, carved into rocky cliffs, are caves.

Creole Coteaux

Arnos Vale Road past the hotel continues to curve upwards through rolling countryside planted with the short, leafy banana palms which are, strictly speaking, large herbs. About a kilometre (half a mile) or so past the hotel is a sign on the right for Franklyn's Road, a hilly, bumpy track which eventually emerges in the hill village of **Les Coteaux**.

But just after the turn, on the right, practically hidden by thick undergrowth, is the original **Arnos Vale Water Wheel** ❼ (daily 8.30am–10.30pm; tel: 639 2881/2). Its deep-red bricks covered with creeping vines, the wheel dates back to 1857 and is now the focal point of a nature park with trails, a small museum, two Amerindian sites, an old slave village and a restaurant noted for excellent cuisine and cultural shows.

The track leads past Franklyn's Estate, now a modern vacation home surrounded by a high pink wall and wrought-iron gate, with an unlikely stand

of pine trees. Past that are small houses with neat yards, and many deep cuts.

Arnos Vale Road continues through low dry hills, reminiscent of Indonesia or Africa, past the ubiquitous tethered livestock and into the village of Les Coteaux, a crossroads of comparatively goodly size in this area of Tobago.

The sounds of crowing roosters and klaxons make every day sound like Sunday, and the residents will happily offer directions, whether or not they know the way and whether or not you can interpret the dialect.

The name of their home, an obvious leftover from the days of French colonisation, is pronounced by locals as something more akin to "Leckito". If you give it a French pronunciation, you risk misunderstanding.

Les Coteaux, like Moriah *(see page 322),* is one of the villages where the African heritage, from drumming and dancing to folklore and storytelling, has survived. These are villages which have changed very little over the past 200 years and where authentic Tobago culture, untouched by tourism, continues at its own leisurely pace.

At Les Coteaux three roads meet: to the left the road leads up north along the shore, to the right down through lush hills and streams to Scarborough, and straight ahead (sort of) it twists off toward, the Hillsborough Dam. Keep left to explore the northern shore.

The bad mountain road leads over rocky terrain with ravines crowded with the immortelle, vivid orange in dry season, and terraced hillsides fringed by the pale green of bamboo stands. Little iridescent lizards, baby dinosaurs, dart across the road, which is often washed out in places, and periwinkle-blue morning glories carpet the road banks.

For **Culloden Bay**, at the fork take Culloden Road, leading south through the

There is a 5-hectare (12-acre) Adventure Farm and Nature Reserve (weekdays 7am–5pm; tel: 639 2839) on Arnos Vale Road. It has a citrus orchard, where you can pick your own fruit and see iguanas. It is also a good place for birdwatching.

BELOW: Arnos Vale Water Wheel.

Some of the best scuba diving and snorkelling can be had at Buccoo Reef, Mount Irvine, Arnos Vale, Culloden Bay, Englishman's Bay and Castara Bay.

BELOW: a beach house peeps through palm trees at Castara Bay.

tiny hamlet of **Golden Lane**. There are beautiful vistas out to sea across hills dotted with palms and breadfruit trees. Take a sharp right turning at the Moriah/Arnos Vale junction in Golden Lane, and an extremely rocky track leads to the bay. Culloden Bay is a fishermen's pebbly cove with the charm of the utilitarian. The fishermen here catch redfish, bonito and albacore, among other things, and if you care to venture down (there are some amazing trees along the way) you might persuade one of them to take you fishing very early one Sunday morning for a lot less than the organised tours will charge. The boats are fibreglass dinghies and the methods uncomplicated – trolling with heavy line and massive hooks – but the fishermen know how to read the waters and skies for schooling fish.

Return the way you came, past the small settlements of pastel houses on stilts, some with flags that resemble those of the Hindus but signify Shango (an African cult) houses, and small grocers marked by Carib beer signs. North of **Moriah** the coastal road traverses steeper and steeper hills as it climbs toward the small fishing villages and perfect beaches of Castara and Parlatuvier.

A tropical Amalfi coast

The easiest access to the Leeward (northern) coast is to follow Northside Road direct from Scarborough. The Plymouth route can be impassable at times, depending on road and weather conditions. Travelling up from Scarborough will take you through Mason Hall Village, before Moriah, and on to nearby **Mason Hall Falls**, Tobago's second highest waterfall at 50 metres (160 ft).

As it follows the Leeward coastline Northside Road offers some of the most spectacular views and passes stunning shores, glimpsed around hairpin turns, as the glittering navy sea shades into turquoise near the shore hundreds of feet below. At the height of the road you might simply dive into clouds like the unbroken expanse of sparkling water. **King Peter's Bay**, on the way, named for a Carib *cacique* (chief), is not particularly good for swimming.

The Sisters Rocks appear offshore, surrounded by white foam, right before the road spins down headily to Castara Bay. On the beach you might imagine yourself on the Amalfi coast, with sharp dark-green cliffs enclosing the village and bay, and the blue water glittering like diamonds. **Castara ❽**, like most of the northcoast settlements, is a fishing village, and most of the 500 or so residents support themselves by a combination of fishing, farming and government work, most notably road repair. It is a Tobago conundrum that a great number of island men work on the roads yet many still remain deeply potholed, although there has been a marked improvement in recent years.

Castara has changing rooms, showers and toilets, but mostly you will find fishermen liming in their sheds while they mend nets and wait for the tide to change. The long wide beach, edged by low thick palms, often has nets laid out to dry, and wooden dinghies float offshore with their bamboo rods balanced like insect antennae. If you are hungry visit Henry Jackson's **First and Last** *roti* stand, just up the road from the beach, where he sells tasty goat, chicken and potato *roti*, cold drinks, alcohol and sundry items

Map on pages 306–7

such as bay rum and toothpaste. Sit on the shaded bench and watch shy smiling children pass while friendly bony dogs beg at your feet for scraps. Or there is the No Problem food supply store nearby.

North of Castara the views are equally stunning, as the road winds inwards through jungle, up and down steep hills and back out towards the coast. The second rocky bay past Castara is **Englishman's Bay ⑨**, below the railing on the coastal side. Drive down to where the road is straight and then take the track to this beautiful secluded beach, obscured from the road by trees.

Next is **Parlatuvier ⑩**, a leisurely 30-minute drive from Castara. Parlatuvier has a perfect crescent beach curving away towards pretty pastel houses and palm-fringed hills, a little elementary school shaking with the noise and concentration of children, a tiny shop or two, and not much else. Teenage boys lounge under palm trees, burly fishermen drag in their seines, and the sea rolls quietly on the sand. Parlatuvier is village life at its simplest.

Beyond the beach, Northside Road crosses a small bridge over a reedy estuary and heads up the hill towards the left. Further on, the road is often impassable but it does provide quiet green views and perhaps motmots or cocricos in the bushes until it peters out entirely on a curve above a mossy green ravine. The right fork leads to a crossroads, after a bumpy ride on a wide track, and the right turning there leads over the top of the mountain to **Roxborough**.

After Parlatuvier is the remote village of L'Anse Formi and the north side. The road is a beautiful drive through jungle past **Bloody Bay**, the site of a long-ago battle which legend states stained the waters red. After L'Anse Formi the road, which is being relaid, descends from the heights above **Man O' War Bay**, where pirates secreted their booty, down to tranquil Charlotteville. ❑

If you plan to spend time at isolated Englishman's Bay, it would be wise to go in a group, and to lock valuables away in the car if you want to take a dip.

BELOW: view over Parlatuvier Bay.

Map on pages 306–7

THE NORTH, CENTRAL AND THE ATLANTIC COAST

An idyllic rural interior reveals lush green forest land, while the Atlantic Ocean laps the eastern coastline and peaceful picturesque villages offer sanctuary

Scarborough

Tobago's interior is rich in nature and wildlife, and in the north and along the Atlantic coast tranquil rural and fishing villages dot the landscape. Even in Scarborough, which is busier because most visitors head for the delightful capital, there is a no-rush attitude to life. This part of the island offers the chance to relax on the pretty beaches, hike through the verdant vegetation of the Tobago Forest Reserve and visit picturesque villages along the way. Lovely Charlotteville in the far north, Speyside, Roxborough and Scarborough all offer peace and a chance to explore nature at her best.

There are a number of overland routes to the south side from the west. The Parlatuvier–Roxborough road is about a 45-minute drive through the interior through the magnificent **Tobago Forest Reserve** ⓫ above steep ravines filled with bamboo and birds. Declared a Crown Reserve in 1776, this is the oldest protected rainforest in the western hemisphere. The road climbs over the Main Ridge – the spinal mountain ridge rising to 580 metres (1,900 ft) – Tobago's highest altitude, which runs down the eastern two-thirds of the island.

At the summit's Forestry Division lookout you can savour the superb views over the forest canopy down to the Caribbean Sea in the east, and sample some of the local snacks and juices on sale. This point also marks the start of the **Gilpin Trace** nature trail which (with a guide) will take you to the heart of the forest. As you descend towards Roxborough a low cocoa grove is a signal that you have reached the Windward Road.

Another overland route southeast is via the **Hillsborough Dam**. This is a much longer and rougher journey, which can take almost two hours to complete. At the north end of Les Coteaux continue straight on to **Mason Hall Road**. After the bridge bear right down a track and you are on your way south.

Like much of Tobago, this area was made up of cocoa and coffee estates and is still cultivated for those crops, though on a much smaller scale. You can still see coffee-drying houses with their corrugated roofs that slide on rafters to expose the beans when it is sunny and cover them when it rains. The huge iron pots in some yards used to be (and sometimes still are) used for boiling sugar. Neighbourhood dogs were allowed to lick them clean and so are called "pot hounds".

The bumpy track passes soft hills and isolated houses where young girls walk three miles a day just to fetch water and do the family laundry. When the road becomes paved take a left turning, past neatly tended gardens and small glades, and you are at the dam.

A surprising mixture of pines and palms surrounds

PRECEDING PAGES: a little girl paddles in the sea, Castara. **LEFT:** on the beach. **BELOW:** ferns at the Tobago Forest Reserve.

TIP

If you want to hike or hunt in the interior around the Hillsborough Dam you would be wise to employ a guide who knows the area well. Check with your hotel reception before setting out, or the tourism office (TIDCO) in Scarborough (tel: 639 4333) for recommendations and permits required.

the quiet lake, and if you walk out across the dam you might see a cayman (a peaceful relative of the South American alligator) nosing about the reeds. The dam is a good place to begin a hike or a hunt, but do not set out without a guide.

The journey from the dam down to the Windward Road at **Studley Park** takes an hour. First pass the lush growth of palms and bamboo supported by streams trickling through mossy beds, and stop the car to listen to the loud noise of balisier leaves rubbing together. Pass a gravel quarry and then wind down through the small town of Studley Park, just five minutes' drive above the water.

Back to civilisation

The interior on the west side of the island is more populated and less wild, situated as it is between Plymouth and Scarborough. The ride between the two towns is only 20 minutes or so, provided that you do not stop to pick up hitch-hikers or a beer along the way.

Scarborough ⑫ is Tobago's capital. Besides being the largest and most important town, it is a market centre and port where 17,000 of the island's 50,000 inhabitants live. Compared with some of the more European-style cities in the Caribbean, Scarborough still has an essentially rustic appearance, although it has been spruced up. The port is a regular cruise-ship stop, and tourists come ashore at the deep-water harbour and head immediately for the beach. As a centre of island life it is certainly worth an afternoon's scrutiny.

Ranged up and down a steep hill overlooking **Rockly Bay**, Scarborough became the capital in 1779. The town is divided into Upper and Lower Scarborough, the latter having been a Dutch depot in the 17th century. Nowadays the ferry from Port of Spain docks here, as do fishing and cargo boats, though over

BELOW: view of Scarborough from Rockly Bay.

Maps:
Area 306
Town 329

the years ships' captains have cursed the sharp red rocks of the harbour which give the bay its name. The town consists largely of tin-roofed shops, shacks selling a variety of clothing and local produce, and some more solid cement buildings housing several well-known larger stores.

A diminutive town square sits below government buildings and the **Department of Tourism** on Jerningham Street, and the narrow streets crawl with slow-moving traffic, schoolchildren and professional limers. On Friday and Sunday an open-air fruit and vegetable market brings villagers to town.

Any number of undistinguished and sometimes unnamed bars and restaurants serve fried chicken, beer, *roti* and fish and chips. The **Old Donkey Cart House** restaurant, on the road east toward Bacolet, has more expensive Creole food and a relatively expensive German wine list. In an old Victorian house overlooking Bacolet and Rockly bays, the restaurant is tarted up with Christmas lights and taped music.

In Lower Scarborough there is a modern mall encompassing a school and other buildings, and though the brick and concrete modern architecture seems out of keeping with the rest of town, it houses a number of useful resources including the bus station, post office, banks and the island's main library. The mall forecourt and car park are used for parties by Trinidadian DJs.

The library offers a periodical section on the main floor with a wide selection of Caribbean magazines and newspapers. The Caribbean book section upstairs contains many British and American books on Trinidad and Tobago, some impossible to find elsewhere, as well as all monographs and books written by Trinidadians and Tobagonians on Tobago. This is a cool, quiet place to spend the hot midday hours (until school ends and students come here to flirt).

Adjoining the mall in Lower Scarborough is the market, a scene of constant action particularly on Friday and Saturday. The market specialises in fish, fruit and vegetables, and there are vendors selling reasonably priced local food.

BELOW: a cruise ship off the coast at Scarborough.

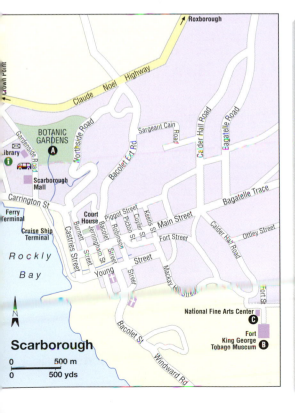

Scarborough

The Jig *by Luise Kimme, National Fine Arts Center.*

Scarborough also has a **Botanic Gardens** Ⓐ (daily; free), near the approach highway, where you can stroll amid cultivated versions of plants and trees which grow wild on the island but are sometimes difficult to find.

Fort King George Ⓑ, high above Scarborough, was built by the English in 1779 to protect the town, and was later captured by the French. Like Tobago itself it changed hands a number of times, and now lies in partial ruins above the hospital, surrounded by palms, ferns and lawns. The views, particularly at sunset, are breathtaking.

The **National Fine Arts Center** Ⓒ (tel: 639 6897) stands at the entrance to the Fort compound. Above in the main Fort the burnt-out powder magazine survives, while other buildings on Barrack Square serve as offices for the Tobago House of Assembly Culture Division and also house the excellent **Tobago Museum** (Mon–Fri, 9am–5pm, doors close at 4.30pm; tel: 639 3970). The small Museum of Tobago History *(see page 315)* was moved from Mount Irvine and integrated into the Tobago Museum in 1989, bringing with it exhibits of shells, pre-Columbian and European tools, buttons and tableware from pirate ships and colonials, potsherds and a host of other archaeological finds from all eras of Tobago's history. In the years following the move the collection expanded to include military relics, colonial maps and documents.

Bacolet and coconuts

From the Fort, continue on the Windward Road, past the Old Donkey Cart House restaurant and apartment complex, between low hedges and neat palm groves, a tropical version of rural England, to within 90 metres (100 yards) of the Windward Road junction at the Bacolet River. Continue down a small paved

BELOW: the view from Fort George.

track on the right, and at the intersection take a left turning, and then another to the end of the road. Walk 15 metres (50 ft) towards the sparkling water, and you are on beautiful **Bacolet Beach**, one of Tobago's most famous.

A long, rough, beautiful crescent fringed with tall palms and littered with coconut husks and tree trunks, the dark-sand beach is set in a residential area of large seaside homes with well-groomed yards, though a deep coconut grove separates it from nearby houses. Pounding surf creates a misty spray of rainbows and haze around the palms, and the beach is often deserted.

In the grove you might see coconut pickers and their rickety ladders balanced on the beds of old-fashioned pick-up vans. The pickers' ability to launch themselves into the fronds, 12 metres (40 ft) above an absolutely straight trunk, is astounding and rare. Coconut sellers used to climb the trees in search of the best fruit, but now, lament old-timers, most wait until the nuts drop of their own accord.

Winding up the Windward

The drive from Buccoo in the south to Charlotteville at the far end of the Windward Road would probably take three or four hours without stops, but as it passes some of the most enchanting beaches on the way there is little chance that you will make the trip in three hours. Ideally, one could take two or three days to explore, taking the road in stretches, returning home each night by a slightly different route, or staying at one of the hotels or small guesthouses on the Windward Road.

The Windward is also one of the most used roads on the island, much more so than the Northside Road, and so you may encounter mild inter-village traffic which, combined with hair-raising turns over breathtaking prospects, slows

Maps:
**Maps:
Area 306
Town 329**

Bacolet Beach was the setting for the movie version of The Swiss Family Robinson.

BELOW:
Bird of Paradise Island from the Windward Road.

The pretty, hilly fishing village of Pembroke, past Barbados Bay and before Roxborough, is becoming well known for its annual Salaka Feast, a celebration of African ancestors with song, dance, drumming and story telling, which forms part of the Tobago Heritage Festival held from mid-July to early August.

one's progress considerably yet pleasurably. East of Scarborough the road is a tropical combination of California's Highway One and Italy's Amalfi coast.

Beyond Bacolet and the **Dwight Yorke Stadium**, the Windward Road curves to and from the shoreline, offering glimpses of long misty beaches or sparkling water, with coconut and cocoa groves and watery estuaries between the road and the beaches. You can swim pretty much anywhere, and if you spot an inviting beach be assured that there is a footpath leading to it. **Hillsborough Bay** and **Barbados Bay** offer many bathing sites. Overlooking the Bay is the village of Mount St George, Tobago's first short-lived capital, Georgetown, founded in 1762 but abandoned in favour of Scarborough by 1769. Further down the coast, at **Granby Point**, all that remains of the fort built to protect the capital is a soldier's gravestone.

There are only a few lodging places at this end of Tobago; and all are small, and most unassuming. Village life reigns supreme here, and the roads are traversed by strong Tobago women, renowned for their broad shoulders and ample girth, with bundles on their heads or umbrellas unfurled against the sun and passing showers. The ubiquitous schoolchildren are cheekier here, and boys may shout unintelligible but highly amusing (to them) remarks to the sightseer passing through. In time-honoured Tobagonian (and African) tradition, these light-hearted verbal assaults are meant as much for amusement as energy releasers and an acceptable form of criticism. This *picong* is not meant seriously.

Towns are small and perched precariously on cliffs overlooking stunning Caribbean seascapes, and on the days when light rain comes and goes there may be three or four rainbows at once, stretching from slope to sea, from treetop to pastel house. There are few foodstalls or restaurants, and those that exist are

BELOW:
catching the
waves on the coast.

closed at the weekend after 4pm, or at any other time that the owner would rather be elsewhere.

Richmond restored

Continue on the coast road past **Pembroke**, and just outside the hamlet of **Belle Garden** keep an eye out for the wooden sign to **Richmond Great House** (tours; tel: 660 4467). One of many old estate houses, Richmond is one of the few to have been restored. A typical 18th-century plantation house, it was bought in a state of disrepair by a Professor Lynch of Columbia University in New York City. After extensive restoration the house opened as a guesthouse, offering a sense of history and local atmosphere for a small number of visitors.

The square whitewashed brick house sits on top of a knoll overlooking rolling land to the sea, with mountains behind and palm trees and jungle as far as the eye can see. The Great House's chief charms are its location: isolated and a short ride or 15 minutes' walk from the beach; its design, which permits cool breezes to blow through the rooms even on the hottest of days; and, for visitors interested in African art, the professor's extensive collection of objects. It is also a good place for nature lovers, with an abundance of birds and plant life.

Beyond Belle Garden is the track leading to the **Argyle Waterfall** ⓭ (entrance fee), at 54 metres (177 ft) the highest in Tobago. A short way down the tree-lined track is the Roxborough Visitor Service Co-op office, where guides can be hired for the 15-minute walk to the falls. There are three pools; a climb to the top pool reveals that although the smallest it is the deepest and ideal for swimming.

The road from Belle Garden passes old cocoa plantations to **Roxborough**, the only sizeable settlement on the Windward coast and site of the bloody 1876

Climb the Argyle Waterfall in the rainy season (June–Dec) with an official guide.

BELOW: a welcoming smile.

Map on pages 306–7

Diving at Speyside.

BELOW: a couple at Tyrrel's Bay, Little Tobago, enjoy the view northeast to Speyside.

Belmanna Riots *(see page 38)*. The town remains virtually untouched by tourism (although you'll find the island's only decompression chamber here), and is a good place to see Tobagonians conducting life in their own style, or just to sit at a small seafront rumshop and commune with the Atlantic waves.

Continue to the village of **Delaford**, and just outside look for a sandy carpark on the left. This is the entrance to the **King's Bay Waterfall**, once spectacular but reduced to a trickle by the damming of the King's Bay River. High above the path to the falls, in the branches of tall trees, look for the pendant nests, resembling socks filled with sand, of the crested orapendula. These birds permit rice grackles to live in the nests, as they eat parasites off the chicks' bodies.

Royal sands and birds of paradise

Down King's Bay Depot Road is the approach to **King's Bay Beach**. This sheltered beach has deep-grey sand and a soft pebbly bottom. There are some facilities provided, though most beachcombers are townspeople from Delaford, or local fishermen. A small restaurant next to the beach is a comfortable place for an informal meal – when it is open. Yachts sometimes dock offshore to use the - sheltered harbour and enjoy the verdant scenery. Enclosed by the jungle-covered hills as it is, King's Bay seems cooler and wilder than more westerly beaches.

After King's Bay, the Windward Road turns inland until the drop into **Speyside** 🄸, with its spectacular views over the village and **Tyrrel's Bay** beyond. This tiny village with its brightly painted seafront cottages has developed as a scuba-diving centre, but the diving shops located at the far end of the village have not intruded on the tranquillity. On the roadside here you will also find local favourite, **Jemma's Restaurant**, and the starting point for trips to **Goat Island** and **Little Tobago** 🄸. The latter has been known as **Bird of Paradise Island** since 1909 when ornithologist Sir William Ingram brought 24 of the rare exotic birds from New Guinea in an attempt to save them from extinction. Sadly the birds have not survived, but the island is now a sanctuary for seabirds.

Recent hurricanes have diminished the bird population, so it is unclear how many birds remain. You might want to check with the game warden on the island about the bird count, since tour boatmen will all tell you there are plenty to be seen. It's a 20-minute boat ride to any of the three offshore islands, and you can swim at the beach in front of the playing field.

Blue Waters at Batteaux Bay

Beyond Speyside, towards the tiny enclave of **Lucyville**, is the remote and romantic **Blue Waters Inn** 🄸, a small hotel on its own bay, across from Goat Island. After climbing a side road for about a hundred metres, you will see on your right the entrance to the Inn, a small track. Drive towards it and you will think that you are about to fly off into the blue, the declivity is so steep. It is a thrilling vista, and one that can make you want to jump right into the ocean once you arrive. The Inn has air-conditioned rooms fronting the small beach, and an airy, open dining room. The narrow beach is confined by sea grapes like natural cabanas, and birdwatching is almost unavoidable.

The end of the road

Between Speyside and Charlotteville the road winds across the mountains through dense wet deep-green jungle. Curving and mountainous, it can be treacherous during sudden heavy downpours, and though it is only about 6 km (4 miles) between the two villages, the drive takes a good half an hour. Midway is a scenic vista from a metal lookout tower placed at Tobago's highest point, **Flagstaff Hill**. Bird of Paradise Island is distinctly visible across forest and water.

Charlotteville ⓱ is the most picturesque village on Tobago. Isolated by the mountains to the south and the impassable road to the west, it sleeps undisturbed on sharp, steep cliffs above a deep-blue bay. Some of the best fishing on the island can be found offshore, and most male inhabitants are fishermen. There are beach facilities and a beach club offering music at night, and there are cabins for hire on the beach, with porches from which to watch the sunset.

More extensive than it seems at first, Charlotteville is made up of numerous unmade and paved tracks winding back and up along the mountainside. Beyond and to the west is the continuation of the north road, no more than a track, but it is being upgraded.

Everything is covered in a carpet of soft green vegetation, with orchids and bromeliads growing from trees, support wires, telephone poles or anything else that provides purchase. Tree frogs chirp ceaselessly, and small perfect waterfalls edge the roadside. Parrots fly above, as does the cocrico, the island's national bird. The effect is of being in an enormous misty arboretum. It makes the south end of the island seem positively arid.

If there are too many deep muddy potholes, turn back, because it might be hours until someone else passes. And days before a breakdown van can come. ❑

Map on pages 306–7

The beach near Blue Waters Inn.

BELOW:
Charlotteville tumbles down the hill to Man O' War Bay.

Travel Tips

✻ INSIGHT GUIDES Phonecard

One global card to keep travellers in touch. Easy. Convenient. Saves you time and money.

It's a global phonecard

Save up to 70%* on international calls from over 55 countries

Free 24 hour global customer service

Recharge your card at any time via customer service or online

It's a message service

Family and friends can send you voice messages for free.

Listen to these messages using the phone* or online

Free email service - you can even listen to your email over the phone*

It's a travel assistance service

24 hour emergency travel assistance – if and when you need it.

Store important travel documents online in your own secure vault

For more information, call rates, and all Access Numbers in over 55 countries, (check your destination is covered) go to **www.insightguides.ekit.com** or call Customer Service.

JOIN now and receive US$ 5 bonus when you join for US$ 20 or more.

Join today at

www.insightguides.ekit.com

When requested use ref code: **INSAD010**

OR SIMPLY FREE CALL
24 HOUR CUSTOMER SERVICE

UK	0800 376 1705
USA	1800 706 1333
Canada	1800 808 5773
Australia	1800 11 44 78
South Africa	0800 997 285

THEN PRESS ⓪

For all other countries please go to "Access Numbers" at **www.insightguides.ekit.com**

* Retrieval rates apply for listening to messages. Savings base on using a hotel or payphone and calling to a landline. Corre at time of printing 01.03

(INS001)

powered by **ekit**

"The easiest way to make calls and receive messages around the world"

CONTENTS

Getting Acquainted

The Place

Area: 5,128 sq. km (1,980 sq. miles). Trinidad 4,828 sq. km (1,864 sq. miles). Tobago 300 sq. km (116 sq. miles).
Capital: Port of Spain (Trinidad); Scarborough (Tobago).
Population: 1.3 million.
Language: English.
Religion: Christian 61 percent (Roman Catholic 32 percent, Protestant 29 percent); Hindu 25 percent; Muslim 6 percent; other religions 8 percent.
Time Zone: GMT minus 4 hours; one hour ahead of Eastern Standard Time.
Currency: Trinidad and Tobago dollar (TT$).
Weights and measures: metric.
Electricity: 110 and 220 volts/ 60 cycles.
International dialling code: 868.

Orientation

Trinidad and Tobago lies at the southern end of the Caribbean island chain, a few miles off the South American coast. Because Trinidad was once joined to South America it has a similar variety of flora and fauna which confirm this link. Trinidad and Tobago are only 33 km (21 miles) apart, and both lie south of the hurricane belt.

Trinidad, the most southerly of the Caribbean islands, is just 11 km (7 miles) off the coast of Venezuela, across the Gulf of Paria, and lies 10 degrees north of the Equator. It is the larger of the two islands and is home to all but 50,000 of the combined population of 1.3 million people.

Trinidad has a range of mountains along the north coast called the Northern Range, the main peaks of which are El Cerro del Aripo, rising to 940 metres (3,084 ft), and El Tucuche, 936 metres (3,072 ft). The flat central area is characterised by savannahs, rivers and swamps, and is mostly used for growing sugar cane. The south with its gently rolling, forested hills is home to the Pitch Lake and the Devil's Woodyard, the site of a small mud volcano, one of many in the southern area but the most accessible to the public.

Tobago, unlike its sister isle Trinidad, is a coral island with complex reef systems. Its shape, interpreted differently by many, has been compared to a fish and a cigar. It is 42 km long and 11 km wide (26 miles by 7 miles), with a central chain of forested hills rising to 549 metres (1,800 ft). The birthplace of footballer Dwight Yorke, Tobago has become known as an exclusive tourist haven. Excellent beaches, diving, sailing, snorkelling are all features of a holiday on the island.

The People

The population of Trinidad and Tobago is roughly divided between equal numbers of those of African and East Indian descent, and much smaller percentages of Chinese, European and Syrians. The diversity, which has resulted in the country being dubbed "the Rainbow Nation", is mainly confined to Trinidad, however; in Tobago over 90 percent of the people are of African descent.

In Trinidad over half the population resides along the east-west corridor which stretches from Chaguaramas in the west through Port of Spain, the capital, to Sangre Grande and Arima in the east. In Tobago the population is concentrated in the west part of the island, surrounding the island's capital, Scarborough.

Religion

Christianity is the largest faith, with the traditional denominations like Roman Catholic and Anglican but also a growing number of Spiritual Baptists and other evangelical denominations. There is quite a significant number of Hindus (25 percent), a small percentage of Muslims and an even smaller number of those who follow traditional African faiths like Orisha. Trinidad and Tobago, however, probably has the largest number of Rastafarians in the Caribbean after Jamaica.

Culture

CARNIVAL

Trinidad and Tobago is the home of the Caribbean's most famous Carnival. Every year, from the Sunday before Ash Wednesday until Shrove Tuesday, the streets burst into colour and music – calypso, soca, ragga-soca, rapso and steelpan, which are all indigenous to these islands. Other art forms of no less significance that Trinidad and Tobago can claim to have invented are chutney soca and chutney *parang*: Hindi folksongs, sung at birth and wedding ceremonies, fused with *parang* (derived from Venezuelan Christmas carols) and soca (a modern party version of calypso which places emphasis on its fast catchy dance beat).

The testament to Trinbagonian talent and artistry is arguably best seen at Carnival when the culmination of a year's work by mas' men takes to the street; leading a band means visualising a concept and bringing it to life through colour and design, requiring months of research, and skills of drawing, wire-bending and copper beating. One of the finest talents is Peter Minshall, who designed the opening ceremonies for the 1992 Barcelona Olympic Games and the 1996 Atlanta Games. Another is Gerald Hart, who designed the winning national costumes at the 1998 and 1999 Miss Universe pageants.

LITERATURE

Before arriving on Trinidad and Tobago's shores, one can gain a clear picture of the culture and the daily lives of the islands' people by reading the work of authors such as Samuel Selvon, C.L.R. James and Michael Anthony. Trinidad and Tobago's literary tradition also includes other notable names like Nobel Laureate Sir V.S. Naipaul and his lesser known brother Shiva, the first prime minister, Dr Eric Williams, and Commonwealth prize-winning novelist Earl Lovelace.

THEATRE & DANCE

Dance and theatre are popular art forms, but performances are not regular. The small commercial theatre in Port of Spain, the Central Bank auditorium, deals in "Run for Your Wife" type farces.

The Trinidad Theatre Workshop (TTW) founded by St Lucian Nobel Laureate, Derek Walcott, is one of the few producers of serious drama, but output is low. Occasionally the TTW put on small concerts and recitals. The Centre for Creative and Festival Arts at the University of the West Indies (UWI) St Augustine campus, also stages theatre performances once or twice a year.

Comedy and calypso shows attract large crowds year-round, they are usually staged at the National Stadium in Port of Spain, or similar venues in Chaguanas, San Fernando or Tobago. Entertainment tends to concentrate on local issues; the comedy is raunchy and politicised, but visitors can still enjoy the experience. Popular comic entertainers include Tommy Joseph, Sprangalang and Nikki Crosby.

The calypso shows are also culturally specific, focussing on local concerns and current events showcasing the talents of well known calypso artists such as 3Canal, Singing Sandra, Pink Panther and the Original DeFosto.

There are also a number of Indo-oriented chutney and mas' (masquerade) shows, featuring singers and comedians such as Adesh Samaroo, Nirmal "Massive" Gosine, comedian Kenneth Seepersad and Bollywood singers.

Etiquette

The culture in Trinidad has traditionally been relaxed, but local people appreciate good manners, such as formal greetings, please, thank you and common courtesy.

The laid-back nature of the country is slowly being eroded, as crime and violence increase. Visitors should always ask permission before trying to take anyone's picture, and be polite, but firm with people whose attention is not welcome.

As a general rule in Trinidad and Tobago, time seems to be enlarged. If your Trini friends say they will pick you up at 8pm, they will probably arrive closer to 9pm. Don't worry about other appointments because the whole country is on the same schedule. If you really do need something to be done in a hurry, however, be polite but persistent.

Climate

The climate is tropical, meaning that it is warm all year round. The average temperature is 29°C (84° F), though there are blisteringly hot days of 36°C (97°F) and 24°C (75°F) during the night.

There are two seasons: the Wet, which runs from June to December, and the Dry, which runs from end of December/January to May. During the Wet season, rain is not monsoon-like, and ranges from little drizzles to heavy showers which generally do not last for more than an hour.

Government

Trinidad and Tobago became fully independent from Britain in 1962, and declared the Republic into being in 1976, when the president replaced the British monarch as head of state. The presidential role is largely ceremonial and symbolic. Executive power resides with the elected government, headed by the prime minister. Tobago's legislative body, the House of Assembly, sets domestic policy for that island.

The democratic system has functioned well in Trinidad and Tobago since Independence, with two hiccups. One was in 1970, when dissident army officers tried to break out of their camp at Chaguaramas with the intention of heading into Port of Spain to unseat the government. They eventually surrendered.

The more serious challenge to democracy came 20 years later, in 1990, when a militant Muslim group, the Jamaat-al-Muslimeen, stormed Parliament, holding the then prime minister, A.N.R. Robinson, and several of his ministers hostage for five days. The group was eventually persuaded by the army to give up. Several people died in the assault on Parliament and the fire-bombing of the nearby police headquarters, including one MP. The prime minister himself was injured, though not seriously.

In the October 2002 election, the PNM was returned to power. The government is led by the prime minister, Patrick Manning. The country's president and head of state is Maxwell Richards, former Principal of the Trinidad and Tobago campus of the University of the West Indies (UWI).

Economy

Trinidad and Tobago is the region's biggest producer of oil and gas, and has the most industrialised economy in the Caribbean. Manufacturing, heavy industry and the sugar business are well established in Trinidad, whereas Tobago, historically an agricultural economy growing cocoa, sugar and coffee, has become more dependent on tourism since the 1970s. A law allowing foreigners to buy land in Tobago has brought about a rise in the construction industry, using local labour to build new homes and hotels.

Diversification of the economy away from dependence on oil and gas has been given high priority by successive governments. For Trinidad, not yet established as a tourist location, tourism is expected to make a much greater contribution to growth and employment in the years ahead.

Trinidad and Tobago hosted the 1999 Miss Universe pageant, which was broadcast in more than 80 countries, therefore improving the country's international profile.

Trinidad promotes itself as a Carnival destination, and has links to annual festivals in several North American cities. The Carnival is an important part of the national heritage and its importance cannot be understated. Preserving the islands' musical and cultural identity is important, which was highlighted by Trinidad's response to American attempts to patent the steel drum in 2004. Old festivals were revived and new ones sprung up, including the world steelband festival, the world calypso competition, world mas' competitions and international carnival conferences.

While there is no permanent calendar of events, the yearly schedule is impressive. For more information about what's on and when, visit the tourism websites listed on *page 343.*

Business Hours

Opening hours vary from business to business and area to area, but as a general rule the following apply:
Government Offices: 8am–noon, 1–4.30pm Mon–Fri. Closed at weekends.
Banks: 8am–2pm Mon–Thur; 8am–noon, 3–5pm Fri.
Republic Bank on Long Circular Mall, St James, Trinidad, has extended opening hours until 6pm.
First Citizens' Bank at the Piarco Airport operates a Bureau de Change, open daily 6am–10pm.
Scotiabank: Ellerslie Plaza in Maraval, open 9.30am–5pm.
Businesses: 8am–4pm or 4.30pm (although some stay open until 5pm or 6pm) Mon–Fri.
Shops: open Sat 8am–2pm; a few, usually in the southern and central areas of Trinidad, open on Sunday 8am–11am or until noon.
Shopping malls usually stay open 8am–8pm Mon–Sat.
Supermarkets open Mon–Thur 8am–7pm, Fri and Sat 8am–8pm, and Sun 8am–11am or noon,

although there is one large supermarket, Extra Foods in City of Grand Bazaar, Valsayn, open from 2pm.

Public Holidays

Trinidad and Tobago has 13 official public holidays and two unofficial days for Carnival celebrations. Public holidays, when offices, banks and most shops close, are:

New Year's Day	January 1
Good Friday	variable
Easter Monday	variable
Spiritual Baptist	
Liberation Day	March 30
Indian Arrival Day	May 30
Corpus Christi	variable, but usually in June
Labor Day	June 19
Emancipation Day	August 1
Eid-ul-Fitr	as decreed
Independence Day	August 31
Republic Day	September 24
Diwali	as decreed
Christmas Day	December 25
Boxing Day	December 26

Whit Monday is no longer an official holiday; it was replaced on the holiday calendar by Arrival Day, later renamed Indian Arrival Day.
Carnival Monday and **Tuesday** (in February or March) have never been official holidays but are observed as such anyway. Even government offices, and all banks, are closed. Everybody is too busy participating in the festival to notice.

Planning the Trip

Visas and Passports

Visas are not required for visits of under three months by British and most European Union nationals, OAS (Organization of American States) passport holders and Commonwealth nationals. North Americans do not need visas for a visit shorter than two months, and Venezuelans can stay for up to two weeks without them. Citizens of Australia, New Zealand, India, Sri Lanka, Nigeria, South Africa, Uganda, Tanzania and Papua New Guinea are exceptions to the rule that Commonwealth countries' nationals do not need visas. Your travel agent should be able to obtain one on your behalf, otherwise contact your nearest Trinidad and Tobago embassy.

Passports are required by all visitors and should be valid for the entire period you intend to stay. You are required to supply the address where you will be staying in Trinidad or Tobago, proof that you can financially support yourself while in the country, and a return ticket.

EXTENDING YOUR STAY

A visa extension of anything from three months to one year costs approximately TT$100. The process of obtaining an extension can be rather time consuming, so be prepared. You will be asked to provide proof of income and the reasons for wanting an extension. For more information, or to apply for an extension, telephone or visit the Immigration Office at 67 Frederick Street, Port of Spain, Trinidad, tel: 625 3571.

BUSINESS VISITORS

Applications for work permits are available from the Ministry of National Security, 18 Knox Street, Port of Spain, tel: 623 2441. Business visitors can work without a permit for a period of one month in each calendar year.

Customs

What you can bring in: the duty-free allowance covers 200 cigarettes, or 50 cigars, or 450 grams (1 lb) of tobacco, one litre of wine or spirits, and gifts of up to TT$1,200.

What you can take home:

US: US Customs regulations allow each resident to take home purchases totalling US$400 without paying duty, provided that the resident has been out of the country for at least 48 hours and has not claimed the exemption within the past 30 days. Family members living in the same household can pool their exemptions. You may also mail home any number of gifts worth up to US$50 each, as long as any one person does not receive more than US$50 worth in one day. But these gifts may not include spirits, perfume or tobacco. For information about US allowances write off for the booklet *Know Before You Go* from the US Customs Service, Washington, DC 229.

Canada: Returning residents of Canada who have been out of the country for over 48 hours may bring back CA$100 worth of merchandise without paying duty. The goods must accompany the resident, and the exemption, claimed in writing, may be taken no more than once per quarter. Canadians who have been abroad for more than 7 days may also bring home duty-free goods worth up to CA$300 once each calendar year. These goods may be shipped separately, but must be declared when the traveller reaches Canada. Canadians are eligible to take both the CA$100 and CA$300 exemptions on separate trips, but the two cannot be combined. The duty-free totals may include up to 200 cigarettes;

50 cigars; 907 grams (2 lbs) of tobacco for residents over 16 years old; 1 litre (34 fluid ounces) of wine or spirits, or 24 cans of beer, if you meet the age regulations of the province where you arrive.

UK: The total exemption for residents returning to the United Kingdom from outside the EU may include 225 grams (9 fluid ounces) of toilet water, 50 grams (2 fluid ounces) of perfume and, for persons over 17 years old, 250 grams (½ lb) of tobacco, or 200 cigarettes, or 100 cigarillos, or 50 cigars. For visitors living outside Europe, double the tobacco limits. Duty-free alcohol allowances include 1 litre (34 fluid ounces) of spirits or 2 litres (68 fluid ounces) of sparkling wine, plus 2 litres (68 fluid ounces) of still table wine.

DUTY FREE AT PIARCO INTERNATIONAL AIRPORT

There are twelve duty-free shops at Piarco International Airport.

Stetcher's Limited – Perfumes, crystals, jewellery etc.

Ray Cool – Sunglasses.

Y. De Lima – Jewellery.

Frederick's Fine Leather – Leather bags etc.

The Craft Gallery – Souvenirs and handicrafts.

Karie's Island Wear – Souvenir T-shirts etc.

Rhyner's Records – All types of recorded music.

T Wee Liquor – All types of alcohol.

Fabi Cosmetique – All types of cosmetic.

Maraj and Sons Jewellers – All types of jewellery.

Noveltees Gift – Books and a variety of gift items.

NON-DUTY FREE

Departure Lounge

Pizza Boys – Restaurant.

Chocolate House – Chocolates.

Nature's Way – Art and craft.

Karie's Craft – Local craft souvenirs.

V's Ceramics – Paintings and ceramics.

Federal Spices – Local seasonings and spices.

Sunjet Inbond – Alcohol and perfumes.

Piarco Airport Florist – Floral arrangements.

Ishmael Khan and Sons Bookstore – Books and magazines.

Convenience Stores and Speciality Shops

Piarco News Stand – Newspapers and magazines.

T & T Handicraft – Handicraft items, dolls etc.

Bee Wee Gift Shop – Watches, clothing etc.

Hong Kong City – Chinese food.

Kentucky Fried Chicken (KFC) – fast food.

Pizza Burger Boys – Burgers, pizzas, doughnuts etc.

Willies – Ice cream.

Ali's Candy Shop – Sweets.

Dairy Bar – Ice cream, cakes, popcorn and soft drinks.

Lakhan Bazaar – Gift shop.

Piarco Airport Florist – Floral arrangements.

DUTY FREE AT CROWN POINT INTERNATIONAL AIRPORT

There are three duty-free shops at Crown Point International Airport.

Stetchers Limited – Perfumes and creams.

Karie's Craft – Souvenir items, steelpan etc.

Lagniapppe – Alcohol.

NON-DUTY FREE

The News Stand – Newspapers, magazines etc.

Christie's – Beachwear, T-shirts and souvenirs.

Native Instincts – All types of recorded music.

Karie's Craft – Local handicrafts.

Health

Vaccinations for smallpox and yellow fever are not required for entry into Trinidad and Tobago unless you have recently passed through an infected area.

Throughout the islands the water is safe to drink, though many locals do boil it before drinking. Both local and imported bottled water are available almost everywhere drinks are sold, from roadside vendors to mini-supermarkets and restaurants. **Dehydration** and heat rashes could be a problem when you first arrive, especially if visiting from a temperate climate – drink lots of fluid and dress in cool tops and T-shirts with shorts or comfortable skirts. Wear ample sunscreen, build tanning time slowly up from 15 minutes in the early morning and late afternoon, and bring a hat or buy one.

Street food is generally tasty and fresh for most of the year, though during Carnival it is probably best to avoid the seafood and meat specials sold from numerous shanties around Queen's Park Savannah. Often the food is cooked at the vendor's home in the morning, and stored without refrigeration all day.

Avoid casual sex (the rate of **HIV** infection is rising) and always use condoms, which are widely available. Steer clear of any procedures which pierce the skin, and remember that alcohol abuse can affect your judgement.

Especially if you visit in the wet season (June–December), but not only at this time, Trinidad and Tobago has mosquitoes and sand flies. Sand flies are harder to see than mosquitoes, and give a smaller, scratchier bite. You can protect yourself by using **citronella oil**, which is available at most pharmacies but which has a strong fruity scent you may not like if going out on the town. People with sensitive skin should avoid the oil, as reactions like skin burning and itching can occur; well-known brands of repellent are available from most pharmacies and some supermarkets, so you should be able to find OFF, Cutter's and other spray and roll-on insect repellents.

Dengue Fever

The *aedes aegypti* mosquito spreads dengue fever, marked by its flu-like symptoms, rash on the torso, severe muscle aches, nausea and vomiting. Dengue fever becomes fatal when it progresses into Dengue Haemorrhagic Fever, a condition usually affecting the very old, very young or very weak. If staying in a guesthouse or renting a beach house or private apartment, consider using aerial insect sprays, citronella candles and mosquito coils to avoid being bitten at all costs. If bitten, soothe bites with petroleum jelly or aloe vera gel.

Insurance

An initial visit with a private doctor or specialist may cost TT$100–300, and if you require any additional treatment expenses may escalate. Therefore a comprehensive travel Insurance policy should be a serious consideration: a package which covers serious illness and repatriation as well as the loss or theft of your possessions – especially money. The best policy would be one which also provides adequate cover for any planned activities such as snorkelling and mountain climbing.

Money Matters

CURRENCY

The Trinidad and Tobago Dollar (TT$) is made up of 100 cents. Notes are in denominations of TT$100, 10, 5 and 1, and coins in denominations of TT$1 and 50, 25, 10, 5 and 1 cents.

Currency Exchange

Foreign currency (mainly Can$, Euro, Sterling and US$) can be bought and sold at banks throughout the country, and at the Unit Trust Corporation in Port of Spain. ATMs at Piarco airport and at a few areas in Trinidad (like Royal Bank, St James) issue US dollars. Local machines accept cards with the Cirrus logo, and bank ATMs and merchants accept major credit cards.

Tax & Tipping

- **Departure/Airport Security tax:** TT$100.
- **Hotel:** 10 percent service charge; 10 percent room tax.
- **VAT** (Value Added Tax)**:** 15 percent on goods and services.

In general 10 percent is the standard tip unless a service charge is included in your bill.

Credit Cards

MasterCard and Visa are accepted by selected banks, shops and most tourist facilities. Many traders charge 5 percent for the use of credit cards. Check with your credit card company for details of merchant acceptability and other services which may be available.

Travellers' Cheques

Travellers' cheques are widely accepted and will often prove the most convenient means of transaction. Banks charge a fee for exchanging them; check for the best rates. To avoid additional exchange-rate charges, visitors are advised to take travellers' cheques in US Dollars or Pounds Sterling.

Currency Restrictions

The import of local currency is unlimited, provided that it is declared on arrival. The export of local currency is limited. There is free import of foreign currency, subject to declaration. The export of foreign currency is limited to the amount declared on entry.

Tourist Information

IN TRINIDAD

TIDCO (Tourism and Industrial Development Company)
10–14 Philipps Street
Port of Spain
Tel: 675 7034/5/6/7
Fax: 638 3560 (Tourism Division)
Email: tourism-info@tidco.co.tt
Mailing Address:
Tourism and Industrial Development Company (Trinidad and Tobago) Ltd

Level 1 Maritime Center
No 29 Tenth Avenue
Barataria
Trinidad, West Indies
Local Information Office:
Piarco Airport, Trinidad
Tel: 669 5196
International Freephone Information:
US: 1 888 595 4TNT
UK: 0800 960 057
Germany: 01 30 86 07 94
Italy: 1 678 77530
Canada: 888 535 5617
International Representatives
Morris Kevan International Ltd
Mitre House
66 Abbey Road, Bush Hill Park
Enfield, Middlesex
EN1 2RQ England
Tel: 020 8350 1009
Fax: 020 8350 1011
The RMR Group Inc.
Tauras House
512 Duplex Avenue,
Toronto M4R 2E3, Canada
Tel: 888 535 5617; 416 485 8724
Fax: 416 485 8256
Keating Communications
350 Fifth Avenue, New York NY
10118, USA
Tel: (212) 760 2400
Fax: (212) 760 6402
Cheryl Andrews Marketing Inc.
331 Almeria Avenue
Coral Gables, FL 33134, USA
Tel: (305) 444 4033
Fax: (305) 447 0415
For press enquiries.

IN TOBAGO

Department of Tourism
Tobago House of Assembly
NIB Mall, Carrington Street,
Scarborough
Tel: 639 2125/4636
Freephone only in US and Canada:
1 888 689 1884
Fax: 639 3566
At Crown Point Airport:
Tel: 639 3566
TIDCO Tobago
Unit 26, TIDCO Mall,
Sangster's Hill, Scarborough
Tel: 639 4333/4514
TIDCO Trade Division
Unit 24, TIDCO Mall
Sangster's Hill, Scarborough
Tel: 639 3668/3151
Tobago Bed and Breakfast Association
c/o Federal Villa
1–3 Crooks River
Scarborough
Tel: 639 3926
Fax: 639 3566
For bed and breakfast bookings in
private homes.

ON THE INTERNET

TIDCO:
www.entertainTNT.com
www.investTNT.com
www.tradeTNT.com
www.visitTNT.com
www.tidco.co.tt
Trinidad Hotels Restaurants and Tourism Association
c/o Trinidad and Tobago Hospital
Institute, Airways Road,
Chaguaramus, Tel: 868 634
1174/5, Fax: 868 634 1176;
email: info@tnthotels.com;
www.tnthotels.com

Getting There

BY AIR

Piarco airport in Trinidad is 5½
hours' flying time from New York,
3½ hours from Miami, 5 hours
from Toronto and 9½ hours from
London. Crown Point airport in
Tobago is just 12 minutes away
from Trinidad by air.

In Tobago, besides the
scheduled British Airways and
Virgin Atlantic flights from London
in the UK, several regular charter
flights from various countries bring
visitors directly to Crown Point.
Excel Air has charters from the UK,
TransMeridian from the US, and
SkyService Zoom from Canada.
These carriers change from time to
time. Intra-Caribbean routes are
handled by LIAT and BWEE.

The Trinidad to Tobago domestic
air route is operated by the locally-
owned airline Tobago Express,
which flies between Piarco airport in
Trinidad and Crown Point airport in
Tobago more than ten times a day.
BWEE (formerly BWIA) is Trinidad and
Tobago's national airline, which
services the main international
centres of New York, London, Miami
and Toronto several times a week.
Routes via other cities, such as
Manchester in the UK and Frankfurt
in Germany, are used periodically.

BWEE flies to Piarco airport from
London five times a week, from
New York daily, from Miami daily,
from Caracas daily, from Toronto
five times a week, and from Guyana
daily. Connections to Trinidad from
other Caribbean islands are also
possible through LIAT and BWEE.

The following companies provide
a regular service:
American Airlines
69 Independence Square
Port of Spain
Tel: 627 7013
Air Canada
Piarco Airport
Tel: 669 4065
BWEE
30 Edward Street
Port of Spain
Tel: 625 2470
LIAT
9–11 Edward Street
Port of Spain
Tel: 627 6274

Linea Aeropostal Venzolana
110–12 Frederick Street
Port of Spain
Tel: 623 6641
Surinam Airways
Cruise Ship Complex
Port of Spain
Tel: 627 4747

BY SEA

Trinidad and Tobago is developing its assets as a cruise destination. A dedicated cruise-ship berth and shopping area have been established at the Port of Spain port, and Scarborough harbour has been upgraded to be able to handle two cruise ships simultaneously. This, combined with a boom in the cruise industry, means more options for travellers and more cruise lines with one or both islands on their routes. Check with a specialist travel agent before booking.

The main problem with taking the sea route is the difficulty in extending your stay beyond the few hours the ship is docked. Most cruise-ship tickets are sold for complete voyages, and you will probably want to avoid the logistical manoeuvring involved in a change.

The ships from the following cruise lines stop at Trinidad and/or Tobago:
Cunard Cruise Lines, tel: 800-728 6273; www.cunardline.com
Fred Olsen Cruise Lines, tel: 01473 742424; www.fredolsen.co.uk
Holland America Line, tel: 206-281 3535; 877-724 5425; www.hollandamerica.com
Ocean Village, tel: 0845 358 5000; www.oceanvillageholidays.co.uk
Princess Cruises, tel: 800-421 0522; www.princess cruises.com
NB Toll free from the US only.

Practical Tips

TELEVISION AND RADIO

There are four local television channels: TV6, IETV, Gayelle, The Channel and Synergy TV. TV6, which is attached to the Caribbean Communications Network (CNN), is the only national station. The others are available only through the local cable company (Cable Company of Trinidad and Tobago), which covers just half the island.

Programming on the local stations varies from all local (Gayelle) to music videos (Synergy), and American sitcoms, talk shows, documentaries and entertainment shows on IETV and TV6.

Local shows are mainly talk and phone-in affairs, with live coverage of concerts and cultural events in the north of the island. The cultural events in the central and southern areas – which are strongly influenced by South Asian culture – receive less coverage.

The limited programming on the local television stations has made cable TV and DirecTV very popular in Trinidad and Tobago. DirecTV is available in larger hotels, and cable TV in some of the smaller ones. CableTV offers over 60 channels, including premium movie, sports and 24-hour news channels, Asian TV and educational channels such as Discovery and Discovery Kids.

There more than 21 FM and two AM radio stations, with more due to launch in the future. Some of the more popular include GEM radio 93FM, which broadcasts around the Caribbean; Love 94, a gospel station; Power 102, for political debates, some local music and social commentary; women's radio on 107.7FM; several Indian music stations on 106FM, 90.5FM and 103FM; mainly Christian religious format on 98.1 FM; and 96.1FM for rap, reggae dancehall, R&B, rapso and occasionally (but more common at Carnival time) soca.

In Tobago, Radio Tambrin on 92.1FM plays a diverse range of music including calypso and soca, and covers primarily Tobagonian news. Tambrin can also be picked up in the northeastern regions of Trinidad.

The phenomenon of talk radio sweeping through the Caribbean is a controversial aspect of the local radio landscape; several stations have been threatened with legal action because of racist content.

PRINT

The three daily newspapers published in Port of Spain and distributed throughout Trinidad and Tobago are the *Trinidad Express*, *Trinidad Guardian* and *Newsday*. There are several weekly and bi-weekly papers, some of which may be prone to lurid stories and bathing beauty photos – *Punch* and *Blast*. Others which feature lively investigations and political debates include the *TNT Mirror*, *Bomb* and *Heat*. The Trinidad and Tobago Roman Catholic Church publishes *The Catholic News*. *The Tobago News* is published weekly in Scarborough, and is entirely devoted to local events.

International news magazines such as *Time*, *Newsweek* and *The Economist* are easy to find and are available at supermarkets, bookstores and the airport. Foreign newspapers, however, are not readily available.

The Trinidad and Tobago Postal Corporation (TTPost) is managed by a postal company from New Zealand, which is improving the postal system and service.

Most of the old post offices have been given facelifts. In

some, Western Union money transfers and other services are available, including bill payment, internet access and stationery is on sale. Most post offices are open during business hours. The St James office on Tragerete Road, near the Roxy Roundabout, is open on Saturday morning until noon.

There is also an Express Mail Service, described as "cheaper (than Fedex or UPS) but a day later", and a countrywide courier service for the delivery of small packages throughout Trinidad and Tobago. Fedex, UPS and DHL Worldwide operate in both Trinidad and Tobago, offering 24-hour delivery services and other express services to destinations worldwide.

Telecommunications

Telecommunications Services of Trinidad and Tobago Television (TSTT) provides local and overseas telephone, fax, telegram and other services. Visitors can make calls or send faxes from the company's offices at 54 Frederick Street and 1 Edward Street in Port of Spain. International direct dialling is available throughout the country. Charges for operator-assisted overseas calls are based on a three-minute minimum. For person-to-person or transferred-charge calls there is a three-minute minimum plus a one-minute surcharge.

Dialling Codes

To the UK: dial 011, then 44 and the area code without the first zero, finally the number eg. 011 44 20.
To the US and Canada: dial 1 then the area code and number.
To Australia: dial 011, then 61, then the area code and number.

Airport Courtesy Phones

Courtesy phones are located at the Piarco and Crown Point international airports. This service provides travellers with immediate access to businesses within the tourism industry – hotels, car rental agencies etc. The user simply dials the relevant code (displayed) which routes the call to the desired party.

Operator Services

- **Local operator:** dial 0
- **Overseas operator:** dial 0
- **Directory enquiries:** dial 6411

Cellular Phone Services

The island's cellular phone network will support most GSM phones on the 1800 frequency. If the phone is SIM-locked, local technicians may be able to unlock it. Visit www.tstt.co.tt for cellular phone information.

Call Centres

International call centres exist throughout the island and offer the best rates for international calls to the US, UK and other places. The centres can be found in all major urban centres – Port of Spain, San Fernando, Arima and Chaguanas – a less expensive alternative to the regular phone company rates.

Phonecard Service

Sold in denominations of TT$20 and TT$60, TSTT phonecards allow users to make local phone calls from specially designated public pay phones. Local cards cannot be used for international calls (*see Companion Calling Cards below*). The telephone booths usually have bright signs that read "Phonecard". There are many more phonecard booths than coin ones so it makes sense to invest in a phonecard. They can be purchased from TSTT offices and everywhere the Phonecard sign is displayed.

TSTT Companion Calling Card

The TSTT's Companion Calling Card service allows customers to make international calls from any touch-tone telephone. Cards are sold at all TSTT offices and at authorised dealers where the TSTT Companion Calling Cards signs are displayed. The Calling Cards are available in denominations of TT$10, TT$30, TT$60 and TT$100.

No charges are made to the telephone number from which the call is made; the cost of the call is deducted from the TSTT Companion Calling Card.

Home Country Direct Service

TSTT's Home Country Direct Service allows visitors to Trinidad and Tobago to keep in touch with their businesses, friends and family using an international carrier of their choice such as MCI, AT&T, Teleglobe or British Telecom. All calls made using this service are charged by calling card, credit card or collect. Callers utilising this service can use special telephones at any of the following:
Piarco International Airport (luggage/arrival/departure areas).
Cruise Ship Complex, Port of Spain.
Peake Marine Marina, Chaguaramas.
Trinidad & Tobago Yachting Association, Chaguaramas.
Trinidad Hilton, Port of Spain.
Kapok Hotel, Cotton Hill, St Clair.
Moniques Guest House, Saddle Road, Maraval.

TSTT Customer Service Centres, Independence Square, Port of Spain; St James Street, San Fernando; Caroline Building, Scarborough.

Cybercafés

It is possible to find internet cafés in virtually every town and village. For those travelling with their laptops, public wireless access is not yet available everywhere in Trinidad. Only two places have wireless internet access: MovieTowne in Port of Spain (available to customers), and the University of the West Indies, St Augustine.

The local phone company Telecommunications Services of Trinidad and Tobago (TSTT) has a service that allows non-subscribers to access the internet by dialling: 619-EASY. Long-term visitors can open an account with a local provider such as Rave, CableNett, TSTT or Carib Link.

Diplomatic Representation

EMBASSIES

US: 15 Queen's Park West
Port of Spain
Tel: 622 6371–6
Venezuela: 16 Victoria Avenue
Port of Spain
Tel: 627 9821

CONSULATES

Barbados: Honorary Consul
12 Mayfair Gardens
Santa Cruz
Tel: 638 8431
Guyana: Park Plaza, Room 310A
64–70 St Vincent Street
Port of Spain
Tel: 627 1692
Surinam: Honorary Consul
Cruise Ship Complex
Port of Spain
Tel: 627 4747

HIGH COMMISSIONS

Canada: 3–3A Sweet Briar Road
St Clair
Tel: 622 6232
Jamaica: 2 Newbold Street
Port of Spain
Tel: 622 4995–7
United Kingdom: 19 St Clair Avenue
Port of Spain
Tel: 622 2748

Gay Travellers

Although there is a large gay and lesbian community in Trinidad and Tobago, it is illegal to have gay sex, and attitudes towards gays and lesbians can still be described as hostile. As an underground scene, gay clubs, bars and hang outs are not publicised, and you really need to be a part of the community to find out what is going on. For a traveller this of course can be difficult, but the internet has made it easier to make friends and find out where to go long before you reach the island. You can join a mailing list, the two most popular

being Trinicontact at Listbot.com and Caribbeangaymale at Egroups.com. There are also two websites that give some insight into what the gay/lesbian scene is like in Trinidad and Tobago:
gaytrinidad.cjb.net, where you can join both the lists mentioned, and:
www.geocities.com/gaytrinidad.

Medical Treatment

The public health system in Trinidad is unreliable and visitors should seek private medical attention if the need arises. There are private hospitals in the following centres: **St Clair Clinic**, Port of Spain, tel: 628 1452; **St Augustine Private Hospital**, Curepe, tel: 663 7274; **Gulf View Medical Centre**, South Trinidad, tel: 652 7102. In addition, there are many doctors with private practices. These can be found in the phone book or through referrals. If an ambulance is required, call **990** to access the public Emergency Health System.

HOSPITALS

Trinidad
The main public hospitals include:
Port of Spain General Hospital
56–57 Charlotte Street
Port of Spain
Tel: 623 2951–6; 625 3622;
623 7715
San Fernando General Hospital
Lady Hailes Avenue
San Fernando
Tel: 652 3580; PBX: 652 3581-6
Eric Williams Medical Sciences Complex (Mount Hope)
Uriah Butler Highway
Champs Fleur
Tel: 645 HOPE; 640 2640–9
Community Hospital of Seventh-Day Adventists
Western Main Road
Cocorite
Port of Spain
Tel: 622 1191–2; 628 8330–2

Tobago
Scarborough Regional Hospital
The Fort
Scarborough
Tel: 639 2551–4

Scarborough Medical Associates
Triangle Building
Scarborough
Tel: 639 1115

PHARMACIES

Late-night Opening
4am Drugs Limited
14 Southern Main Road, Curepe
Tel: 662 4858
Open 7am–10.30pm daily, including Sun and public holidays
Alchemists
57 Duke Street, Port of Spain
Tel: 623 2718
Open daily until 1am
Bhagan's
Broadway, Port of Spain
Tel: 627 5541
Open until 11pm Mon–Thur, midnight on Fri and Sat, and 10pm on Sun and public holidays.
Kappa Drugs Limited
Corner of La Seiva and Saddle Roads, Maraval
Tel: 628 0545
Open 7.30am–10.30pm Mon–Fri and 8am–10.30pm Sat, Sun and public holidays.
Valini's Drug Mart Limited
58 Sutton Street, San Fernando
Tel: 657 6444/1053
Open 7am–midnight every day

Security and Crime

The crime rate in Trinidad is growing at an alarming rate, which has resulted in negative travel advisories being issued by the US and UK governments. Visitors should observe common sense rules and take appropriate precautions to ensure safety during their stay.

For the moment Tobago remains relatively untouched by the rising crime on its sister island.

Leave your hotel key at the desk when you go out; stay off deserted streets, especially after dark; do not leave valuables unattended on the beach or in your room; avoid conspicuously displaying money. It makes sense to "break" hundred-dollar notes into small bills so that you do not have to pull out wads of money, and remember that what is flashy on the street will not be the same in a restaurant.

Avoid accepting lifts from strangers, do not tell everyone where you are staying and avoid taking strangers back to your hotel room. Do not go sightseeing at night, especially if you have to travel by taxi. Not knowing exactly where you are going can make you a target at night.

Port of Spain is a big city, and big-city precautions should be observed. Do not under any circumstances cross Queen's Park Savannah at night, except during Carnival (and then only if it is well lit and full of people), watch out for pickpockets, and always compare taxi and other prices before you commit yourself.

Certain areas of Port of Spain are safer than others. The Independence Square area has been reborn as the Brian Lara Promenade and is now drawing crowds back to the city centre after dark. Hanging out here can be, as the locals say, "a nice lime", but don't do it alone. Streets east of Henry Street should, generally speaking, be avoided. Policemen and security personnel are now more visible in the main urban centres of Port of Spain and San Fernando, and this should give comfort to locals and visitors alike.

Drugs are illegal in Trinidad and Tobago, and even a small amount in your possession (including marijuana) can get you into serious trouble, including deportation, heavy fines and even a long jail sentence.

Getting Around

Public Transport

BUSES

The Public Transport Service Corporation (PTSC) runs the national bus service. The system is not particularly comfortable or efficient so wherever possible, visitors should rent a car for touring, travel by route-taxi or, as a last resort, maxi-taxi. Always negotiate a fare before embarking on a taxi journey. If you must travel by bus be patient.

Buses go to all parts of both islands and are reasonably priced. Tickets, which must be purchased beforehand because drivers do not accept cash, are available at the main bus depots and from small shops around Trinidad and Tobago.

Buses assigned to the main trunk routes in Trinidad (from Port of Spain to San Fernando, Chaguanas, Arima, Sangre Grande and back) are air-conditioned, play music and only allow seated passengers. Board buses at the City Gate terminus on South Quay, Port of Spain. The non-air-conditioned buses, which go to rural areas, are yellow and red, and accommodate both seated and standing passengers. If using the **Rural Transport**, as it is called, be prepared for overcrowding and a sometimes uncomfortable ride.

In Tobago there is a bus stop directly across from the airport, and the main terminal is located in Scarborough – on Greenside Street behind the NIB Mall. **Blue transit** or **Super Express** buses are used, which are bigger than Trinidad's rural transport buses

but no less uncomfortable. On either island the public bus service cannot be described as reliable, and buses break down-causing sudden changes in the timetable and sometimes stranding passengers in odd and isolated locations.

MAXI-TAXIS

These colour-coded mini-buses follow particular routes on both islands. They can be boarded anywhere along the route by sticking out your hand. Once there is space they will stop. Passengers can also stop maxis anywhere along the route by pressing a bell, one of which is located above each window. Most maxis display the rates on the main door or in the centre of the windscreen.

In Trinidad

Yellow band maxis are for western areas. They leave from a terminus on the corner of South Quay and Wrightson Road going towards Diego Martin and Petit Valley; from the corner of Park and St Vincent Street (Green Corner) going to St James, Carenage, Westmoorings and some to Chaguaramas; and also from Oxford Street going to Maraval.

Red band maxis are for eastern areas – Morvant, Barataria, Curepe etc. They operate along the Eastern Main Road, the bus route or the highway and are boarded at the City Gate Terminus.

Green band maxis service Chaguanas and San Fernando. They are boarded at the City Gate Terminus.

Black band maxis operate from San Fernando to Princes Town, and from Princes Town to villages on its outskirts, located along the Naparima Mayaro Road, such as New Grant, Indian Walk, Tableland, Rio Claro and Mayaro. Maxis are boarded at the corner of Coffee and Prince of Wales Streets in San Fernando, and in Princes Town from the car park next to a fast food outlet called Chicken Delight.

Brown band maxis operate from San Fernando into southwestern areas such as La Romaine, Penal and Point Fortin. Board the buses in San Fernando at the bottom of High Street for Point Fortin and on Prince of Wales Street for La Romaine.

In Tobago

Blue band maxis – no fixed stand.

ROUTE TAXIS

Route taxi cars carry up to five passengers along set routes from fixed stands to various destinations. The vehicle registration plate always begins with the letter H. Sometimes drivers will digress slightly for visitors if the car is not full. Unless they render special services, drivers do not expect tips.

In Trinidad

Some of the main taxi stands in Port of Spain include:
Cascade: corner of Charlotte and Prince Streets. The cars circle Queen's Park Savannah.
Chaguanas: South Quay, opposite Chacon Street.
Curepe/Tunapuna/Arima/Sangre Grande: lower Henry Street, south of Independence Square.
Diego Martin/Petit Valley: Abercromby Street, south of Independence Square.
Maraval: corner of Duke and Charlotte Streets.
San Fernando: corner of Broadway and South Quay.

In Tobago

Scarborough: route taxi stands are located across from the bus terminal and central shopping plaza.

Private Transport

HIRE TAXIS

Like route taxis, hire taxis have an H on their licence plates, but they are essentially private taxis, carrying only you and your companions to where you want to go. Hire taxis do not have meters

and are rather expensive. In Tobago the fare from the airport to Speyside is approximately TT$240, to Scarborough TT$60. Usually rates are equivalent between drivers, but you can sometimes strike a bargain if you use the same driver for a number of trips or as a guide for a narrated tour of the island. Always agree on the fare in advance. Also note that fares in Tobago double after 9pm.

Hire taxis wait near most large hotels. Below are a few services:
Independence Square Taxi Service
Independence Square
Tel: 625 3032
Phone-a-taxi
Tel: 628 8294; 652 8294;
671 8294; 672 8294
Piarco Airport Taxi Co-op Society
Tel: 669 1689
St Anthony's Taxi Cab Co-operative
Tel: 648 3941
St Christopher's Taxi Co-op Society Ltd
Tel: 627 2257; 624 3560 (Hilton hotel head office); 625 4531 ext. 1541 (Holiday Inn)
Tobago Taxi Cab Co-op Society Ltd
Tel: 639 2707/2659 (Carrington Street); 639 2742 (Milford Road); 639 8252 (Store Bay)
Tobago Taxi Owners and Drivers Association
Tel: 639 2692 (Scarborough)

RENTAL CARS

Car rental in Trinidad and Tobago is handled by numerous local fleets. Many accept credit cards for both rental fees and the substantial deposit (up to TT$1,000) that is required. Day rates for non-air-conditioned cars with manual transmission begin at about TT$150, weekly rates at about TT$1,000 (see On Arrival page 348).

BICYCLES

Mountain bikes are popular in Tobago, but mopeds are more advisable for the inexperienced rider. There are a number of places in the Lowlands (southeast) where

visitors can hire bicycles. You must be certified to ride a motorcycle or scooter on your driver's licence in order to hire one. Try:
Cherry Scooter Rental
Sandy Point Beach Club
Crown Point

Driving Regulations

Visitors with valid driving permits issued in any of the countries listed below may drive in Trinidad and Tobago for a period of up to three months. They are, however, entitled to drive only motor vehicles of the class specified on their permits or licences. Drivers must at all times have in their possession:
1. Their International Driving Permit or equivalent.
2. Any travel document on which is certified their date of arrival in Trinidad and Tobago.

Visitors whose stay exceeds the usual three-month period are requested to apply to the Licensing Department (Wrightson Road, Port of Spain, tel: 625 1031) for local driving permits. This applies to all signatories to the Convention on International Drivers' Permits including the US, Canada, France, the UK, Germany and the Bahamas. Excluded are China, South Africa and Vietnam, whose nationals require passports, International Driving Permits and national licences.

In Trinidad and Tobago it is important for visitors to remember that vehicles drive on the **left**. Trinbagonians are not known as the world's best drivers, and cars often stop without warning, and go through red lights, while pedestrians cross without caution. Wearing seatbelts in the front seats is compulsory.

On Arrival

TRINIDAD

Piarco Airport is about 19 km (12 miles) from Port of Spain. You can take a taxi into town; go by bus, which may involve carrying your own bags some distance; or arrange to pick up a rental car, which will probably take a bit of organising. If you are travelling alone at the weekend, when the business districts of Port of Spain are fairly deserted, it is advisable to take a taxi.

Piarco International Airport is serviced by the Airport Taxi Drivers' Co-operative. You can arrange a pick-up with the taxi dispatcher at the Customs exit. Check the fare; it will probably be about TT$115. Beware of the drivers who rush up to offer their services; some are not above grossly overcharging. Driving time from the airport to Queen's Park Savannah is about 30 minutes with minimal traffic; during rush hour it can take over an hour.

Taking a bus from the airport to Port of Spain is the cheaper option; it costs TT$4.00. Unfortunately the service is not very frequent: two departures in the morning, at 7.15 and 7.45–7.50; two departures in the afternoon, at 3.45 and 5. The bus will take you to City Gate, where you can take another bus if staying outside the capital and in an area serviced by buses or a maxi-taxi. City Gate is in the heart of Port of Spain, and most stands are accessible from this point.

Car Rentals

There are seven car-rental agencies at Piarco International Airport:
Auto Rentals Ltd, tel: 669 2277
Singh's Auto Rental, tel: 669 5417
Southern Sales, tel: 669 2424
Sue's Auto Rentals, tel: 669 1635
Kalloo's Car Rentals, tel: 669 5673
Econo Car Rentals, tel: 669 2342
Thrifty's, tel: 669 0602

TOBAGO

Check with your hotel, which may have its own airport transfer service. It should also be able to say how long the drive is from the airport. Several of the hotels near Store Bay and Crown Point are in easy walking distance if you travel light; others are a long and costly taxi ride away. Consult the dispatcher, check the table of rates and agree on the fare with the driver before setting out. Most taxi drivers are also well-informed guides.

Car Rentals

Several car-rental agencies operate out of Crown Point Airport:
Auto Rentals Ltd, tel: 639 0644
Baird's Rentals Ltd, tel: 639 7054
Econo Car Rentals, tel: 660 8728
Thrifty/Rodriguez Car Rental Ltd, tel: 639 8507/8062

Bus Service

There is an hourly bus service to and from Crown Point International Airport. The fare for this service is TT$2.00 one way.

Travel between Trinidad and Tobago

BY AIR

Every day there are flights every two hours run by BWIA and Tobago Express from Piarco (Port of Spain) to Crown Point (Tobago). During peak seasons (especially Carnival time) flights are heavily booked.

BY SEA

There is a fast ferry service from Trinidad to Tobago on a modern catamaran (2 hours), or a conventional ferry (5 hours). Each vessel makes one return trip per day, usually departing daily from Port of Spain in the afternoon and Scarborough in the late evening, or vice versa. Check the schedules for weekend sailing times.

Tickets are on sale at the Port of Spain and Scarborough offices of the Port Authority, and at branches of the Royal Bank in Arima, Chaguanas, San Fernando and Point Fortin. The office in Port of Spain is open Mon–Fri 7.30am–4pm.

Passenger ticket sales are closed two hours before departure time; vehicles must be on board two hours before sailing. Tickets are valid for 90 days from the date of purchase. Prices may be subject to change; check the rates table

For further information telephone the Port Authority:
Port of Spain, tel: 623 2901–2 ext. 160/1
Tobago, tel: 639 2417

Where to Stay

Accommodation

Traditionally Trinidad has not had many hotel rooms, but with the island's increasing economic prosperity the number is growing. The country is acquiring a reputation as a centre of commerce, with a large influx of a expatriates who staff multinational companies based here.

Business travellers favour the Hilton, Normandie, Crowne Plaza, Cascadia and Kapok hotels, and also the Courtyard Marriott, Ambassador, the Chancellor.

Carnival time is the most popular and expensive time to visit, with some rooms at least doubling in price. A minimum stay is usually imposed by most hotels and guesthouses during the festivities, and some also offer special packages, so if you plan to visit for Carnival book well in advance. It is also useful to note that rooms in Trinidad and Tobago are subject to a 10 percent room tax and 15 percent VAT, so when booking check the price of a room including all local taxes.

Hotels

TRINIDAD

The Ambassador Hotel
99a Long Circular Road
St James
Port of Spain
Tel: 628 9000
Fax: 628 7411
www.ambassadortt.com
Large hotel and conference centre located 10 minutes from downtown Port of Spain and near to the sport stadium, Oval Cricket ground and several shopping malls. Rooms are simple but comfortable with internet access. **$$$**

Cascadia Hotel
Ariapita Rd
St Ann's
Tel: 623 4208
www.cascadiahotel.com
Located on 10 hectares (25 acres) of hillside surroundings in the St Ann's Valley, the hotel is only 8 minutes away from Port of Spain, and 3 minutes from the historic Queen's Park Savannah. Facilities include access to an outdoor pool, waterslide and sun-deck, and a meeting and banquet room. Sporting and recreational facilities include a gym and squash and tennis courts. The lounge has nightly entertainment and one of the most popular nightclubs in Trinidad, **Club Coconuts**. Free newspapers are delivered to each room daily. **$$$**

The Chancellor
5 St Ann's Avenue
St Ann's
Tel: 623 0883
Fax: 623 0883
www.the chancellorhotel.com
Large hotel in a residential neighbourhood, just 5 minutes from the centre of Port of Spain. Rooms are comfortable with tropical decor, tiled floors and internet access. Swimming pool and conference facilities available. Bistro and bar on the property. **$$$**

Courtyard Port of Spain
Invaders Bay
Audrey Jeffers Highway
Port of Spain
Tel: 627 5555
Fax: 627 6317
www.marriott.com
Large, comfortable hotel spread over four floors, with parking, wheelchair access, a casual restaurant on site and in-room internet facilities. The A La Bastille restaurant is nearby. **$$$**

Crowne Plaza
Wrightson Rd
Port of Spain
Tel: 625 3366
Fax: 625 4166
Email: eoffice@crowneplaza.co.tt
www.crowneplaza.com
Crowne Plaza is a large business hotel in the heart of Port of Spain, opposite the Cruise Ship Complex

and within walking distance of the Parliament buildings, Hall of Justice, museums, libraries, cathedrals and one of the main shopping areas. With 245 rooms, a Presidential Suite and 12 one-bedroom suites, all air-conditioned, with private bath and balcony, radio and satellite TV. There is also a pool, a gym, a paddle tennis area, shuffleboard, a children's pool, conference facilities and a business centre. **$$$**

Hilton Trinidad and Conference Centre
Lady Young Road
Port of Spain
Tel: 624 3211
Fax: 624 4485
Email: hiltonpos@wow.net
www.hiltontrinidad.com
Claims to be the world's only upside-down hotel. The public areas and pool deck are on top while the 380 rooms are on lower levels. The Hilton has restaurants, bars, tennis courts, badminton, a gym, a conference centre, a ballroom, an executive suite and frequent entertainment. **$$$**

The Kapok Hotel
16–18 Cotton Hill
St Clair
Tel: 622 5765
Fax: 622 9677
Email: stay@kapok.co.tt
www.kapokhotel.com
Geared more towards the business traveller, the Kapok Hotel has 94 rooms with satellite TV, air conditioning, telephone with voice mail and data port, bath/shower and a hairdryer. Some rooms have private balconies. There are nine studios and six suites with kitchenettes, designed for extended stays. There are also conference facilities and a well-equipped guest computer

room allowing access to the internet. A doctor on-call service is available. On-site are the **Tiki Village** (Oriental and Polynesian) restaurant and the **Bois Cano** wine and coffee bar. **$$$**

The Normandie Hotel and Restaurant
10 Nook Avenue
St Ann's
Tel: 624 1181
Fax: 624 0108
Email: normandie@wow.net
www.normandiett.com
Originally established as a small guest house, the Normandie has been extended to provide 53 rooms, 12 studio-style lofts, standard and superior rooms and a swimming pool. Locals know it as a place to go to purchase local craft and fashion. Its restaurants **La Fantasie** and **Café Trinidad** and **The Cascade Club** are very popular. **$$$**

The Royal Palm Suite Hotel
7A Saddle Road
Maraval
Tel/Fax: 628 6042; 628 5086–9
Email: royalpalm@trinidad.net
www.royalpalm.co.tt
Located in Maraval, among the Maraval Hills, and is 15 minutes from central Port of Spain. It is within walking distance of three shopping malls, four banks, fast food outlets and a supermarket, and Trinidad's most popular beach, Maracas Bay, is only minutes away. There are also tennis courts, golf and horse-riding facilities nearby. All rooms and suites have cable TV, direct dialling, private baths and kitchenettes. **$$$**

Hosanna Hotel
2 Santa Margarita Circular
St Augustine
Tel: 662 5449
Fax: 662 5451
www.hosannahotel.com
The owners describe this as the Christian Hotel of the Caribbean. The Hosanna is a small family-operated hotel for single travellers or married couples only. All couples are required to provide proof of marriage to register as guests. Located just 15 minutes from both the airport and Port of Spain, the

Price Guide

The price categories are for the cost of a double room; check whether breakfast is included:
$ up to US$70
$$ US$70–100
$$$ over US$100

Hosanna Hotel is in an easily accessible location. The premises are tobacco and alcohol free, and all rooms and suites are air-conditioned. There is cable TV, an outdoor gazebo and a whirlpool. **$$**

Maracas Bay Hotel
Maracas Bay
Tel: 669 1914
Fax: 669 1643
Email: maracasbay@tstt.net.tt
www.maracasbay.com
A modest, locally-owned, beachfront hotel located less than an hour's drive from the busy centre of Port of Spain. The rooms are basic, but comfortable and all have air-conditioning; some have satellite TV for an additional charge. **$$–$$$**

The Piarco International Hotel
Piarco
Tel: 669 3030
A 35-room hotel complete with 24-hour service, three bars, two restaurants, a swimming pool and a conference room, only five minutes from the airport and ideal for in-transit passengers. The hotel offers a complimentary shuttle service to and from the airport. A choice of smoking and non-smoking rooms is available. **$$**

Paria Suites
Tel: 697 1442
www.pariasuites.com
Overlooking the Gulf of Paria, this is one of San Fernando's few exclusive hotels. The rooms are all fully air-conditioned, and on-site are a restaurant lounge, conference facilities, a swimming pool and a mini zoo. Locals often "hang out" here for the entertainment. **$$**

Pelican Inn
2–4 Coblentz Avenue
Port of Spain
Tel: 627 6271
Fax: 623 0978
The Pelican Inn offers 14 affordable air-conditioned rooms, a restaurant serving international cuisine, squash courts and a popular pub. **$**

Eco-Spots

Asa Wright Nature Centre and Lodge
Arima
Tel: 667 4655
Fax: 667 0493
Email: asawright@caligo.com
www.asawright.org
In the US call:
Toll Free: 800-426 7781
Tel: (914) 273 6333
Fax: (914) 273 6370
Described as a "Birdwatcher's Paradise", the Centre and lodge are located on a 81-hectare (200-acre) conservation estate, established to provide a protected area to preserve and study tropical wildlife in north Trinidad. Fourteen species of hummingbird have been recorded at the Centre, and it has the world's most accessible colony of oilbirds. Field trips are organised to other birding locations, including the Caroni and Nariva swamps.

With 24 twin-bedded rooms, private balconies and bathrooms. All rooms have disabled access. Airport transfers can be requested for a fee. **$$$**

The Mount Plaisir Estate
Tel: 670 8381
Fax: 670 0057
Email: info@mtplaisir.com
www.mtplaisir.com
Situated on the northeast coast of Trinidad, on the beach in the village of Grande Rivière 88 km (55 miles) from Piarco Airport and 116 km (72 miles) from Port of Spain, the Estate has remoteness as its most obvious attraction. Ten suites face the Caribbean, with landscaped gardens and the rainforest to the rear. Each suite can accommodate from four to six persons, and guests are encouraged to arrange the furniture "to suit their taste and comfort". The room furnishings, which are entirely the work of local craftsmen and artisans, are also available for sale. Guests can canoe along the Grande Rivière river, find a quiet beach, or hike deep into the rainforest. **$$–$$$**

Reservations

Reservations will make your travels run smoother. Many hotels now have websites that facilitate on-line booking and provide information about their services. You can even see what your preferred hotel looks like before you book.

Despite this you will probably have no problem finding a room in Port of Spain and in Tobago without advance reservations, though you may not get your first choice.

However, during the Carnival season (Feb) it is absolutely essential to reserve a room, especially if you want to stay close to Queen's Park Savannah.

Pax Guesthouse
Mount St Benedict
Tunapuna
Tel: 662 4082
Fax: 645 4232
Email: stay@paxguesthouse.com
www.paxguesthouse.com
Twenty minutes from Piarco Airport and 25 minutes from Port of Spain, Pax is located on the 243-hectare (600-acre) **Mount St Benedict Monastery Estate**, which comes complete with its own rainforest, nature trails and birdwatching spots. It is home to over 140 species of bird, 17 species of mammal and 13 species of reptile. Established in 1916, this is the oldest guesthouse in the country.

Its 18 rooms are furnished with European antiques and furniture handcrafted by the monks. There is a popular **tea garden** where an assortment of teas, pastries and cakes are served; restaurant specialises in Caribbean dishes. Just 5 minutes from the University of the West Indies campus, Pax offers basic laboratory facilities to visiting researchers.

Airport transfers arranged for a fee. Main dishes in the restaurant include fresh seafood, but there are also vegetarian dishes. **$$–$$$**

Salybia Nature Resort & Spa
13¾ Mile Post
Toco Main Road, Salybia Village
Tel: 668 5959
Fax: 691 3210
www.salybiaresort.com.
A nature resort located in the unspoiled north east of Trinidad. It has 18 suites, a penthouse and a seven-room villa. Pool with swim up bar and spa facilities. Hiking and kayaking trips can be arranged. **$$$**

Guesthouses

TRINIDAD

Alicia's Guesthouse
7 Coblentz Gardens
Port of Spain
Tel: 623 2802
Fax: 623 8560
Email: aliciashouse@tstt.net.tt
www.aliciashousetrinidad.com
An ideal location during Carnival since it is within walking distance of Queen's Park Savannah. A converted two-storey home, it has two large rooms near the front door, one where guests can watch TV, read the paper or just lounge around, and the other where meals (ordered the previous day) are served family style.

Rooms are very basic, each with a ceiling fan, bath and bidet, a/c, a telephone and a refrigerator. There is also a pool, a whirlpool and a patio area. **$$**

Carnetta's House & Inn
99 Saddle Road, Maraval
Tel: 622 5165
Fax: 628 7177
Email: carnetta@trinidad.net
www.carnettasinn.com
All guestrooms are air-conditioned, with private toilets and showers and direct-dial telephones. Rooms with kitchenettes available on request. Includes **The Bamboo Terrace** restaurant, with full bar. **$$**

Monique's Guesthouse
114–116 Saddle Road
Maraval
Tel: 628 3334/2351/5511
Fax: 622 3232
Email: info@moniquestrinidad.com
www.moniquestrinidad.com
Comprises air-conditioned rooms

with private baths and telephones. One room has been designed to accommodate disabled guests. Also on the property is **Monique's on the Hill**, which has 10 rooms with balconies, kitchenettes and cable TV. From single to quad occupancy. **$$**

Hotels

TOBAGO

Arnos Vale Hotel
Scarborough
Tel: 639 2881
Fax: 639 3251
www.arnosvalehotel.com
Located on a 182-hectare (450-acre) plantation with rooms, suites and cottages. All guest quarters have private baths and are air-conditioned. Cottages are set in the gardens with a view of the sea; some rooms are close to the beach; there is a pool with a swim-up bar called the **Pirate Blenny** and the **MahiMahi** beach restaurant. Princess Margaret honeymooned here, staying in the "Crow's Nest" cottage. There is occasional entertainment, but the hotel is home to a number of birds and so has a quiet atmosphere. However, there is local entertainment such as steel bands, calypso or folk ballads during the Carnival and Tobago Heritage Festival season. There are also tennis courts and table tennis. **$$$**

Blue Haven Hotel
Bacolet Bay
Scarborough
Tel: 660 7500
Fax: 660 7900
Toll Free (from the US): 800-237 3237
Email: info@bluehavenhotel.com
www.bluehavenhotel.com
In business since the 1940s, the restored luxury hotel has 55 superior and deluxe rooms and 10 suites on 6 hectares (15 acres) along the southern shore of Tobago. All rooms have private balconies, views of the ocean, air conditioning, ceiling fans, cable TV, telephones and safes. Connecting rooms and suites are available for families. Facilities include a restaurant in a colonial-style villa, a beach bar, a

pool overlooking the ocean, a fitness centre, a floodlit tennis court and a childrens' playground. The 15-minute ride from the airport can be done in style using the hotel's limousine service. **$$$**

Blue Waters Inn
Batteaux Bay
Speyside
Tel: 660 2583
Fax: 660 5195
Email: bwi@bluewatersinn.com
www.bluewatersinn.com
A 38-room beachfront low-rise hotel about 1¼-hour taxi ride away from the airport in a quiet part of Tobago, far from the island's main tourist areas. It is situated on its own secluded bay amongst 19 hectares (46 acres) of lush tropical land.

The Blue Waters Inn is a good place to learn scuba-diving, and was the first resort to obtain status as a full service PADI International Gold Palm (5-Star) Resort and Training Facility. Other activities include kayaking and windsurfing, hiking and birdwatching; also there are floodlit tennis and basketball courts. **$$$**

Coco Reef Resort
Coconut Bay
Scarborough
Tel: 639 8571
Fax: 639 8574
Email: cocoreef-tobago@trinidad.net
www.cocoreef.com
Almost all rooms have ocean views. Amenities include direct-dial telephones, refrigerators, air conditioning, bathrooms, wall

Wildlife at Blue Waters

The Blue Waters Inn is geared towards nature lovers and scuba-divers. It is opposite Little Tobago (Bird of Paradise Island), the island's largest bird sanctuary. The hotel can organise trips to the sanctuary, offering guests the opportunity en route to view the rich birdlife and also to get close to giant manta, nurse sharks, moray eels and many other creatures.

Price Guide

The price categories are for the cost of a double room; check whether breakfast is included:
$ up to US$70
$$ US$70–100
$$$ over US$100

mounted hairdryers, satellite TV and a twice-daily maid service.

Coco Reef offers guests the choice of two restaurants, **Tamara's** and **Bacchanals**, and two bars: **The Gallery** and **Bobsters**. **$$$**

Grafton Beach Resort
Stonehaven Bay
Black Rock
Tel: 639 0191
Fax: 639 0030
Email: sales@grafton-resort.com
www.grafton-resort.com
There is a choice of rooms in low-rise blocks, including two deluxe suites with private jacuzzis. Rooms are air-conditioned with ceiling fans, mini refrigerators, bathrooms, satellite TV and 24-hour room service. All-inclusive option includes an ocean-view room, all meals, drinks (excluding wines by bottle and champagne), non-motorised water sports – kayaks, step jets, snorkelling and one introductory scuba session in the pool – use of air-conditioned and floodlit squash courts, all entertainment. Conference facilities. **$$$**

Kariwak Village Hotel
Store Bay Local Road
Crown Point, Scarborough
Tel: 639 8442
Fax: 639 8441
Email:kariwak@tstt.net.tt
www.kariwak.co.tt
The Kariwak Village Hotel and Holistic Haven has 18 poolside and six garden rooms set in lush tropical gardens. Excellent Caribbean cuisine, and holistic activities including yoga, Qi Gong and massage. **$$$**

Le Grand Courlan Spa Resort
Black Rock
Tel: 639 9667
Fax: 639 9292
Email: legrand@trinidad.net
www.legrandcourlan-resort.com
Rooms at the resort include satellite TV, two telephones, air conditioning and ceiling fans, mini bars, and the choice (depending on the type of room) of an indoor or outdoor jacuzzi. Valet and room service add to the resort's complement of services, which also include a spa and health club with sauna, steam room and whirlpool. **$$$**

Hilton Tobago
Lowlands
Scarborough
Tel: 660 8500
Fax: 660 8503
Email: tobhilt@tstt.net.tt
www.hilton.com
Located on the 300-hectare (750-acre) Tobago Plantations development, the large 200-room hotel exudes tropical luxury and style with its neo-Creole architecture and private balconies. Facilities include an 18-hole golf course, fitness centre with sauna, beach front pool and a PADI dive centre. **$$$**

Manta Lodge
Speyside
Tel: 660 5268
Fax: 660 5030
Toll free: 800-544 7631 (US only)
Email: info@mantalodge.com
www.mantalodge.com
The Speyside lodge was designed with the scuba-diver, birdwatcher, nature enthusiast and families in mind. Twenty-two air-conditioned rooms with choice of ceiling fans, en-suite facilities, daily maid service and private verandahs with views of the Atlantic Ocean; a freshwater swimming pool, sandy beach with sun beds and sun umbrellas, restaurant and bar, local water taxi, nature trails, scuba-diving and PADI training, and snorkelling. **$$$**

Plantation Beach Villas
Stonehaven Bay
Black Rock
(mail to: PO Box 435, Scarborough)
Tel: 639 9377
Fax: 639 0455
Email: plantationbeach@tstt.net.tt
www.plantationbeachvillas.com
Spacious, two-storeyed three-bedroomed houses with large open verandahs. The master bedrooms, on the ground floor, have four-poster twin beds and en-suite bathrooms, with air conditioning and ceiling fans. The other two air-conditioned bedrooms, all with queen-size four-poster beds and en-suite bathrooms, open onto balconies. Rollaway beds, cots, and high chairs are available on request. Each villa has a fully-equipped kitchen with table settings for eight. All electrical equipment runs on 115V/60 cycles. Daily maid service, although the laundry room has a sink, and an automatic washer and dryer. Baby-sitting service available.

In-villa catering service offering Caribbean cuisine prepared by local cooks for some or all midday and evening meals. **$$$**

Tropikist Beach Hotel
Crown Point
Tel: 639 8512–3
Fax: 639 9605
Email: tropikist@wow.net
www.tropikist.com
Upgraded hotel located only five minutes from the airport and minutes from two of the most popular beaches – **Store Bay** and **Pigeon Point**. There are 10 deluxe rooms and one mini suite. All rooms are air-conditioned, with small refrigerators, telephones, radios and cable TV. There is a pool with poolside bar. **$$$**

Wood and Water

Manta Lodge is located between the Atlantic Ocean and the montane rainforest in the village of Speyside, where directly offshore are some of the Caribbean's finest coral reefs, the **Tobago Dive Experience** (tel: 660 4888) operates daily dive charters to the lush reefs from the Lodge.

Birdwatchers and hikers staying at the Lodge can explore the flora and fauna around the estate by themselves, or they can arrange a guided bird-watching and nature tour of the nearby montane rainforest, which is the western hemisphere's oldest rainforest preserve.

Price Guide

The price categories are for the cost of a double room; check whether breakfast is included:
$ up to US$70
$$ US$70–100
$$$ over US$100

Crown Point Beach Hotel
Crown Point
Tel: 639 8781–3
Fax: 639 8731
Email:CrownPoint@SunSurfSand.com
www.CrownPointBeachHotel.com
One of the most attractive hotels in the affordable price bracket, with a view of the ocean and spacious grounds, often used for weddings. All rooms and villas have air conditioning, kitchenettes, cable TV, telephones and patio areas. Airport transfers can be arranged at no extra cost. The hotel has an award-winning restaurant, **The Best of Thymes**, and is also a great place to stay during popular Tobago events such as the annual Du Maurier Great Race held at the end of July, and Sailing Week, when the sailing village is set up in the hotel grounds. **$$**

Arthur's by the Sea
Crown Point
Tel: 639 0196
Fax: 639 4122
Email: arthurs@trinidad.net
www.trinidad.net/arthurs
Or for reservations in the US:
International Travel and Resort
4 Park Avenue
New York NY 10016
Fax: (212) 251 1767
Arthur's is close to Store Bay and the Pigeon Point resort and only a 15-minute drive from Scarborough. Rooms have private patio, shower, air conditioning and TV. There is an open-air dining room, a swimming pool, and a gift shop in the lobby. Children under 5 years old sharing a room stay free of charge. **$**

Belleviste Apartments
Sandy Point
Scarborough
Tel/Fax: 639 9351
Email: bellevis@tstt.net.tt
www.trinidad.net/belleviste
Twenty self-contained apartments

with air conditioning, cable TV, kitchenettes and private balconies. **$**

Hotel Coconut Inn
Store Bay Local Road
Bon Accord
Tel: 639 8493
Fax: 639 0512
Email: annholten@tstt.net.tt
A small hotel set in a 1-hectare (3-acre) tropical garden with a pool and its own private lounging area. Only a 5-minute drive from the airport, the Inn provides free airport transfers for all guests. There are 16 self-contained apartments in a two-storey building. Each apartment is air-conditioned, with a kitchen, bedroom, bathroom and a private terrace or balcony overlooking the swimming pool. Adjoining the apartments are 16 air-conditioned rooms with bathrooms and private balconies or terraces. **The Coconut Inn Guesthouse** is more economical than the hotel. It comprises six large private bedrooms with fans and handbasins. The kitchen, lounge area with cable TV, showers and toilets are shared. Also includes the **Copratray** bar and restaurant. **$**

Ocean Point Apartment Hotel
Milford Road
Hampden, Lowlands
Tel: 639 0973
Fax: 660 8892
Email: info@oceanpoint.com
www.oceanpoint.com
Near the Tobago Hilton, this recommended small family-owned and operated apartment hotel has self-contained apartments with kitchenettes, air conditioning and private patio areas. Studio apartments can accommodate three people, and the upper-floor suites sleep five. **$**

Sandy Point Village/Sandy Point Beach Club
Crown Point
Tel: 639 8533
Fax: 639 8534
Reasonably priced for all the facilities and services offered. Guests have access to complimentary daily shuttles to and from Pigeon Point Beach, daily newspapers and entry to the club's disco, **The Deep**. All apartments are

air-conditioned with kitchenettes. **The Steak and Lobster Grill** offers US-style steak, local fish steaks and lobster meals for as little as US$15. Every Wednesday there is a "complete curry Indian dinner" with your choice of curried shrimp, chicken or beef for the same price. The manager also hosts a rum punch party on Wednesday. Comfortable and friendly, the Club also has a swimming pool, mini gym, small conference room, satellite TV and access to car hire on-site. Close to the airport and airplane flight path. **$**

Eco-Spots

Cuffie River Nature Retreat
PO Box 461
Scarborough
Tel: 660 0505
Fax: 660 0606
Email: cuffiriv@tstt.net.tt
www.cuffie-river.com
Situated on the edge of Tobago's rainforest and surrounded by wild heliconias, bamboo groves and forest. At its back is a chain of mountains with streams and pools.

This family-run retreat has ten rooms, home-cooked meals, pure spring water, bird-watching, and waterfall baths. Also transport to and from Crown Point Airport and the Scarborough Deep Water Harbour, guided nature walks, beach outings and excursions. Can cater for special dietary needs. Wedding and honeymoon packages available. **$$–$$$**

Footprints Eco Resort
Culloden Bay Road, via Golden Lane
Tel: 660 0118
Toll free (in US only): 800-814 1396
Email: info@footprintseco-resort.com
www.footprintseco-resort.com
Constructed with locally grown woods or others which are native to the region. The roofs of the building are made from the leaves of the timit palm, the material used by the indigenous Amerindians to thatch their *ajoupas* (huts). With ocean-front rooms and suites. **The Cocoa House** restaurant has a retractable thatched roof, and **R&C Divers' Den** provides underwater excitement, including snorkelling. **$$–$$$**

Bird Spotting

Spot a wide variety of birds around the cottages at Man-O-War Bay: blue tanagers, big-eyed thrushes, blue herons, flycatchers, yellowtails, bananaquits and hummingbirds can be seen hopping from tree to tree.

Man-O-War Bay Cottages
Man-O-War Bay
Charlotteville Estate
Tel: 660 4327
Fax: 660 4328
www.man-o-warbaycottages.com
The Cottages are on 2 hectares (5 acres) of beachfront, part of Charlotteville Estate, a former 405-hectare (1,000-acre) cocoa plantation. Visitors can wander the nature trails and explore a few of the untouched beaches left in Tobago. Birdwatching and nature trips arranged, also swimming and snorkelling off two small reefs directly in front of the cottages, as well as off two larger reefs within the bay. **$$–$$$**

Villa Limbo Vacation Rental
(reservations in the US)
Tel: (815) 477 7539
Fax: (815) 459 8325
www.villalimbo.com
Situated on a 8-hectare (21-acre) estate on the **Grafton Caledonia Wildlife Sanctuary**, the villa is part of Sanctuary Villas and is rented during the months that owners are away. Few of the other villas are rented, so guests stay in a residential setting. It sleeps four and is beautifully decorated in batik and bamboo, with the walls adorned with local art. Air-conditioned, with plunge pool, living room, dining room, barbecue, cable TV and CD player. **$$$**

Guesthouses

Hampden Inn
Milford Road
Hampden, Lowlands
Tobago
Tel/Fax: 639 7522
Email: hampden-inn@excite.com
This inexpensive 12-room bed and breakfast accommodates children of

2 years old and under free and 2–10 years old at half price. Rooms have private baths, air conditioning and cable TV. There is also a porch with a hammock, a restaurant, a bar and a swimming pool. **$$**

House of Pancakes
Corner of Milford Road and John Gorman Trace
Crown Point
Tel: 639 9866
Email: kittycat@tstt.net.tt
The House of Pancakes is a 5-room guesthouse catering for families with small children and for those on a limited budget. Clean and affordable, it also has a cybercafé and car-hire service. Close to the airport and the beaches at **Store Bay** and **Pigeon Point**. **$**

Old Grange Inn
Mount Irvine
Scarborough
Tel/Fax: 639 9395
www.trinidad.net/grangeinn
Located in Grange Bay, overlooking Mount Irving golf course, the Inn is a 10-minute drive from Crown Point Airport and an 8-minute walk from **Grange Bay Beach**. Its 18 rooms are quite large with air conditioning, private baths and balconies and views of the **Buccoo Reef** and **Nylon Pool**. Also on the property is the **Papillon Restaurant**. **$**

Bed and Breakfast

The Trinidad and Tobago Bed and Breakfast Co-operative Society has on its books about 100 rooms which have been inspected and approved. Rates range from US$50–US$100 per day for a double room, with children under 12 given a 12 percent discount in some homes. Contact:
The Trinidad and Tobago Bed and Breakfast Co-operative Society
Cruise Ship Complex
1 Wrightson Road
Port of Spain
Tel: 627 2337
or PO Box 3231
Diego Martin
Trinidad and Tobago, W.I.

Where to Eat

What to Eat

Travellers from the budget-conscious student to the business executive can find food to suit their tastes and pockets, though food prices on the whole are relatively high. The more expensive hotels tend to serve a kind of bland continental cuisine, but some offer special Creole meals.

Restaurants run the gamut, from *roti* shops frequented by office workers to sophisticated restaurants in restored Victorian mansions, serving the best French, Creole, Indian and Asian cuisines. Roadside stands proliferate, as do American fast-food outlets, such as Pizza Hut and Kentucky Fried Chicken (KFC).

Price Guide

The price categories are for the cost of a meal for one person, excluding drinks.
$ = under TT$30
$$ = TT$30–60
$$$ = TT$60–100
$$$$ = over TT$100

Restaurants

TRINIDAD

Port of Spain & Environs

A La Bastille
Corner of Ariapita Avenue and Verteuil Street, Port of Spain
Tel: 622 1789
Parisian-style brasserie with French classics on the menu and up to 100 imported French wines. French chef, proprietor Gérard Mouillé, has adventurous dishes. Open Mon for dinner, Tues–Sat from 7.30am.
$$–$$$

Anchorage
Hart's Cut, Point Gourd Road
Chaguaramas
Tel: 634 4334
Email:
info@theanchoragetrinidad.com
www.theanchoragetrinidad.com
Overlooks Chaguaramas Bay.
Specialises in seafood. **$$$–$$$$**

Apsara
13 Queen's Park East
Port of Spain
Tel: 623 7659
Email: apsara@wow.net
www.caribscape.com/apsara
Claims to be the only authentic
Indian restaurant in Trinidad and
Tobago. Specialising in Northern
Indian cuisine, it offers a wide
selection of well-known sub-
continental dishes including
Tandoori, curries and Indian breads
such as stuffed *paratha*, *naan* and
roti. Private dining facilities are
available on the upper floor, and
meals can be ordered à la carte or
from the restaurant's fixed-price
buffet menu. Open Mon–Sat
11am–11pm. **$$$–$$$$**

Botticelli's
Grand Bazaar
Uriah Butler Highway
Valsayn
Tel: 645 8733
Fax: 663 8733
Considered an elegant Italian
restaurant. Open daily
11am–11pm. **$$$–$$$$**

La Boucan
Hilton Hotel
Tel: 624 3111
This manor-style restaurant at the
Trinidad Hilton serves lunch daily,
tea Wed–Fri and dinner nearly every
evening. Specialises in international
and West Indian cuisine. **$$$**

Buccoo Rouge
West Mall
Westmoorings
Tel: 632 4601
Fax: 632 4072
Email: buccoo@wow.net
www.caribscape.com/buccoorouge
French cuisine and Caribbean
seafood. Claims to mix the flavour
of French cooking with the widest
variety of seafood in the Caribbean
region. Serves lobster and oysters
live from the tank. Diners can

expect classic seafood dishes such
as Gumbo, Lobster Thermidor or
Newburg, Oysters Rockefeller and
grilled red snapper, as well as as
Alaska king crab cocktail and
grilled wild Atlantic salmon. It also
serves meat appetisers and
entrées, with beef, lamb, veal and
poultry. Open Mon–Sat
11am–11pm. **$$$–$$$$**

China Palace
Ellerslie Plaza
Maraval
Tel: 622 5866
Fax: 622 6921
Chinese food to eat in or a
takeaway service. You can call in
your order and pick it up. If you
intend to dine in you must make a
reservation. Open Sun–Thur
11am–10pm, Fri and Sat until
11pm. **$$$–$$$$**

El Pecos on the Grill
68 Ariapita Avenue
Woodbrook
Port of Spain
Tel: 628 9908, 680 1319
Specialises in jerk, barbecue and
rotisserie chicken, with side dishes
such as cassava, rice and potato
salad. **$$–$$$**

Gourmet Club
Ellerslie Plaza
Maraval
Tel: 628 5113
Specialises in Italian food. Open
Mon–Fri 9am–2.30pm and
6–10.30pm. Only open for dinner
on Sat. **$$–$$$$**

Laughing Buddha
86 Frederick Street
Tel: 627 0100
Japanese menu includes sushi,
sashimi and a Teppanyaki bar. Open
daily for lunch and dinner.
Reservations. **$$–$$$$**

Il Colesso
16 Rust Street
St Clair
Tel: 628 1494
Classic Italian cuisine with live
music Wed and Sat evenings.

La Fantasie
The Normandie Hotel
10 Nook Avenue
St Ann's
Tel: 624 1181–4
A mix of French and Caribbean
cuisine. **$$$–$$$$**

La Ronde
Crowne Plaza Hotel
Wrightson Road
Port of Spain
Tel: 625 3361
Serves à la carte continental food
7.30–11pm daily. **$$–$$$**

Olympia
Crowne Plaza Hotel
Wrightson Road
Port of Spain
Tel: 625 3361/8
Offers buffet breakfast and lunch
and à la carte dinner. **$$–$$$**

Pelican Inn Restaurant
2–4 Coblentz Avenue
Cascade
Tel: 627 6271
The Pelican offers lunch Mon–Sat
noon–3pm. In the pub area (*see
Nightlife*) lasagne, shepherd's pie,
chicken casserole and crab meat,
served in little cups. **$$–$$$**

Plantation House (Da Vinci's)
38 Ariapita Avenue
Woodbrook
Tel: 628 5551
Fax: 623 0731
Specialising in French Creole, Cajun
and a Louisiana-style menu; the
Plantation House's most popular
dish is its Cajun-style blackened
fish. Open daily 11.30am–2.30pm
and 6.30–10.30pm. Reservations
are necessary. **$$$–$$$$**

Rafters
6A Warner Street
Newtown
Tel: 628 5108/9258
Fax: 628 9258
Housed in a 100-year-old grocery
store with a 9-metre (30-ft) ceiling,
it offers fresh local seafood,
including lobster, sea conch, squid
and shrimp, and a buffet on Mon
and Fri. Business Luncheon Buffet:
Mon–Thur. Prix Fixe dinner menu
specials feature Caribbean/

Continental fusion cuisine. There is a good salad bar, and an à la carte menu which includes US steaks, local entrées and speciality sandwiches in the **Lounge Bar**, which attracts a cosmopolitan clientèle for cocktails. Open for lunch 11.30am–3.30pm and dinner 7–11pm. **$$$**

Singho
Level 3, Long Circular Mall
St James
Tel: 622 1628; 628 2077
Fax: 622 3228
The restaurant specialises in Chinese food. Buffet dinner every Wed 7.30–11pm with live entertainment. Open daily 11am–11pm. **$$–$$$**

Solimar
6 Nook Avenue
St Ann's
Tel: 624 6267
With a garden-style ambience, a small waterfall surrounded by bamboo and banana plants creates the setting for diners to enjoy an international menu which includes dishes such as the seafood platter of locally caught fish and shrimp, sautéed in lime-garlic butter, and the English roast saddle of lamb and mignottes of tenderloin topped with black peppercorn and red wine sauce. Chef and owner Joe Brown hosts a food festival every month where guests can enjoy anything from Indian and Southeast Asian curries to lobster feasts, North Italian food or French provincial cuisine. Reservations recommended. **$$–$$$**

Tamnak Thai Restaurant
13 Queen's Park East
Port of Spain
Tel: 625 9715/0647
Fax: 623 7510
Serving oriental cuisine, the restaurant comes well-recommended with its menu of Thai-style duck, lobster dishes, curries etc. Diners can try, among other specialities, marinated chicken on bamboo skewers grilled and served with peanut sauce and vegetable pickles (salay gai), or pla rad prik – deep fried fish fillet accompanied with three tasty chilli sauces. Take-out service available. Open daily 11am–11pm. **$$–$$$**

TGI Friday's
Corner of Queen's Park West and Victoria Avenue
Port of Spain
Tel: 624 8443; 627 8768
Casual restaurant and bar with American-style dishes and a good children's menu. **$$**

Tiki Village
Kapok Hotel
Maraval
Tel: 622 5765
Offers oriental cuisine with a Polynesian twist. Dim Sum on weekends and public holidays. Buffet lunch on Wednesday and à la carte lunch and dinner. Open daily 11.45am–10.15pm. **$$–$$$**

Tony Roma's
51 Cipriani Boulevard
Tel: 627 7427
An American chain restaurant known for its barbecued ribs. The menu also includes chicken, beef and seafood. An upscale ambience and reasonable prices. **$$–$$$**

Trotters
Corner of Maraval and Sweet Briar roads
Port of Spain
Tel: 627 8768
Overpriced meals and drinks in fashionable liming spot. **$$–$$$**

Valpark Chinese Restaurant
Valpark Shopping Plaza
Morequito Avenue
Valsayn
Tel: 662 4540
Fax: 645 5474
Cantonese dishes and Omaha steaks. Chinese buffet every Wednesday evening and Sunday lunchtime. Open daily 11am–11pm. Live entertainment daily. **$$–$$$$**

Veni Mangé
67A Ariapita Avenue
Woodbrook
Tel: 624 4597
A popular restaurant well known for its Creole cuisine. Also offers International dishes, and caters for vegetarians. Check out the "Friday After Work Lime" with DJ music. Open Mon–Fri 11.30am– 3pm, Wed for dinner 7.30–10pm. **$$–$$$**

The Verandah
10 Rust Street
St Clair
Tel: 622 6287
Set in an old colonial house, it serves dinner both indoors and outdoors. Food described as "freestyle Caribbean". This restaurant comes well-recommended. Open Mon–Fri lunch 11.35am– 1.45pm, Thur–Sat dinner. **$$$**

Woodford Café
62 Tragarete Road
Woodbrook
Tel: 622 2233
Fax: 622 7319
Specialises in Creole cuisine, in a plantation-style café on one of the busiest roads in Port of Spain. Open Mon and Tues 11am–3.30pm, Wed–Sat 11am–10pm. **$$–$$$$**

Wok 'N' Roll
Highland Plaza
Glencoe
Tel: 637 6858
Freephone (in Trinidad and Tobago): 800-BOYS. For express delivery. Highly rated Chinese cuisine. Can deliver to your door if you are staying in the area. **$$$**

San Fernando

Horace's Garden Restaurant
6–8 Farah Street
San Fernando
Tel: 657 8331
Long-established Chinese eatery in the south. Open Mon–Thur 11am–10pm, Fri and Sat 11am–11pm. **$$–$$$$**

Le Petit Bourg
Paria Suites
Southern Main Road
Claxton Bay
Tel: 659 2230
Continental and local food served daily 6am–10pm. **$$–$$$**

The Pagoda Restaurant and Lounge
59 Independence Avenue
San Fernando
Tel: 657 6375
A family-orientated Chinese restaurant. Open Mon–Thur 10.30am–10pm, Fri–Sat 10.30am–10.30pm. **$–$$**

Soong's Great Wall
97 Circular Road
San Fernando
Tel: 657 5050 or 652 WALL
Fax: 653 3834
The Soong family has been offering southerners Chinese cuisine for generations. This is their flagship outlet, offering a wide range of Chinese-style seafood dishes, including stuffed crab backs, lobster and shrimp cocktails, as well as wontons, low meins, Chinese soups and beef and poultry dishes. **$$$–$$$$**

Blanchisseuse

Surf's Country Inn
North Coast Road
Blanchisseuse
Tel: 669 2475
Resort restaurant overlooking the Caribbean Sea. Serves both local and international cuisine. Open Mon–Fri 10am–5pm, Sat and Sun from 9am. **$$–$$$$**

Cafés

TRINIDAD

Café Trinidad
Normandie Hotel
10 Nook Avenue
St Ann's
Tel: 624 1181
Fax: 624 0108
Great place to have a quiet lunch, a snack or just a cup of tea, just off the Normandie Hotel's shopping centre. **$$$**

Restaurants

TOBAGO

Arnos Vale Hotel
Plymouth
Tel: 639 8084
The old Plantation House is the location of the hotel reception, restaurant, bar and lounge. Enjoy food prepared with fresh produce from the gardens and from the sea. **The Plantation House** opens every evening at 4pm when, throughout the unique tea service, numerous tropical birds join you to be fed by hand. The restaurant and the bar are

open throughout the day for hotel guests, offering refreshments, fresh salads and grilled entrées. **$$–$$$$**

Le Beau Rivage
Mount Irvine Golf Club
Tel: 639 8871
Fax: 639 8800
An open-air restaurant overlooking the golf course, serving gourmet French and Nouvelle Creole cuisine. Diners can choose from an extensive collection of vintage wines and champagnes from the restaurant's cellar. Open daily 7–11pm. **$$$$**

The Best of Thymes
Crown Point Beach Hotel
Crown Point
Tel: 639 0207/8781
Award-winning restaurant offering seafood, local and East Indian dishes. Overlooks the hotel pool. **$$–$$$**

The Black Rock Café
Black Rock Main Road
Tel: 639 ROCK (7625)
Serves anything from flying fish to lobster, poultry to prime and beer to Bordeaux. Open daily 3–11pm. **$$$–$$$$**

Blue Crab
Main and Robinson Streets
Scarborough
Tel: 639 2737
The Blue Crab specialises in seafood. Open Mon–Fri 11am–3pm for lunch. Dinner is strictly by reservation and usually begins around 7pm. **$$–$$$$**

Blue Note Bistro
Store Bay Local Road
Crown Point
Tel: 639 8492
Delicious local dishes accompanied by the owner's excellent jazz collection. **$$**

Café Coco
Store Bay Road
Crown Point
Tel: 639 0996
New World cuisine: Caribbean, Mexican and Cajun food served under the open sky. **$$$**

Conrado Beach Hotel
Milford Extension Road
Pigeon Point
Tel: 639 0145
Local food in air-conditioned comfort, with a view of the sea. **$$$**

Dillon's Seafood Restaurant
Crown Point
Tel: 639 8765
Specialising in fresh Tobago fish and lobster dishes, Dillon's is open daily from 6pm. Reservations are recommended. There is usually live entertainment. **$$$–$$$$**

The Fish Pot
Blue Waters Inn
Batteaux Bay
Speyside
Tel: 660 4341
Fax: 660 5195
A beachfront restaurant specialising in seafood and local cuisine. The menu does offer some international dishes tastefully put together with local ingredients. Open for breakfast 8–10am, lunch noon–3pm and dinner 6.30–8.30pm. Reservations are recommended. **$$$–$$$$**

Golden Star
Crown Point
Tel: 639 0873
A popular nightspot (*see Nightlife*), with a restaurant which is open for as long as the entertainment is happening. Serves local and international cuisine. **$–$$$**

Green Moray
Manta Lodge
Windward Road
Speyside
Tel: 660 5268
Fax: 660 4320
Part of **Manta Lodge**, the restaurant and bar are set on the beach amidst one of the oldest rain-forest reserves in the world. Open daily for breakfast 7.30am–11am, lunch 12.30–3pm and dinner 7–9.30pm. Afternoon tea is served 3.30–5.30pm, and cocktail hour is 6–7pm (2 for 1). The bar is open 10am–11pm daily. To accommodate divers with families there are children's menus available, and early dinners can be arranged. Special theme nights. Regular evening entertainment. **$–$$**

House of Pancakes
Milford Road and John Gorman Trace
Crown Point
Tel: 639 9866
Part of the House of Pancakes small guesthouse (*see Tobago guesthouses page 355*), the restaurant specialises in Cajun and

Creole cuisine with a strong emphasis on local ingredients. One of its most popular features is the homemade fruit and buttermilk pancakes. The menu caters for the vegetarian as well as the meat lover. Dishes include breadfruit salad, pumpkin soup, seafood or okra gumbo, blackened fish and chicken Jambalaya. **$$–$$$**

Jatt's Harbor Wok
Milford Road
Tel: 639 2745
Serves Creole food 8am–8pm daily. Food sold in portions. **$–$$**

Jemma's Sea View Kitchen
Speyside
Tel: 660 4066
A small restaurant in a tree house, overlooking the sea. Best known for its Creole food but also serves seafood and steaks. **$$–$$$**

Kariwak Village
Store Bay Local Road
Crown Point
Tel: 639 8442
Well-recommended. Caribbean cuisine cooked with herbs and spices grown on the Kariwak grounds. This hotel restaurant also has an excellent breakfast buffet on Sunday and live entertainment at weekends. **$–$$$**

The Kiskadee
Rex Turtle Beach Resort
Courland Bay
Tel: 639 2851
A resort restaurant serving a mix of local and international cuisine. Open daily for breakfast 7.30am–10am, lunch served in the coffee-shop area 12.30–3pm and dinner 7–9.30pm. **$$–$$$$**

Leandros Mediterranean Bistro
Le Grand Courlan Resort
Black Rock
Scarborough
Tel: 639 9667
Fax: 639 9292
An intimate bistro located at Le Grand Courlan Spa Resort adjacent to Grafton Beach Resort, Leandros features dishes from the Mediterranean and Caribbean regions. Good seafood specialities too. Open daily for breakfast, lunch and dinner 6–10.30pm. **$$$$**

Marcia's
Store Bay Local Road
Bon Accord
Tel: 639 0359
Local food. Reservations for lunch advisable. **$$**

Old Donkey Cart
Bacolet
Tel: 639 3551
Local and international cuisine. Housed in an old-fashioned Tobago home. Open noon–2.30pm for lunch, and 7pm for dinner. **$$–$$$**

Papillon
Old Grange Inn
Mount Irvine
PO Box 297
Scarborough
Tel/Fax: 639 9941
Email: grangeinn@trinidad.net
Offers local, international and continental à la carte dining. Specialises in seafood, including the Papillon Seafood Platter (fish, shrimp, lobster), Jumbo Shrimps with Garlic-butter Sauce, Lobster Thermidor and Mountain Stream Langoustine (crayfish). There is a choice of over 25 main courses. **$$–$$$**

Patinos
Shirvana Road
Tel: 639 9481
Offers both local and Polynesian dishes, specialising in grilled seafood with dishes such as Lobster Polynesian, Caribbean Pepper Shrimp and Buccoo King Fish. If seafood is not your flavour you can try Patino's Grilled US Tenderloin Steak or Chicken A La Marcia. A full tropical breakfast daily, a lunch and a dinner menu. There is a wide selection of European wines and of cocktails made from local rums and fresh tropical fruits and juices. You can enjoy your dinner within the

restaurant itself, or choose to dine at the poolside in the courtyard surrounded by the tropical foliage and the sounds of the nearby waterfall. Open 6.30pm till late. **$$–$$$$**

Peacock Mill Restaurant and Garden
Friendship Estate
Milford Road
Tel: 639 0503
A restaurant in an 18th-century sugar mill, with international cuisine during the week and barbecue at weekends. **$–$$$$**

The Seahorse Inn
Old Grafton Road
Black Rock
Tel: 639 0686
Fax: 639 0057
Specialises in a variety of seafood dishes, prime-quality steaks, Creole and international cuisine. Located in the hotel of the same name, it overlooks the beach and offers the choice of patio or balcony dining. Open for breakfast 7.30–10.30am, lunch noon–4pm and dinner 6.30–10.30pm. **$$$–$$$$**

Shirvan Watermill
Shirvan Road
Mount Pleasant
Tel: 639 0000
Fax: 639 0534
Dine in the pretty garden pavillion. Cocktails served at 5pm, dinner from 6pm.

Sugar Mill
Mount Irvine Hotel
Mount Irvine
Tel: 639 8871
A casual restaurant housed in an old converted mill. Relaxed atmosphere. **$$–$$$$**

Tamara's
Coco Reef Resort and Spa
Crown Point
Tel: 639 8571
A resort restaurant which serves an international menu. Open daily for breakfast 7am–10am and for dinner 7–10pm. **$$$$**

La Tartaruga Café and Bar
Buccoo Bay
Buccoo
Tel: 639 0940
Specialises in Italian food in response to an increased Italian presence in Tobago. **$–$$$**

Price Guide

The price categories are for the cost of a meal for one person, excluding drinks.
$ = under TT$30
$$ = TT$30–60
$$$ = TT$60–100
$$$$ = TT$100+

Toucan Inn & Bonkers
Store Bay Local Road
Crown Point
Tel: 639 7173
Fax: 639 8933
Bonkers (also a popular nightspot) is open every day from 7.30am. Breakfast, lunch and dinner from a menu of local and international dishes: everything from soups and salads to cakes and homemade ice-cream. Try the smoked duck and salsa salad or succulent sweet curried lamb. **$$–$$$$**

Drinking Notes

Mixed drink specialities in Trinidad and Tobago revolve around rum, and it is not hard to find a rum punch that will infuse any time of year with a bit of Carnival. Trinidad is also home to Angostura Bitters, a secret concoction that has been adding zest to mixed drinks for generations.

Two popular brands of locally-brewed beer are Stag and Carib. There are now also a number of imported beers and lagers available on the islands including Grolsch, Beck's, Polar (from Guyana), Carlsberg and Stella Artois.

Local soft drink favourites include sorrel, ginger beer made with real ginger, and mauby, made from a tree bark.

Culture

Cultural Activities

In addition to Carnival and the indigenous arts of calypso and steelband, there are theatres, museums, art galleries and festivals. Trinidad and Tobago has also produced some of the region's finest writers and performers, and much of the current crop of plays, performance art and choreography is staged regularly. Check the local newspapers for special events.

Art Galleries and Museums

TRINIDAD

Art Creators
Flat 402, 7 St Ann's Road
Port of Spain
Tel: 624 4369
Mon–Fri 10am–1pm, 4–7pm,
Sat 10am–noon
Chaguaramas Military History and Aerospace Museum
Western Main Road
Chaguaramas
Tel: 634 4391
Daily 9am–5pm
Horizons
39 Mucurapo Road
St James
Port of Spain
Tel: 628 9769
Mon–Fri 9am–5.30pm, Sat 9am–1pm
National Museum
117 Frederick Street
Port of Spain
Tel: 623 5941
Tues–Sat 10am–6pm, Sun 2–6pm

TOBAGO

Kimme's Sculpture Museum
Bethel Post Office
Tel/Fax: 639 0257
Sundays only, 10am–2pm.
Tobago Art Gallery
Hibiscus Drive
Lowlands
Tel: 639 0457
The gallery is a showcase for the work of Martin and Rachael Superville and other artists.
Mon–Fri 9am–5pm. Weekend visits by appointment.
Tobago Museum
Barrack Guard Square
Fort King George
Tel: 639 3970
Interesting and well-stocked museum which also incorporates the Tobago Museum of History. Historical artefacts, military memorabilia and Amerindian tools. Groups should book in advance.
Mon–Fri 9am–5pm (doors close at 4.30pm)

Concert Halls

Queen's Hall
1–3 St Ann's Road
St Ann's
Port of Spain
Tel: 624 1282
Music, fashion shows and other events
Hilton International
Port of Spain
Tel: 624 321/3111
Concerts in the ballroom
Naparima Bowl
19 Paradise Pasture
San Fernando
Tel: 652 4704
Concert hall space

Theatres

Central Bank Auditorium
Eric Williams Financial Complex
Independence Square
Port of Spain
Tel: 625 4921 ext 2665
Little Carib Theatre
Corner Robert and White streets
Woodbrook
Port of Spain
Tel: 622 4644

Queen's Hall
St Ann's Road
St Ann's
Tel: 624 1284
Under the Trees
The Normandie Hotel
10 Nook Avenue
St Ann's
Tel: 624 1181

Music

For those who want to hear steelband music, panyards dot the city; these are open lots where the bands practise regularly – particularly in the weeks leading up to Carnival. They do not stage shows, since this is truly practice space, but there is something about hearing the sparkling sound of a steelband at night that is more thrilling than staged events. This way you can decide on your favourites before the competition begins. The following is a randomly selected list of panyards. Usually the music starts around 7pm.

TRINIDAD

North
Amoco Renegades
17A Oxford Street, Port of Spain
Blue Diamonds
George Street, Port of Spain
Carib Tokyo
Plaisance Road, St John
Humming Birds Pan Groove
George Street, St James
Kool
25–27 Baneres Road, St James
Laventille Sound Specialists
Eastern Quarry, Laventille
Neal and Massy All Stars
Duke Street, Port of Spain
North Stars
63 Bombay Street, St James
Pandemonium
3 Norfolk Street, Belmont
Pan Vibes
St François Valley Road, Belmont
Petrotrin Invaders
Tragarete Road, Port of Spain
(opposite the Oval cricket ground).
Phase II Pan Groove
13 Hamilton Holder, Woodbrook
Starlift

187 Tragarete Road, Port of Spain
T&TEC Power Stars
14 Western Main Road, St James
Valley Harps
Morne Coco Road, Petit Valley
Witco Desperados
Laventille Community Centre
Laventille

South
Antillean All Stars
8–10 Carib Street, San Fernando
Couva Joylanders
Railway Road, Couva
Fonclaire
Dottin Street, San Fernando
Hatters
Lady Hailes Avenue, San Fernando
Jah Roots
Warden Road, Point Fortin
Pan Patriots
Charlo Village, Penal
Petrotrin Deltones
Railroad Road, Siparia
Skiffle Bunch (Pan Round the Neck)
Lambie Street Vistabella
San Fernando
T&TEC Motown
Navet Road, San Fernando
Tropical Angel Harps
Enterprise Village, Chaguanas

East
Birdsong
Corner Conel and St Vincent
streets, Tunapuna
Exodus
Eastern Main Road, Tunapuna
Harmonites
Churchill Roosevelt Highway,
Barataria
Klondykes Pan Sounds
Macoya Road, Tunapuna
Melodians
Bellamy Street, Cocorite Road
Arima
National Quarries Cordettes
Moonoo Street, Sangre Grande
Potential Symphony
Upper Sixth Avenue, Malick, Barataria
Scherzando
Evans Street, Curepe
Textel Pantastic Sounds
Old Southern Main Road, Curepe
Tunapuna All Stars
Railway Road, Tunapuna

TOBAGO
Carib Dixieland
Mount Pleasant
Katzenjammers
Black Rock
Tobago Buccooneers
Buccoo
T&TEC East Side
Zion Hill, Belle Garden
Trintoc Tobago All Stars
Wilson Road, Scarborough
West Side Symphony
Patience Hill

Film Fun

There are two cinema complexes in Trinidad: MovieTowne at Invaders Bay in Port of Spain, and Caribbean Cinemas 8 at the Trincity shopping centre. Both show first-run movies contemporaneously with the US. MovieTowne is expensive and upscale, while Caribbean Cinemas is less pricey.

There are also several more cinemas in Port of Spain and in other towns, scattered around the island, which show double features. Check the local press for locations and show times.

Outdoor Activities

For touring the Islands you will find more information and telephone numbers for Trinidad and Tobago's main visitor attractions in the walking and driving tours that make up the *Places* section of the book *(see pages 203–335)*.

If your main stop is Trinidad, do not leave without spending some time in Tobago – or vice versa.

TOURS FOR CRUISE-SHIP PASSENGERS

Trinidad and Tobago re-emerged as a Caribbean cruise ship destination after the Cruise Ship Complex was established at the Port of Spain port in 1989 and improvements were made to the port of Scarborough in Tobago. About 100 ships call at Trinidad and Tobago's ports each year. Trinidad has been developing special tours to encourage cruise visitors who want to see more than the cruise-ship-terminal shops but have limited time to spend.

There are currently three main tours popular with cruise ship passengers, each lasting about four hours and so leaving ample time for getting back to the ship before it sails. The tours are normally pre-agreed between the local tour operators and individual cruise lines, so it is advisable to check at the start of the cruise to find out what is available. Tours include:

The Maracas Swim Tour
A short drive through Port of Spain, taking in the Botanic Gardens located at Queen's Park Savannah and the Magnificent Seven buildings, then on to Maracas Beach for a swim and back to the cruise ship.

City Saddle Road–Maracas Tour
A short drive through Port of Spain taking in the Botanical Gardens and the Magnificent Seven buildings, but turning around at Maracas without a swim stop and returning to the ship via the Santa Cruz valley and a cocoa plantation.

City Cultural Tour
A drive through Port of Spain via the Botanical Gardens, then to a cultural presentation either at the Queen's Hall or at the Little Carib Theatre. Can also include Indian dancing, folk music, steelband and Carnival costumes.

Eco-Tour
There is also an eco-tour which is particularly popular with nature lovers, but not suitable for cruise ship passengers because of its length. It takes about 12 hours and includes a morning at the Asa Wright Nature Centre, lunch, then a visit by boat to see the scarlet ibis at Caroni Swamp.

More tours are planned, including a deep-sea fishing tour in which visitors will be transported by car to Chaguaramas and taken off shore by yacht; a golf tour; a visit to the Benedictine Monastery at Mount St Benedict, and a tour of Trinidad's gas-based industrial heartland at Point Lisas.

Specialist Tours

With the growth of cruise-ship tourism, organised tours have increased substantially in Trinidad, most of them geared towards eco-tourism.

TRINIDAD

Briko Air Services in Piarco (tel: 636 1168) can arrange plane and helicopter sightseeing trips within Trinidad and Tobago and to other nearby islands.

Tours & Hikes
For further information on guided tours and hikes in Trinidad contact:

Trinidad and Tobago Field Naturalists' Club
c/o Secretary, Rosemary Hernandez
Tel: 624 8017
PO Box 642
Port of Spain
www.wow.net/ttfnc
Chaguaramas Development Authority
Tel: 634 4312/4364
Guided tours.

TOBAGO

Buccoo Reef
For special tours to Buccoo Reef contact:
Buccoo Reef Co-operative Society
Buccoo Point
Tel: 639 8582
Hew's Tours
53 Coral Gardens
Buccoo
Tel: 639 9058.
Well-recommended for nature tours and hikes in Tobago:
Pioneer Journeys
Man-O-War Bay Cottages
Charlotteville
Tel: 660 4327 (Pat Turpin)
Nature Tours
Scarborough
Tel: 639 4276 (David Rooks)
Educatours
Carnbee
Tel: 639 7422 (Margaret Hinkson)

Shopping on Tour

The cruise-ship complex has a 40-booth handicraft market. Suggested best buys include: Hand-painted T-shirts (US$25) Earrings, steel pans, key chains etc in copper (US$5) Calabash handbags (US$5–10) Ceramic pots (US$5–15) Leather sandals/belts (US$15) Straw hats (US$2)

Tour Operators

The following tour operators in Trinidad are approved by TIDCO:

A's Travel Service
177 Tragarete Road
Port of Spain
Tel: 622 7664/5502
Fax: 628 6808
Email: as-travel@trinidad.net

AJM Tours
PO Box 471
Port of Spain
Tel/Fax: 625 3732
Email: ajmtours@trinidad.net
www.ajmtours.com

Banwari Experience
64 Prince Street
Port of Spain
Tel: 621 5893
Fax: 675 1619
Email: banwari@tstt.net.tt

Blue Emperor Tours
Springflow Road
Blue Range
Tel: 637 4246
Fax: 632 5863
Email: emperor@carib-link.net

Caribbean Discovery Tours
9B Fondes Amandes
Port of Spain
Tel: 624 7281
Fax: 624 8596
Email: caribdis@wow.net
www.caribbeandiscoverytours.com

Classic Tours & Travel
Crown Point Airport
Tobago
Tel: 639 9891
Email: info@classictoursltd.tstt.net.tt
www.classictoursltd.com

Joy Tours
Chaguaramas Convention Centre
Chaguaramas
Tel: 634 2379 ext. 1516
Fax: 633 4733

Nanan's Bird Sanctuary Tours
Bamboo Grove Settlement #1
Tel/Fax: 645 1305

Rooks Nature Tours
c/o 44 La Seiva Road
Maraval
Tel/Fax: 622 8826
Email: rooks@pariasprings.com
www.pariasprings.com/rookstours

The Travel Centre Limited
2 Uptown Mall
Edward Street
Port of Spain
Tel: 623 5096; 625 1636
Fax: 623 5101
Email: trvlcentre@wow.net

T&T Sightseeing Tours
12 Western Main Road
St James
Tel: 628 1051
Fax: 622 9205

TOBAGO

AJM Tours
Crown Point Airport
Tel: 639 0610
Tel: 639 8918

Almandoz Tobago
PO Box 151
Scarborough
Tel: 639 3691

Libby Tours
32 Meerut Street
Scarborough
Tel: 622 2493
Fax: 627 2666

Rooks Nature Tours
Lambeau Hill
Email: rookstobago@trinidad.net

Ted's Sunshine Enterprises
Store Bay Local Road
Tel: 639 0547
Fax: 639 9906
Email: sunshine@trinidad.net

Nightlife

Popular Pubs and Clubs

TRINIDAD

The Anchorage
Point Gourd Road, Chaguaramas
Tel: 634 4334
Also a restaurant, the Anchorage is known as a great place to party with the fish and hear an occasional live pop-rock band. Opening times vary, and parties are usually by invitation. Call for party dates and invitation information.

The Attic
Shoppes of Maraval, Maraval
Tel: 622 8123
Open daily from 4pm to 4am; The Attic's liveliest nights are Tuesdays and Thursdays.

Club Zen
Corner of Keate and Frederick streets
American-style nightclub. Open nightly. Be warned there are long lines to enter the club.

Cocktail Lounge
City of Grand Bazaar, Valsayn
Tel: 662 5631 or 665 1283
Open from 10am daily, The Parrot stays open until midnight on every night except Thursday, when it closes at 1am, and Friday, when doors shut at 4am. Fridays and Saturdays are party nights, and there is an admission fee at the door. Music supplied by a DJ. The restaurant and cocktail lounge are open for lunch and dinner, and meals include roast beef, grilled chicken, red fish or snapper and your choice of potato (baked, grilled, boiled).

Cricket Wicket
149 Tragarete Road, Port of Spain
Tel: 628 4193; 622 9762
Popular liming spot opposite the Queen's Park Oval.

51 Degrees
51 Cipriani Boulevard
Port of Spain
Tel: 627 0051
Upscale nightclub.

Hi RPM
Gulf City Mall, La Romaine
Tel: 652 3760
Hi RPM, known as one of the home of pop-rock music parties, is open from Monday to Sunday. On Mondays and Tuesdays it is open from 1pm; Wednesdays and Thursdays from 2pm; Fridays and Saturdays from noon; Sundays from 4pm. Wednesdays are pop-rock nights, with drink specials. Affiliated with local radio station 95.1FM.

Jazzy's Restaurant and Bar
48 Western Main Road, St James
Tel: 628 6355
A lively night spot in the heart of St James, Jazzy's is open Monday to Sunday from 10am, closing when the crowd disperses. Thursday nights are for karoake, and Friday and Saturday are party nights. But on any week night there is a "lime" going on, and patrons can sample a variety of food from Jazzy's kitchen (Indian, Creole, Chinese) while they drink and dance.

Jenny's on the Boulevard
Cipriani Boulevard
Very decorous restaurant; after-work limes in the bar.

The Parrot Steak House and The Tunnel
Ramsaran Street, Chaguanas
Tel: 671 4819
Located in Central Trinidad, The Tunnel may be a bit difficult to get to without a car. Open Thursday to Saturday from 10pm, Thursday is Ladies' Night where women enter free and drink free all night. You must have an invitation to enter the club on all nights, and you can telephone for information.
Invitations can be picked up on the night of the party.

The Pelican Inn
2–4 Coblentz Avenue, Cascade
Tel (Pub): 624-RHUM (7486)
A very popular English pub Caribbean-style, especially on those Wednesday nights, when there is a live band, and Friday nights, which start with a regular Trini after-work

lime and heat up around 8pm with a DJ and a cover charge to enter. The Pelican is open daily from 11am, usually closing during the week around 2am but staying open at weekends as long as there is a crowd.

Pier One
Western Main Road, Chaguaramas
Tel: 634 4472
Email: pier1@rave-tt.net
www.pier1-tt.com
Pier One is only open on Thursday and Friday nights from 9pm–3am. Thursdays are Latin music nights and Fridays TGIF, meaning Thank God It's Free Drinks. Despite its name and location, Pier One is not a marina, and apart from the parties visitors can do a merengue or salsa dance lesson there during their stay on the island. Call for further information and for party invitations.

Poleska Cocktail Bar
Trinidad Country Club, Champs Elysées, Maraval, Port of Spain
Tel: 622 2112
Elegant ambience with occasional live entertainment.

Smokey and Bunty
Tragarete Road, St James
No telephone
The quintessential example of the Trini liming spot, Smokey and Bunty, a bar, is open all night, and patrons generally hang out on the sidewalk drinking, eating from the many surrounding food vendors (who offer anything from *roti* to black pudding) and just having a great time amidst the St James crowd and traffic. St James is described as the city that never sleeps. Smokey and Bunty is a must if you are ever to get the hang of "liming".

Trotters
Corner Maraval and Sweet Briar roads, Port of Spain
Tel: 627 8768
Huge sports bar that is very popular on Friday night.
Other spots include:

Club Celebs or Celebs Night Club and Sports Café
Gulf City Shopping Mall
La Romaine
Tel: 652 7641
Located in southern Trinidad. During the week patrons can play pool or

darts, or just hang out. There are Friday after-work limes, and free-drink parties during the weekend. Telephone for details.

Club Liquid
Roundabout Plaza,
Maritime Centre, Barataria
One of the fashionable nightspots.

Karaoke Lounge
Carlton Centre, St James Street
San Fernando
Tel: 652 2749
Nightly entertainment; and probably the best place to hear calypso and pan outside carnival time.

Mas' Camp Pub
corner of French Street and Ariapita Avenue
Woodbrook
Tel: 623 3745

Race Rock Sports Bar
City of Grand Bazaar
Tel: 663 9271
Club and bar located in the City of Grand Bazaar shopping centre in Valsayn.

Shakers
MovieTowne, Invaders Bay
Lively al fresco bar, which closes around 1am.

Tasca Latina
16 Phillips Street, Port of Spain
Tel: 625 3497

TOBAGO

Copratray
Store Bay Local Road, Crown Point
Tel: 639 8493
The Copratray is open Monday–Saturday evening from 6.30pm and is very popular with both locals and foreigners. There are three pool tables and a resident DJ, who plays everything from reggaerock to calypso and soca. Adjoining the bar is the Copratray Restaurant which is open daily 8.00–10.00am for breakfast, and from 6.30pm Monday–Saturday for dinner.

The Deep
Sandy Point Village, Crown Point
Tel: 639 8533
In Tobago on Sunday nights there is a party known as "Sunday School" in Buccoo Village where partygoers hang out in the beach facilities and the disco until the small hours. This

has become a tradition especially during the Tobago Heritage and Great Race holidays. Most of the bigger hotels and restaurants offer nightly entertainment like calypso, steelband, folkdancing and singing.

Golden Star Restaurant and Bar
Crown Point
Tel: 639 0873
Open daily from 7am. Nightly entertainment including live steelband on Wednesdays with a barbecue from 8pm and from 10pm a dance with a DJ that lasts till dawn. This is a very popular spot.

Kariwak Village Hotel
Store Bay Local Road, Crown Point
Tel: 639 8442
Live entertainment every Friday and Saturday night 9–11pm.

Lush
Shirvan Road, Canaan
Tel: 639 9087

Toucan Inn & Bonkers
Store Bay Local Road, Crown Point
Tel: 639 0916/7173
Tuesdays there is old time calypso, Wednesdays GMC steelband, Thursdays Les Couteaux Dancers, Fridays Native Spirit, Saturdays old time calypso and Sundays solo steelpan.

Casinos

Casinos have become quite popular in Trinidad and Tobago during recent years. Trinbagonians love to gamble, and the daily Play Whe and Pick 2, the twice weekly Cashpot and the weekly Lotto are testaments of that.

Here are a few of the more popular casinos:

Crystal Palace
corner of Milford and Mt Marie roads, Tobago
Tel: 639 9747

Club Casanovas
10 Macoya Road, Tunapuna, Trinidad
Tel: 662 1050

D'Cabin
Parly 2, St James Street
San Fernando
Tel: 652 5288

Island Club Casino
City of Grand Bazaar
corner of Churchill-Roosevelt &

Uriah Butler highways
Valsayn, Trinidad
Tel: 645 3333

Ma Pau
corner of French Street and Ariapita Avenue, Woodbrook
Tel: 624 3331

Platinum City II
69 Western Main Road
St James
Tel: 628 8813

The Ritz
19 Buen Intento Road
Princes Town
Tel: 655 0636

Festivals

General festivals include Carnival, the Steelband Music Festival (every two years), the annual Hindu festivals of Phagwah and Diwali, the Muslim festivals of Eid-ul-Fitr and Hosay, the Best Village Folk Festival (October–December), annual Flower and Orchid Shows (March and October), La Divina Pastora in Siparia (April), the Santa Rosa Festival, honouring the original Amerinidian inhabitants of Trinidad, and Tobago's Heritage Festival (in July). For powerboat lovers there is the Du Maurier Great Race between Trinidad and Tobago (last weekend in July).

Carnival is usually held in February. The busiest days are Carnival Monday and Tuesday, although preparations and celebrations begin months in advance, as early as November, but things really hot up any time from New Year's Day. There are lots of parties or "fêtes" to attend in the run-up to the event. *See the Festivals page 155 for a closer look at T&T's many celebrations.*

Carnival

Forthcoming Carnival Monday and Tuesday dates:
2006: 27–28 February
2007: 19–20 February
2008: 4–5 February
2009: 23–24 February
2010: 15–16 February

Shopping

What to Buy

Indian silver and gold jewellery, competitively priced imported fabrics, batik and tie-dye T-shirts and wrap skirts are just a few of the items visitors should not leave Trinidad and Tobago without. From the smallest trinket – miniature steelpans, copper hibiscus and hummingbird-inspired earrings – to larger mementos like calabash bags and beautiful wooden wall plaques and hangings, there is something to suit every taste and budget.

To remember T&T's culinary achievements, think about taking home bottles of local pepper-sauce, Indian kutchela, preserved mangoes, plums and cherries, or a bag (or two) of local spices. Can't forget those nights at the Pelican Inn Pub or at Smokey and Bunty? – take a bottle of White Oak, Black Label or Vat 19 rum to keep the memories warm back home. None of these would be complete, of course, without a bottle of Angostura Bitters. Trinidad and Tobago also has some of the world's finest cocoa and coffee – they are sold, pre-packaged, in a variety of flavours in souvenir shops. Brand names to look for include Caribbean Coffee House, Caribbean Select Coffee and Hong Wing.

BOOKS

RIK Services
87 Queen Street, Port of Spain
Tel: 623 4316
102–4 High Street, San Fernando
Tel: 652 4824/3830
There are also branches in City of Grand Bazaar, West Mall and Long Circular Mall

A Different View
9 Warren St, Woodbrook
Tel: 622 3648
S & Dees Bookstore
10 Saddle Road, San Juan
Tel: 674 4685
City of Grand Bazaar
Valsayn
Tel: 662 5516
Lexicon Trinidad Limited
Boundary Road, San Juan
Tel: 675 3395
Publishers and wholesalers; books
at bargain prices.
Metropolitan Book Suppliers
Colsort Mall, 11–13 Frederick
Street, Port of Spain
Tel: 623 3462
Great for local cookbooks etc.
Paper Based
At the Normandie Hotel
St Ann's
Tel: 624 1181

LOCAL CRAFTS

There are handicraft studios and
shops all over Trinidad and also in
Tobago producing authentic and
good quality locally-made items.
Keep an eye out for leather
sandals, belts and bags; copper
jewellery; calabash bags, ceramics,
straw and canework.
Ajoupa Pottery
326 Chickland Road, Upper
Carapichaima
Tel: 673 0604
Alkebu-Lan
13 Ariapita Avenue, Woodbrook
Tel: 627 1060
Bambu Gift Shop
Level 2, West Mall
Tel: 632 7567
Kapok Hotel, 16–18 Cotton Hill
St Clair
Tel: 628 4003
Crown Point Hotel, Crown Point
Tobago
Tel: 639 9721
Blind Welfare Association
118 Duke and Edward Street
Port of Spain
Tel: 624 1613
Chic Shak
27 Jerningham Avenue
Port of Spain
Tel: 625 4214

Cruise Ship Complex
1D Wrightson Road, Port of Spain
Tel: 62 SHIPS (627 4477)
All items purchased here are duty
free upon production of a current
passport and airline/cruise ship
ticket.
Maca Fouchette
Level 2, West Mall, Port of Spain
Tel: 633 1278
Selection House
corner of Prince and Frederick streets,
Port of Spain
Tel: 623 7088
United Craft Workers' Co-op
Frederick Street, Port of Spain
Piccadilly Street, eastern Port of
Spain

DESIGNERS

Heather Jones
35 Eastern Main Road, Barataria
Tel: 638 6092
Meiling
Kapok Hotel, 16–18 Cotton Hill
St Clair
Tel: 628 6205
Radical Designs
Valpark Shopping Plaza, Valsayn
Tel: 662 3542
3 Frederick Street, Port of Spain
Tel: 627 6110
58 Frederick Street, Port of Spain
Tel: 627 4425
Branches in West Mall and Gulf City.

MUSIC

Rhyner's Record Shop
54 Prince Street, Port of Spain
Tel: 62 KAISO (625 2476)
Crosby's Music Centre
54 Western Main Road, Port of Spain
Tel: 622 SOCA (622 7622)
Cleve's One Stop Music Shop
Mall 58, Frederick Street
Port of Spain
Tel: 624 0827
Just CD's
Level 1, Long Circular Hall,
51–53 Long Circular Road,
St James
Tel: 622 7516
Starlite Shopping Plaza
Four Roads, Diego Martin
Tel: 633 7516

Movie Towne, Audrey Jeffers
Highway, Port of Spain
Tel: 625 3472
Music Shak
Aboutique Mall, Frederick Street,
Port of Spain
Tel: 623 0665

T-SHIRTS

Native Spirit
7 Victoria Square E, Port of Spain
Tel: 627 3648
NIFTEES
West Mall, Port of Spain
Tel: 633 TEES (633 8337)
Ellerslie Plaza, Port of Spain
Tel: 622 5711
There are also other branches at
City of Grand Bazaar and Valpark
Shopping Plaza.
NIFTEES Kids
Tel: 637 1264
Zoom Caribbean
Long Circular Mall, St James
Tel: 628 7873
Pigeon Point, Tobago
Tel: 639 7873
(other branches at West Mall, City
of Grand Bazaar and Gulf City)

SWIMWEAR

Swimwear can be bought from malls
throughout Trinidad: Gulf City in the
south; Price Plaza in central; and
West Mall and Long Circular Mall in
the north.
Chaos Enterprises
24 Borde Street, Port of Spain
Tel: 623 6472
Island Casuals
43 Long Circular Road, St James
Tel: 622 2412

Sport

Sport

Trinidad and Tobago can claim to have produced many world-class athletes: Brian Lara, the West Indies cricket batsman, holds the world record for the highest score in test match and first class cricket. The world's oldest powerboat race, the Great Race, is held annually between Trinidad and Tobago.

Though a lack of facilities and money impede the population's interest in sport, in Trinidad games like cricket, football and basketball are among the most popular. Tobago, on the other hand, is the perfect place for any kind of watersport, from kayaking, deep-sea fishing, scuba diving and snorkelling to windsurfing, diving and sailing. When it comes to finding a diving shop in Tobago, ask around and go with the one with the best reputation, or organise it through your hotel. On both islands most of the facilities for games like golf, squash and tennis are housed in the larger hotels.

Apart from the places listed below, telephone the following associations for details of forthcoming events or for well-recommended members:
Cricket: T&T Cricket Board of Control Tel: 636 1577
Football: T&T Football Federation Tel: 622 1445
Game Fishing: T&T Game Fishing Association Tel: 624 5304
Golf: T&T Golf Association Tel: 625 3531 cxt. 445
Hockey: T&T Hockey Board Tel: 625 3520/9 ext. 4131
Powerboat racing: T&T Powerboats Association Tel: 634 4427
Sailing: T&T Yachting Association Tel: 634 4210/4519

Squash: T&T Squash Association Tel: 649 3573
Tennis: Tennis Association of T&T Tel: 628 0783
Windsurfing: Windsurfing Association of T&T Tel: 628 8908

Cricket

Test matches are played at Queen's Park Oval, west of Queen's Park Savannah, Port of Spain. For information telephone the **Queen's Park Cricket Club**: 622 2295/3787.

Golf

Mount Irvine Bay Hotel and Golf Club
Scarborough, Tobago
Tel: 639 8871
Golf: 9-hole and 18-hole.
The course opens at 6.30am, last client allowed on the greens at 4pm
St Andrew's Golf Club
Moka, Maraval
Tel: 629 0066
Trinidad's best 18-hole golf course
Chaguaramas Golf Course
Bellerand Road, Chaguaramas
Tel: 634 4349
9-hole golf course, open 6.30am–7pm.

Horse-racing

There is horse-racing at Santa Rosa Park, Arima, about 15 km (9 miles) outside Port of Spain. For information telephone the **T&T Racing Authority** on: 646 1986 or the **Arima Race Club** on: 646 2450–1

Squash

Grafton Beach Resort
Black Rock, Tobago
Tel: 639 0191
Use of facilities by appointment only. Telephone to make day or nighttime reservations. Fees are charged for 45 minutes on the court, for 2 balls, and racquet hire is available.
Pelican Inn
2–4 Coblentz Avenue, Cascade
Tel: 637 4888, 627 6271
Open 24 hours a day, 7 days a week, the Pelican Inn squash facilities are available to visitors

through temporary membership. Call at the telephone number above for details.
Cascadia Hotel
Ariapita Rd, St Ann's
Tel: 623 3511
Reservations recommended for use of the Cascadia squash courts. Offices are open between the hours of noon and 9pm for bookings, and the courts themselves between 6am and 11pm. Guests of the hotel can play free of charge but visitors must pay a fee for 45 minutes court time. Balls and racquets also on sale.

A Holistic Approach

At the Kariwak Village Hotel in Tobago *(see page 353)* they take an holistic approach to fitness and health. There are stretch and relaxation classes several times per week, and also yoga, TaiChi and Qi Gong. Also available at the hotel are massage and reflexology treatments. For more information about Kariwak's fitness centre, activities and classes call 639 8442.

Swimming
Hilton International Hotel
Lady Young Road, Port of Spain
Tel: 624 3111
Open from 7am to 6pm, there is a charge to use the swimming facilities at the Hilton. A further refundable deposit is required for use of towels.
Cascadia Hotel
Ariapita Rd, St Ann's
Tel: 623 3511
Swimming facilities are open from 9am–6pm. Daily fee.
Chutes and waterslides.
La Joya Complex
st Joseph
Tel: 662 6929
Open 9am–6pm.

Tennis
Arnos Vale Hotel
Plymouth, Tobago
Tel: 639 2881
Facilities for guests of the hotel only.

Blue Waters Inn

Batteaux Bay, Speyside, Tobago

Tel: 660 4341/4077

Resident guests at the hotel can use the tennis courts free of charge at any time during the day, and only pay a minimal fee for nighttime usage. Non-resident guests pay TT$100 per hour and must make a reservation beforehand, and for them the facilities are open between 6am and 8pm daily.

Cascadia Hotel

Ariapita Rd, St Ann's

Tel: 623 3511

Courts open 5am–9pm.

The Hilton International Hotel

Lady Young Road, Port of Spain

Tel: 624 3111

Open 6am–10pm daily, the Hilton's tennis courts can be used for an hourly and per person fee. Racquet and ball hire, and tennis lessons are also available.

Mount Irvine Bay Hotel

Scarborough, Tobago

Tel: 639 8871

Visitors are charged by the hour during the day, with an extra flat fee for use of the court light at night.

Trinidad Country Club

Champs Elysees, Maraval

Tel: 622 3470

The offices of the Trinidad Country Club are open 8am–7pm, but the tennis facilities can be used from 6.30am to 10.30pm. The fee for use of the courts is charged per hour.

Tranquillity Square Lawn Tennis Club

Tel: 625 4182

Private members' club that offers temporary membership to visitors. Telephone for details.

Further Reading

Further Reading

The books listed below are non-fiction, historical or biographical accounts. By themselves they will give the reader a general outline of the facts of Trinidad and Tobago's history.

Anthony, Michael and Andrew Carr. David Frost Introduces Trinidad & Tobago. London: Andre Deutsch, 1975.

Anthony, Michael. Towns and Villages of Trinidad and Tobago. Circle Press, Trinidad, 1988.

Besson, Gerard and Brereton, Bridget. The Book of Trinidad. Paria Publishing, Co. Trinidad, 1992.

Boomert, Arie. "The Arawak Indians of Trinidad and Coastal Guyana, ca 1500–1650." Journal of Caribbean History 19:2. University of the West Indies, 1986.

Borde, Pierre Gustav. History of the Island of Trinidad under the Spanish Government. Vols. I & II. Port of Spain: Paria Publishing Co., 1982.

Brereton, Bridget. Race Relations in Colonial Trinidad 1870–1900. Cambridge: Cambridge University Press, 1979.

Brereton, Bridget. A History of Modern Trinidad 1783–1962. London: Heinemann, 1981.

Calder-Marshall, Arthur. Glory Dead. London: Michael Joseph, 1939.

Carmichael, Gertrude. The History of the West Indian Islands of Trinidad and Tobago. Port of Spain: Columbus Publishers, 1986.

Ffrench, Richard and Peter Bacon. Nature Trails of Trinidad. Trinidad & Tobago: S.M. Publications, 1982.

Gomes, Albert. Through a Maze of Colour. Port of Spain: Key Caribbean Publications, 1974.

Hargreaves, Dorothy and Bob. Tropical Tree. Kailva, Hawaii: Hargreaves Co., 1965.

Jacobs, Richard. Butler Versus the King. Port of Spain: Key Caribbean Publications, 1975.

James, C.L.R. Life of A.A. Cipriani. Lancashire: Nelson, 1932.

James, C.L.R. Beyond a Boundary. Jamaica: Sangsters, 1963.

Jones, Anthony, Mark. The Winston "Spree" Simon Story. Port of Spain: Educo Press, 1982.

Lewis, Gordon K. The Growth of the Modern West Indies. New York: Monthly Review Press, 1968.

Lewis, W.A. Labour in the West Indies. London: New Beacon Books, 1977.

Martin, Tony. The Pan African Connection: From Slavery to Garvey and Beyond. Massachussets: The Majority Press, 1983.

Murray, Eric John. Religions of Trinidad and Tobago. Outline of the basic beliefs and numbers of most of the religious bodies. It is not much more than a collection of statements supplied by the bodies themselves, plus a few statistics, but it is a useful reference.

Naipaul, V.S. The Middle Passage. Harmondsworth: Penguin Books, 1962.

Naipaul, V.S. The Loss of El Dorado. Harmondsworth: Penguin Books, 1973.

Naipaul, V.S. Finding the Centre. London: Andre Deutsch, 1984.

Newson, Linda. Aboriginal and Spanish Colonial Trinidad. London: Academic Press, 1976.

Nunley, John W. Caribbean Festival Arts: Each and Every Bit of Difference. London and Seattle: Saint Louis Art Museum in association with The University of Washington Press, 1988.

Quevedo, Raymond. Atilla's Kaiso: A Short History of Trinidad Calypso. St Augustine: University of the West Indies, 1983.

Ramdin, Ron. From Chattel Slave to Wage Earner. London: Martin Brian & O'Keefe, 1982.

Robinson, Arthur N.R. Mechanics of Independence.

Rohlehr, Gordon. Calypso and Society in Pre-Independence Trinidad. Trinidad, 1990.

Ryan, Selwyn. *Race and Nationalism in Trinidad and Tobago*. Toronto: University of Toronto Press, 1972.

Ryan, Selwyn. *The Politics of Succession*. St Augustine: University of the West Indies, 1979.

Sander, Reinhard W., ed. *From Trinidad: An Anthology of Early West Indian Writing*. London: Hodder & Stoughton, 1978.

Warner, Keith. *The Trinidad Calypso*. London: Heinemann, 1982.

Williams, Eric. *History of the Peoples of Trinidad and Tobago*. Port of Spain: PNM Publishing Co., 1962.

Williams, Eric. Inward Hunger: *The Education of a Prime Minister*. London: Andre Deutsch, 1969.

Williams, Eric. *Forged From the Love of Liberty: Selected Speeches*. Port of Spain: Longmans Caribbean, 1982.

Creative Writing

To get a feel for the experience of that history, the reader must turn to the country's creative writers, for only they can transform knowledge into understanding. A short list must include:

Antoni, Robert. *Divina Trace*. New York: Overlook Press, 1989.

Antoni, Robert. *Blessed Is The Fruit*. New York: Henry Holt & Co. 1997.

Bellour, Helene; Chock, Jeffrey; Johnson, Kim and Riggio, Milla.*Renegades: The History of Renegades Steel Orchestra of Trinidad and Tobago*. London: Macmillan, 2002

Boissiere, Ralph de. *Crown Jewel*. London: Pan Books, 1981.

Burnett, Paula, ed. *The Penguin Book of Caribbean Verse in English*. Harmondsworth: Penguin Books, 1986.

Lovelace, Earl. *The Dragon Can't Dance*. London: Andre Deutsch, 1979; Salt. Faber and Faber, 1996.

Mittelholzer, Edgar. *A Morning at the Office*. London: Heinemann Educational Books, 1974.

Naipaul, V.S. *The Mystic Masseur*. Harmondsworth: Penguin Books, 1964.

Naipaul, V.S. *The Suffrage of Elvira*. Harmondsworth: Penguin Books, 1969.

Naipaul, V.S. *A House for Mr Biswas*. Harmondsworth: Penguin Books, 1969.

Naipaul, V.S. *The Mimic Men*. Harmondsworth: Penguin Books, 1969.

Ramcharitar, Raymond. *Breaking the News: Media and Culture in Trinidad*, Lexicon Trinidad, 2005.

Resistance, Brother. *Rapso Explosion*. London: Karia Press, 1986.

Riggio, Milla Cozart (ed) *Culture in Action, The Trinidad Experience*. New York, Routledge, 2004

Scott, Lawrence. *Witchbroom*. Heinemann, 1993.

Scott, Lawrence. *Aelred's Sin*. Allison & Busby, 1999.

Scott, Lawrence. *Night Calypso*. Allison & Busby, 2004.

Selvon, Samuel. A Brighter Sun. London: Longman Books Ltd., 1979.

Walcott, Derek. *Collected Poems*. Faber & Faber, 1988.

Finally, the reader should listen to the wit and wisdom of Trinidad and Tobago's calypsonians. Their oral history and poetry, social commentary and bawdiness, nonsense rhyme and satire, scandal mongering and fantasy has no parallel in any other art form.

Other Insight Guides

There are more than 400 titles in the three series of guidebook: Insight Guides, Compact Guides and Pocket Guides, including many covering the Caribbean region. Companions to this volume include Insight Guides to the Caribbean, Caribbean Cruises, Cuba, Barbados, Bahamas, Bermuda, Dominican Republic and Haiti and Jamaica.

Feedback

We do our best to ensure the information in our books is as accurate and up-to-date as possible. The books are updated on a regular basis, using local contacts, who painstakingly add, amend and correct as required. However, some mistakes and omissions are inevitable and we are ultimately reliant on our readers to put us in the picture.

We would welcome your feedback on any details related to your experiences using the book "on the road". Maybe we recommended a hotel that you liked (or another that you didn't), as well as interesting new attractions, or facts and figures you have found out about the country itself. The more details you can give us (particularly with regard to addresses, e-mails and telephone numbers), the better.

We will acknowledge all contributions, and we'll offer an Insight Guide to the best letters received.

Please write to us at:

Insight Guides
PO Box 7910
London SE1 1XF
United Kingdom

Or send e-mail to:

insight@apaguide.co.uk

ART & PHOTO CREDITS

Picture Spreads

Index

Numbers in italics refer to photographs

INSIGHT GUIDES

The classic series that puts you in the picture

Alaska
Amazon Wildlife
American Southwest
Amsterdam
Argentina
Arizona & Grand Canyon
Asia's Best Hotels & Resorts
Asia, East
Asia, Southeast
Australia
Austria
Bahamas
Bali
Baltic States
Bangkok
Barbados
Barcelona
Beijing
Belgium
Belize
Berlin
Bermuda
Boston
Brazil
Brittany
Brussels
Buenos Aires
Burgundy
Burma (Myanmar)
Cairo
California
California, Southern
Canada
Caribbean
Caribbean Cruises
Channel Islands
Chicago
Chile
China
Colorado
Continental Europe
Corsica
Costa Rica
Crete
Croatia
Cuba
Cyprus
Czech & Slovak Republic
Delhi, Jaipur & Agra
Denmark

Dominican Rep. & Haiti
Dublin
East African Wildlife
Eastern Europe
Ecuador
Edinburgh
Egypt
England
Finland
Florence
Florida
France
France, Southwest
French Riviera
Gambia & Senegal
Germany
Glasgow
Gran Canaria
Great Britain
Great Gardens of Britain
  & Ireland
Great Railway Journeys
  of Europe
Greece
Greek Islands
Guatemala, Belize
  & Yucatán
Hawaii
Hong Kong
Hungary
Iceland
India
India, South
Indonesia
Ireland
Israel
Istanbul
Italy
Italy, Northern
Italy, Southern
Jamaica
Japan
Jerusalem
Jordan
Kenya
Korea
Laos & Cambodia
Las Vegas
Lisbon
London

Los Angeles
Madeira
Madrid
Malaysia
Mallorca & Ibiza
Malta
Mauritius Réunion
  & Seychelles
Mediterranean Cruises
Melbourne
Mexico
Miami
Montreal
Morocco
Moscow
Namibia
Nepal
Netherlands
New England
New Mexico
New Orleans
New York City
New York State
New Zealand
Nile
Normandy
North American &
  Alaskan Cruises
Norway
Oman & The UAE
Oxford
Pacific Northwest
Pakistan
Paris
Peru
Philadelphia
Philippines
Poland
Portugal
Prague
Provence
Puerto Rico
Rajasthan

Rio de Janeiro
Rome
Russia
St Petersburg
San Francisco
Sardinia
Scandinavia
Scotland
Seattle
Shanghai
Sicily
Singapore
South Africa
South America
Spain
Spain, Northern
Spain, Southern
Sri Lanka
Sweden
Switzerland
Sydney
Syria & Lebanon
Taiwan
Tanzania & Zanzibar
Tenerife
Texas
Thailand
Tokyo
Trinidad & Tobago
Tunisia
Turkey
Tuscany
Umbria
USA: The New South
USA: On The Road
USA: Western States
US National Parks: West
Venezuela
Venice
Vienna
Vietnam
Wales
Walt Disney World/Orlando

INSIGHT GUIDES

The world's largest collection of visual travel guides & maps